Human Rights as War
by Other Means

PENNSYLVANIA STUDIES IN HUMAN RIGHTS

Bert B. Lockwood, Jr., Series Editor

A complete list of books in the series
is available from the publisher.

HUMAN RIGHTS AS WAR BY OTHER MEANS

Peace Politics in Northern Ireland

Jennifer Curtis

PENN

UNIVERSITY OF PENNSYLVANIA PRESS

PHILADELPHIA

Published by
University of Pennsylvania Press
Philadelphia, Pennsylvania 19104-4112
www.upenn.edu/pennpress

Printed in the United States of America on acid-free paper
10 9 8 7 6 5 4 3 2 1

Library of Congress Cataloging-in-Publication Data
Curtis, Jennifer (Jennifer Gail)
  Human Rights as War by Other Means: Peace Politics in Northern Ireland / Jennifer
Curtis. — 1st ed.
    p.   cm. — (Pennsylvania studies in human rights)
  ISBN 978-0-8122-4619-3 (hardcover : alk. paper)
  1. Human rights—Political aspects—Northern Ireland. 2. Political violence—
Northern Ireland. 3. Social conflict—Northern Ireland. 4. Peace-building—Northern
Ireland. 5. Northern Ireland—Ethnic relations—Political aspects. 6. Northern
Ireland—Politics and government—1994– I. Title. II. Series: Pennsylvania studies in
human rights.
JC599.G7C87   2014
941.6083—dc23   2013046740

For Nathaniel

CONTENTS

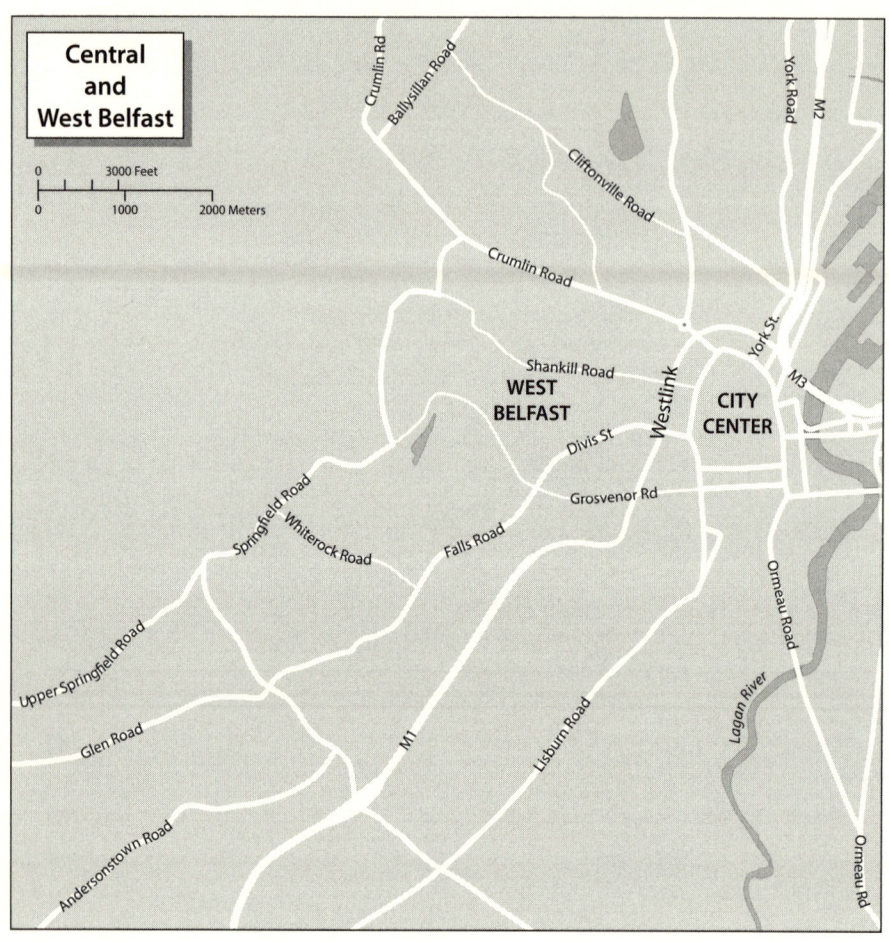

Central
and
West Belfast

Ireland
and
Northern Ireland

Londonderry/ Derry

NORTHERN
IRELAND
(U.K.)

Omagh

Belfast

Dundalk

IRISH

SEA

Dublin

IRELAND

Galway

ATLANTIC

OCEAN

Waterford

Cork

| 0 | | 50 | | 100 Miles |
| 0 | 50 | 100 Kilometers | | |

CHRONOLOGY

1916	Easter Rising. Irish republicans seeking independence from Britain staged a rebellion, primarily in Dublin. British forces suppressed the insurrection, then court-martialed and executed the rebellion's leaders.
1919–1921	Irish War of Independence. The IRA fought British forces for Irish independence.
1920	Partition was enacted by the Government of Ireland Act 1920, establishing two territories on the island of Ireland. Partition was reinforced by the Anglo-Irish Treaty of 1922.
1922–1923	Irish Civil War. Republicans who favored the treaty with Britain and the partition of Northern Ireland from the new state battled republicans who opposed both the treaty and partition.
1964	Campaign for Social Justice (CSJ) formed, a civil rights group that campaigned against anti-Catholic discrimination in Northern Ireland.
1966	Northern Ireland Civil Rights Association (NICRA) formed.
1968	October: Rioting at a civil rights march in Derry inspired formation of People's Democracy (PD), a radical student civil rights group.
1969	January: PD attempted the "Long March" from Belfast to Derry and was attacked by loyalists and police. In subsequent months, civil unrest spread across the region.
1969	August: Massive intercommunal rioting caused civilian deaths and displacement of thousands of families, especially in west Belfast.
	December: Members of the Irish Republican Army (IRA) split from the organization, forming the Provisional IRA (PIRA) to take a more aggressive approach to the conflict. The remaining organization was called the Official IRA.
1970	July 3–5: Falls Road curfew. A curfew was instituted in the lower Falls Road area after a British army raid searching for IRA weapons and personnel erupted in rioting, gunfights, and civilian casualties. The curfew was broken by women from the upper Falls areas, who marched to the area with supplies for residents.

1971   August 9–10: Internment. Government introduced internment with-
                out trial for suspected paramilitaries. The British army carried out a
                wave of arrests called Operation Demetrius, resulting in widespread
                rioting and displacement in nationalist west Belfast. The policy con-
                tinued until December 1975, during which time almost 2,000 people,
                mostly nationalists, were interned without trial.

1972   January 30: Bloody Sunday. British paratroopers monitoring a civil
                rights march shot dead thirteen unarmed civilians; seventeen others
                were injured, one fatally. The killings caused widespread local and
                international outrage.

                March: Direct rule. British government dissolved the Northern Irish
                parliament and established direct rule, after the unionist government
                refused to cede security decision making to Westminster in the wake of
                Bloody Sunday.

                July 31: Operation Motorman. The British army moved into nationalist
                areas of Belfast, Derry, and other towns, with 22,000 troops, to retake
                "no-go" areas from republican paramilitary control.

1973   December: Sunningdale Agreement. An agreement among nationalist
                and unionist political parties outlined power-sharing arrangements for
                the region.

1974   January–May: The power-sharing government established by the Sun-
                ningdale Agreement operated.

                May: Ulster Workers' Council (UWC) strike. Unionist opposition to
                the Sunningdale Agreement mobilized in a major strike, large demon-
                strations, and riots. After two weeks, the head of the power-sharing
                executive resigned along with his unionist colleagues. Direct rule was
                restored.

1980–1981   Hunger strikes. Republican prisoners protested revocation of their
                political prisoner status with a series of hunger strikes. The strikes
                ended in October 1981, after ten men had died.

1985   Anglo-Irish Agreement. The governments of the UK and Ireland estab-
                lished cooperative arrangements regarding Northern Ireland. The agree-
                ment stated that the constitutional status of Northern Ireland would not
                change without the consent of its residents, while establishing a consul-
                tative role for the Republic in the governance of Northern Ireland.

1994   Paramilitary ceasefires. PIRA declared a ceasefire on August 31. The
                Combined Loyalist Military Command, including the Ulster Volunteer
                Force (UVF) and the Ulster Defense Association (UDA), declared a
                ceasefire on October 13.

1996   February 9: PIRA ended its ceasefire after progress toward peace talks stalled.

1997   July: PIRA resumed its ceasefire after the new UK Labour government made plans for negotiations.

            September: Sinn Féin entered the multiparty peace negotiations after affirming principles of nonviolence formulated by former U.S. senator George Mitchell.

1998   April 10: The Good Friday Agreement (GFA) was reached in the multiparty peace talks.

            May 22: Voters in Northern Ireland and the Republic endorsed the GFA.

            June 25: Elections were held for the new Northern Ireland Assembly.

            July 1: The new assembly met for the first time and began to operate in "shadow" form.

            August 15: Twenty-nine people died following a bombing in Omagh. The bomb was placed by republicans who opposed the peace process.

1999   December 2: Powers of government were devolved to the new assembly.

2000   February 11–May 30: Devolution was suspended after disagreements about paramilitary decommissioning of weapons. After plans for decommissioning were agreed, devolution was restored in May.

2001   July 1: First Minister David Trimble, a unionist politician, resigned in protest at lack of progress on PIRA decommissioning. In an attempt to resolve the dispute, Britain ordered two twenty-four-hour suspensions of devolution, on August 10 and September 22.

            November 4: The Royal Ulster Constabulary was renamed the Police Service of Northern Ireland, and police reform moved forward.

            November 5: Devolution was restored after PIRA put forward a plan for decommissioning, and the Independent International Commission on Decommissioning (IICD) affirmed that decommissioning had begun.

2002   October 15: Devolution was suspended once more when unionists refused to share power with republicans due to allegations that Sinn Féin party members were spying for PIRA.

2003   November 26: Although the assembly was still suspended, elections were held. The more hardline republican and unionist parties eclipsed moderate parties in the elections.

2005   July 28: PIRA announced an end to its armed campaign, and its commitment to democratic and political organizing.

September 26: International observers affirmed that PIRA decommissioning was complete.

2006   Following negotiations between the largest political parties, the Northern Ireland (St. Andrews Agreement) Act (2006) dissolved the assembly and established a transitional assembly.

2007   March 7: Elections were held for a new assembly.

March 26: Devolution was restored to the assembly.

May 10: The assembly parties formed a power-sharing government. Sinn Féin boycotted the executive for a period because of disagreements about devolution of policing and justice powers; the executive did not meet from June 19–November 20, 2008.

2009   June: UVF decommissioning was completed.

2010   January 6: UDA decommissioning was completed.

April 12: Policing and justice powers were devolved to the assembly, with an Alliance party member serving as justice minister.

CHAPTER 1

Whose Rights and Whose Peace?

I saw, in fact, history being written not in terms of what
happened but of what ought to have happened according
to various "party lines."

—George Orwell, "Looking Back
on the Spanish Civil War"

"We have peace," declared "Séamus," a taxi driver in national west Belfast.
"And they can have their culture, or whatever they want to call it, as long as
it's not in my face. And I can have mine, and I hope I'm not in their face."[1]
Séamus was explaining to me his attitude toward loyalists and the new, separate peace in Northern Ireland in May 2010, while he showed me around
the West Belfast Taxi Association's new taxi terminal in Belfast city center.
The spacious new terminal, its outer walls decorated with murals from Irish
legends, serves as a sort of bus station for what are locally called black taxis.
Black taxi services began in the 1970s as a grassroots initiative to provide
transportation in areas where widespread violence restricted buses' regular
operation. Of course, then, the taxis—one of the radical cooperatives of the
period—were illegal and unlicensed. Enterprising activists drove used London hackney cabs up and down main arteries to the west of the city, charging
passengers a shilling per journey.

More than a decade after the Good Friday Agreement (GFA), black taxis
are legitimate. The Northern Ireland minister for regional development
appeared at the new terminal's opening in 2010. The association serves the
area of nationalist west Belfast. In addition to providing cheap, reliable transportation, the association offers historical tours, nicknamed "terror tours,"

in partnership with some loyalist black taxi drivers. (There are similar black taxi services in loyalist west Belfast, but they do not serve as large an area and populace.) Drivers are understandably proud of their new status. The terminal, the history tours, and recognition as a transportation provider are part of a peace dividend for west Belfast.

As the political context changed more than a decade since the GFA, Séamus's perspective on the conflict changed as well. When our conversation turned to the Protestant drivers on the loyalist Shankill Road segment of the tours, we talked about the Shankill bomb in 1993. This Provisional Irish Republican Army (PIRA) operation killed ten people, including the bomber and two schoolgirls.[2] "It was terrible," he said, "but I wouldn't have said that twenty years ago. Twenty years ago I'd have been, like, 'Fuck them.'" With this new, separate peace, sympathy, like terror tours, was possible. Having survived injuries from a loyalist attack in his youth, Séamus's newfound sympathy was a major shift.

But others are less sanguine about the soundness of this peace and more cynical about enterprises like terror tours. "The problem is that it [the conflict] isn't over," another research participant explained a few days after I visited the new taxi terminal. "Ruth" was a long-time activist in the loyalist Shankill area, who, like Séamus, had experienced loss during the conflict. Now working for a parenting education program, she had been a community activist for decades, often meeting with foreign researchers, politicians, donors, and filmmakers—including me. Ruth admired the success of development efforts like the taxi terminal and tours, but she had reservations about nationalist interpretations of the peace process: "Some [nationalists] seem to really think that the war was won on their behalf, and the IRA were winners in that way. But there were no winners. We all lost."

For all the changes in Northern Ireland since the settlement, she said, outsiders struggle to understand that peace is not complete. An American once asked her opinion about "taking the peace wall down." Ruth replied, "Which one? What do you mean? There's 88 of them. What are you suggesting?" She claimed that some community organizers make their living monitoring interface areas between nationalist and loyalist neighborhoods, where walls and other defensive architecture have been erected to protect people and property from vandalism and violence. Meanwhile, taxi drivers, Catholic and Protestant, make a living taking tourists to see the walls. But the walls, phone networks, and tours, she argued, are not emblematic of past conflict and present peace; instead, they are persistent expressions of divisions that still require walls to protect people from their enemies—their neighbors.[3]

Ruth's and Séamus's comments articulate differences that characterize postconflict politics in Northern Ireland. Their views on peace are part of wider disagreements about what the settlement has achieved—indeed, what actually caused the conflict. A facile analysis would characterize these as simple nationalist and unionist divides, but the distinctions are finer than that. Different political factions within the broader categories of nationalism and unionism attach profoundly different political values to the "facts" of the settlement, its consequences, and the peace process more generally.

Within republicanism, although most people accept the GFA as a settlement of the conflict, some dissidents argue that the PIRA was defeated because it did not achieve the goal of a united Ireland. Instead, the peace process merely allowed Sinn Féin to become part of the political elite. Some constitutional nationalists—whose representative party, the Social Democratic and Labour Party (SDLP), rejected the legitimacy of armed struggle—see the current agreement as hardly different from a failed settlement two decades earlier, the Sunningdale Agreement. Like the GFA, that short-lived settlement (December 1973–March 1974) consisted of a regional power-sharing legislature and government, as well as cross-border bodies. Therefore, decades of armed struggle to attain essentially the same plan were pointless and tragic.

Meanwhile, some unionists see the settlement as a defeat of unionism and a capitulation to political violence.[4] Other unionists argue that the GFA has secured union with Britain, making any change to sovereignty dependent on a referendum, and it forced republicanism to embrace political means rather than armed struggle. Further complicating these differences, some unionists and nationalists in each of these camps argue that loyalist discontent with the process stems merely from losing unfair privileges over Catholics. These are only summaries of the differences, of course, but they help as an introduction to contemporary conflicts about what the peace process actually accomplished.

In the midst of these different perspectives, a more cohesive, albeit contested, narrative has emerged, one that commands respect among some politicians, scholars, and many ordinary people. This popular history establishes a central role for rights—political, economic, and human—as a cause and cure of the conflict. The outlines of this narrative are these: after partition in 1921, the new state in Northern Ireland systematically denied civil and economic rights to Catholics and maintained Protestant dominance.[5] In the late 1960s, when peaceful civil rights demands were met with both loyalist and state violence and state reforms failed, the republican movement was forced into armed struggle. During the conflict, the British state engaged in human rights violations, further compromising the legitimacy of UK governance. In the late 1990s, republicans, unionists, and the British state settled the conflict by agreeing to new political institutions that ensured equal rights for all.

This success story of rights denied by the state, violent reactions, and a peace created by collective commitment to human rights is a political one. As such, it has been exported to dramatically different conflicts such as Iraq and Afghanistan (see Finlay 2010; Wilson 2010). Its analysis echoes local appropriations of human rights discourse since the 1960s, as well as linkages of human rights and peace that have prevailed globally since the 1990s. Since then in Northern Ireland, human rights have been foregrounded in political rhetoric, the GFA, and its implementation. This account depicts the inevitable triumph of human rights over social and political abuses, echoing the utopian *telos* of other contemporary human rights discourse (see Moyn 2010).

My analysis here of grassroots rights discourse in Belfast, based on over fourteen years of research, moves away from this contemporary narrative to highlight the historical contingency of rights politics in Northern Ireland. I argue that rights talk has functioned as war by other means, during both the conflict and the peace process, and that the contradictory uses and consequences of rights talk must be acknowledged to assess the role of human rights in resolving political conflicts.

Before this contemporary narrative was constructed about human rights, civil rights activism in Northern Ireland emerged in the 1960s. An uneasy coalition of students and middle-class Catholics protested the injustices of the Stormont regime, which had been dominated by the unionists since partition and had presided over systemic anti-Catholic discrimination in economics and politics. The discourse of civil rights was quickly appropriated in the most communally divided working-class locales of the city that, not coincidentally, endured the most intense political violence from 1969 to 1998 (McKittrick et al. 1999; Shirlow and Murtagh 2006). The result was that rights of different varieties quickly became the lingua franca for political demands. In the 1970s and 1980s, these demands focused on economic rights, shifting to the language of political and human rights after the early 1990s.

At the grassroots level, rights talk was translated into everyday advocacy by highly mobilized networks of community organizers. This book traces how local activists appropriated changing transnational understandings of rights and how these appropriations coalesced with communally based politics. Local appropriations of rights talk exacerbated an ethnopolitical tendency to treat two broad "communities," nationalist and unionists, as collective subjects of rights. As a consequence, activists pursued social, political, and economic justice through rights talk—yet their efforts also helped sustain the political conflict. This history of rights discourse demonstrates that rights politics do not play a simple causal role in conflict, nor do they automatically promote peace. Indeed, many of the community organizers I talked to were also combatants in the conflict and acknowledge that some rights-based approaches supported their narrower ethnopolitical goals (see also Shirlow and McEvoy 2008; McAuley et al. 2010). Recognition of this ambiguity facilitates richer understanding of Northern Ireland's peace process and a critical tension of any peace process: those who must make peace are those whose lives are most enmeshed in conflict. In other words, sometimes, peace processes may appear to be war by other means.

My ethnographic engagement with these communities began in the summer of 1996, during predoctoral fieldwork. On the day I arrived in Belfast, the European Union announced significant funding for community-based organizations, proclaiming a central role for these groups in the peace process (see chapter 4). That summer, local academics and activists introduced me to a number of activists in the city. When I returned to conduct doctoral research from 1997 to 2000, I worked with grassroots organizations in the Falls and Shankill areas of west Belfast.[6] Initially, I was interested in whether and how this community activism contributed to peace. These neighborhoods presented the opportunity to observe the work of both nationalist and loyalist groups.[7] Separated from the city center by a motorway and from one another by "peace walls" and interfaces, the Falls (nationalist, approximately 80,000 residents) and Shankill (unionist, approximately 30,000 residents) are broad areas of geographic and communal coherence, comprised of many smaller, distinct neighborhoods (see Curtis 2008). In the late 1960s, these areas of Belfast became epicenters of civil rights protest and political violence. Over the decades of conflict, many residents of these communities were victims of violence, and many served prison sentences for their activities.[8] In addition to high levels of violence and poverty, these neighborhoods were home to numerous community organizations, the groups that policymakers framed as integral to a grassroots peace process (see NICVA 1993, 1994).

Since 1997, I have conducted long-term fieldwork, oral history interviews, and archival research focusing on grassroots activism in west Belfast. Hundreds of community groups in these neighborhoods have changed their names and goals over the years, yet often the same individuals drove these different incarnations, some since the late 1960s. These groups are dedicated to a range of issues, including economic development, education, housing, health services, recreation, child rearing, and gender issues. Their shared characteristic is being founded and operated by local residents. In practice, their activities can range from arranging pensioners' luncheons to running daycare centers, from delivering government-sponsored training programs to operating raves for young people. I conducted participant-observation of the routine day-to-day activities of organizations and social gatherings of activists, as well as public meetings held by community groups, conferences, events such as festivals, and annual general meetings held by various groups. I also conducted interviews and oral histories with activists, local residents, state workers, and civil servants.

Over the course of my initial research, 1997–2000, research participants impressed upon me the importance of the civil rights movement for these communities—not in terms of causing conflict but as a catalyst for political mobilization and direct action. Along with this historical consciousness, I was struck by the centrality of rights—civil, political, and economic—to their contemporary understandings of politics and the unfolding peace process. From 1999, I began to explore these connected historical happenings—a grassroots peace process and rights politics—through archival materials. I consulted archival collections at the Linenhall Library, Public Records Office Northern Ireland, West Belfast Economic Forum, and the Northern Ireland Council for Voluntary Action. Subsequently, I conducted follow-up ethnographic and archival research in 2006, 2010, and 2011. However, in 2010, I shifted my research emphasis from the geographical area of west Belfast to a single organization, Belfast Pride, a lesbian/gay/bisexual/transgender (LGBT) group.

At that time, during the implementation of the GFA, debates about rights seemed to ossify around nationalism and unionism. Yet the GFA also facilitated tremendous legal changes, and public debates, regarding LGBT rights. Belfast Pride had become the largest cross-communal organization in the north. When I approached the group, board members helped me organize both participant-observation and interviews with activists. Jeff Dudgeon, plaintiff of the landmark case *Dudgeon v. United Kingdom*, organized access to his papers held by the Public Records Office, as well as other documents he collected during his years as an activist and historian. This research allowed me to trace the history of rights discourse, conflict, and peace along another path, still connected to the 1960s civil rights movement. This path is as partial as any of the others I describe here. Shifting my attention to LGBT rights was determined by circumstances, especially the increasing visibility of LGBT issues after the GFA—just as the announcement of peace funding for community groups steered me toward grassroots activism in 1996. However, as chapter 6 explains, LGBT activism does not exist in isolation from the city's broader community networks, and some research participants were active in both local groups in west Belfast and LGBT groups. LGBT activism illuminates other dimensions of rights discourse and other ways the logic of rights has permeated everyday politics since the 1960s. This activism also envisions dramatically different postconflict possibilities than the hardened blocs of communalized rights; as such, it enriches this historical account while bringing it to a more satisfying, albeit partial, conclusion.

Histories are provisional as well as partial, and stories like the ones in this book do not end, even with the deaths of individuals. Furthermore, especially in Ireland, history incites passions. Questions engaged by historians are not "merely" academic; rather, they are central to politics (see McBride 2001). Academic debates bleed into newspapers and popular history journals. For example, trenchant critiques are still leveled in such venues against the late historian Peter Hart (1998, 2003), whose study of Ireland's wars from 1916 to 1922 concluded that the violence was more ethnic than political in character.[9] This "meta-conflict" about the nature and cause of the conflict is perennially contested, and conclusions are received as a political statement of one kind or another (McGarry and O'Leary 1995). Yet as this much-studied conflict continues to inspire and provoke, conventional conclusions require scrutiny. Bew (2007) writes, "Given the scale of the emotional investment that has traditionally been made [in Irish history], it is difficult to contemplate the possibility that, for all its sound and fury, the tale might not entirely have the comforting significance attributed to it" (ix).

I have written this ethnographic history conscious of these considerations and of the fact that critique can be construed as cynicism. The diminution of political violence, paramilitary demobilizations, the IRA's decommissioning in 2005, and loyalists' decommissioning in 2009 and 2010 are significant achievements of the peace process. Nevertheless, the contemporary political narrative about human rights in the conflict and peace process poses more profound social risks than critiques like mine—namely, it perpetuates perilous conditions for a fragile peace, overlooks actual achievements of rights advocacy, and, by extension, generates flawed prescriptions for other conflicts.

This book has two broad aims. First, I aim to describe local rights talk and activism over time, which are selectively included and glossed over in the new postconflict narrative of human rights. Second, I analyze the course of this activism and what it tells us theoretically and practically. In post-conflict Northern Ireland, political realities formed by a logic linking rights and peace potentially undermine the peace process's greatest success—the tremendous reduction in political violence. Inasmuch as the settlement's arrangements work by balancing the collective rights of opposed communal groups, it reproduces the limited political interests of unionism and nation-alism and institutionalizes ethnopolitical conflict in the mechanics of post-conflict politics. Furthermore, without a means to address past violence, the past remains both subject and terrain of conflict. Together, these conditions establish a minimalist peace and implicate rights talk in the continuation of war by other means.

War by rhetorical means is certainly preferable to physical violence. However, rhetoric and practice are not neatly separable, and contemporary rhetoric creates vulnerabilities for the future.[10] The settlement and this new narrative history do not acknowledge how institutionalizing long-standing enmities sustains the potential for violent conflict. Furthermore, by promot-ing the Northern Irish solution as a model for other conflicts, local achieve-ments are overstated, while the particular circumstances that produced them are underexplored—leaving general conclusions and prescriptions based on them open to question.

New Histories, Old Certainties

> The days of humiliation, of second-class citizens and
> of inequality are over and gone forever. . . . The Good
> Friday Agreement and the basic rights and entitlements of
> citizens that are enshrined within it must be defended and
> actively promoted by London and Dublin.
> —Gerry Adams, Speech to Sinn Féin convention,
> Navan, December 2004[11]

Shortly after midnight on October 5, 2010, a car bomb exploded outside a bank in Derry, leaving a massive dent in the reinforced concrete walls, scat-tering glass and metal across the road, and knocking a police officer at the security cordon off his feet. The explosion occurred about an hour after a telephone warning that provided just enough time to evacuate houses and businesses on one of Derry's busiest roads. Two months earlier, a two-hundred-pound car bomb detonated outside the Strand police station in Derry, twenty-three minutes after a warning. More than decade after the peace settlement, there were ninety-nine bombing incidents in 2011, nearly double the number for 2009–2010 (PSNI 2011: 5).

Of these ninety-nine bombs, only one resulted in a human casualty, killing a young Catholic police officer whose car had been booby-trapped. Yet these almost-"spectaculars" seemed to indicate that republican opponents of the Good Friday Agreement were gaining support, especially in Derry—the constituency of Sinn Féin Deputy First Minister Martin McGuinness.[12] McGuinness angrily condemned bombings of the city where he once commanded the Provisional IRA. Calling the dissidents "Neanderthals" and "conflict junkies," McGuinness denounced the same means—violence—and the same ends—unification of Ireland—that he once embraced. The timing of the bomb seemed calculated to embarrass McGuinness, appearing for the first time at a Tory conference. Instead, unfazed, he argued that changing times had made armed struggle obsolete.

Later that day, members of the legislative assembly (MLAs) rushed to condemn the attack.[13] Sinn Féin MLAs echoed McGuinness, in a profound shift from their earlier refusals to condemn republican violence. The debate captured in a singular moment the new historical narrative about human rights and the conflict that has emerged in recent years and illustrated its logic with striking clarity.

Sinn Féin MLA Martina Anderson, herself convicted of explosives offenses and released under the GFA, offered a robust defense of past PIRA campaigns and attacked the illegitimacy of current violence. In the past, she said, violence had been the only means to protest the injustice of "a state whose institutions were designed and sustained in the interest of one dominant ruling class, . . . a Protestant Parliament for a Protestant people . . . an Orange state . . . 50 years of oppression" (Northern Ireland Assembly 2011: 40). Yet "The Good Friday Agreement changed all of that," she said. "It is quite clear that the conditions that we endured in the past no longer exist" (40). If the conflict was simply due to a lack of rights, then "curing" the conflict by ensuring rights is possible. For some republicans I worked with, this is tantamount to heresy—they did not fight for equal rights within a British state but for Irish sovereignty.

Unionists, of course, were incensed at suggestions that the conflict was necessary. An Ulster Unionist Party (UUP) MLA sarcastically thanked

Anderson for her "jaundiced and misplaced lesson on the history of this Province," arguing that "There is no excuse for violence in this Province: there never has been any excuse, and there never will be" (Northern Ireland Assembly 2011: 40). SDLP MLA Pat Ramsey reminded the chamber of a civil rights demonstration in Derry on the same day in 1968 and asserted that "the people of Derry will overcome" (39). He called the dissidents "born-again Provos," whose violence is neither more nor less legitimate than PIRA's.[14]

Unionists and dissident republicans, some of whom continue to defend armed struggle while others do not, are not the only public skeptics. Henry McDonald, the Ireland correspondent for the prominent British newspaper the *Guardian*, grew up in a working-class, nationalist community, and he is particularly scathing about the argument that armed struggle was necessary to reform the local state: "The idea that thousands would have to die and thousands more go to jail or themselves lose their lives so we could have an Irish Language Act or the control of policing and justice powers *within* the Northern Ireland state is a gross, deliberate distortion of history" (see also McDonald 2008; emphasis original).[15]

In this section's epigraph, Gerry Adams, former internee, alleged PIRA leader, and president of Sinn Féin since 1983, treats the GFA as a foundational document that ensures equal rights for citizens with opposed national aspirations.[16] Such characterizations are part of this new political narrative, explaining both the past and future of the conflict in terms of rights. The political power of this narrative lies in its encapsulation of ordinary understandings of the conflict, bolstered with reference to historical facts.

This narrative power became apparent to me soon after the GFA was ratified. "Angela," a republican community activist from Ballymurphy, was thrilled after the vote to support the GFA in the spring of 1998. I spoke with her frequently in the months following the agreement, and she eagerly discussed current events as they unfolded, such as elections to the new assembly and its televised first session. Part of her excitement about the GFA, she confided, was because she finally felt she had equal rights. She described what it had changed in terms of both abstract ideals and concrete, everyday experiences. It meant, she said, that her Irish nationality was acknowledged as legitimate and that her son could wear the uniform of his Irish-language primary school in downtown shops with pride and without fear of harassment.

I was wary of her enthusiasm. Surely a single document did not eliminate the risk of sectarian abuse overnight? But my concerns about aggressive teenagers in shopping centers seemed misdirected as the summer of 1998 unfolded. In July, loyalist protests at the rerouting of an Orange parade in the town of Portadown escalated into violence and intimidation, and hundreds of families were displaced from their homes. The violence ended when three brothers, aged nine, ten, and eleven, died after a petrol bomb was thrown into their home in Ballymoney. The murders took place in the early hours of July 12, the annual holiday celebrated by unionists and the Orange Order.[17] As the holiday dawned and news of the deaths spread, both parade supporters and opponents were shocked. That day, another controversial Orange Order parade along Belfast's Ormeau Road was met by a silent protest with black balloons, a sharp shift from assertive protests in previous years. The murders appeared to have shaken even GFA opponents such as the hardline Democratic Unionist Party's (DUP) Ian Paisley, who had been stridently proclaiming that the Portadown parade must not be rerouted. But the calm did not last. In August, dissident republicans bombed the market town of Omagh, killing twenty-nine people.

Apparently, not everyone had been notified that the conflict was over. Angela was both grief-stricken and outraged. It quickly became apparent that the Omagh bomb's planning had occurred in the Republic of Ireland, where dissidents regrouped in protest at Sinn Féin's acceptance of the Mitchell Principles in 1997.[18] Angela imagined confronting the dissidents herself: "If you feel that the war needs to go on, . . . why did you go to Dundalk for twenty-five years? Why did you go to Cork? Why, if you feel the war should go on, why are you not in the middle of it, fighting it? . . . Because I would like to know. I've watched it. I've watched all the suffering. I have watched the effects of what the bomb does and what the bullet does. And the armed strategy. I've watched all that and I never want to see it again." The political power of the GFA, then, lay in its promise of an ending as much as the much-touted beginning of peace—a longed-for conclusion of violence.

The horrifying violence of summer 1998 seemed to sharpen the resolve across political parties as well as the populace. But the violence also indicated that the deeper causes of conflict are not easily removed. In one sense, Angela and proagreement republicans are correct; the GFA recognizes the aspirations of unionism and nationalism as irreconcilable, stating, "We acknowledge the substantial differences between our continuing, and equally legitimate, political aspirations" (GFA, Declaration of Support, item 5). Yet the GFA and the Northern Ireland Act (1998) that enacted the settlement address this problem with a rhetorical sleight of even-handedness: "the power of the sovereign government with jurisdiction there shall be exercised with rigorous impartiality on behalf of all the people in the diversity of their identities and traditions and shall be founded on the principles of full respect for, and equality of, civil, political, social and cultural rights, of freedom from discrimination for all citizens, and of parity of esteem and of just and equal treatment for the identity, ethos, and aspirations of *both communities*" (GFA, Constitutional Issues, item 1, my emphasis).

In this fashion, the GFA avoids a broader social reckoning regarding conflict and human rights, framing "both communities," the opposed collectivities of unionists and nationalists, as primary subjects of rights. Inclusive references to all citizens, diversity, identities, traditions, and parity of esteem obscure, but do not conceal, the extent to which the GFA's institutions and implementation entrench collective subjects of rights. The GFA's pragmatic recognition of profound differences between the political aspirations of unionists and nationalists also reproduces those differences, central to the conflict, as the basis for the new rights politics that will ostensibly resolve it. This approach limits the way rights are claimed in postconflict politics, in the same way that rights debates were reduced to assertions of communal entitlements during the conflict. Thus, recognition of "both communities" fails to transform both institutional and everyday debates about rights and provides continuity with the past, rather than an end or a beginning. In the postconflict era, these basic assumptions about two collective subjects of rights also constrain recognition of other subjects of rights and political subjectivities— echoing another politically oppressive feature of the conflict.

Scholarship about the peace process, as much as conventional political wisdom, emphasizes guarantees of rights as a driver of the settlement and downplays the vulnerabilities outlined above. Harvey (2001) argues that due to the agreement's "explicit basis in the progressive values of human rights, equality and democratic governance . . . the normative basis for a new beginning is clearly established." Furthermore, he says, the new institutions aim to "construct a human rights culture" (113). Other legal scholars emphasize the centrality of human rights within the GFA (e.g., Bell 2000, 2006). Some work emphasizes the role of human rights nongovernmental organizations (NGOs) in the peace process, supporting paramilitaries' move to democratic politics and making human rights central in the negotiations themselves (e.g., Bell and Keenan 2004; McEvoy 1999, 2001; Mageean and O'Brien 1999). Whitaker (2010) asserts that human rights processes since the GFA, particularly the Bill of Rights debates, facilitated discussions of politics beyond the divisions of nationalism and unionism. Finlay (2010) offers a rare dissent, arguing that postconflict human rights processes have failed in their objective to create principles about which diverse political actors share consensus.

Furthermore, the logic implicating human rights specifically in the conflict's resolution has been projected causally onto past rights mobilizations. For example, Bell (2006) characterizes the 1960s civil rights campaigns as "essentially demands for more human rights" (358). In contrast, Dickson (2010) contends that early mobilizations made few appeals to human rights principles (15–16). Indeed, he states that subsequent human rights discourse distorts causality, leading "some people" to believe the conflict "was totally focused around human rights and equality issues," rather than stemming from the lack of consensual political institutions (22).

The facts of causality matter, as the diagnosis of causes determines remedies. In this instance, the solution of human rights and equality is not a completely post hoc rationalization. As both cause and solution, however, the role of rights in the conflict was contested well before the peace process. White (1989) is an earlier example of the argument that state repression in the face of peaceful demands for civil rights led to violent conflict. Heated academic debates have raged as to whether civil rights violations, such as institutionalized anti-Catholic discrimination, were the direct cause of the conflict, as in the six-year exchange between Denis O'Hearn (1983, 1985, 1987) and Christopher Hewitt (1981, 1983, 1985, 1987) in the *British Journal of Sociology*. This is not to argue that serious scholarship on rights and conflict in Northern Ireland are simply expressions of a zeitgeist; that would be disingenuous and dismissive. Rather, it is to underscore that both political rhetoric and academic analyses have changed over time.

One important change is in terminology. As Dickson (2010) notes, the 1960s protesters in Northern Ireland appealed to civil rights, not *human* rights. Yet no matter how rights have been designated over time, as civil, political, economic, or human, the discourse of rights has enduring *puissance*. Williams (1991) captures this quality: "For the historically disempowered, the conferring of rights is symbolic of all the denied aspects of their humanity" (153). This is evident in Northern Ireland, as, for example, when Gerry Adams spoke of "the days of humiliation" being over. Here, Adams evoked historical understandings of Irish Catholic experiences under British and unionist governance (see Cullen 1986). Such claims about how the GFA works indicate the cultural and political power of "rights" in the settlement. However, distinctions about types of rights are analytical as well as descriptive. Moyn (2010) argues that, as human rights became a utopian political project in the late twentieth century, clarity about their definition and legal basis was diminished. Over time in Northern Ireland, distinctions about different kinds of rights and the subjects or bearers of rights have been blurred in the service of the new narrative about the role of human rights in the conflict.

Human Rights in Law and Discourse

Philosophically and legally, human rights are fundamental liberties and entitlements people possess because of their humanity. In the aftermath of World War II, the newly created United Nations adopted the Universal Declaration of Human Rights in 1948. In the 1960s, two covenants were negotiated and became effective in 1976: the International Covenant on Civil and Political Rights and the International Covenant on Economic, Social, and Cultural Rights. Together, these three documents are the basis for international human rights law. This splitting of political and economic rights into separate documents, writes Ignatieff (1999), was a consequence of the Cold War, reflecting "philosophical disagreement between the *legal and political* rights tradition of Western liberalism and the predominantly *social and economic* rights tradition of the Marxist world" (317; emphasis original). Civil rights and political rights include principles such as freedom from torture and freedom of expression. Economic, social, and cultural rights are principles such as rights to subsistence and to housing. The covenants contain overlaps regarding rights to self-determination, privacy, and nondiscrimination; and, in practice, rights do not have simply political or economic consequences. For example, education provision (a social right) affects the capacity of citizens to exercise political as well as economic rights.

Both Ireland and the UK ratified the UN declaration and covenants.[19] Additionally, the UK and Ireland are signatories to the European Convention on Human Rights. The convention is similar to the UN declaration but incorporates some basic social and economic rights. Postwar European states developed the convention, which also has enforcement powers. It established the European Court of Human Rights, a judicial body that allows individuals to seek redress from signatory states who violate these basic rights. The UK was an original signatory nation, ratifying the convention in 1951.[20] Ireland ratified the convention in 1953. It was enacted in UK domestic law in 1998 and in Irish law in 2003. Both states also signed the European Social Charter, a complementary treaty expanding social and economic rights.[21] The social charter was revised in 1996, and an enforcement procedure was established in 1998. The UK and Ireland are signatories.[22]

Anthropologist Richard Wilson (2006) explains that, in legal forms like the UN declaration and covenants or the European convention and charter, human rights "do not provide the basis for a fully worked out moral or political philosophy" (78). His point introduces another distinction, one between human rights activism, often called rights discourse, and law (see Wilson 2007: 350). NGOs and social movements do the political work of embedding human rights norms in social life, and the term "discourse" is frequently used to distinguish their activities from law and legal cases, as above in Dickson (2010). With increasing human rights advocacy during the late twentieth century, defining and securing rights became part of everyday politics. Yet appeals to fundamental human rights frequently mask this politicization. McEvoy (2011) writes that the primary weakness of human rights talk is "its tendency to deny the quintessentially political nature of its argumentation" (377). Even the most dedicated defenders of human rights as a project acknowledge its limitations and ambiguities. For example, Ignatieff (2001) recognizes contemporary human rights "idolatry" and states that "rights inflation—the tendency to define anything desirable as a right—ends up eroding the legitimacy of a defensible core of rights" (90).

Critics point out that the malleability of this discourse facilitates co-optation—for example, human rights have been invoked to justify less-than-liberatory projects, such as the substitution of truth commissions for retributive justice (e.g., Feher 1999; Wilson 2001) and as a rationale for military interventions like the Iraq war (e.g., Orford 2003). The ubiquity of human rights NGOs has allowed groups like the Catholic Family and Human Rights Institute to enter UN consultation processes, bringing their politics to bear on the United Nations Population Fund's contraception policies—politics that some see as diminishing economic and social rights for large numbers of humans (see Buss and Herman 2003). An even larger problem sketched by current critics of human rights discourse is that the ideology and rhetoric of human rights masks oppressive political-economic processes (e.g., Gledhill 2003). Some scholars such as Brown (2004) detect a profound disingenuousness whereby human rights politics disable other visions and promote "unchecked globalization of capital, postcolonial political deformations, and superpower imperialism" (461).

"Discourse" and "talk" are sometimes problematic terms to distinguish certain activities from law (see Wilson 2007). One problem is these terms' lack of descriptive specificity. "Discourse" in contemporary usage often echoes Michel Foucault's thought on power and resistance, departing from conventional definitions of "discourse" as patterning in language above the level of the sentence (see Curtis and Spencer 2012; Sherzer 1987). In some uses, "discourse" seems to indicate something more like "hegemony" or a slightly modified Althusserian "ideology." In another vein, using "discourse" in a more linguistic sense to distinguish talk from law is flawed from the perspective of pragmatic linguistics, since a binary opposition of law and talk does not convey the degree to which law itself is linguistically constituted (see Richland 2013; Mertz 1994). Furthermore, framing discourse as a separate category from law betrays an undertheorization of language in use, treating language as mere epiphenomenal representation, rather than as "a constitutive element of material social practice" (Williams 1977: 165). Thus, the term "discourse" can obscure a range of practices that take place, such as research, documentation, lobbying, and education, while setting "talk" in the realm of something less real than law. Yet some terminology is necessary to describe practices outside law or legal proceedings. As Helsing and Mertus (2006) note, "the reality of the human rights field . . . relies heavily on extralegal mechanisms and on the promotion of human rights norms through diplomacy, the building of human rights institutions, education and postconflict reconstruction and reconciliation" (9). Now, as Dembour (2010) observes, discursive approaches constitute a "school" within the study of human rights (2, 19). As such, "discourse" is an inescapable lingua franca for describing the advocacy and activism considered here.

Ethnographic analysis has contributed to the study of human rights discourse, especially regarding social processes at the nexus of law and politics (see Goodale 2009a, b; Goodale and Merry 2007; Cowan et al. 2001; Wilson 1997a; Wilson and Mitchell 2003). Wilson (1997a) characterizes this program: "part of anthropologists' brief is to restore the richness of subjectivities and chart the complex fields of social relations, contradictory values and the emotional accompaniment to macro-structures that human rights accounts often exclude" (15). Notable works such as Merry (2006b) describe and conceptualize the globalization of human rights advocacy and its outcomes.[23] In the discourse vein, anthropological work on human rights has made visible its political origins and effects in different social contexts. For example, Speed (2008) argues against simply accepting prior assumptions about rights talk's political or antipolitical effects: "We can learn more by looking at the various reappropriations of the discourse of human rights, and the ways that they emerge in particular interactions: the way the tool is held by particular social actors in particular contexts" (181).

Despite contradictions and unforeseen consequences, rights talk, especially human rights talk, animates a range of political movements. Such discourse, however, merits scrutiny, rather than reflexive acceptance or dismissal. This scrutiny must critically trace the sources, varieties, and consequences of rights talk, to understand what has been achieved and what has not, and what, if anything, might be useful for general theory or application in other regions. To that end, and to situate the themes of this book, the next two sections consider some substantial political challenges that are not addressed by contemporary narratives about human rights and peace in Northern Ireland.

"Sunningdale for Slow Learners"

> Orwell would have appreciated the way 'an "agreed"
> Ireland' turned out to mean the very opposite of a "united
> Ireland," while "power-sharing" came to denote "separate
> spheres," not reconciliation.
> —Roy Foster, "Partnership of Loss," 2007

In 2003 "Anthony," a commissioner on the new Northern Ireland Human Rights Commission (HRC), resigned his position. He was one of six commissioners to resign or withdraw from the commission in 2002 and 2003. He and his colleagues cited multiple reasons related to the commission's lack of authority and resources, its approach to drafting a new Bill of Rights, and its approach to handling a contentious dispute between residents of a north Belfast neighborhood. The new commission—created by the GFA—had struggled to establish itself since being set up in 1999. Legal proceedings had made public the commissioners' internal disagreements about loyalist protests in 2001 at the Holy Cross Primary School (a Catholic girls' school) in Ardoyne, an area of north Belfast. Although the commission as a whole voted not to become involved, its casework committee committed the HRC to supporting a lawsuit on behalf of some families of the pupils. The suit alleged that policing of the protest violated their human rights.

In Anthony's view, the scandal and squabbling were part of a broader problem: the commission had become captive to political debates about collective, communal rights and had devolved into a forum for pursuing grievances. The problem, he said, was that society was concerned with only Catholic rights and Protestant rights, fixated on identity issues—human rights were peripheral, even within the body established to promote them. In his view, these circumstances allowed human rights to be a proxy for ethnopolitical conflicts between nationalists/Catholics and unionists/Protestants. Concerns outside these categories were systematically marginalized. Anthony's commitment to a culture of human rights was indisputable. A lawyer trained at Queens University in Belfast, he had advised the UN, government ministers, and civil servants on human rights policy. He was also actively engaged with NGOs and grassroots groups, and, in the early years of the GFA's implementation, he conducted public workshops for activists and NGOs to explain the new legal and political structures.

The preoccupation of the HRC with conflicts like the Holy Cross dispute was part of a broader trend. Institutional commitments to parity of esteem between two communities quickly facilitated antagonism soon after the new institutions began to operate. For example, during this period, the Department of Health and Social Services implemented plans made under direct rule to close the City Hospital maternity unit in south Belfast. On its face, this was a sensible rationalization of services, since the hospital was just a mile from the Royal Victoria Hospital, where maternity services were centralized. Belfast's geography, however, meant that the closure became a political debate about the distribution of both health services and public employment. The City Hospital's front entrance is on the Lisburn Road, where both nationalists and unionists reside, but it backs onto a loyalist enclave. The Royal is located in the nationalist Falls area. Women from loyalist areas lobbied to keep the City Hospital maternity unit open, arguing that Protestant families would be fearful about traveling to the Royal for prenatal care and delivery.[24] The decision was also seen as forcing associated nonmedical workers (janitors, porters, cleaners) to an area where working-class Protestants would not want to travel to work. Both arguments made some sense in the context of increasing segregation in activity and residence since the ceasefires (Shirlow and Murtagh 2006). But their logic was grounded in the GFA's balancing act approach to putative Catholic and Protestant "rights."

Other conflicts reached the level of farce. In 2001, Sinn Féin proposed a floral display of Easter lilies at the Northern Ireland Assembly, with lapel lilies sold in the lobby to benefit the National Graves Association. Not only are lilies a republican symbol of the 1916 Easter Rising, worn on the lapel by republicans at Easter, but the National Graves Association is dedicated to maintaining memorials to republican dead. The rationale was that, if lapel poppies could be sold to commemorate Remembrance Day, then parity of esteem required lilies to be displayed at Easter.[25] A furious DUP recalled the assembly from its spring recess for an emergency debate about the matter. Ultimately, Easter lilies were displayed, but the sale of lapel lilies did not go forward.[26] Lest one think these were merely the predictable difficulties that accompany the learning curve of governance, in January 2011, the European Court of Human Rights refused to hear the complaint of a republican prisoner that his human rights were violated when the prison service did not allow him to wear a lily outside his cell.[27]

The GFA is based on the work of political scientist Arend Lijphart (1977, 1999, 2002). His consociational model prescribes the management of conflict through power sharing among parties defined in ethnic or communal terms. Kerr (2006), a proponent of the system, argues that the power-sharing model is now the globally preferred prescription for constitutional arrangements after conflict, although Finlay (2010) argues that the model's flaws have become apparent internationally. In Northern Ireland, a proportional voting system is in place, and a governing executive branch consists of ministers selected according to their parties' numbers in the assembly—the d'Hondt method. The settlement dictates that local assembly members must designate themselves as either "unionist," "nationalist," or "other" upon entrance. "Key decisions" must be ratified on a "cross-community" basis—with either a majority of nationalists and of unionists voting in favor or a "weighted" majority with 60 percent overall approval and 40 percent of these designations (see *Agreement Reached* 1998: 5–6). Key decisions are identified by either the Office of the First Minister and Deputy First Minister (OFMDFM) or by petition from a "significant minority."

This model is nothing new. Since civil conflict led to direct British rule and the suspension of the post-partition parliament in 1972, consociationalism has been offered as a solution for Northern Ireland. In 1973–74, unionist protests brought down a short-lived experiment in power-sharing; that experiment came out of the Sunningdale Agreement and is the origin of the SDLP's Séamus Mallon's dig at both unionists and republicans when he called the GFA "Sunningdale for slow learners."[28]

However, an innovation of the GFA is that it also makes human rights central to the broader consociational framework, with the entirety of section 6 devoted to "Rights, Safeguards and Equality of Opportunity." It mandates the creation of a national human rights institution (NHRI), following a recent international practice that balances oversight of state policy with recognizing the extralegal dimension of human rights promotion. The result was the HRC, established to advise the state on legislation and a bill of rights, promote broader public awareness of human rights values, and pursue investigations and legal challenges regarding human rights breaches. The predecessor of the HRC, the Standing Advisory Commission on Human Rights in Northern Ireland, existed since 1973, but local activists had deplored it as impotent during its twenty-five-year history. Gay rights activists, who clashed with the committee in the 1970s regarding sodomy legislation, jokingly called it "saccharine," comparing its superficial authority to artificial sweeteners.

During and after the peace process, the convergence of consociational institutions and continuing divisions within the society embedded human rights discourse into local political conflicts. This outcome must be understood in the broader history of peace and human rights, in practice and in scholarship. Similarities, overlapping objectives, and conflicts between the two endeavors are apparent. For example, both peace and human rights are often traced conceptually to Enlightenment thought (see Howard 2000; Hunt 2008). A recent trend in scholarship on war—organized collective conflict—emphasizes its decline over the course of human existence (e.g., Goldstein 2011; Pinker 2011; Mueller 2004), and this work locates causality for contemporary peace, of sorts, in the growth of modern, democratic states and Enlightenment humanism. Similarly, one strand of historical scholarship on human rights traces an arc of progress (e.g., Hunt 2007; Ishay 2008; Lauren 2011). These analyses of peace and human rights share a broad progressive orientation to history, particularly regarding the Enlightenment and modernity. Yet claims such as Pinker's (2011) that modern states have progressively led to peace are open to critique; for example, one may reasonably ask how, and for whom, high rates of incarceration in the United States constitute peace. In this vein, valorizing histories of human rights, such as Hunt (2007), have also received sharp critique (e.g., Moyn 2007, 2010).

Nevertheless, since World War II there has been widespread recognition that violent conflict produces violations and denials of human rights. Commonsensically, the resolution of conflict entails recognition of human rights to prevent the recurrence of conflict and to create legitimacy for postconflict institutions. Yet the truism that these practices are interdependent is challenging in practice. Many scholars locate the difficulty of reconciling conflict resolution practice and human rights principles in a clash between the pragmatic (conflict resolution) and idealist (human rights) impulses of the fields (e.g., Helsing and Mertus 2006). Nevertheless, argues Bell (2000), their continuing linkage in theory and actual peace agreements reflects a broader association of justice— regarding representation, state institutions, and past violence—with peace, despite contradictions between conflict resolution's *realpolitik* and human rights ideals. Much of the work linking conflict resolution and human rights empha- sizes a mutually reinforcing reciprocity or "synergy" between the two areas of practice (e.g., Galant and Parlevliet 2005). Said and Lerche (2006) go farther, arguing that peace itself should be recognized as a universal human right.

The practical challenges of protecting such a right are immense, how- ever, as Donnelly (2006) argues. Other scholars share his reserved perspec- tive on human rights principles and conflict resolution. In fact, human rights advocacy has been shown to be counterproductive for reconciliation in some postconflict societies. For example, in South Africa, human rights discourse has been linked to the substitution of a truth and reconciliation commission (TRC) for retributive justice (see Wilson 2001). In another case, demands for human rights and disagreements about how to define and secure them have caused returns to violence in Sri Lanka (see Keenan 2006, 2007).

Nevertheless, human rights advocacy and conflict resolution practice share overlapping concerns. These come from a conscious or unconscious concern with a term Said and Lerche (2006) use, "robust peace"—that is, peace beyond the absence of violence. A minimal or negative formulation of peace exists when violence or war is neither present nor imminent. In con- trast, "robust peace," writes geographer Peter Taylor (1991), exists when "the fundamental social structures of the social system negate violence" (80; see also Elias and Turpin 1994). Institutions and processes that allow the pursuit of disagreements through politics, rather than war, are important character- istics of such structures. A robust peace, then, is not the absence of conflict but the presence of legitimate institutions that facilitate nonviolent political debates and negotiation. This institutional element is where consociational- ism becomes a tool for conflict resolution. Similarly, human rights advocates are concerned that postconflict law and institutions are both legitimate and just. National human rights institutions are a relatively recent attempt to aug- ment the judicial protection of human rights. As the Northern Ireland HRC's aims make clear, NHRIs also move beyond the realm of state and law to the more nebulous and contested terrain of society and culture (Smith 2006).

There are also correspondences in theory and practice regarding social spheres. Conflict resolution theory and practice recognize the incomplete- ness of institutional settlements, acknowledging the roles of nonstate and nonparty actors, including grassroots groups, in promoting broader social changes and reconciliation. These are often conceptualized as "track two" diplomacy, which complements official, "track one" efforts (e.g., Gidron et al. 2002). Curle (1990) devised a model to capture this dimension, calling it "conflict transformation." Lederach (1995a, b, 1997, 2005) became the leading theorist and proponent of the concept, arguing that "resolution" is not "sufficiently concerned with the deeper structural, cultural, and long-term relational aspects of conflict" (1995a: 201).[29] Much of conflict resolution literature emphasizes modeling in terms of temporal phases of conflict; conflict transformation is intended to capture the longer-term, open-ended processes of social change necessary to end violent conflicts. As such, it acknowledges that settlements are not endings, and that elite-focused negotiations do not neatly determine broader social changes that negate violence.

Correspondingly, human rights discourse, as discussed earlier, includes a range of activities that are positioned in a sphere of politics beyond the state. In particular, advocacy and mobilization have been treated as a way to embed political norms, beyond law, which promote human rights—mirroring the claim that conflict transformation creates values that promote peace beyond institutions. For example, Stammers (2003, 2009) argues that social movements were a primary force in shaping current understandings of human rights. Much of this work emphasizes the transnational circulation of human rights and its translation into local cultural consciousness and norms (e.g., Merry 2006b; Goodale 2009b; Risse et al. 1999; Mertus 1999).

These overlapping themes are echoed in the GFA. Conflict transformation entered the lexicon of my Northern Irish research participants in the 1990s, much as human rights had in previous decades. In some ways, the GFA engages with a transformative approach, recognizing that the basic political conflict regarding sovereignty cannot be resolved. The tenets of conflict transformation allowed paramilitaries to accept their irreconcilable differences and seek other means to pursue political and cultural change (McAuley et al. 2010; Shirlow and McEvoy 2008). Meanwhile, the influence of rights discourse is evident in the GFA's commitment to "parity of esteem . . . for the identity, ethos, and aspirations of *both communities*" (*Agreement Reached* 1998: 4; my emphasis). Yet as the previous section makes clear, human rights discourse also opens up new fronts of conflict. To a large extent, the peace process has been an institutionally focused affair, while social divisions and sectarianism continue under its "semi-benign apartheid" (McAuley et al. 2010: 36). Rather than transforming divisions, human rights discourse has helped reproduce them.

This situation has been strongly critiqued in scholarship. Arguing from the conventional premises of liberal individualism, Wilson (2010) asserts that the GFA's model makes violence more, not less, likely. Finlay (2010) draws from a Foucauldian critique of liberal individualism to argue that the agreement reproduces ethnopolitics through bureaucratic management. These critics emphasize the compulsory dimension of the GFA's two-communities model (nationalist, unionist, with the occasional nonnormative "other") and its foreclosure of other forms of political collectivity. Finlay (2008) is scathing about the GFA's potential for reconciling politics or people: "All there is, is the constitutional right to hold simultaneously both a British and an Irish passport" (288). Some scholars defend the model by suggesting that group rights simply recognize social reality (e.g., Harvey 2003). Meanwhile, Whitaker (2010) asserts that a "communalization of rights" has not occurred and that processes like the Bill of Rights consultation created spaces for alternative political debates (26). Others predict future benefits, arguing that consociationalism will allow stability to develop over time, embed equality in law, policy, and everyday life, and ultimately increase choice regarding identity and politics rather than compulsion (e.g., McGarry and O'Leary 2004).

The practical institutionalization of collective rights has led to public and academic debates much farther afield than Northern Ireland, of course. The emergence of liberal multiculturalism in the 1990s is a well-known source of collective rights debates. Advocates such as Taylor (1994) and Kymlicka (2001) call for recognizing group rights because group membership is a primary producer of political subjectivity. In this analysis, recognizing groups as bearers of rights is a move toward a more just society, an institutional protection against pervasive structural injustices rooted in difference. Allowing perceived members of a group the option to self-identify in other ways, a "right of exit," guards against communal compulsion (Kymlicka 2001). This position has been criticized from many angles.

One critique suggests that defining the subjects of rights collectively is a challenge to a fundamental conception of human rights as individual rights (see Donnelly 2003). A different response is that situating community as a locus of political rights reduces the complexity of political identification to one category (e.g., Appiah 1994). Anthropological scholarship suggests that collective rights models fail to recognize that rights claims produce political subjectivity as much as groups produce rights claims (see essays in Cowan et al. 2001; Wilson and Mitchell 2003; Wilson 1997b). Cowan (2006) points out that liberal theorizing not only ignores how mobilization is productive of groups but that rights of exit are grounded in inadequate awareness of the compulsion and social processes that constitute "choice" in everyday life. These studies underscore warnings that the GFA model may reproduce ethnopolitics over time.

This scholarship sheds light on both the reasoning behind the GFA and the contradictions that have emerged as it was implemented. The Holy Cross case that precipitated the HRC's first public crisis was an example of broader communal conflict translated into the language of the agreement. A street-level confrontation, much like those during the conflict, became a globally publicized conflict of rights. In June 2001, loyalists from the Glenbryn estate began picketing Holy Cross Primary School in nationalist Ardoyne, north Belfast. The school entrance was located just on the Glenbryn side of a famous "peace line." Police in riot gear were deployed to protect small girls as they walked to school past lines of enraged adults. The dispute continued for four months, with violent conflicts during the summer break and a resumption of the pickets when the new term began in the autumn. Riots spread throughout north Belfast that autumn and winter, along with attacks on children travelling to other schools. Murals in the area compared the girls' plight to desegregation efforts in the United States in the 1950s.

Reasons given for the protests varied. Protagonists in the conflict framed the dispute in terms of collective rights and alleged that these rights were being differentially allocated by the state. Families of the girls argued that the protests subjected them to inhuman and degrading treatment—violations of their human rights. Furthermore, they said, police did not use force to stop the protests because the girls were Catholic, but they would have ended any such protest by nationalists. Therefore, police acted in a discriminatory fashion. Loyalists claimed that free assembly was an unconditional right, irrespective of sectarian content or whether violence might be a consequence. They also argued that the dispute was entangled with the disputed Drumcree parade. Since Orangemen in Portadown were no longer allowed to walk on a stretch of road through a nationalist estate, they argued the girls' right to walk to school near their estate was also conditional.

Parents' claims became the basis for an unsuccessful challenge of police conduct under the Police (Northern Ireland) Act 2000, and under Articles 3, 8, 13, and 14 of the European Convention. As noted earlier, the Human Rights Commission supported the court case, but its chief commissioner disagreed with that decision. His dissent became public when a letter he sent to the chief constable was published in legal proceedings. The commission's conduct in the dispute has since been called "a disaster" because the HRC and individual commissioners took contradictory public positions and became increasingly divided—the HRC became part of the conflict rather than public advocates for either the protection of vulnerable people or fundamental rights (Livingstone and Murray 2004: 156). The incident also compromised public perceptions of its independence from police and other arms of the state. The court case failed before a high court, the Court of Appeal, and the House of Lords, and finally was ruled inadmissible by the European Court.[30] Its long legal journey ended in 2010, when the European Court of Human Rights declared that the case was "manifestly ill-founded" and that, horrific as the protests were, there was no evidence of European convention breach.

The GFA framers could have anticipated the difficulties such a body would face. As former HRC chair Brice Dickson (2010) writes, "The reality is that human rights, like so many concepts, had by 1981 become a propaganda tool in the war of words between all sides to the conflict in Northern Ireland" (22). Nevertheless, from this inauspicious beginning, the HRC soldiered on. Since the Holy Cross debacle, the HRC has made some unpopular decisions, like initiating a judicial review of the local ban on gay adoption; the challenge to the ban was upheld in 2012. It has fulfilled its brief to advise and consult on the Bill of Rights (Whitaker 2010; NIHRC 2008).[31] Yet after the HRC submitted its advice in 2008, the government conducted its own consultation.

The combination of consociational institutions and collective rights politics has not transformed Northern Ireland's ethnopolitics. Instead, post-conflict rights discourse extended its function as war by other means. The incorporation of human rights discourse into the peace process and the minimal peace being promoted produce other vulnerabilities. These contribute not just to present divisions but to the broader contradictions that both human rights law and discourse create regarding past and future violence.

Casualties of Peace

> The consciousness of being at war, and therefore in
> danger, makes the handing over of all power to a small
> caste seem the natural, unavoidable condition of survival.
> —George Orwell, *Nineteen Eighty-Four*, chapter 9

One March morning in 1998, a few weeks before the GFA was unveiled, I met a research participant for coffee. "Tommy," an IRA volunteer and ex-prisoner, was agitated. The night before, he said, the IRA had punished a friend's son who had bought some cannabis for himself and a friend. Paramilitaries burst into his flat, called him a drug dealer, and beat him, taking both the cannabis and the money his friend had brought to reimburse him. In a further insult, Tommy said, they also took a pornographic video and a jar of loose change. "That's what the revolution has come to," he lamented. "Stealing a jar of change, some blow [cannabis], and a blue movie!" The young man was fortunate his offense was so slight—he could have suffered far worse. At the time, republicans had executed several people condemned as drug dealers under the cover name "Direct Action Against Drug Dealers" (DAAD). Tommy had been frustrated by the practice of punishment attacks for many years. In the early 1980s, a teenager asked him to arrange for an ambulance behind a local recreation center at a specific time because he was scheduled to be shot in the knees and feared bleeding to death.[32]

In the weeks after the Agreement was ratified in May, I met another man outraged by punishment attacks. "Billy" was an affable loyalist, aligned with the paramilitary Ulster Volunteer Force (UVF), yet he seemed more interested in fishing than politics. When compatriots shot his brother in the knees, however, he became distraught. His brother's offense had been to oppose UVF decommissioning after the GFA was ratified. A man in the area had recently lost both legs after a punishment attack, and Billy feared that his brother would as well. As he wept, he repeatedly lamented the fact that his brother was shot by his own friends.

Republicans have long treated the practice of punishment attacks as an assertion of the right to police their own neighborhoods, a popular sovereignty of sorts. Because many nationalist residents regarded the Royal Ulster Constabulary (RUC), now the Police Service of Northern Ireland (PSNI), as an illegitimate police force, investigations of petty crimes were often impossible, due to a lack of local cooperation. Yet without a police service, people were vulnerable to crime. Thus, punishment attacks were viewed by many nationalists of west Belfast as an unfortunate necessity (Hamill 2011).

Loyalists, caught in a bind of loyalty to the state, argued that the police were lax about investigating "ordinary" crimes and treated their communities as ghettos. All paramilitary groups at the time engaged in the practice of beating and even shooting those accused of antisocial behavior—usually young men, who, although undoubtedly disruptive, came of age in profoundly traumatic circumstances. In the years following the ceasefires, while official paramilitary operations against enemies diminished, punishment attacks rose (see Kennedy 2001; Hamill 2011).[33] Government tolerance of such attacks during the GFA's implementation demonstrated how the *realpolitik* of conflict resolution clashes with the ideals of both human rights law and discourse. But it also illustrates more profound contradictions created by human rights discourse as it was incorporated within the peace processes.

From the 1970s to the present, punishment attacks have been a feature of life for the people who experienced the highest levels of violence during the conflict. After the ceasefires, punishment attacks sustained legitimacy for armed groups. In the absence of pursuing their military raison d'être, armed groups asserted their authority and relevance through the practice. Indeed, for a brief period in the mid-1990s, when local political parties envisioned a possible settlement in an expansive fashion, some paramilitaries believed they would become part of a new postsettlement policing service. Later, attacks were linked to policing dissent, as Billy came to realize. More recently, republican dissidents have taken up the practice to build legitimacy for their position, engaging in high-profile attacks in parts of west Belfast and Derry.

In the late 1990s and early 2000s, the media increasingly covered the ongoing punishment attacks. In a communicative culture where caustic wit is highly valued, their persistence during the ceasefires was a source for black humor. In 1996, novelists Robert McLiam Wilson and Glenn Patterson took grim aim at the ceasefires' conceits with a documentary called "Baseball in Irish History" for Channel 4's *War Cries* series.[34] Noting a dramatic surge in baseball bat sales since the ceasefires, despite Northern Ireland having only one baseball team, Wilson went to darkly comic lengths to underscore ongoing violence. On camera, he went to a sports shop and bought a bat, making it clear to the clerk he would not be playing baseball. He went to the Sinn Féin office in the Falls Road area of west Belfast to inquire about joining the local baseball team. (Of course, there was no baseball team in the area.) In both everyday consciousness and media coverage, punishment attacks undermined rather than sustained the legitimacy of key actors in the peace process—the combatants themselves.

The practice of punishment attacks in the post-ceasefire and post-settlement periods in Northern Ireland underscores the vulnerabilities that human rights discourse introduces vis-à-vis past and present violence. Unsurprisingly, not everyone was convinced of paramilitaries' commitment to human rights when they began to organize restorative justice projects during the late 1990s.[35] One young research participant who had unpleasant encounters with paramilitaries explained to me that it was difficult to listen seriously to talk of rights for victims of petty crime—after all, paramilitaries used to walk around his estate with baseball bats, not to mention their more violent activities during the conflict. Contradictions between human rights discourse and behavior are not new, of course. The U.S. struggle for independence, with its appeals to liberty, was won in part by slave owners. Such contradictions obviously undermine the credibility of human rights advocates. Local social and historical contexts, as well as the historical uses of rights discourse, determine the degree of skepticism that greets such discourse just as much as the intent of human rights advocates.

More importantly than the problem of disingenuousness, however, the attacks, the political culture they reproduce, and the vulnerability of working-class communities to both petty criminality and paramilitary authority underscore larger problems within the new narrative about human rights and peace. Extralegal attacks by armed, nonstate actors highlight the extent to which the agreement left in place the structures and practices of paramilitarism and a capacity for violence in neighborhoods where an economic peace dividend remains elusive. The new culture of human rights has limits that require acknowledgment.

Punishment attacks undermine the rhetoric of peace, and pose broader questions about the nature of the peace and who actually experiences it. Answers to these questions, in turn, show that human rights proponents have taken different approaches to political violence, contributing to skepticism rather than society-wide attachment to its principles. Claims about the efficacy of human rights within the peace process do not fully acknowledge the contradictory effects of such advocacy. In short, as both a legal and normative framework to describe or address political violence in Northern Ireland, the political effect of human rights also produces legitimacy for a minimal, profoundly differentiated statist "peace." This quasi-peace and its skeptics are influenced by the GFA's approach to human rights, the way human rights principles have been translated in rights talk, and particular characteristics of the context of reception.

Human rights laws concern the actions and obligations of states. Paramilitary organizations and transnational corporations do not sign human rights treaties. However distant a given state's authority may be from the daily lives of putative citizens, legally a state is responsible for violations that occur within its jurisdiction.[36] The 1948 Universal Declaration of Human Rights was, as Alston (2005) puts it, so concerned with state sovereignty that its assumptions are not adaptable to changing conditions in which states are "competing with quite a few others as the embodiment of power and even authority" (4). Occasionally, McCorquodale (2010) writes, treaty-monitoring bodies like the UN Committee Against Torture attempt to define nonstate actors as "sufficiently 'state-like'" to merit the status of violators, but, to do so, they must use "a form of legalized imagination" (107–8). Multiple claims against the British state for violations of the European Convention have been successful during the conflict, such as *Ireland v. UK*.[37]

However, nonstate actors inflicted the majority of casualties in Northern Ireland, which is unusual for a regional conflict. Recognizing this stark fact is crucial for understanding how rights talk can undermine public confidence in both human rights institutions and the broader peace process. McKeown (2009 [2001]) attributes 2,013 fatalities to republican paramilitaries (55.71 percent), 1,018 to loyalists (28.02 percent), and 378 to security forces (10.46 percent) in the period 1969–2001 (14).[38] McKittrick et al. (1999) attribute 2,139 deaths to republican paramilitaries (58.8 percent), 1,050 to loyalists (28.9 percent), and 367 to security forces (10.1 percent) between 1966 and 1999 (1482).[39] Sutton's (1994) earlier analysis yields similar proportions. Of course, positivism cannot convey or contain the subjective experience of violence (Ross 2002; Wilson 2003). Yet outlines of nonstate combatants' roles, as well as the larger challenges their activities pose for a human rights-based approach, are evident in even the roughest figures. The lethality of nonstate actors indicates a central challenge for human rights discourse in Northern Ireland.

Meanwhile, scholars frequently focus on state actions rather than engage with the problems that nonstate lethality creates for human rights certainties. Possible and proven instances of collusion by state actors and loyalist paramilitaries, as well as republican informers paid by security agencies, offer more straightforward examples of human rights violations.[40] For example, Rolston's (2000) analysis of an increase in loyalist killings between 1990 and 1994 concludes that 56 percent are likely to have involved collusion. Bell and Keenan (2005) argue that "these figures leave open the 'dark figure' of collusion" between loyalist paramilitary and state actors" (72). But focusing on state collusion with paramilitaries does not eliminate the problem of how human rights talk can acknowledge nonstate violence. McEvoy (1999, 2001) notes that humanitarian law—international law regarding armed conflict—seems an attractive alternative for acknowledging the violence of nonstate actors in

Northern Ireland. But he concludes that this vehicle embroils human rights groups in the parsing of "legitimate" targets, debates about which population groups suffered most, and the legitimacy of different causes.

For many of my research participants, the collision of principles with particular circumstances makes *both* human rights law and talk inadequate to acknowledge or describe important qualities of the conflict. "I was burned out of my home by Protestants. . . . My brother-in-law was shot dead by the British Army, and my best friend, who was in the police, was shot by the IRA. Who am I the victim of?" one woman asked me rhetorically in 2010, frustrated by ongoing debates about past violence. Each violent episode presents its own challenges. For example, in 1997, Darren Bradshaw, an RUC constable, was shot dead by the Irish National Liberation Army (INLA) at a gay bar while he was suspended from duty. Gay rights activists suspect he was a soft target as well as a "legitimate" one, by the paramilitaries' standards.

The Bradshaw case demonstrates how context is lost in the logic of both human rights law and talk. A police officer was killed by a nonstate organization; this may be a terrorist action or a legitimate military action, depending on perspective, of course. The targeting of a gay man was politically problematic for a group that positioned itself as leftist, and a gay spokesperson justified the operation to the media. In addition to these political dimensions, the shooting demonstrates the intimate dimensions of the conflict, through which victims frequently became vulnerable to targeting. At the time, conservative Belfast had only one gay bar. Bradshaw was most likely targeted through proximity and social knowledge in a gay community that at the time was discreet.[41] Furthermore, from the standpoint of gay activists, homophobia casts a shadow of suspicion on the killing, in light of republican bombings of gay clubs during the years of conflict. Such subjective, social dimensions of violence, like the conduct of nonstate actors, are lost in legalistic understandings of human rights.

McEvoy (2011) has described how legal practice was shaped by the small size of Northern Ireland. So, too, was violence. This meant that daily life was permeated by fear and suspicion, particularly in the areas where I conducted research, where most residents had connections with both victims and perpetrators. The proximity of combat also engendered allegations of cooperation between enemies, in addition to state collusion. For example, some claim that IRA and loyalist contact enabled the 1982 killing of loyalist Lenny Murphy (who was responsible for some of the most horrifying murders of the

1970s) and the 1987 killing of Ulster Defence Association (UDA) leader John McMichael. More mundane connections also existed: the young republican who died planting the Shankill bomb was enrolled in a job training program alongside young people from the loyalist area; indeed, the loyalist who ran the program told me he had been concerned about the young man and contacted his mother a few weeks before the bombing.

Fear and actual risk, then, combined with geography to create a social paradox: profound segregation, which has intensified in the postconflict era, exists alongside the intimate knowledge that characterizes life in small places.[42] I was introduced to this sense of knowing one's enemies, or at least having grounded suspicions about them, in typical Belfast form—a joke. A pro-GFA loyalist community organizer once informed me that he had been threatened frequently by the INLA when the group increased armed operations in opposition to the agreement. But, he said, darkly, "Last night, they called me on my mobile, and I says, 'Right, lads, if youse call me again, I'll fucking kill both of youse.'" He watched my face and laughed as I absorbed his slight to their membership numbers—as well as the implication that they had his cell phone number.[43] Acknowledging this social dimension of the conflict is not intended to depoliticize; rather, it is to highlight the contradictions that are glossed over by both human rights discourse and the GFA's solution. The existence of possible and actual enemies beyond the state, living within communities of civilians, create conditions in which human rights discourse appears contradictory or even disingenuous.

In an attempt to address the issue of nonstate violence, international human rights NGOs began including nonstate actors in their research and documentation on the conflict the late 1980s and early 1990s. They published reports scrutinizing abuses by the British state, republicans, and loyalists—three broad "sides" containing many fine distinctions (e.g., Helsinki Watch 1991; Amnesty International 1994). In July 2011, I interviewed a former Amnesty International staff member about a shift in organization policy regarding lesbian/gay/bisexual/ transgender (LGBT) rights. His explanation of the organization's policy on gay rights led to a defense of another contentious decision made by Amnesty in 1991: to acknowledge abuses by nonstate actors. He argued that as an NGO, rather than a legal body, the group need not be limited by legal definitions. For example, he said, a beating produces similar subjective pain whether inflicted by the RUC or a paramilitary group, and requires recognition in either instance. Yet McEvoy (1999, 2001), an experienced practitioner and scholar, has argued that shifts like Amnesty's were problematic both in terms of reporting on the conflict and in practice for local NGOs. He writes that, for local human rights advocates, extending attention beyond the state would have been untenable for maintaining the organization's local credibility. Such a change could have involved greater condemnation for loyalist paramilitaries than republicans and thus undermined the group's influence.

Nevertheless, local NGOs' emphasis on state violence convinced many unionists that human rights are a nationalist issue. Generally speaking, many loyalists interpreted human rights criticisms of the state as opposition to union with Britain. Since the basis of republican rhetoric was a challenge to the legitimacy of the post-partition state and British jurisdiction, the focus of human rights discourse on state violations seemed aligned with that larger political project. Efforts by international NGOs to consider nonstate violence intensified critiques of local campaigns' silence, contributing to the longer-term skepticism that is problematic in the postconflict era.

Today, human rights skepticism exists beyond loyalism. Most strikingly, it is apparent among people charged with upholding human rights standards in the postconflict era. Attorney General John Larkin, the first attorney general since Sunningdale, has argued that rights claims are ubiquitous in the region and that these claims trivialize human rights. Addressing a Human Rights Commission conference in 2010, he noted that the public housing agency had recently asked residents of a particular housing development not to wear pajamas outdoors. Residents' response to the rule, he said, was "This is our culture," to which they had a human right. Larkin argued that "Perhaps the outdoor wearing of pyjamas is a useful emblem of our contemporary malaise" regarding human rights and concluded that "Wearing pyjamas outdoors should be left for regulation simply to social courtesy and social decency (and a strong sense of the ridiculous)" rather than treated as a human rights issue (16).[44] In a less humorous example, in February 2011 the policing federation's newsletter decried the policing board's "one-sided" approach to human rights. The newsletter claimed rules regarding human rights protections disregard the rights of police officers facing threats from both rioters and dissident republicans. The editorial condemned legal advice not to publish photographs of wanted rioters under age eighteen as "human rights nonsense."[45]

Punishment attacks underscore key problems of human rights discourse as peace promotion and highlight the multiple contradictions of rights talk. These contradictions are not merely the result of undisciplined NGOs interpreting legal principles incorrectly. They are also linked to disjunctions between the terms of legality and actually existing experience. How human rights are received and how effectively they can be pursued are not determined simply by how clearly legal and social advocates speak. The effects of discourse are also produced by context-specific circumstances. Complex conditions of production frame contradictory claims for human rights as both a weapon of war and a tool for peace—including, of course, my own claim that rights discourse has functioned as a form of war by other means. This is why the social life of rights discourse over time requires scrutiny, particularly to understand the historical trajectory of different political projects being treated as human rights promotion and then conflated with peace. This history, in turn, explains the consequences and reception of rights discourse in the present.

Rights Discourse over Time

The peace process began when the first stone was thrown.
—Loyalist community activist, August 2010

Human rights have been central to Northern Irish politics, international litigation, and scholarship on the conflict. The civil rights movement, prisoners' rights campaigns (e.g., protests for political status culminating in the hunger strikes), and extrajudicial killings inspired court cases, media coverage, and academic monographs on both legal and grassroots mobilizations (e.g., Dickson 2010; Ross 2012). However, a historical account of human rights focused only on well-known cases and campaigns obscures important ways rights discourse has worked in everyday politics. Most important, such an approach does not address how rights talk became central to community activism and a vehicle for conflict as well as peacemaking. To acknowledge and explain the ambiguous politics of human rights in Northern Ireland, this book looks at that more subtle historical process: how rights discourse came to permeate grassroots politics and activism, how it transformed these politics, and how rights discourse itself was transformed. This history explains the susceptibility of human rights talk to ethnopolitical appropriation, provides a caution regarding its potential to promote peace, and highlights less recognized contributions of rights discourse to broader reconciliation.

To introduce this history, in Chapter 2, "The Usual Suspects," I trace the adoption of rights discourse in everyday politics. In the 1960s, both the U.S. civil rights movement and the global student movements of 1968 influenced a local civil rights campaign in Northern Ireland. As in these movements, campaigners faced both state and civil violence. In Northern Ireland, however, civil violence became widespread and routine. In subsequent years, grassroots NGOs in the most polarized areas appropriated both the rhetoric and tactics of civil rights to express grievances about housing and communal space. This was, as I argue, a crucial moment when rights talk became central to everyday political understandings and actions. The rhetoric of rights subsequently became a common political tool in grassroots politics. Chapter 3 considers campaigns for economic rights in the 1980s. I argue that economic injustice mobilized activists in the most deprived and violent areas of the city. However, as campaigners became focused on the relative deprivation of nationalists versus loyalists, an inclusive campaign for economic rights fractured, and a comprehensive critique of economic injustice failed to materialize. In Chapter 4 I examine the contradictory consequences of rights discourse as peace appeared possible during the 1990s. When ceasefires were established and, eventually, peace talks began, previously unthinkable discussions also took place among political opponents at the grassroots level. These efforts were justified and sustained by defenses of political rights to association. At the same time, however, rights to assembly fueled ongoing violent conflicts, creating bitterness that lingers more than a decade after the GFA. Chapter 5 moves into the post-GFA years to explore a significant lacuna of the settlement; that is, the GFA included no institutional provisions for systematically addressing past violence by either state or nonstate actors. Its lack of either an amnesty or a truth commission—that is, some official form of truth recovery—has been rapidly filled with discursive efforts to record history (such as community-based oral history projects), and selective accounts of the past have become a means of waging war in the theater of history. Chapter 6 shifts from the failures of rights discourse to consider local LGBT advocacy since the GFA. In contrast to the GFA's shortcomings regarding past violence, the settlement presented gay rights activism with legal opportunities. Although the GFA rights language is focused on parity of esteem for "two traditions," it provided tools that LGBT activists used to expand legal and social equality for LGBT persons. This unexpected consequence of the GFA's human rights provisions hints at new possibilities for rights discourse to support both justice and reconciliation.

Chapter 7, "Ethnopolitics and Human Rights," concludes the book with a return to history. I examine the Irish Enlightenment's outcome, the bloody United Irishmen Rebellion of 1798, in order to revisit debates about who is the subject of rights. To think critically about political subjectivity, the human subject of rights, and the GFA, I consider the fact that Irish campaigns for rights have repeatedly fractured along communal lines. Historically in Ireland, political actors outside the state have been profoundly influential. Yet political subjectivity has usually been mobilized for ethnopolitical projects that privilege certain subjects and restrict other dimensions of political subjectivity. State institutions, like those established by the GFA, may not always dictate political practice, but they can reflect, favor, and reproduce certain practices. As the LGBT case demonstrates, institutions may also create, or at least tolerate, spaces in which new political associations and subjects are mobilized.

The history here is not one of inevitable progress from rights violations to rights institutions or from violence to peace. Neither is it a simple critique of postconflict processes. Instead, it is a history of the ambiguities of rights discourse during conflict. It is also a history of how political actors in Northern Ireland embraced different conceptions of rights to conduct, conclude, and, in some ways, continue the conflict.

Appendix

Paramilitary Punishment Attacks (Shootings and Assaults) 1994–2011
1994–1995: 203 (PSNI 2004: 5)
1995–1996: 252 (PSNI 2004: 5)
1996–1997: 332 (PSNI 2004: 5)
1997–1998: 198 (PSNI 2004: 5)
1998–1999: 245 (PSNI 2004: 5)
1999–2000: 178 (PSNI 2004: 5)
2000–2001: 323 (PSNI 2004: 5)
2001–2002: 302 (PSNI 2004: 5)
2002–2003: 309 (PSNI 2004: 5)
2003–2004: 298 (PSNI 2004: 5)
2004–2005: 209 (PSNI 2012a: 5)
2005–2006: 152 (PSNI 2012a: 5)
2006–2007: 74 (PSNI 2012a: 5)

2007–2008: 52 (PSNI 2012a: 5)
2008–2009: 61 (PSNI 2012a: 5)
2009–2010 (2010): 127 (PSNI 2012a: 5)
2010–2011 (2011): 83 (PSNI 2012a: 5)
2011–2012 (2012): 79 (PSNI 2012a: 5)

CHAPTER 2

The Usual Suspects

Street politics were made fashionable by the Civil Rights
Movement, and that was a good thing. . . . If people
couldn't articulate what they felt in words then they
could forcibly demonstrate what they felt with bricks and
bottles. Street politics changed the very consciousness of
the people, and opened to them prospects which were
before vague dreams, i.e., jobs, houses, justice. . . . Street
politics were exhilarating, dangerous and to a degree
effective; they were also bloody, brutal and murderous.
—Joe Nicholas, letter to the editor,
Sunday Press, November 1, 1970

At the bottom of the Falls Road, in the Divis area of west Belfast, one wall
has become a dedicated site for murals. It is called the "international wall,"
and the murals there draw connections between Northern Ireland and other
countries. Periodically, the murals are changed; exemplary paintings have
commemorated the Basque struggle, expressed sympathy with besieged
Gazans, and celebrated historical figures like Che Guevara. A long standing
trope of the murals is comparison of nationalist experiences in Northern Ireland with African American experiences in the United States. So, for example, in 2010, nine years after the Holy Cross protests discussed in Chapter 1,
a mural juxtaposed images of the Holy Cross children and Elizabeth Eckford,
one of nine black students who attended the desegregating Little Rock High
School in Arkansas, as she was harassed by white students in 1957.

Comparisons of Irish experiences in the north with the U.S. civil rights struggle have persisted since the 1960s, when local civil rights campaigners appropriated the strategies of the U.S. activists. The civil rights movement began in protest of practices under the unionist-dominated Stormont parliament—including gerrymandering, limited enfranchisement, and anti-Catholic discrimination in public services, especially housing. Their demonstrations and marches were met with violent opposition from police and loyalists. Street politics spiraled into violent conflict. In this sense, rights discourse was implicated in the conflict's emergence.

Those living in the most impoverished and violent areas of the city quickly embraced the protest tactics of the civil rights movement, as working-class nationalists and unionists in west Belfast incorporated rights discourse into their political vernacular. This appropriation, as much as the civil rights movement itself, was an early determining influence on the contemporary function of rights talk as war by other means. The appropriations of rights talks in the 1970s swiftly translated grander assertions of civil rights into more quotidian claims for socioeconomic rights, such as the right to public housing in communally identified areas of the city. Territorial boundaries of political and communal blocs hardened, and swathes of people were put out of their homes, often violently. As riots, mass displacements, bombings, and shootings became everyday events, rights talk, especially about housing rights, became inseparable from profound social and political cleavages, as well as new forms of political action.

Rights Enter the Lexicon

"Patrick," a former member of People's Democracy (PD), one of the 1960s civil rights organizations, still recalls some of their work with a sense of accomplishment. But he is also rueful and contemplative. The subsequent loss of life, he says, makes his heady days of student activism seem naïve. In 2011, he still questions PD's role in the conflict, and he is still shaken by memories as he makes his way through the city. Recently, he says, driving past the Divis area, he remembered Patrick Rooney, the first child to die, killed in his bed as police fired on Divis Flats during the riots of 1969.[1] He began to cry and pulled to the side of the road to compose himself. Questions and doubts plague him, not about the injustices of the Northern Irish state they confronted but about the different paths they might have taken. "It's not whether those things didn't happen; it's whether the response to them could have been different," he said sadly.

In contrast to Patrick's doubts about civil rights strategies and categorical rejection of violence, contemporary accounts of the peace process causally link past violence to the postpartition state's rights deficits. The curative potential of human rights is celebrated for helping end the conflict. A pivotal moment in this account is the late 1960s campaign for civil rights, the violent reactions of police and loyalists, and the subsequent street-level, intercommunal violence that escalated in 1969. But the movement from rights protest to violent civil conflict was not a straightforward historical trajectory—the journey was more complex, just as the role of rights discourse in peacemaking is more ambiguous.

The commonly understood impetus for civil rights grievances is the way unionists dominated government in Northern Ireland after partition in 1921. Under the devolved Stormont regime, anti-Catholic discrimination occurred in private and public employment and public services, particularly those provided by local councils. Although some debate the character of the postpartition state in both politics and scholarship, a broad consensus agrees that, from 1921 to 1968, the devolved political system supported and legitimated widespread discrimination against the Catholic minority (e.g., Darby 1976; Whyte 1983).

State discrimination was most pronounced in local government. Local authorities preferentially allocated public housing to Protestants, and the system for voting in local elections meant housing discrimination had electoral consequences. That is, under Northern Irish voting laws, only "ratepayers"— either property owners or public housing tenants, both of whom paid a local property tax called "rates"—or their nominated representatives could vote in local elections. Private tenants did not pay rates—their landlords did—so these tenants were not automatically entitled to a local council vote. These rules applied only to local council elections; all adults were enfranchised for Northern Irish and UK parliamentary elections. Yet this system, combined with discrimination against Catholics in public housing, amplified the political representation of unionism. Ratepayers' provisions also entitled owners of commercial property to nominate special voters (non-ratepayers) for each £10 ($28) value of the property, for up to six voters.[2] Given disproportionate Protestant ownership of commercial property, this, too, increased unionists' political representation (see Darby 1976). Furthermore, the practice nurtured a culture of patronage within unionism, as nonratepaying Protestants were dependent on property owners for nominations to vote in local council elections. There was also a pattern of gerrymandering, whereby electoral boundaries were drawn to ensure unionist dominance, most strikingly in Derry. Policing and justice also operated in a biased fashion, with the Civil Authorities (Special Powers) Act 1922 allowing internment without trial.[3]

Brice Dickson (2010), a respected human rights scholar and advocate (he was a founding member of the Committee on the Administration of Justice and the former head of the Human Rights Commission), makes clear the underlying difficulty of approaching Stormont's repressions as human rights violations. Although these practices disenfranchised the minority, he explains, international frameworks that define human rights do not prescribe particular political or voting arrangements. In this sense, these frameworks offer limited tools. For Dickson (2010), stretching human rights principles to denounce the Stormont regime's practices obscures the essentially political nature of its abuses (15). Extending this observation helps clarify a central insight: rights conflicts were political from the moment of their emergence in Northern Ireland. Broader narratives took longer to emerge, such as identifying human rights violations as causes of conflict or, later, human rights culture as a cause of peace.

In the 1960s, however, political and economic shifts occurring throughout western Europe dramatically changed the region's politics. A growing Catholic middle class and radicalized university students (from both Catholic and Protestant backgrounds) challenged the region's governance. The civil rights movement they created, and opposition to it, became a catalyst, rather than a simple cause, for the conflict. The local movement combined tactics from both the U.S. civil rights movement and European student uprisings. These tactics were introduced at a moment of increasing local tensions, as nationalists and unionists, respectively, celebrated the fiftieth anniversaries of the Easter Rising and the World War I Battle of the Somme.[4]

In the 1960s, pressures for state reform were acknowledged by some of the unionist elite. Northern Ireland Prime Minister Terence O'Neill, who took office in 1963, attempted to reform the state by proposing the elimination of the commercial owners' vote and a boundary commission in 1966. Two years later he added review of the Special Powers Act and fair public housing allocation to his reform proposals. Civil rights campaigners felt the reforms were too modest, and unionists felt that any concessions were dangerous. O'Neill's efforts appear motivated more by a concern to preserve and modernize the unionist state than by a commitment to civil rights (Dixon 2001).

An early civil rights group was the Campaign for Social Justice (CSJ), formed by middle-class Catholic residents of Dungannon, County Tyrone, in 1964. Their main concern was discrimination in the Dungannon Urban District, where the council gave Protestants preferential treatment in public housing allocations (McCluskey 1989). With leadership from Dr. Conn McCluskey, a general medical practitioner, and his wife Patricia, the CSJ began organizing protest marches. The group's first publication, "Northern Ireland: The Plain Truth," compiled figures on housing allocation, council employment, and political representation according to political identification in Londonderry, Enniskillen, and Dungannon districts (CSJ 1964).

The CSJ also initiated legal challenges, including applications to the European Court of Human Rights, but they were unsuccessful (Dickson 2010; McEvoy 2011). Although Dickson (2010) contends that the group's U.S. lawyers provided inadequate counsel, the CSJ members believed state denial of their legal aid application also hurt the cases (CSJ 1966). Alongside CSJ, other civil rights groups began to emerge in the 1960s, such as the Derry Housing Action Committee (DHAC). The movement quickly realized legal challenges were not an effective tactic (McEvoy 2011). Direct actions, such as marches and protests, became their preferred approach, along with rhetorical appeals to audiences in Britain, North America, and Australia (Maney 2000).

In 1966 and 1967, a new group emerged to coordinate the various civil rights groups: the Northern Ireland Civil Rights Association (NICRA). The Wolfe Tone Societies, republican groups established in 1964 to commemorate the leader of the 1798 United Irishmen Rebellion against Britain, were a primary force behind the creation of NICRA (Purdie 1990: 122). The Wolfe Tone Societies' engagement with civil rights activism was a break from the republican ideology of armed struggle. In the 1960s, many republican groups, including the IRA, increasingly embraced leftist and Marxist ideology and became receptive to other political tactics (see Moloney 2007). Nevertheless, this early alliance of civil rights activism with republicanism added to unionist suspicions of the movement, even among the Protestant working class who could benefit from civil rights reforms. In 1967, NICRA publicized five objectives shared by civil rights groups: "To defend the basic freedoms of all citizens; To protect the rights of the individual; To highlight all possible abuses of power; To demand guarantees for freedom of speech, assembly and association; To inform the public of their lawful rights" (NICRA 1978: 20). In 1970, the group created a more specific list of demands: the individual franchise in local government elections, an independent boundary commission

for local constituencies, a points system for housing, fair employment legislation, and a bill of rights. (Inclusion of the first demand, individual franchise,
was mostly a propaganda device, since it had been established more than a
year earlier in April 1969.)

The civil rights movement's rhetorical appeals for international sympathy
established a tactic that subsequent activists used for a variety of causes. Yet
appropriating rights discourse is not a simple task, especially when movements in other places and times are treated as comparable to different situations. So, for example, civil rights activists in Northern Ireland faced a
significant rhetorical challenge when they compared arcane local council
voting practices or discrimination in public housing allocation to U.S. laws
disenfranchising African Americans (e.g., poll taxes and literacy tests), to
systematic, state-mandated racial segregation (Jim Crow laws), and to the
historical legacies of the mass kidnap, transport, and enslavement of African
peoples.[5] At the same time, the Irish Americans who supported the Northern Irish campaign, but not the U.S. civil rights movement, were discom-
fited by these comparisons (Maney 2000; Dooley 1998). James C. Heaney of
the American Congress for Irish Freedom warned in a letter to Dr. Frank
Gogarty, a civil rights campaigner, "There is not a single Irish American
group in the United States which has worked with the Colored Civil Rights
movement. . . . So don't expect this of any of us."[6]

The other primary tactic, street protests, catalyzed broader political conflict throughout 1968 and 1969. On October 5, 1968, the DHAC, with support from NICRA, organized the first civil rights march in Derry. Police and
loyalists attacked the protestors, and intercommunal rioting raged across the
city and the region for two days. These events inspired the formation of a
new, more strident civil rights group, People's Democracy (PD).[7] On October
9, to protest these events, about 3,000 students and staff from Queens University attempted a march to Belfast City Hall and were blocked by loyalist
counterdemonstrators. PD was formed following this incident, and Northern
Ireland's 1968 arrived. PD initially outlined a list of conventional civil rights
demands regarding voting, housing, employment, and civil rights (Arthur
1974), yet from the beginning it was more explicitly oriented to a class-based
analysis than was NICRA. On October 24, marking the United Nations Declaration of Human Rights Day, PD was allowed to hold a three-hour sit-in at
Stormont (see Arthur 1974).

Student radicals introduced several fissures in the civil rights movement.
Purdie (1990) writes that the PD coalition with civil rights campaigns was a

temporary, instrumental move, because members were "almost as hostile" to middle-class nationalist elements within the movement as they were to Stormont (198). Arthur (1974), a PD leader from October 1968 to Easter 1969, argues that PD members were not seeking revolution and in the beginning innocently believed that, once civil rights reforms were achieved, they could retreat from broader politics. What is certain is that, during 1968 and 1969, PD members disagreed repeatedly with NICRA members, pushing for more street marches. NICRA's (1978) account reflects the suspicions that PD members were attempting to undermine the group and push a more leftist agenda.

The PD quickly began organizing protests the other groups found controversial. In January 1969, a small number of PD activists staged what they called the Long March, walking from Belfast to Derry. However, they never reached their destination. An organized loyalist contingent brutally attacked the marchers at Burntollet Bridge outside Derry. PD participants said the police did nothing to defend them. Conflict intensified after this event. As summer approached, both nationalists and loyalists lived in fear of their neighbors. Nationalists told me they had feared a sectarian onslaught from loyalists; loyalists said they were anxious the IRA was going to mount a full military campaign for a united Ireland.

On August 12, 1969, violence escalated in Derry and Belfast. Nationalists in the Bogside and Creggan areas of Derry directly engaged police and loyalists after a loyalist parade. By the next day, rioting had spread across the region. After two days, with police staff strained to the breaking point, the British Army stepped in at Derry. In Belfast, the rioting intensified, and intense sectarian battles led to six deaths. The most intense riots took place in mixed neighborhoods located between the lower Falls and lower Shankill areas of west Belfast. In Bombay Street, forty-four houses owned by Catholics were burned to the ground by loyalists. A barricade was set up between the Falls and Shankill Roads, the IRA surged, and conflict escalated from this point throughout the 1970s. The cityscape became a patchwork of embattled "communities," separated by makeshift walls, later institutionalized as "peace lines."

The political reforms proposed in the 1960s were ultimately implemented, but only after conflict had erupted. Individual franchise in local elections came earlier, in April 1969, but sporadic street violence had already become widespread civil disorder. Other reforms followed in the next decade, also too late to forestall the violence and conflict. The Northern Ireland Housing Executive (NIHE), established in 1970, gradually took over administration of public housing from elected representatives (see Brett 1986). The Fair Employment Act banned discrimination in 1976.

In 1972, the most violent year of the conflict, 496 people were killed, and some of the most horrifying violence occurred (McKittrick et al. 1999: 138). Potentially lethal violence became a daily occurrence: police records show 1,853 bombs and 10,631 shooting incidents in 1972 alone (PSNI 2012b: 2). At the beginning of the year, on January 30, civil rights marchers in Derry protested the practice of internment. Shockingly, British paratroopers monitoring the march shot dead thirteen unarmed civilians; seventeen others were injured, one fatally. The incident became known as "Bloody Sunday." These killings were seen by nationalists as conclusive evidence of the local state's failure. In March, devolution was suspended, and Britain instituted direct rule, dissolving the Stormont parliament. Local authorities were restricted to governing matters such as refuse collection, recreation, and community services. Yet the abuses of the Stormont era remained a potent rhetorical weapon in political battles for decades.

After Bloody Sunday, civil rights campaigners organized fewer marches, understandably reluctant to expose themselves to further state violence. As the conflict escalated, NICRA turned to more conventional advocacy, lobbying the UN regarding internment, policing and justice, and treatment of prisoners.[8] The PD became overtly associated with republicans as it attempted to become a working-class movement. After conflict became endemic in 1969, some PD members aligned themselves figuratively and literally with the beleaguered residents of the Falls. Arthur (1974) recalls that attempts at activism in working-class communities fell on deaf ears among the Protestant working class, who associated civil rights with nationalism. Certainly, PD efforts in west Belfast never became as influential as citizen's defense committees and paramilitaries. But PD did introduce New Left concepts, such as people's cooperatives and people's councils.

Many individuals within PD became influential figures in political and academic spheres in the years that followed. Kevin Boyle became a widely respected human rights lawyer. Michael Farrell, also a human rights lawyer, served on the Irish Council for Civil Liberties. Eamonn McCann, a young leftist from Derry, became a respected journalist and an active member of the Socialist Workers Party. Bernadette Devlin, famously elected an MP at age twenty-one in 1969, was influential in the formation of the Irish Republican Socialist Party (IRSP). Jeff Dudgeon pursued a successful challenge to sodomy law before the European Court of Human Rights and remains an internationally recognized gay rights activist. Paul Bew became a respected academic historian and eventually advised the Ulster Unionist Party during the peace process.

Although consensus about the nature of the Stormont regime eventually emerged, the role of the civil rights movement in the conflict is more contentious. Unlike Bell (2006), who treats the movement as part of a trajectory toward human rights values, others implicate activists in the genesis of conflict. For example, Prince (2006, 2007) suggests that the civil rights movement, shaped by the "global revolt" of 1968, was partially responsible for the violence that followed its rise. Because civil rights brought street politics to sectarian Northern Ireland, with the ensuing state brutality and intercommunal violence, Prince argues that "its legacy was more one of civil strife than of civil liberties" (2006: 875). Politicians also claim that civil rights demands inevitably led to conflict. Conor Cruise O'Brien, who careened between unionism and republicanism in his long political career, argued in 1981 that the movement's outcome "in Northern Ireland conditions could only be, as usual, Catholics versus Protestants" (cited in Ranelagh 1999: 268).

Other scholars and participants view the movement as a catalyst rather than a cause of conflict, treating violence as a symptom of an irredeemable system, unmasked by the movement. White (1989, 1993) explores how membership in or support of the civil rights movement influenced some to join the IRA. It is overly simplistic, however, to treat the movement as a straightforward route to armed struggle or as a direct cause of the conflict. Furthermore, a number of factors determined west Belfast community activists' subsequent appropriation of civil rights tactics, especially direct protest and rhetorical appeals.

Although large numbers of civil rights activists did not embrace violence, the fact that some high-profile activists eschewed the nonviolence of Martin Luther King was a crucial factor in perceptions of the civil rights movement as a cause of the conflict. The role of the republican Wolfe Tone Societies in NICRA's formation and the presence of paramilitary stewards at some marches led many to believe the movement was aligned with republicanism. Certainly, some of my research participants embraced both the civil rights movement and a philosophy of armed struggle. Furthermore, after conflict erupted, some more radical tendencies in the broader movement advocated armed struggle, and individual activists such as McCann appeared sympathetic to PIRA at times (1980: 129).[9] Nevertheless, the mobilization for civil rights, through the assertion of basic rights to assembly, did not inevitably cause the conflict. It was, however, a catalyst for some of what followed. One consequence was that the language of rights became an integral part of institutional and everyday politics.

The contemporary function of rights discourse as war by other means is determined by how rights talk is received by different social groups as much as by the intentions of advocates. Current reception of rights talk is partly shaped by historical perceptions that, despite legitimate grievances, the civil rights movement was implicated in the conflict. Prominent campaigners' contradictory positions about political violence aggravated these perceptions. However, the contemporary politics of rights discourse are shaped even more by the way working-class activists swiftly appropriated rights talk. In territorialized communities where the violence of the conflict was most intense, the example of the civil rights movement provided rationales, tactics, and language for claiming basic social and economic rights. The community politics of rights that followed were contingent rather than inevitable: they were shaped by historical political conditions, structural changes linked to deindustrialization, the intentions of the activists, and the very particular concerns and fears of people living through extreme violence with scarce material resources. In this crucible of poverty and violence, rights talk became inseparable from ethnopolitical conflict.

"Beyond the Capacity of Maps": Poverty, Violence, and Political Consciousness

> So it came about that, by 1970, a first-class housing
> crisis was one of the principal contributory factors to the
> Troubles.
> —C. E. B. Brett, *Housing a Divided Community*, 36

During pervasive intercommunal violence in 1969 and 1970, riots, direct violence, and intimidation displaced thousands of people from their homes. The upheaval intensified profound associations of people and place, leaving behind a cityscape that was "beyond the capacity of maps."[10] In the aftermath, west Belfast residents retreated behind protective barricades into the safety of ethnically homogeneous neighborhoods. The destruction of houses and displacement of people created additional demands for housing in areas of the city where housing supply was limited and substandard. The Stormont government had been slow to introduce the postwar welfare entitlements established in Britain, and public housing was scarce. As part of the 1960s reforms, local government devised redevelopment plans that would increase public housing in the western part of the city. However, the plans were primarily designed to attract foreign investors as traditional industries declined. To provide new factory and commercial sites, the plans proposed razing and redeveloping large swathes of Victorian housing and moving people to newly constructed public housing. This process was already underway when conflict erupted.

As conflict brought additional threats to working-class life in the city, wide-scale resistance was mobilized against redevelopment. Increased housing demand and new resentments animated this resistance, as well as fear. Angry residents combined the direct action and rhetorical appeals of the civil rights movement with neighborhood defense groups, emerging paramilitarism, and desperate self-help projects. Rights-based consciousness and language converged with violent upheaval and preexisting grievances about housing. This new, community-based activism brought rights politics into the everyday terrain of loss and survival. Although these new housing campaigns made valid claims on the state, under conditions of increasing violence and territorialization, housing rights activism appropriated rights talk to maintain or rebuild communally identified neighborhoods. These embattled communities effectively became collective subjects of rights, establishing an important antecedent of present rights politics.

This new activism translated grand claims for civil rights and rights to national self-determination, often intermingled, into more quotidian assertions of residents' rights to determine the location and design of public housing. Such claims were what Sally Merry (2006a) calls a "vernacularization" of human rights. Merry argues that such discursive processes offer liberatory possibilities when advocates "draw more extensively on local institutions, knowledge, idioms, and practices" (48; see also Merry 2006b). Merry (2006a, b) also asserts that local social movements become translators in the process of vernacularizing rights, and this dynamic also emerged in Northern Ireland.

In 1970s west Belfast, new NGOs proliferated, creating an infrastructure of local self-help and advocacy groups. Activists and scholars of the period called the emerging NGO practices "community action" (Lovett and Percival 1978; Griffiths 1975a). These new community groups translated struggles for neighborhood survival into the language of rights; housing rights became a central issue throughout the 1970s (McCready 2001; Griffiths 1978; Wiener 1976). These claims were grounded in prior patterns of social life in the urban spaces of west Belfast, and translated by activists as the rights of "communities." This term, "community," had powerful local resonance, conveying the profound associations among places and people at stake in superficially straightforward housing claims.

"Community"—emplaced social relationships—carries multiple communal and ideological associations in contemporary Northern Ireland. Bryan (2006b) explains that "Real people, along with a range of agencies, are active participants in the reproduction of community boundaries," despite the term's exploitation by "ethnic entrepreneurs" under the GFA's consociational arrangements (604–5). These boundaries sharpened in the late 1960s and early 1970s. Houses and streets—central to everyday life—were burned and barricaded in the conflict. The redevelopment plan threatened to displace more people and permanently alter the areas—the lower Falls and Shankill areas—where some of the most intense violence took place. Local opposition to redevelopment intensified alongside increasing violance. One Shankill activist told me that residents saw redevelopment as a state plot to dismantle their community "brick by brick, but also taking it apart in terms of its community structure, the actual social structure." To explain the political power of "community" in the past and the present, and its elevation as a subject of rights, I must describe its historical meaning and the changes that elevated its importance to my research participants over time.

Today, Belfast is an unprepossessing, deindustrialized, provincial city. Approximately 275,000 people live in the urban area and about 580,000 in the greater metropolitan area. Yet, beyond the city center and its more monied southern environs, Belfast's past endures in a series of working-class and poor enclaves. In these areas west and north of the city center, people recount local histories as distant as seventeenth-century settlement. Others describe more recent upheavals like the blitz of World War II. Many young men from Belfast fought in World War I, and people still recount stories of soldiers naming their trenches after streets in Belfast—Sandy Row, Royal Avenue—superimposing a map of the city onto the Flanders battlefields. The development of distinctive identities in these west Belfast communities is tied to rapid industrialization in the nineteenth century. Rural people moved to the city for linen and shipbuilding jobs when Belfast was a thriving port and industrial center. Historical studies have documented the development of distinctive local identities in the Falls, Shankill, and Springfield areas as early as the nineteenth century (e.g., Porter 1973), and political geographers have documented the long-term phenomenon of "territoriality" in these areas (Boal 1969, 1978).

Throughout the late twentieth century, Northern Ireland remained one of the poorest regions of the UK and Ireland, with west Belfast topping tables for unemployment, welfare dependence, and other deprivation indices. Since the 1970s, various agencies and academics have analyzed the spatial occurrence of deprivation in Northern Ireland (Boal et al. 1973; BAN Project Team 1976; Robson et al. 1994; Noble et al. 2001; NISRA 2010). West Belfast ranks as a severely impoverished, disadvantaged area from the beginning of such reporting to the present. This poverty was not limited to Catholics; indeed, in the 1970s, Rose noted, "given their larger numbers in the population . . . there are more poor Protestants than poor Catholics in Northern Ireland" (1971: 289). Poverty intensified social affiliations in these areas both before and during the conflict, even before deindustrialization caused dramatic levels of unemployment from the 1970s onward.

Yet the neighborhoods my research participants wanted to defend and preserve cannot be characterized simply by the broadly drawn blocs of communalism, although they are largely communally homogeneous. In everyday life, a kind of pointillism prevailed, where people formed their solidarities street by street. In the Falls and Shankill areas particularly, people identified their neighborhoods in precise geographic terms, as small as a single street (see Curtis 2008).

Both loyalists and republicans refer to pre-conflict communities as "great places," in terms not of material conditions but of cohesive relationships and mutual assistance that made coping with poverty possible. "Ivan," a housing campaigner in Shankill in the 1970s, told me, "The poorer you were, the more 'community' you had." Solidarity was a positive effect of difficult material circumstances. "Sadie," from a mixed neighborhood situated where the motorway now divides west Belfast from the city, said, "You were always reared with the idea it wasn't a question of being forced to help your neighbor; it was something you done automatic." When a neighboring Catholic family's male breadwinner lost his job, Sadie's Protestant mother learned of their circumstances and discreetly prepared extra food to take over, saying she had "made too much." "It wasn't cause she hadda do it," Sadie said. "It was because she had a feeling for the community."

The physical structures of housing shaped social relationships. In west Belfast, central to the physical environment were the house and the street.

Much of the housing in inner west Belfast (nearest the city center) consisted of Victorian terraced houses, the smallest, most common type being the "two-up, two-down" or "kitchen house."[11] Most had an outdoor toilet and no bath. Whether publicly owned or rented by private landlords (often mill owners or the Catholic Church), the houses were often in poor states of repair. Dampness and flooding aggravated the difficulties of scarce space and poor facilities.

In the 1970s, kitchens in these areas usually had gas stoves and cold-water sinks. Residents heated water on the stove or in large portable water heaters that ran on electricity, like giant kettles. Heat came from coal fires, but most residences had no central heating systems. Many kept buckets upstairs to avoid winter journeys to outdoor toilets in the night. Indeed, people seem to relish their stories of an almost Victorian existence ("Sure, we'd've kept coal in the bath, if we'da had one," one man said).

With high birth rates—among Protestants as well as Catholics—compared to Britain and Europe, the size of these houses posed challenges for families (McWilliams 1993). In one conversation, a woman deplored the houses, pointing out that "you couldn't swing a cat in there." Her neighbor reprimanded her, recalling a widow in their street who had "raised thirteen children in a house like that, and they were always immaculate." Yet another neighbor pointed out that the family with eight children next to him had served their dinners with children ranged up the stairs, and sitting in the "coal hole." "Or sometimes they fed 'em in shifts. I always wondered how they done it, but I didn't believe it till I seen it," he said.

The size of traditional terraced houses did not nurture contained, nuclear households. With neither front yards nor back gardens to extend private space outdoors, a street culture emerged. Children roamed and played in the streets, and family-like relationships developed beyond individual households. Residents fondly reminisce about a time when "everyone's door was always open." Intricate networks of extended families lived in these little streets ("people were related in ways you would never have believed"), yet even unrelated people shared informal childcare arrangements. In both nationalist and loyalist areas, women who worked in the linen mills ("millies") were assisted by unrelated older women acting as second mothers to their children. Today, adults still refer lovingly to biologically unrelated people as their brothers and sisters or even mothers.[12] The physical structures of the houses necessitated other forms of intimacy. Lack of bathing facilities meant that adults often used public bathhouses to groom, a Friday night ritual before going out to a dance.

Although the pleasures and struggles of working-class life were often similar on the Falls and in Shankill, there were differences along communal lines. For nationalists, discrimination in the allocation of public housing led to overcrowding, with adult children remaining in the family home, unable to acquire housing for their own families. "Kevin," a PIRA ex-prisoner and community activist, says of his family home in Iveagh, "We had a bathroom, actually. Our side of the street had bathrooms, and the other side had outside toilets. So, relatively speaking, we weren't too bad. But it was only a two-bedroom house, for my parents and seven children. And one of the rooms downstairs developed into a bedroom as well. But for a period, I was living in my mother's house, and my wife was living in her mother's house. 'Cause there wasn't enough room in either house for the two of us."

Protestants faced substandard housing conditions more often than overcrowding. Sadie says of her family home,

> Literally, in my street, when it rained, it rained in the back door and out the front door. We were flooded two or three times every year. One year, someone forgot to open the gates of the river, and it rained very heavy and we were flooded to a depth of five feet. . . . I mean, I can remember coming down as a young woman—I have a great fear of cockroaches—and when the lights went out in our house, the whole floor was covered in hundreds and hundreds of cockroaches. They came out of the damp. And I can remember if you had to go to the toilet, which our toilet was outside, I remember coming down the stairs, running along the settee and taking a big jump into the scullery, so that I would step on as little of them as possible. . . . People wouldn't live in those conditions today.

In these circumstances, public housing was a deeply contested political and social commodity well before people began driving neighbors from their homes. Local government's patronage approach to public housing intersected with the importance of homes in working-class communities. Preferential housing allocations for Protestants created persistent consciousness of inequality. When "Marie," a Catholic from Ardoyne, married a Protestant in the 1950s, she began to understand the way housing inequality worked:

> We were living in a large five-bedroom house on the Cavehill Road. And this was in '59. And there was only my husband and myself and

one baby and his mother and father living in a five-bedroom house. And his brother had a flat [in an area] where we wanted one and a flat became vacant and we were told about it. And his father went and seen the City Hall and we got the flat. In the meantime, I . . . had chums who were Catholics who'd got married and they were living eight, ten, maybe twelve in a two-up, two-down in Ardoyne. And then later I thought, "Oh, it's because you're Protestant. You get a house quicker."

However, the civil rights movement made some loyalists uncomfortably aware of their own housing needs, and they realized that their supposed advantages were often marginal. "Tim," a Protestant, was twenty-eight in 1969, still living with his parents and two adult sisters in Ardoyne. He resented the protests:

I can assure you as a Protestant I'm ashamed of some of the things that's been done in my name. But I'm also ashamed that certain—. . . a lot of the things that was supposed to be done by us were not actually done by us, and we were all accused of being bigots. And every one of us had flashy cars and big houses and so on and so on, and the truth of the matter was we lived in exactly the same conditions as they did. We didn't have any of those rights the marchers wanted. And we should have asked for them too. But we didn't know that. Because we were told that these people were gonna steal our country, they were gonna do this to us, they were putting us into a united Ireland. . . . I didn't have a vote, nor did my two sisters.

Ivan says such realizations were a shock for many loyalists. "Traditionally the Protestant community believed that it was looked after and being looked after by its unionist governors," he says:

There's an element in which that was true. In that, with the right connections, being in the right lodge, being in the Masons, you know, will get you a deal, get you a house, get you a job. To a degree. But you were living in shit. . . . But you know what the transformation was, the transformation was that when civil rights broke out in the Catholic community and went working-class eventually, I remember there was TV coverage of houses in the Bogside and the Falls Road and suddenly, this is true, the Shankill woke up. "Jesus, they're the same as our houses. We thought we had better houses."

The civil rights movement brought home how public housing was linked to political rights under prior electoral arrangements. The political importance of houses and streets then increased with violence and mass displacements in 1969.

Intercommunal violence has recurred often over centuries in Belfast. In the nineteenth century, intense sectarian violence broke out in 1835, 1841, 1857, 1864, 1872, and 1886 (Hepburn 1990; Bardon 1982). In the early twentieth century, violence took place in 1907, and from 1920 to 1922 intense violence accompanied Ireland's partition. The Depression brought another period of sustained intercommunal violence, particularly in 1935. Yet Brett (1986) reports that, following World War II, "many parts of Belfast, and of most other Ulster towns, had become genuinely mixed in religious complexion" (63). This mixing made some families especially vulnerable when more intense violence arrived in August 1969.

The 1969 riots were accompanied by forced evictions—through direct violence, such as arson and physical beatings, or threats of violence. Unlike previous clashes, however, the 1969 crisis led to decades of sustained conflict. The locus of the riots was the western edge of the city center, in the neighborhoods between the lower Falls and lower Shankill areas. People fled intimidation and attacks in mixed communities and escaped to more homogeneous neighborhoods. Minority members of neighborhoods that were predominantly loyalist or nationalist were expelled or fled. If not burned out, people would often burn the houses they left so the "other side" could not have them. Residents erected barricades to bar state and enemy incursions.

Research participants' recollections of August 1969 shed light on how the violence was interpreted by protagonists and the increasing role of place in the conflict. Since January 1969, there had been repeated clashes among civil rights marchers, police and loyalists. In Belfast, Catholics feared an imminent invasion of their neighborhoods. Meanwhile, Protestants feared the IRA was about to recommence a military campaign not simply for a united Ireland but for the elimination of the British "presence"—which they interpreted to include themselves. In this feverish and fearful environment, both nationalists and loyalists argue that their actions were defensive.

On August 13, approximately 500 nationalists assembled and held a protest at the Springfield Road police station. Kevin, a participant, says, "At that time Derry was under a lot of pressure, and so we were talking about, 'well, we can do something down the road somewhere [i.e., the Falls], we can take the pressure off Derry. . . . And that was the whole idea." They then marched down the Falls Road to another police station, where youths broke away and attacked the station with stones and petrol bombs. In response, riot police mobilized on the scene. The police and IRA exchanged gunfire, and disorder spread in the Divis and Falls areas. Nationalists burned down a Protestant-owned car dealership and a Catholic-owned betting parlor.

The next night, nationalists again assembled in the Divis area, and some attacked the police station once more. Loyalists expected the protest and had gathered in Dover and Percy Streets. Some of those present told me they feared nationalist battles with the police would progress to attacks on themselves. When police and nationalist protesters clashed again, with stones and petrol bombs raining down from Divis Tower, these loyalists began to push into Divis from their gathering place. Participants I spoke to called this a defensive gesture; nationalists living in these areas called it a pogrom. Under fire from the IRA, the police began to fire machine guns indiscriminately. Loyalists surged past barricades into the neighborhoods of Divis and Clonard, and began burning houses.

Kevin says, "I, along with hundreds of others, witnessed policemen baton-charging people, shooting people down like dogs. Going along with loyalist mobs into Catholic streets and burning them to the ground. Watching all this. Clonard, Bombay Street. Down Conway Street. I watched a cop actually throwing two petrol bombs into . . . a pub on the corner of Dover Street, the Argyll Inn." "Andrew," an IRA activist at the time, reports that the paramilitary group did attempt to defend these areas, but "We were useless, running around Clonard with rusty guns."[13] Meanwhile, in Ardoyne, loyalists began to attack houses near the now famous Holy Cross Church, and nationalist residents scrambled to defend the area.

Republican research participants view their initial protests as defensive, originating in solidarity with Derry. Loyalists also regard their actions as defensive. "Hugh," a UVF member originally from the lower Shankill, said that, in the days before August 13, "The tension was so high that, you know, everybody heard rumors it's going to start here, and so everybody was wound up and waiting for it to start. Word had come down that it [the nationalist protest] was going to start in Belfast, to weaken the police. And the reaction from the loyalist community at that time was, well, we'll defend the police." Loyalists were frightened, he says, and believed that the IRA was about to invade: "My perspective on it [was that] it was an attack on my community. It was the beginning of it. I can remember, I was eleven, and I can remember standing on the street corner, terrified, watching tracer bullets flying up the street. . . . [A]t that time I thought that was the IRA shooting down my street." He later found out the tracer bullets came from the B-Specials, a police auxiliary that was disbanded in 1970, firing randomly.[14] Yet he admits, "I don't think the people on the Falls had anticipated such a high level of reaction. Like Bombay Street, and all that, they hadn't anticipated that, they hadn't realized the kind of tensions that was stewing within the loyalist community."

The full-scale fighting ended when the British Army was deployed into the streets. Nationalists initially welcomed them as protectors, but this was not to last. Hugh says that, on the loyalist side of the barricades, "I think when the army came in, they seen the damage that was done in the nationalist areas and seen us as the aggressors. And were fairly hostile towards the loyalist community in the early stages. . . . [T]here was [a] level of hostility, that the soldiers wanted to teach the Protestant community a lesson. Not only was the first policeman shot [by loyalists], but there was two loyalist casualties shot dead. Those were the early impacts." Meanwhile, for Kevin, who joined PIRA, the horror of those few days was clear evidence that civil rights reforms were insufficient: "When you see agents of the law breaking the law, actually cutting people down, murdering people, there's no way the state can be reformed. So . . . there was a stampede to the IRA." Later events, such as internment in 1971 and Bloody Sunday in 1972, led to further recruitment to the new republican paramilitary group, PIRA.

Entire streets where nationalists once lived were burned down; in Bombay Street, forty four houses inhabited by Catholics were destroyed. The mixed area between the districts of the lower Falls and lower Shankill was replaced by a barricade. In September 1969, the state built the first "peace line," a wall between the Falls and Shankill areas, replacing barricades set up by residents. In the following months, people living as minority members of districts fled to the safety of communities homogeneous to themselves. In 1970, disturbances rocked upper Springfield, and there were shifts of population in the newer, more westerly estates. Another wave of violence followed the reintroduction of internment in August 1971, and the few remaining mixed areas were subsumed into homogeneous communities. Outbreaks of intimidation continued sporadically in certain areas, such as Lenadoon.

Population movement in the city during the 1970s was the largest in Europe since World War II (that is, until Yugoslavia fragmented). While hatred was a component of these conflicts, it must be remembered that many people were simultaneously victims and perpetrators of violence and that, as perpetrators, people were also motivated by fear and a desire for the safety of communally homogeneous zones.

The Northern Ireland Community Relations Commission (NICRC), a short-lived state agency, conducted research into population movement in the 1969–1973 period, and found state records for the movement of 8,000 families.[15] Furthermore, the commission concluded that in total about 15,000 families were displaced in greater Belfast, by studying additional data from informal relief organizations (NICRC 1974: App. K). The commission estimated that 8 percent of Belfast's population had been displaced. Although figures vary somewhat, rough estimates show that, in the first wave of displacements in 1969, the communal breakdown among the displaced was approximately 80 percent nationalist, 20 percent loyalist (Poole 1971; NICRC 1974: 59); and, in the second wave in 1971–1972, 60 percent nationalist, 40 percent loyalist (NICRC 1974: 59).

In the context of the street-by-street communities, expulsion came as a crushing betrayal, at once severing bonds and calling into question their prior sincerity. One research participant, "Cheryl," had been displaced to a newer loyalist estate on the edges of the Shankill. She kept a photo of her family home in Ardoyne, taken as they fled in the second wave of displacements in 1971; the photo showed mostly smoke and flame, giving little sense of the house itself. Her loss was not of a house but of an entire way of life and childhood friends and neighbors. "We would have been put into a back bedroom," she explains, describing the actions taken during violent episodes, "with mattresses and beds against the windows. Because friends of ours that we'd grew up with were stoning the windows and there was shooting up the street. Stuff like that, you know. So you're talking five children lying in a room, you know, screaming, with their mother and their father downstairs, trying to make sure nobody's going to get in any of the doors, you know. I mean we weren't the only family that experienced it. Everybody in that area [did]."

Like many others who fled, her father set the fire that destroyed their home as they left. Such an action is unsympathetic on its face, but the NICRC assessed the practice in a more sensitive fashion: "To give up a home where one has lived for years, and which is in itself a symbol of security, for the insecurity of squatting, which many did, is an act of desperation: to damage one's home on leaving, or allow others to do so, is an act of despair" (NICRC 1971: 1).

Direct assaults, like the burning of Bombay Street in 1969 or Cheryl's situation, may have been the most violent means to convince people to flee, but they were hardly the only means. While not burnt out, a few days after the riots in August 1969, "James" was intimidated into leaving his home in an area where he and his wife were part of a Catholic minority. While Cheryl doubted her prior bonds of friendship, in hindsight James was certain he had been naïve to live in a predominantly loyalist area. "There's a lot of people moved out and I remember friends of mine went out to get a lorry and I sat out, shitting myself, the next day, I think it was the 16th, 17th of August, and I heard the kids in the street shouting, 'The Fenians are coming, the Fenians are coming,' and it was all my mates on the back of this lorry, to get me. So it was just, into the house, fuck the furniture out, and very quickly away. Just threw it into the back of this lorry. The house was burned that night."

Variation in the style of intimidation does not, however, correlate with varying senses of grievance and betrayal. It did not matter how evacuation came about:

> The crunch itself, when it does come, has no stereotype. There have been cases where individual families of minority groups have been directly intimidated by marauding mobs; . . . there has been community pressure of a more subtle nature in many estates; some of the most volatile estates have experienced no pressure against individuals at all. . . . It is important to observe that the effects of general violence can be every bit as intimidating as the gunmen standing at the door. (NICRC 1974: 71)

Those who remained were subject to sanctions for nonconformity, such as tarring and feathering or punishment beatings or shootings. The ugly side of solidarity was never far from the surface. Sadly, the NICRC report's conclusion still sometimes rings true today: "This is pressure against any nonconformist in the area—the man who criticizes the IRA, or the family which refuses to pay its UDA dues, even the drug addict or the sexually promiscuous. In a desperate search for security, anyone who is not completely conformist is at risk" (72).

Ultimately, memories of prior communities and their imperiled state in the 1970s had ramifications for how people voiced their grievances. The street became not just the place for child's play, social life, and riots, but also for protest. Although the civil rights movement had marched, organized responses to the violence opened up the streets as a venue for other forms of political protest (as opposed to communal, territorial rioting), and the material conditions that created solidarity—that is, poor housing—became reasons for protests.

Politics on "Our" Streets

> Under street-lamps by all the city's walls, writing gleams:
> IRA, INLA, UVF, UFF. . . . The city keeps its walls like a
> diary. In this staccato shorthand, the walls tell of histories
> and hatreds, shriveled and bleached with age. *Qui a terre a*
> *guerre*, the walls say.
> —Robert McLiam Wilson, *Eureka Street*, 212

Despite his grief at the violence and loss of life, Patrick's radical PD past still shapes his memory of the period between 1969 and Operation Motorman in 1972 as a time that also contained promise and possibility.[16] Before Motorman, he says, everyone was talking, even the defense associations and paramilitary groups. Behind the barricades, Patrick says, a revolution appeared within reach, as grassroots activism emerged on a wide scale. Defensiveness created greater cohesion, as residents stayed out at all hours, minding barricades, watching for assaults, and, more important, talking deep into the morning hours. People wrote and distributed newsletters and pamphlets and formed new organizations. People's councils were formed to introduce direct democracy. New economic cooperatives, like the black taxis, began, and systems for distributing household necessities sprang up; those who owned vans took shopping orders, traveled to supermarkets, and delivered supplies. Behind the barricades, cooperative movements took hold, partly for survival.

These nascent efforts were swiftly formalized into NGOs and residents associations; local practices were quickly given a formal name by activists, "community action." A new infrastructure of activism emerged and became the vehicle for rights claims in these areas. Scholarship from the period defines community action loosely, as the formation of groups to address "an issue or condition which is presumed to have some significance or importance for the community" (Griffiths 1975a: 191). Many early initiatives were cooperative responses to evacuations and displacement. Sometimes minorities in one area swapped houses (technically called squatting) with those who were minorities in another. Occasionally, these exchanges were organized by local "defense associations" and were orderly affairs. For example, in 1970, an organization of about 1,000 men, both Protestant and Catholic, patrolled the area, and coordinated the movement of people when intercommunal rioting took place in upper Springfield (De Baróid 1989: 48; NICRC 1974: 41).

"Sandra," from the loyalist Springmartin estate, says, "At that stage, the whole area was in an uproar. And there was the New Barnsley estate, which was mixed, there was the Springmartin estate which was mixed, and in one weekend, people actually went out on the road and negotiated: 'You keep your house safe, and I'll keep my house safe, and we'll actually transfer houses.' So in one weekend, New Barnsley became a Catholic ghetto, and Springmartin became a Protestant ghetto."

So, if conflict had fragmented community, it also became another source of solidarity. Emergency efforts established relief centers to provide food and shelter. As areas received their coreligionist refugees, new networks of cooperation and activism further enhanced solidarity. For example, the Co-ordinating Centre for Relief established fifteen centers for displaced persons, providing assistance in applying for state compensation, housing, welfare benefits, and legal aid. Much of this activity was necessary because the conflict rendered state services nonexistent or partial in these areas. "No-go areas" for the police and the British army were set up in both loyalist and nationalist neighborhoods. Gun battles between the army and paramilitaries, bombings, and shootings became commonplace, as did rent and rate strikes.[17] The neighborhoods of west Belfast continuously erected and reerected barricades to protect themselves from attack by communal enemies or state forces.

Andrew, who joined the PIRA faction when the IRA split in 1969, says, "You had the clear political and civil rights emerging; you also had the economic issues beginning to surface again." Andrew says these efforts dovetailed with armed struggle, which he called, "politics by other means." By controlling territories of west Belfast, he believed that republicans had displaced state authority: "In the '70s after internment, there was no police, they couldn't exercise their writ, they couldn't collect their money, they couldn't bring people to court, they couldn't tax their cars, rents didn't have to be paid, electricity bills didn't have to be paid. And yet they still had to provide them."

By 1973, there were more than 300 community-based organizations in Belfast alone (Wiener 1976). Early on, they often used the tactic of street protests; women took the lead in organizing. In nationalist west Belfast, for instance, women organized large demonstrations against security-force actions, protesting raids in Clonard and imprisonments in Ardoyne and upper Springfield. Contemporaneous newspaper accounts support research participants' memories of events. In July 1970, 2,000 women broke the Falls Road curfew by marching from the upper Falls to the lower Falls (for some, a journey of up to four miles) carrying bread and milk to residents confined to their homes by the army. In loyalist west Belfast, women also were active in street protests, in blocking roads, and in marching. Loyalists also organized protests against security forces. During the disturbances that led to the expulsion of Protestants from Ardoyne in 1971, more than 300 women went to the police station to protest against inadequate protection.

Community groups also organized rent and rate strikes. More than 16,000 public housing tenants in nationalist west Belfast withheld rent and rates from the NIHE following internment in 1971. Shankill loyalists organized strikes over rent increases and housing conditions as early as 1969 and continued until the early 1980s. Protests in both areas occurred against the Payments for Debt (Emergency Provisions) Act of 1971, which authorized deductions to be made from social security payments—or wages in the case of state workers—to cover rent and rate arrears. The act was later extended to apply to utility arrears. When NIHE imposed a dramatic rent increase in 1975, tenants' groups from the Shankill and the Falls joined together to block roads and protest the decision.

Following emergency efforts to assist refugees and the routine organization of street protests, activists formed more grounded, ongoing projects. Some of the earliest efforts centered on young people. For example, "Bernadette," from the nationalist Newhill area, first organized a shopping van for the area. As the conflict continued, she began to worry about her children and their friends becoming involved in the conflict or being attacked wandering into unsafe neighborhoods: "There was absolutely nowhere for young people to go. Nowhere. And they were all kept in their own areas, so were the adults, too. . . . Ghettoized, you could say." As a solution, she helped young people form a youth club, starting up a disco in a vacant building, initially with borrowed sound equipment. By charging a small fee, they earned the money to buy their own equipment. Other parents later helped the young people begin a broader program that included boxing, football, drama, and snooker.

Similarly, on the Shankill, Ivan said that young people were bored and restless. He was young himself—nineteen—and his friends who had participated in riots were now barred from church-based youth clubs. They banded together and took over a vacant council house to begin their own youth club.

Collecting wood from houses that were being razed for redevelopment, they began making window boxes and selling them. Observing the spirit of the times, they also began a placard business—using reclaimed wood to provide signs to the various protest groups springing up. Ivan says, "I remember this so clearly. . . . And it just blew my mind. I mean this was not organized, this was not—this just *happened*."

Gaining confidence from projects like the shopping vans and youth clubs, activists began organizing self-sustaining cooperatives. These provided jobs and steered local consciousness and action toward self-help. For example, the Turf Lodge Development Association (TLDA) conducted an employment survey and seized vacant buildings for economic ventures. In Ballymurphy, local residents set up a knitting co-op in 1971, which expanded into a commercial knitting factory. Although Ballymurphy Enterprises, as it was called, struggled, efforts to establish worker-run industry persisted. A cooperative building company, Whiterock Industrial Enterprises LTD, purchased a twelve-acre site in the Whiterock area and constructed a factory that it then leased to a furniture company. It also constructed a local filling station, franchised by Burmah Oil. The group sold "loan bonds" locally to raise capital. In 1979, however, the army took over the Whiterock Industrial Estate and dispersed the businesses operating there.

One of the most successful offshoots of the co-op movement in both the Falls and the Shankill were the People's Taxis, or black taxis, which are now an institution. In the early 1970s, hijackings and rioting caused the suspension of regular bus service to the areas of the conflict. People began to get lifts from each other, paying car owners a shilling or so per journey. From this phenomenon, the black taxis began. Local drivers bought used London cabs and drove them along the bus routes. By 1972, a service operated from the city center up the Shankill to outlying loyalist estates, sponsored by the UVF. By 1974, the Falls Road Taxi Drivers' Association had 300 full-time drivers making a similar journey up the Falls from the city center (*Irish Times*, August 22, 1974, 6). Despite initial opposition by government transport agencies and security force harassment, the taxis continued to operate. There are now thousands of black taxis on these and other routes, providing cheap, rapid transport between the city center and western and northern estates.

Many of the same activists, a collection of "usual suspects," led efforts during this period and remained active and influential in later campaigns. Indeed, in both the Falls and Shankill, the "usual suspects" was a term often used for the loose network of actors that emerged. The matter of housing became the central focus of both nationalists and loyalists. Civil rights activists' concern with housing allocation and its link to voting rights provided a language to articulate the more visceral demand for a basic standard of housing. As noted earlier, housing was in short supply, demand was exacerbated by displacements, and the emerging anger with urban redevelopment decisively turned this activism toward housing. Early activism coalesced around claiming housing rights and defending neighborhoods from redevelopment. A rights discourse developed about the state's responsibilities regarding housing, along with more fraught claims for the rights of communities to "hold" territory and steer public housing plans, inflected by ethnosectarian territoriality.

Regeneration, Not Gentrification

In 1961, the UK ratified the European Social Charter, a treaty that expanded the social and economic rights contained in the European Convention on Human Rights.[18] The charter sets out basic rights of individuals in respect to housing, health, education, employment, and nondiscrimination. These rights were not enforceable during the 1960s. The European Social Charter was revised in 1996, and the European Committee of Social Rights, a quasi-judicial enforcement mechanism with a collective complaints procedure, was established in 1998 (see Cullen 2009). Nevertheless, like other western European countries in the postwar era, the UK had a system of social entitlements, including public housing. As with other aspects of the social safety net developed in the early and mid-twentieth century, Northern Ireland's government was slow to match British welfare provisions. Adequate and affordable housing was especially scarce. The civil rights campaign, with its emphasis on anti-Catholic discrimination in housing allocation and the link between property ownership and voting rights, barely scratched the surface of profound housing inequalities and deprivation.

Plans to increase public housing provision and address the infrastructural housing difficulties of Belfast developed slowly from the 1950s onward. In the late 1960s, the Ministry of Development and the Belfast Corporation contracted Travers Morgan and the Building Design Partnership (BDP) to produce a roads plan and housing redevelopment plans, respectively. The subsequent plans required massive house clearances, with blocks of flats and fewer houses replacing the old stock and motorways cutting across the city in concentric "ring roads." The plans projected a "car culture," and the Falls and Shankill Roads, beloved of their denizens, would be reduced to arterial routes sprinkled with "district shopping centers" housing large multinational retailers. The plans dictated the destruction of both the physical and social existence of communities, and, not surprisingly, residents in the affected areas found the plans unacceptable. Yet it is unlikely that opposition would have been so forceful, or successful, had conflict not erupted, making direct action a conceivable and viable practice (see Wiener 1976). When the Ministry of Development unveiled the plans in the 1960s, there were few objections at initial public consultations, from either Divis or Shankill residents.

The plan called for local government, and later the NIHE, to purchase large swathes of the poor housing in these areas, which was a mix of public and privately owned rentals. The mill owners and Catholic Church, as major landlords, would receive significant compensation. Meanwhile, tenants would be provided public housing, with far more legal rights over the properties than existing tenants. Yet the plan would displace even more people. Organized opposition to the plan in the 1970s by residents of Divis (lower Falls) and the Shankill cemented rights discourse as an intrinsic part of everyday politics in these areas. Without legal recourse under the European Social Charter of the time, activists used new methods of direct action to mobilize for decent, affordable housing. They also asserted rights of local people to traditional forms of housing, in traditional areas of residence. As activists became more confident, they asserted the right of social housing tenants to direct the planning and construction of housing. Their tactics included direct action, research and documentation, media campaigns, and lobbying professional planners directly.

The NIHE took over the management of public housing from local councils in 1971. In the postwar estates—New Barnsley, Moyard, Springmartin, and Glencairn—construction was so poor that residents developed health problems. New Barnsley children suffered from dysentery because inadequate sewage facilities tainted the water supply. Glencairn children had high rates of asthma, partly because of the inadequate heating systems. Moyard flats and maisonettes were a disaster, with flooding, leaks, vermin, and, again, high rates of dysentery and asthma. In all three areas, residents compiled surveys of conditions and shared their data with the NIHE to lobby for repairs or replacement housing. But they also went to the media with their complaints (*Irish News*, August 16, 1974, 12). This increased emphasis on documentation and publicity became a significant and effective tactic of housing campaigns.

Residents saw the plans as part of a deeper conspiracy between security forces and city planners to engineer out of existence the troublesome interfaces of west Belfast. They viewed the plans as slum clearances, putting nationalists in flats and moving loyalists to outlying estates. Most importantly, the plans would destroy social structures that were inseparable from the physical structure of the terraces and the streets as communal space. The hostility of people in the lower Falls and Shankill to the flats cannot be overstated. Despite the poor condition of terraced housing, campaigners did not want wholesale demolition; they wanted to improve the physical structures that shaped social life—and they wanted to take the lead in planning how to preserve their houses and streets. The initial efforts of local redevelopment groups, however, did little to alter the course of government plans, despite intense lobbying. Large swathes of terraced housing were demolished, and flats were indeed built in the lower Shankill and Divis.

On the Shankill, the belief that "their" government was conspiring against them was shocking to people whose loyalty to Britain was paramount; however, loyalists had become more willing to oppose the state since the advent of conflict. Activists on the Shankill believed that engagement with planners was fruitless, and in 1974 they formed a new coalition called Save the Shankill (STS). With the aid of local paramilitaries, STS barricaded streets and either intimidated construction workers or simply did not allow them into these areas. As one activist put it, "STS had capacity and it had weight. It could say 'No, you're not gonna bulldoze that street,' and that street wasn't gonna be bulldozed." The planners could not impose the envisioned path of destruction up the road.

The STS also took an organized approach to publicity. The group made sure its suspicion of a state conspiracy to clear west Belfast of loyalists was widely heard, distributing fliers alleging a "secret NIO [Northern Ireland Office] report" to that effect, and briefing journalists about their suspicions.[19] It also engaged with sympathetic academics and developed its own proposals for higher quality terraced housing. The combination of force and organization was successful. Midway up the road, NIHE stopped building flats and pragmatically opted for alternative, terraced designs. The early blocks of flats were demolished. By 1980, the NIHE had also come over to the STS point of view and proclaimed that it too wanted to "save" the Shankill (*Newsletter*, March 10, 1980, 6). Today some areas built to STS plans have the longest waiting lists in Belfast, despite the area's legacies of poverty and violence. But the area's population was profoundly changed; of 72,000 residents at the beginning of redevelopment in 1970, only 28,000 remained.

Housing conditions in the lower Falls were also abysmal. The most egregious example of redevelopment was in the Pound Loney area, where terraced houses were razed and replaced with thirteen blocks of flats, including a nineteen-story tower block—the now-infamous Divis flats. Complaints began during the first phase of building in 1968. Again, initial objections had no effect. Many opponents partly blamed the Catholic Church for the block's construction. Like other landlords, the Catholic Church benefited when the NIHE bought up slum properties. Once completed, the new flats were a disaster. Dampness and mold were severe. Elevators failed to function and refuse chutes became blocked, causing rubbish to collect and attract rats. Furthermore, residents suffered from the health effects of asbestos, used not just as insulation but in tiles, window frames, and the very casting of the concrete.

The existing community in lower Falls was torn apart. In Divis the issue was not net population loss. About 2,500 people were housed in Divis, more than a quarter of the 7,000 in the lower Falls and about the same number as before—now in a smaller space (Divis Residents Association 1986). More important, though, these were not the *same* people as before. Long-time residents desperately applied for transfers, and the complex became a place to dump "undesirable" tenants. Antisocial behavior increased, including vandalism, solvent abuse, and joyriding. A British army observation post was placed at the top of the tower block, adding to the alienating, prison-like atmosphere. The earlier community of terraced, albeit poor, housing was destroyed.

In 1972 the Lower Falls Residents' Association (LFRA) was formed. Supported by the Official IRA and, later, the Irish Republican Socialist Party (IRSP), the group had only one demand: the demolition of the Divis flats, to be replaced with culturally appropriate housing, that is, terraced houses. LFRA activists confronted a more difficult situation than did the STS, because the construction of flats was complete. Furthermore, LFRA campaigners took longer to bureaucratize their campaign and engage with city planners because of nationalist reluctance to recognize the state.

Initially, LFRA members used direct action to protest; for example, they collected rats and took them to the housing executive's offices. They also occupied the offices and put the staff out. In 1979, direct action became more militant, with the formation of the Divis Demolition Committee. For fifteen months, the committee vandalized vacant flats to render them uninhabitable for new tenants, in the hope that, eventually, entire blocks would be empty for demolition. Still, the LFRA demands were unmet, and these tactics began to seem counterproductive, further diminishing quality of life in the complex.

In 1981, the Divis Residents' Association (DRA) replaced earlier groups and augmented direct action with the development of alternative proposals. Sinn Féin increased its engagement with this group, as the Provisional IRA moved into its "Armalite and ballot box strategy" after the hunger strikes.[20] The greater power of mainstream republicanism strengthened the campaign. The DRA commissioned academic reports on conditions and publicized the Divis situation in the U.S. and Britain. Finally, in 1981 and 1984, four blocks were demolished. Divis residents received approval for a renewal program with acceptable traditional housing. Only Divis tower remains today. Ironically, having now been rehabilitated (complete with a concierge), the tower has a long list of people waiting for flats.

In both the lower Falls and the Shankill, what was at stake in opposing redevelopment was social, material, and political survival. "Houses, not flats" was not merely a motto or preference but an assertion of the right to determine the shape of new public housing. It was also a plea to restore or preserve the structuring spaces of social life—by extension, social life itself. Campaigners asserted the housing rights of local people in terms of their traditional places of residence; at a time of increasing communal division, these claims were inflected with ethnopolitical territoriality. Given that public housing is now planned along the lines envisioned by early activists, the victories were far-reaching.

Lost in Translation

Patrick left People's Democracy in the early 1970s. In 1972, he says, he ran into one of his former comrades. His friend mentioned the murder of twenty-six people in the Tel Aviv airport by members of the Japanese Red Army. "It's a disgrace to socialism," he recalls his friend saying. Patrick remonstrated that Northern Resistance, a group linked with PD, was not bringing credit to the Left. "We weren't committed to nonviolence either," he told his friend. "But this struggle is legitimate," his friend insisted. For Patrick, this was the worst outcome of civil rights—providing a cloak of legitimacy for violence. He was deeply critical of armed struggle yet, for forty years, remained a community activist in the west of the city, working easily with people aligned with various factions of paramilitarism.

As noted earlier, contemporaneous and contemporary analyses frequently treat the civil rights movement as at best a catalyst, at worst a cause for conflict. Meanwhile, many portray PD activists in particular as provoca-teurs who, either naïvely or disingenuously, ushered in more than thirty years of conflict (e.g., Prince 2006, 2007). Despite his commitment to nonviolence, Patrick is more nuanced in assessing both the tactics of the movement and its consequences. Although he is genuinely distressed by the violence that followed, he is sanguine about provocation as a tactic—"all the student move-ments were provocative. They made state violence visible," he told me in 2011. The crux of the matter is not that the civil rights movement introduced human rights to Northern Ireland, leading to both conflict and its ultimate resolution. Rather, it is how rights talk came to reproduce the collective com-munal protagonists of the conflict over time.

Some scholarship on the transnational circulation of human rights dis-course is optimistic that these efforts can produce new, potentially liberatory, political subjectivities (e.g., Speed 2008; Goodale 2009b). Others have reser-vations regarding the production of liberatory political subjectivities, while acknowledging that human rights instruments "are some of the only tools available to struggle for rights of the disenfranchised" (Merry 2006a: 49). The civil rights movement in Northern Ireland brought rights-based political mobilizations into public consciousness. People's consciousness of their rights vis-à-vis the welfare state, especially to public housing, increased dramatically. However, legal approaches offered little satisfaction for civil rights or housing campaigners, and they embraced direct and discursive tactics. Protests and publicity became tools to claim rights, simultaneously radicalizing and profes-sionalizing a generation of grassroots activists in 1970s west Belfast.

Housing rights activism was liberatory in the sense that it demonstra-bly improved the lives of its subjects. But in the context of conflict it was also fused with ethnosectarian territoriality. Everyday appropriations of rights talk incorporated the logic and language of the local conflict, rather than resituating local understandings of the conflict in terms of international laws and norms. Antipathies and their accompanying constitutional politics helped subordinate new social movement politics and their imperatives to the national conflict. The profound role of ethnocommunal territoriality within housing activism and the conflict itself meant that housing rights became part of a political contest between collective communal entities. While hous-ing rights talk and direct action were sometimes successful, they also enabled rights talk to extend and sustain the primacy of ethnopolitics over all others.

This hidden history of rights discourse was partly determined by public perceptions of the civil rights movement as concerned only with Catholic civil rights—despite the disenfranchisement, poverty, and political exclusion of a substantial number of Protestants. Furthermore, the appropriation of rights talk by community activists is a direct antecedent of the current rhetoric of rights. Thus, the origins of rights talk left enduring legacies for the pursuit of political change in the present. In the context of increasing civil violence and social division, rights talk created new terms and terrains for the conflict. It worked in synergy with communal political subjectivity and failed to displace the comforting certainties of national identity with universal individual subjects sharing common humanity.

CHAPTER 3

Peace Sells—Who's Buying?

I was fed, housed, and educated by the British state—and
for this I remain profoundly ungrateful.
—Nationalist community activist, October 1997

During my fieldwork in west Belfast, research participants frequently
described triumphs over state agencies, especially welfare bureaucracies.
"Sarah," a community activist from the Shankill, recounted a particularly
funny story about "doing the double" (working in the informal economy
while claiming welfare benefits). In the 1980s, her husband claimed unemployment while secretly driving a taxi. One bright summer day, her family
went for a rare beach outing, paddling and exploring tidal pools. But on
returning home, their mood darkened when her husband found a summons
to the dole office. They hurried the children back into the car and rushed to
arrive before the office closed. On the way, a storm broke, and they ran into
the office rain-soaked and harried. Only then did they notice the children
were still barefoot. Surveying the bedraggled, shoeless family, the adviser not
only renewed her husband's unemployment benefit without question, she
also issued an emergency check to buy shoes.

Sarah was not sheepish about the incident; rather, she laughed about acci-
dentally besting the adviser. In her neighborhood, working while claiming
benefits was more than tolerated: it was a way to survive a brutal economy
and paltry welfare entitlements. From her perspective, welfare benefits were a
basic state duty—not charity for individuals.

This perspective on the state's economic obligations to citizens became an
important part of community activism in the early 1980s. Welfare rights and a

broader critique of economic inequality became central in community groups' practices and rhetoric. Over the course of that decade, both conflict and high unemployment became more entrenched. In response, public and private agencies proposed economic subsidies to resolve the conflict, or at least palliate its effects. Community groups in west Belfast began to vie for, and administer, new funds designated for economically oriented projects. These funding processes increased local competition, and community groups increasingly promoted local economic initiatives in terms of ethnopolitical parity. Thus, the broader policy treatment of poverty as a cause of conflict, and development as a cure, exacerbated local grievances regarding Catholic and Protestant relative inequalities. Nationalist community activists became more focused on anti-Catholic discrimination in employment, not as part of a broad economic critique but instead as an ethnopolitical critique of local injustices. Policies and rhetoric that treated economics as a cause of conflict displaced local activists' deeper structural arguments about basic entitlements, state subsidy, and economic inequality and muted substantive claims for economic rights. In sum, in the 1980s, both policy and local rights discourse about economics as a cause and cure of conflict reduced economic rights activism to another ethnopolitical contest about Catholic and Protestant inequality.

Economic Conditions, Conflict, and Cures in the 1980s

In economically and socially marginalized areas of Belfast, welfare rights activists of the late 1970s and 1980s began to formulate economic rights claims. Activists and academics alike treated economic deprivation as a cause of conflict. Economic conditions were particularly harsh in the 1980s. Inequality rose sharply, and Northern Ireland suffered extremely high unemployment rates for years (Coulter 1999). Official figures for male unemployment remained over 20 percent until the late 1980s, when they dropped to the high teens (Harrington Kilbride PLC 1989). Female unemployment also remained in double digits throughout the decade, with a similar, modest decline after 1988. Rates of long-term unemployment (persisting more than a year) were disproportionately high, constituting more than 58 percent of the unemployed. In the working-class districts where I conducted fieldwork, unemployment was far higher than official data. Robson et al. (1994) found that nine of the ten most impoverished wards were in north and west Belfast.

In these wards, Protestant male unemployment was 37 percent and Catholic male unemployment 49 percent (Breen and Miller 1993).[1]

Although industrial decline began after World War II, it accelerated after the recession of 1973–1974. Linen, engineering, shipbuilding, telecommunications, and tire plants closed or reduced their workforces. The conflict aggravated poor economic conditions, with high state expenditures for security force operations and surveillance and losses across the economy from paramilitary bombing campaigns. Neither local development nor inward investment replaced jobs lost to deindustrialization.

During the early 1980s, the accelerating European unification project and experiences of deprivation and deindustrialization produced local campaigns for welfare as a basic right. Against local activists' increasing assertiveness regarding welfare, however, the policies of the 1980s Thatcher government decreased welfare expenditure while emphasizing the responsibilities of citizens rather than the state. By the mid-1980s, community-based campaigns began to emphasize development projects more than basic welfare rights, positioning themselves for funding in this changing policy environment.

By the late 1980s, responding to dire economic circumstances in areas where violence was most intense, international aid funds also supported economic development as a cure for the conflict. These new funds for entrepreneurial and self-help approaches appealed to Belfast activists. Private and public funding to support both employment and entrepreneurialism increased throughout the 1980s, and small community groups pursued both "job training" funds and enterprise grants and administered them from local community centers. Yet embracing these policies for funding gains resituated economic rights within the politics of patronage rather than basic state responsibilities. As a result, this shift also returned the matter of economic rights to communal political calculations, muting the emergence of a coherent challenge to either Thatcherism or the Republic of Ireland's later Celtic Tiger model of catering to inward investors.

Alongside efforts to promote economic development as a cure for the conflict, activists' rhetoric intensified the causal linking of violence and economic injustice. Campaigns reasserted the civil rights movement's emphasis on anti-Catholic discrimination, highlighting the nationalist unemployment rate twice that of Protestants and linking this to widespread discrimination. While articulating a valid analysis of this devastating problem, renewed emphasis on anti-Catholic discrimination also displaced more expansive analyses of economic rights and basic entitlements. Critiques of political economy were once more situated in terms of local divisions.

Thus, in the 1980s, local rhetoric, self-help projects, and even peace funding intensified communal comparisons of economic deprivation. In the early 1980s, campaigns for welfare rights and employment offered a momentary opportunity for understanding deprivation in terms that included but were much more expansive than ethnocommunal inequality. Yet this chance to grasp a more structural analysis and comprehensive political project was ephemeral. Its loss was accelerated by the reemergence of discrimination as a rights issue. Although discrimination was not a new issue, in the 1980s, activists focused on private sector discrimination more than public employment and services. In addition to shifting their rhetoric this way, activists also adjusted their rhetoric when presenting grievances to an international audience, especially in the United States.

From the perspective of policymakers and donors, economic aid was effective in some ways as a tool for managing conflict and correcting economic injustices. Certainly, policies addressing anti-Catholic discrimination eventually began to correct the unemployment differential between Catholics and Protestants. By the mid-1990s, the class structure of Catholic and Protestant workers had begun to converge (Breen 2000).[2] Whereas Catholic men had been twice as likely to be unemployed as Protestant men in the 1980s, by 2012, Catholic and Protestant blocs had similar proportions of poor, working-class, and middle-class people. Yet this equality of sorts must be understood in light of the fact that Northern Ireland is one of the most sharply unequal regions of the UK (Shuttleworth and Shirlow 1999: 79).

These 1980s shifts in the rhetoric of economic rights endure in the post-conflict era. Ordinary people in nationalist areas like the Falls and Ardoyne continue to understand their experiences of poverty and unemployment as the product of anti-Catholic discrimination. Meanwhile, loyalists suffering high unemployment in areas like the Shankill believe the peace process simply swapped anti-Catholicism for anti-Protestantism. The certainties of past rights rhetoric continue to explain scarce or poorly compensated work more neatly than the complexity of financialized capitalism, postindustrial economics, and state austerity. In the 1980s, policy and academic explanations of economics as cause and cure for the conflict amplified the common sense of discrimination as a cause of violence; local campaigns cemented the persuasive power of such explanations. The rhetoric of discrimination allowed a constrained vision of ethnopolitical inequality to displace broader critiques of economic injustice, rather than creating a politics that acknowledged the interdependence of political and economic rights. The debates of the 1980s reinforced rights talk as a mode of war by other means and nurtured grievances that persist in the present. Economic explanations reemerge as attractive and true in moments of crisis—and as justifications for violence.

Economic Rights and the Causes of Conflict

> Another reason to be proud, this being a citizen! . . . The majestic quality of the law which prohibits the wealthy as well as the poor from sleeping under bridges, from begging in the streets, and from stealing bread.
> —Anatole France, *The Red Lily*, Chapter 7

Political scientist Ted Gurr's (1970) seminal work *Why Men Rebel* considered material deprivation's causal role in conflict. Gurr used the term "relative deprivation" to describe the gap between a group's actual material circumstances and the circumstances that group members believe they should enjoy (24). He did not propose that this sort of deprivation automatically caused political violence, acknowledging other factors, such as cultural orientations to political violence and perceptions of state legitimacy. Nevertheless, Gurr's analysis treated deprivation as a central factor in conflict, and this association became conventional wisdom for policymakers in many countries in the following decades.

In 1980s Northern Ireland, the perceived links between deprivation and violence energized grassroots rights discourse and practice, policy prescriptions, and analytical debates.[3] For example, in the "meta-conflict" of academia, long-running exchanges took place about the extent to which discrimination against Catholics caused political violence (e.g., Hewitt 1981, 1983, 1985, 1987; O'Hearn 1983, 1985, 1987). These debates are not straightforward discussions of economic rights in the sense of minimal economic guarantees made by states to citizens, as found in the International Covenant on Economic, Social and Cultural Rights or the European Social Charter. Rather, they are discussions of the extent to which the state in Northern Ireland, before and after direct rule, promoted or tolerated systematic anti-Catholic discrimination by private employers and local government. Therefore, such discussions, whether in political rhetoric or academic debate, are about equal protection and the political question of state legitimacy, rather than the state's minimal guarantees of living standards.

In a variety of ways, causal linkages of economy and violence often perpetuate standard modes of political dispute, rather than making sense of causes and solutions. Shirlow and McGovern (1996) argue that, in political practice, "the conditions of capitalist production are continually understood in relation to competing sectarian and social identities" (380). As such, "the economy continues to be a weapon used to support, renew and reproduce the mode of political operation and cultural contestation" (Shirlow and Shuttleworth 1999: 32). Similarly, Smith (1999) argues that material explanations for the conflict in Northern Ireland become inherently political, in communal rather than class terms, due to the broader context of political rhetoric. He writes that the "commonly accepted view of the nature of the violence as a reflex to systemic conditions has, in fact, been assiduously cultivated by the IRA and other paramilitaries to promote their own agendas" (96).

Nevertheless, policy prescriptions of the 1980s that emphasized economic solutions to the conflict contained a material analysis of the conflict, although not always in terms of anti-Catholic discrimination. The driving factor for both British subsidies and U.S.-led aid efforts was the neoliberal economic assumption of an individual's economic self-interest, which Shirlow and Shuttleworth (1999) neatly summarize: "social conflict is caused by deprivation but enlightened self-interest in pursuit of economic benefits will reduce the potential for division" (79). Policymakers reiterated this economic approach to the conflict's causes and solutions long after it was demonstrated to be ineffective (Shirlow and Shuttleworth 1999; Shuttleworth and Shirlow 1999). Indeed, even during the peace process of the 1990s, political leaders, from local representatives to U.S. president William Clinton, repeatedly stressed the importance of economic development. Whether labeled liberal or neoliberal, policies in the 1980s promised a peace dividend of prosperity as both a consequence of conflict resolution and a driver of further reconciliation. Of course, this analysis also inspired skepticism. Darby and MacGinty (2000) point out that a peace dividend would merely compensate for a "peace deficit," caused by shrinking conflict-related areas of the economy such as security (91–92).

In the 1980s, policy and funding programs converged with grassroots efforts to promote local economic development. Local projects, however, were initially animated by the developing European politics of economic rights rather than economic neoliberalism. The origin of these politics of economic rights lies in the growing European unification project during the 1970s and 1980s. Although the 1975 Helsinki Accords, a declaration for improved relations between Western and Communist countries, privileged the U.S. vision of human rights as political rights, this was hardly the end of European advocacy for social and economic rights (Ignatieff 1999; Moyn 2010). This advocacy became increasingly influential in the 1990s and 2000s (Chong 2010; Cullen 2009).

As noted in the previous chapter, the European Social Charter was a 1961 treaty that established basic economic and social rights as a complement to the European Convention on Human Rights. Characterizations of this charter are part of ongoing debates about European approaches to economic rights. Whelan and Donnelly (2007) label as "ludicrous" recent claims that Western governments treated economic rights as subordinate in the establishment of the postwar human rights regimes (910). Their arguments, particularly regarding U.S. stances, have sparked debate among other scholars. For example, Kirkup and Evans (2009) claim that Whelan and Donnelly conveniently ignore both the role of structural forces and disjunctions between law and practice. In this vein, Kang (2009) argues that the existence of social welfare systems do not constitute a substantial normative commitment to social and economic rights. Kang notes that the European Social Charter has been subordinate to the European convention in practice, and that the charter did not develop enforcement mechanisms until 1996. Critiques of Whelan and Donnelly, however, are on firmer ground when restricted to U.S. politics and policy. In Western Europe, the norms of entitlement—especially to medical care—are deeply established, even within the less social democratic United Kingdom.

Debates over the importance of social and economic rights are part of broader arguments in law, policy, and scholarship regarding the definition and universality of human rights. Just as policymakers and academics contest the positions of Western governments regarding the status of economic rights, so too do activists contest the place of these rights. Chong (2010) notes that established human rights lawyers and NGOs remain skeptical about economic rights, while their advocates use rights discourse for more expansive political and legal purposes. In Chong's view, this advocacy is more liberatory and successful than the human rights establishment expected.

Making economic rights central to human rights involves collective understandings of basic human entitlements that are part of a recent tendency within human rights work, which Goodale (2009b) characterizes as "political developments in which the framework of human rights was mobilized in order to address the problem of power as it expresses itself through inequalities" (116). Goodale argues that these attempts "reframe profound political-economic problems in terms of human rights" (119). In 1980s Northern Ireland, there were similar attempts to reframe rights advocacy in terms of political economy—drawing from rights that were formally present in both British law and European treaties.

The philosophical and legal underpinnings of basic economic rights were central to the activism that collided with and succumbed to the 1980s prescription of economic development for peace. Local approaches to entitlement were also partially fuelled and shaped by European welfare standards and opposition to the Thatcher government's policies to limit welfare entitlements. Yet local experiences of poverty and deprivation remained central to activists' understandings of different policy approaches. Thus, Belfast activists drew upon and developed complex political and rhetorical arguments in their campaigns.

"Who Do These People Think They Are?"

During the 1974 Ulster Workers' Council strike, British Prime Minister Harold Wilson angrily labeled residents of Northern Ireland "spongers" and wondered, "Who do these people think they are?"[4] His speech raised an issue that still resonates: British expenditure in Northern Ireland, frequently called "transfer payments." Northern Ireland is a net recipient of, rather than contributor to, British taxation—a condition that has prevailed since the end of World War II (Munck 1993). Discussions of these transfer payments (e.g., Munck 1993; Kennedy et al. 1988; Rowthorn and Wayne 1988) frequently do not explore the broader redistributive logic of taxation. Yet redistribution— sometimes couched in the language of welfare rights and employment rights— has been central to politics in Northern Ireland. In the postwar period, as Northern Irish dependence on transfer payments increased, local acceptance of redistributive logic also increased. Furthermore, by the 1980s, dependence crossed classes, with 40 percent of the workforce directly employed by the state, from civil servants to garbage collectors (Coulter 1999; Rolston and Tomlinson 1988).

Discrimination in employment complicated the economic landscape. Since formal measurement began until the 1980s, aggregate Catholic male unemployment was approximately twice that of Protestant males (Murphy and Armstrong 1994). Unemployment rates for Catholic women were 1.5 to

1.8 times higher than those of Protestant women (Murphy 1996). As antidiscrimination policies were introduced in the 1970s and expanded in the 1980s, the unemployment gap began to shrink significantly. As noted earlier, by the mid-1990s, the class structure of Catholic and Protestant workers had converged (Breen 2000). In 2010, fair employment statistics showed that Catholics were 45.4 percent of the monitored workforce, matching their proportion of the available labor pool (Equality Commission 2010). Although increased Catholic upward mobility was an important economic shift in the 1990s and 2000s and is related to both antidiscrimination campaigns and legal reforms, in the 1980s, the unemployment gap for Catholics loomed large.

Yet deprivation remained concentrated in certain areas. Since the 1970s, various publications have analyzed poverty indices spatially (e.g., BAN Project Team 1976; Robson et al. 1994; Noble et al. 2001; NISRA 2010). West Belfast has consistently been one of the most deprived areas of the region. Activists and scholars argue that a peace dividend has failed to materialize for west Belfast (e.g., O'Hearn 2000). Recent spatial measures of deprivation across the region support this point, consistently listing the nine places of highest deprivation as the areas of north and west Belfast where violence of the conflict was greatest: Whiterock, Falls, New Lodge, Shankill, Crumlin, and Ardoyne (NISRA 2010: 27).[5]

These indices are particularly important with reference to poverty among Protestants. Despite Protestant advantage at the aggregate level, working-class areas like the Shankill had a lesser share in this advantage, and working-class Protestants felt the decline of industry more sharply due to prior preferential access to industrial jobs. By the late twentieth century, long-term, multigenerational unemployment was firmly established in the Shankill as well as the Falls areas.

Curing Conflict with Cash

It is not lack of money that is the matter with Northern Ireland.
—Margaret Thatcher, discussing the International Fund for Ireland, 1987[6]

Funds for the most deprived sections of Northern Ireland were caught up in domestic and international politics. During the 1980s, successive

Conservative governments in Britain pursued neoliberal goals, emphasizing individualism, privatization, and monetarism (Gamble 1988). In the United States, where significant state funding for Ireland was established in 1986, president Ronald Reagan embraced similar goals. In the U.S., political calculations came into play in several ways. Aid to Ireland united Republican and Democratic legislators courting voters who had strong affiliations to their Irish roots. The Republican Party pursued blue-collar voters who had traditionally voted Democratic, and ethnic appeals to white Irish Americans were an effective tool (Jacobson 2006). Additionally, despite the Reagan administration's public denunciations of terrorism, federal immigration judges quietly treated PIRA as a political movement, creating problems for U.S. relations with Britain (Holland 2001).

Thatcher's policies were neoliberal in a strict sense. That is, a set of prescriptive ideas guided policy using a market logic that valorized individualism and privileged the private sector over the public (see Kipnis 2007, 2008). Stuart Hall (1988) characterizes this agenda as broadly privileging market logic not only in governance but also in relations that others might deem social. Through various programs in both Britain and Northern Ireland, private providers took over previously public services, from hospital cleaning to job training. In Belfast's most divided and impoverished communities, these private providers of the state's social services were often organizations that emerged from the activism in the 1970s.

Frank Gaffiken and Mike Morrissey (1989) have noted the congruencies of Thatcherism with Victorian perceptions of the poor. In their analysis, Thatcherism assumed the market would abolish poverty—if allowed to operate properly, free from the distortions and dependencies of welfare. In this model, the deserving poor would receive relief, while benefit cuts would force idle, able-bodied citizens into work. Reagan's philosophy was similar in that it placed responsibility for poverty on the poor, rather than on structural conditions (Kodras 1997). Brown and Pizer (1987) report that Reagan told schoolchildren that hunger was the fault of the hungry because "the hungry are too ignorant to know where to get it [food]" (189).

This philosophical orientation shaped the way both the U.S. and UK governments directed funds to address both conflict and deprivation in Northern Ireland. Yet less lofty political and economic rationales were also at work. Although Reagan publicly valorized entrepreneurialism, U.S. aid to Ireland initially was steered to large corporations whose profits would, he asserted, eventually trickle down into growth for all. Meanwhile, by putting unemployed people in putative job training programs providing social services, the British government served its broader philosophical objectives while obscuring dramatic unemployment figures. (Those in training were no longer classified as unemployed, and their benefits were no longer unemployment benefits.) This approach led to increased funding for community groups, who administered such training programs locally. Later in the decade, domestic funding for these groups seemed like a desperate attempt to pacify the conflict.

Not coincidentally, in this period small organizations in Belfast began to propose "community enterprise" solutions. To access expanding development funds for the region, organizations began to frame projects in entrepreneurial terms, rather than the Marxist rhetoric of 1970s cooperatives. The International Fund for Ireland (IFI) was one of the most significant international aid efforts that encouraged the enterprise model. The fund was established by the 1985 Anglo-Irish Agreement and financed by the United States, Canada, Australia, New Zealand, and some of the European Community.[7] The U.S. Congress mandated that its initial $120 million contribution be used to promote industry in the private sector and not replicate or replace statutory development funds.

Yet as they applied for funding, community groups also criticized the IFI for not directing money to people in the greatest need—for example, the IFI granted £2 million to a large hotel company as part of a tourism strategy. The fund responded to criticism by eventually directing "community enterprise funds" to the poorest areas (Sheehan 1995). Yet even this action brought more profound challenges. An immediate tension arose between the neoliberalism of IFI's mandate and the collective, social nature of community-based projects. More broadly, the IFI action revealed the difficulties of economic rights in practice, a tension between how neoliberal policymakers define responsibility and apportion economic aid and the social democratic leanings of those who seek funding. Considered even more expansively, the IFI work in the 1980s highlights the difficulty of steering economic development to support conflict resolution.

With increased domestic and international funding, the grassroots activism that flourished in the areas of greatest conflict became more bureaucratic. These groups began to constitute themselves more like conventional NGOs. However, they remained an integral part of the local districts, acting as what are now called "community-based organizations" (CBOs). This trend toward institutionalization accelerated during the 1980s, and, by 1992, their number had increased tenfold, to 3,000 community and voluntary groups in Northern Ireland (NICVA 1992: 1). Paradoxically, then, neoliberalism gave stability to groups run by people who opposed and critiqued the state. Funds were channeled through job training programs and other agencies, stabilizing numerous existing groups and inspiring the creation of new ones.

Yet Belfast activists began the decade embracing a very different political and economic understanding of poverty and basic state responsibilities. In the late 1970s, the first European Anti-Poverty Programme gave activists a more robust analysis of poverty's consequences (McCready 2001). The program considered umemployment as merely one measure of deprivation, alongside low wages, high living expenses (for essentials such as food and heating), low educational attainment, poor housing conditions, poor health, and high levels of debt and benefits receipt. A key premise of the program was that these conditions excluded poor people from social and political, as well as economic, power. Therefore, poverty as exclusion denied citizens of their fundamental rights because, for example, people marginalized from economic life cannot effectively exercise political rights. Supported by funding from this program, local activists began to embrace its definition of poverty emphasizing its exclusionary effects—from social, economic, and political life.

These more expansive understandings of poverty as exclusion drove shifts in activism. Local groups expanded their focus from housing to the totality of conditions in neighborhoods. Campaigns for welfare rights and employment emerged alongside job training, service provision, and enterprise schemes. But Belfast activists and groups treated public expenditure as an entitlement rather than charity; furthermore, these economic rights and entitlements were increasingly linked to the exercise of fundamental civil and political rights. These changes arose in benefits-dependent communities, in which survival often meant welfare dependence. Workfare programs treated welfare as "conditional" and replaced public providers with private, albeit nonprofit, ones; international funds placed responsibility for economic development, and thus peace, on the poor themselves. But community activists' acceptance of this largesse was shaped by their own cultural understandings of long-standing economic dependence at the individual and regional level, as well as the deeply engrained tendency to treat a variety of issues as zero-sum conflicts between unionist and nationalist blocs.

Doing the Double

Statistics make unemployment abstract and not too
uncomfortable. The human being is different. To be
hungry is different than to count the hungry.
—Meridel LeSueur, "Women Are
Hungry" (1934)1990, 145

As I learned to navigate west Belfast, one early guidepost I used was a neatly painted wall message reading "DHSS TOUTS WILL BE SHOT." Unlike graffiti, tidy messages in white paint were usually "official" paramilitary communications. The message concisely explained the consequences of reporting ("touting") benefits fraud to state authorities—in this case, the Department of Health and Social Services (DHSS).

Benefits dependence is not just a fact written on the walls. It has long shaped the temporal rhythms of life in these areas. One sunny day, I passed a pub where chairs and tables formed an ad hoc café on the sidewalk. An extraordinary number of women were milling about. "Ah, Child Benefit day," my companion remarked. He meant many women went into pubs on Mondays because child benefits were paid that day. Similarly, I observed an influx of men in pubs on Tuesdays, when unemployment benefits were dispensed. This is not to say that poor people fecklessly waste benefits on alcohol— rather, that, on receiving their benefits, some sought relaxation and company.

The DHSS distributes different benefits—from Child Benefit to Disability Living Allowance—on different days; in fact, the benefits are now deposited in bank or post office accounts. For recipients, they structure activity in time, from socializing to grocery shopping. These patterns can be traced to the tremendously high unemployment rates in west Belfast during the 1980s.

Many activists I met, whether of the old-fashioned voluntary variety or in paid community development positions, had intimate knowledge of the perilous existence of life structured by benefit payments. Many of them personally experienced unemployment during the 1980s. They describe the dilemmas facing the people with whom they work far better than I can. "Frank," an IRA ex-prisoner and community activist, said, "The whole economic culture of this place has been ducking and diving or surviving in the black economy, . . . The security, and I'm using that [word] advisedly, the security of the benefits system, as opposed to the insecurity of self-employment." As Gledhill (2003) observes, "Defrauding the welfare system or participating in the black economy . . . may still provide individuals who pursue such lifestyles with superior subjective senses of personal worth as socially situated actors and improved material opportunities to participate in the culture of consumerism that hegemonic values so tirelessly promote" (221). In other words, economic stability, even if obtained in questionable ways, provides a sense of worth for an individual, allowing him or her to participate in a world that continually promotes consumerism.

Yet welfare dependence does not necessarily produce compliant subjects. Many individuals instead combine work and welfare to make ends meet. They work in the informal economy ("off the books") and receive benefits from the state, a practice called "doing the double." Working off the books subjects people to low wages and poor conditions, with few legal protections, as described in Leonard's (1994) research on Northern Ireland's informal economy. Rather than idleness, doing the double requires initiative, ingenuity, and diligence. Men and women juggle benefits eligibility with labor that is often physically demanding, usually at undesirable hours, working as construction workers or nightclub bouncers, cleaners or hairdressers.

Other practices include "giro drops"—addresses used simply to collect benefits because actual household circumstances reduce benefits eligibility—and compensation claims. More than one acquaintance of mine sustained injuries in ordinary circumstances ranging from brawls to rearranging household furniture, and, on noticing street or sidewalk excavations, claimed compensation by attributing their injuries to falls on sidewalk construction. I was told of six men lowering a pensioner with a broken leg into a construction excavation. He had fallen down his own stairs but claimed his injury came from the construction site, and he ended up netting £10,000 ($15,500) in compensation. In addition to ordinary civil liability, the state has a limited compensation scheme for victims of violence.

Doing the double can be, and is seen as, a form of agency in dire circumstances. No one I met, however, overestimated this agency; most people had an acute sense of its constraint. I attended advice workshops run by local NGOs at which community workers warned of the "benefits trap," where simple safety nets like home insurance are unaffordable and predatory lending is a constant temptation. Furthermore, the loss of dignity and hope is debilitating. As "Barbara," a loyalist community worker, put it:

> If you're sitting in an estate that's the pits, and you have no job, and your husband has no job, and the kids are gurning [whining] that they

want this and they want that, and you don't have the money. . . . Maybe you're in debt, way above your head, and you're not gonna sit and say, "Well, now I have a vision for tomorrow." Because why bother? Tomorrow's gonna be the same as today and the next day and the other day.

Hopelessness is compounded by poverty's heritability. "Michaela," a republican youth worker, described her frustrations for young people with long family histories of unemployment: "They're so proud of themselves, like, 'I'm from Ballymurphy, so what.' Right? They can . . . argue with anyone about their political beliefs. But see work? 'Work's not for me. Because we don't get work.'"

As unemployment soared in the 1980s, attitudes toward the state were also changing. These changes emerged from different experiences of nationalists and loyalists, yet these experiences converged in an intensified sense of entitlement. For many nationalists—with lengthy memories of discrimination—"taking the Queen's shilling" did not buy loyalty to the state. Accepting benefits was an act of subversion, laden with colonial resentments.

In the 1970s, republicans had refused any recognition of British sovereignty. Paramilitary defendants declined to respond to charges in court, individual households boycotted the census, and community groups were slow to accept state funds or liaise with even the lowliest state workers. But after the hunger strikes in 1981, the republican strategy of "Armalite and ballot box" influenced actions beyond armed struggle and party politics. Individuals and CBOs began to believe that claiming rights and entitlements did not undermine their broader struggle. Indeed, acknowledging state agencies could expand the sphere of struggle. "Diarmuid," a former republican prisoner, advocated engaging with the state in the 1980s; in his view, lobbying state agencies was not the same as recognizing their legitimacy:

Never vacate the playing field. Contest the space of it on a whole wide range of issues. I am a republican, nationalist, Catholic. I do not want to live in this state. I cannot say that often enough. I do not want to live in this state. But whilst I am living in this state, I am not going to let the state authorities treat me whatever way they want to. . . . They would like nothing better, the state authorities [would like] nothing better, or the dominant political ideology would like nothing better than for me and the likes of me to walk away. And not contest the space on a whole range of issues. I for one am not going to do that.

Diarmuid's view was shaped by different periods of imprisonment. During the 1970s, paramilitary prisoners had de facto political status, and both republicans and loyalists were self-educated, in a sense radicalized, under that regime (see Feldman 1991). The death of ten republican prisoners on hunger strike to regain political status led some ex-prisoners begin to think more strategically about how they approached the state. In the 1980s, many of the early prisoners were released, having served full sentences; like Diarmuid, they began to apply a more instrumental logic to their entitlements from the state. This political sophistication began to influence broader attitudes. As Diarmuid put it, many ex-prisoners were seen, and saw themselves, as the "most able, dynamic, and competent people" in many neighborhoods.

In loyalist areas, the situation was similar, with different catalysts. Fewer ex-prisoners began to take up community organizing, but another shift in consciousness was occurring among loyalists, who were furious over the signing of the Anglo-Irish Agreement in 1985. The treaty acknowledged a policy role in the north for the Republic and stated that unification of the jurisdictions would be subject to a democratic vote. (In this way, it was also unsatisfactory for republicans because it seemed to soften the Republic's territorial claim.) For loyalists, the declaration that Britain had no "selfish strategic or economic interest" in Northern Ireland was a betrayal. While political parties staged protests against the treaty, some loyalists told me they began to believe they had served Britain as mere "wage slaves and cannon fodder." Protestants had once been ashamed of benefits dependence, embarrassed when they used food vouchers in local shops. With the unemployment crisis, Thatcher's cuts, and the Anglo-Irish Agreement, loyalists' relationship with the state became more ambivalent. If their loyalty was ignored, Britain at the very least owed them a debt, and the stigma attached to benefits dependence began to recede. But translating this understanding of basic rights and responsibilities—the bedrock of economic and social rights—into political action was as complex and fraught as doing the double.

Claiming Economic Rights

> It is our duty to look after ourselves and then also to
> help look after our neighbour, and life is a reciprocal
> business and people have got the entitlements too much

in mind without the obligations, because there is no such
thing as an entitlement unless someone has first met an
obligation. . . . There is no such thing as society.
—Margaret Thatcher, interview for *Woman's Own*,
October 31, 1987

"How many of you have a TV license?" "Grace" asked a group of women from
nationalist and loyalist areas in a community hall outside Belfast one day in
the late 1990s. Looking dubiously from her to the flip chart beside her, the
women began to laugh. State-issued TV licenses are required to use a television, and the fees fund the state broadcaster, the BBC. For many poor people,
these seemed a ludicrous waste of money, not simply because of their cost
but also because TV license inspectors avoided both loyalist and republican
neighborhoods. Indeed, even in 2000, inspectors who did venture into such
areas were sometimes attacked.

While the women laughed, Grace pointed again to her flip chart. "Hold
on, hold on," she said. "It's not funny. If you haven't got a TV license, it's
a thousand pound fine." Gesturing at the next items on her list, she said,
"How many of you have house insurance? Life insurance? House insurance
is important. If you get flooded, no one takes care of the property you lose.
And death happens to all of us. But how many of you have got these things?
Raise your hand." In the silence, no hands were raised. Grace, a woman
from a Catholic background who worked in a loyalist community center,
explained that it seemed as if these discussions never changed over decades.
Benefits do not stretch to the expenses middle-class people take for granted;
apparent necessities for many in the contemporary West are luxuries. But,
she reminded them, any victories gained in the rent and rate strikes of the
1970s were pyrrhic—the state deducted strikers' arrears from their social
insurance payments. The state, it seemed, would always find ways to enforce
its contracts.

Campaigns and workshops like this one have been ubiquitous since the
late 1970s. Then, the European Community Anti-Poverty Initiative catalyzed local advocacy for welfare rights. At that time, welfare rights became
a central issue for community activists, with many of their efforts focused
on informing people of their entitlements and assisting them with claims.
Some efforts were devoted to lobbying for increased benefits allowances
and regulatory changes. So, for example, one recurrent proposal called for
unemployment benefits to help people transition from doing the double to

legitimate employment, recommending a gradual reduction of benefits over the period of several years for claimants as they went legitimate with their hairdressing, house painting, or taxi businesses. In the late 1970s, funds from Europe supported the Belfast Welfare Rights Project, which identified low levels of benefits claims in poor districts of Belfast and established centers where workers advised residents of their benefit entitlements. This project led to the establishment of the first local welfare advice bureaus in Northern Ireland. A former project worker explained to me that, dull as filling in forms may sound, this was the moment when Belfast residents began to understand benefits as *entitlements*, in sharp contrast to *charity*.

The new Citizens' Advice Bureaus offered guidance through the complex maze of government bureaucracy. Meanwhile, in nationalist west Belfast, other projects sought out claimants rather than advising visitors from an office. In Ballymurphy, local activists began a systematic campaign: first, they conducted a survey, enlisting respected locals to encourage participation in both questionnaires and interviews. Using the survey to analyze the gap between benefits received and benefits eligibility, campaign workers then helped residents fill in claim forms for all of their entitlements, from income support to heating allowance.

Not surprisingly, the DHSS was flooded with new claims, and that success encouraged the campaign to move on to other estates, including Moyard, Springhill, and Whiterock/Westrock. Welfare rights advocates also organized public protests against the Thatcher government's welfare cuts. One unusual event was the 1984 Belfast Welfare Rights Festival, with workshops, arts exhibitions, and musical performances, a possibly misguided attempt to promote welfare rights.

Although these campaigns helped establish common understandings of basic welfare benefits as fundamental entitlements, recognizing the minimal duties of the state did not become a full-fledged political project. Partly this was because anti-Catholic discrimination had historically determined structural inequality, and people more readily understood their circumstances in terms of discrimination than in terms of the state's economic interventions, in support of capitalists or workers. But even more fundamentally, welfare rights could not address the constancy of unemployment and its daily humiliations. In the 1980s, benefits claimants, civil servants, and high-ranking government ministers all understood that unemployment was at crisis levels, and neither neoliberalism nor economic rights provided sustainable remedies.

Something to Do

Belfast is a city that has lost its heart. A ship-building,
rope-making, linen-weaving town. It builds no ships,
makes no rope and weaves no linen. Those trades died. A
city can't survive without something to do with itself.
—Robert McLiam Wilson, *Eureka Street*, 1996, 215

In the late 1990s, I asked the director of a youth training program how useful his program was if the young people did not get jobs when they finished. He said, "They may never use the skills in work, but having the skills is some use. I mean, boys always like to mess about with cars, and girls like knowing how to decorate the house and do their hair and things." Gender stereotypes aside, his response contains a striking fatalism. The residents of Belfast's disadvantaged enclaves are aware of the dignity associated with work; they are aware of its lack and loss. They are also aware that their own actions have little to do with whether jobs materialize and that people, like cities, must have something to do with themselves.

In the 1980s, Thatcher's neoliberal policies guided a transfer of funds from welfare into job training, or "workfare," through programs such as the Youth Training Programme (YTP) and Action for Community Employment (ACE). These programs required claimants to "earn" benefits, often while providing social services previously delivered by state employees. Under ACE, for example, a claimant performed work of "community benefit" and received a salary payment in lieu of benefits for twelve months. CBOs were allowed to retain a small portion of that payment for overheads. The rationale was that ACE would provide work experience for the long-term unemployed, increase the labor supply, and reduce benefits fraud (Scott 1993). Similarly, YTPs were administered locally for unemployed young people.

Existing and newly constituted community groups began to deliver these programs; workfare replaced public providers with private, albeit nonprofit, ones. Importantly, these groups' acceptance of state largesse was shaped by understandings of their rights and the state's responsibilities, as well as the myriad failures of this fundamental contract. Nevertheless, the administration of "workfare" turned many CBOs into "subcontractors" for public services. At the same time, the role of community activist became a paid occupation.

Organizations administering ACE funds also began to provide public services through what was called Care in the Community, which further increased their funding. ACE workers provided home help, gardening, household maintenance, Meals on Wheels, day center staffing, and a variety of other support services for vulnerable people, allowing the elderly or disabled to remain in their own communities. ACE funding alone more than trebled from 1985 to 1990, to £50.7 million ($78.8 million) annually; the number of ACE workers increased from 430 in 1981 to almost 11,000 in 1991 (Rolston and Tomlinson 1988: 111; Mulrine et al. 1992: 26).

Workfare did more than fund care, however. While some CBOs existed to administer ACE and YTP, a more widespread effect of the policy was that almost every organization I encountered when I first visited Belfast in the 1990s "employed" ACE workers. Organizations included day-care providers, residents' associations, youth programs, women's centers, or arts projects. The priorities and agenda of local community groups steered the work of these organizations. ACE became more than a program that "off-loaded" public services onto NGOs; it also allowed welfare claimants to work on a compensated, rather than voluntary, basis for CBOs.

Many professional community workers I met began their careers in one-year ACE posts when they were unemployed or through YTP placements. In terms of fostering transitions from benefits to permanent employment, success was arguable: only 35 percent of ACE participants found employment (Scott 1993: 5). Obviously, not every ACE worker became a professional community organizer, but many professionals began as ACE or YTP workers. From the standpoint of community organizations, workfare provided labor to create and maintain organizations, increased their standing with local residents, fueled new areas for engagement with policy, and trained individuals to become professional community workers. Workfare helped legitimate community groups and became a vehicle for them to make demands of the state, as well as vice versa.

The story of one small residents association that began in the 1980s illustrates these dynamics. This group operated in a newer, outlying estate near the greater Shankill area, located on an interface that was a site of frequent political violence. Barbara, who was active in the group's formation, had worked in a linen mill since the age of fourteen. Although the housing was modern, she and others felt that "right on the peace line, the authorities had just taken—. . . had gone out of the estate and just abrogated their responsibility. . . . We couldn't get the streets swept, we couldn't get the bins emptied, we couldn't get normal things done." Only about 300 of 800 properties were

inhabited. In short, the estate suffered from "blight," high levels of unemployment and welfare dependence and was situated in a conflict zone.

In the 1980s the linen mill Barbara worked for closed. Before being laid off,
she had done voluntary work but had not seen that as a career. As she put it,

> Now I had a lot of voluntary community work, but it wasn't the same
> as a job. . . . You know, I could have filled my day quite happily doing
> voluntary work. But it wasn't the same as having the motivation to get
> out of bed in the morning and actually go to work—and the whole
> self-esteem of your own [paycheck].

Although she was "devastated" by unemployment, it spurred her to
become part of a local effort to improve conditions in the estate. In 1987, she
and twelve other residents began the often tedious and disheartening process of community organizing. It was labor intensive: conducting household
surveys, counting vacant and inhabited properties, documenting vandalism.
They began to hope that they would get state funds for their area.

They organized many meetings to discuss antisocial behavior and service
needs. A particular complaint emerged from the meetings: vandalism of vacant
properties. Derelict, one-bedroom flats, unsuitable for most families, housed
squatters or were vandalized by unemployed youth. This created a menacing
environment, confrontations, and, inevitably, paramilitary punishments for
"antisocial behavior." When greater numbers of residents became involved, the
group approached state agencies to negotiate for services and infrastructure.
As Barbara put it, though, they had to demonstrate self-help first:

> We coulda' marched to city hall and demanded the houses be fixed up.
> We woulda' got nowhere. Because as the houses were being fixed up
> they were being vandalized. We had to cure this problem before we
> could cure that problem. We had to have meetings and bring people
> in and say, "look this is our area. Nobody gives a damn whether it's
> right or wrong—except us.

To support their self-help effort, they began to lobby for state-funded
youth services. A mere ten months into the effort, they received funding for a
job-training unit for young people, and Barbara became its manager. In that
job, as she explained,

We brought in young people, young men and women, eighteen plus, who had been, perhaps, in trouble with the police. Not big things, [just] throwing stones, or drugs, or whatever. And we brought them in and we simply taught them how to get out of bed in the morning. How to respond to discipline in a work setting. And how to actually take an interest in what they were doing. And . . . it was the happiest four years of my life. I'm proud to say that in four years we put fifty-seven people through the books. Of which forty-nine went on to work.

This group of concerned citizens became a fully constituted NGO, with a board, four full-time employees, an office, and their own ACE worker. The public housing agency donated a vacant flat for the premises. One-bedroom flats were replaced with family housing, and antisocial behavior declined. The group's story unfolded like that of many community groups. Residents became concerned with a social or economic problem, and local meetings, discussions, and plans followed. An important shift in the 1980s was that state funds were available to implement such plans, as illustrated in Barbara's story.

It would be an exaggeration to claim the area became prosperous. Community groups did not transform the broader economy or alter the dynamics of conflict in the 1980s, nor did ACE become a major transit point into private-sector employment. Peace did not materialize. Nevertheless, state funding did motivate and enable people to improve their living conditions and to formulate demands for state subsidy as a minimal entitlement.

Benevolence and Prosperity

I suspect that its [the International Fund for Ireland's] conception was influenced by a muddled, but benevolent, desire to believe that money could buy peace, even in Ireland.
—Charles Brett, "The International Fund for Ireland, 1986–1989" (1990: 431)

"I don't know why we bother trying to get these companies to come here. They come in for five years, then they're off to the next cheap country, and you're back to the same place you were before, sitting on the dole." In the late 1990s "Jeanine," a community worker in the Shankill area, was dismissive about a promised peace dividend. International corporations—such as Michelin—had been in Ireland before and left. Several companies—such as the DeLorean Motor Company—had received state subsidies and failed. When DeLorean failed, the workmanship of Northern Irish employees was blamed. Jeanine was not alone in being completely disillusioned about promises that international corporations would create jobs. She pointed out that Fruit of the Loom was leaving Donegal—foreshadowing the flimsy foundations of the Republic's then-celebrated Celtic Tiger. "Some of those people will never work again, you know. They'll never have a job again," she said.

In the 1980s, however, inward investment still seemed like a solution, and community groups tried to attract major firms to the most deprived areas of Northern Ireland. "Róisín," an activist from Ballymurphy, laughed when recalling one such venture. Local activists invited several British businessmen to Ballymurphy, including bankers and the head of Marks and Spencer, a large UK department store company. Community activists took them on a tour of the area to demonstrate the need for investment and to ask about the skills local people needed to be hired by their companies. "We wanted to see if we could get doors opened. And how to get people trained up and into jobs. But they [the businesspeople] were terrified." The visiting businessmen were so anxious that they would be attacked or kidnapped that a military surveillance helicopter trailed the entourage throughout the visit.

Although inward investment plans yielded few results in the 1980s, and arguable benefits later, state schemes to attract these companies continued. During its first three years, IFI boasted a fund of £105 million (approximately $170 million).[8] As noted earlier, IFI initially supported larger local corporations and subsidized international investors. Criticisms that funds were not going to the most disadvantaged areas, however, led to a focus on funding "community enterprise." One of the early recipients of IFI community enterprise funds in the New Lodge area of Belfast illustrates how such efforts yielded diffuse, unquantifiable effects.

The New Lodge area lies just northwest of the city center, where loyalist west Belfast bleeds into a patchwork of Protestant and Catholic neighborhoods, with multiple peace walls. New Lodge's seven tower blocks loom over the smaller houses that make up most of the area. An enormous Irish tricolor flag used to fly from the top of one tower, and memorials to hunger strikers now decorate the roofs of the towers. The neighborhood is surrounded by loyalist areas, and violence was frequent in the 1970s and 1980s. Life here was profoundly dangerous during the conflict because New Lodge's geography was not as defensible as areas like the greater Falls. Major city avenues and proximity to the city center allowed loyalists to enter and leave the area quickly to carry out killings, and the PIRA engaged the police and military in street battles. One of the most horrific pub bombings of the 1970s took place at McGurk's Bar in New Lodge; fifteen Catholic civilians died, and seventeen more were injured. Rioting was also common in the 1970s and 1980s; from the 1990s until the present, New Lodge has been a site of periodic rioting during summer parade disputes.

New Lodge is and was an area of serious deprivation. The Robson Index (Robson et al. 1994), a spatial analysis of deprivation during the 1980s and early 1990s, ranked New Lodge as the second most deprived ward in Northern Ireland. Recent census analysis, measuring the area in smaller sections, puts New Lodge area 1 as the fifth most deprived area, and New Lodge areas 2 and 3 as fourteenth and fifteenth respectively (NISRA 2010: 27). In the 1980s, residents of New Lodge benefited from the lessons of earlier redevelopment campaigns like those in Divis and the Shankill; when a redevelopment plan made its way to New Lodge, the local housing association engaged with planners and had extensive input in the new housing design. They ensured that existing residents were able to remain in their homes.

From this success, residents made plans to convert an abandoned mill, which had housed a youth club in the 1970s, into an engine for job creation. The space was derelict and dangerous by the mid-1980s, and residents struggled to find ways to redefine it as a community asset. They wanted to combine economic and social functions in the space, but an architectural study concluded the building could not be cost-effectively converted for mixed use. When the local education board promised to build a youth club at another site, locals began planning how the space could be used for economic development.

Three feasibility studies, funded by different charities and state agencies, led to a project funded with a combined loan and grant from the IFI's Community Economic Regeneration Scheme in 1988. The proposal was to renovate the building to house an ACE scheme, rental retail spaces, and transitional workspaces for local entrepreneurs. Local residents began to raise capital, selling about £30,000 ($48,600) of shares to neighborhood residents at £1 ($1.62) per share; thirty-five shares entitled the owner to voting membership in the cooperative. With small grants from other charities and this startup capital, they secured IFI funding.

As in many poor urban areas, grocery shopping involved travel—and was often expensive and time-consuming. The group's multiple feasibility studies showed the area desperately needed a supermarket, but even this definite goal was difficult to attain. Some members of the steering group wanted to rent space to a retailer; others wanted to operate a grocery themselves so that profits would return to the cooperative. Eventually, the group opted to run a market itself under the franchise of a major Irish chain. Unfortunately, when a renovated space for the market opened in 1991, a major retail mall with its own large grocery store opened nearby, and the cooperative grocery could not compete. The area still lacked a convenience store, however, and the project sold the cooperative's inventory to two members who established a corner shop.

The supermarket had been the project's driving focus and flagship, and its failure nearly derailed the entire project. Even with a franchise backing, a community-based effort could not compete with the prices of a multinational grocery chain. The center continued to operate with its state-subsidized projects, the ACE scheme, and "incubator" workspaces. The managed workspaces, housing small businesses like beauty salons or car repair shops, were surprisingly more successful than any retail units; organizers said if they had had more workspaces, they could have collected even greater revenue.

This center still operates in New Lodge, but it is no longer a cooperative because there are no profits to distribute. It operates with subsidies from the European Union, various state agencies, and charities. In some ways, it has become precisely what the founders did not want it to be: a landlord to shops and community groups. "Brendan," a resident who was active in the earlier redevelopment campaign and the enterprise center, reflects on its outcome: "We had wanted to create the profits ourselves, that we could commit to various social projects. We were never able to do that. . . . The reality in disadvantaged areas is [that] the expectation of people becoming entrepreneurs or taking some control of their economic life is just a fantasy." The loan portion of the IFI funding was not repaid.

But Brendan, like many others, came away with a sharper analysis of the economic entitlements of citizens and responsibilities of states:

I think it's a broader political question. . . . I think the state—there's no free market economy anywhere—the state intervenes in a variety of ways. Even in the U.S. And I think the debates should be about how the state makes its investment. I think community activity and this type of thing should be subsidized. . . . But it shouldn't be that they have to engage in activities which support themselves to take care of social provision—you know, social service provision is needed and has to be part of the state investment, too. I think the debate should be around how that investment is made, rather than whether.

The neoliberal vision of "self-help" placed the responsibility for curing the causes of structural violence squarely on its victims, while disguising more substantial forms of state subsidy, such as support for the Hastings Hotel group in this period, as "investment." The New Lodge residents' journey to this analysis was repeated in similar projects in other neighborhoods. The IFI imported from the United States a fervent faith in the power of small business to overcome structural economic forces. In practice, community groups struggled to resolve tensions between commercial and social goals, leaving community-based businesses unable to compete with purely economic ventures.

The funding to create central public assets in this disadvantaged area was not wasted, but to see the investment as effective, economic standards of profit and sustainability must be discarded. The link between economic rights and conflict resolution is more subtle than simply job creation. The center did become what organizers call a social and economic heartbeat for the community. It still provides space for fledgling entrepreneurs to begin businesses, as well as space for state job programs, but, more importantly and ineffably, it became a hub for social life. Its most successful current offshoots are several affordable child care centers, now in multiple locations, which provide a vital service for working families—precisely the sort of service that markets fail to provide. Furthermore, by creating a physical locus for community organizing, for housing, arts, victims' and youth groups, among others, the center became a locus for public discussion and engagement. Brendan calls this the "soft element of peace-building," which has social, economic, and political dimensions—yet none are easily measurable. In neighborhoods like New Lodge, creating this kind of center through either cooperative or entrepreneurial activity remains a "fantasy," as Brendan called it. The necessity of public subsidy returns us to a different conflict that economic approaches to peace building in the 1980s laid bare: that conflict between understanding state expenditure as a matter of economic rights and entitlements and a neoliberal vision of it as charity, even in the sense of benevolently "teaching a man to fish."

Economic Rights and Communal Contest

> The unemployment in our bones
> Erupting on our hands in stones;
> The thought of violence a relief,
> The act of violence a grief.
>
> —Seamus Deane, "Derry," 1988

In 1996, San Francisco mayor Willie Brown brought the economy of Northern Ireland to the attention of the Bay Area, where I was living at the time. In a show of solidarity with Catholics facing employment discrimination in Northern Ireland, he ceremoniously poured a bottle of Bushmills whiskey down a city sewer grate, supporting a "Boycott Bushmills" campaign. That campaign was intended to enlist American sentiments to the cause of Catholic anti-discrimination efforts, much in the same way that the civil rights movement had harnessed U.S. sentiments. The shift from economic rights to the more familiar civil rights discourse about discrimination began much earlier in both the United States and Northern Ireland than Brown's belated whiskey performance. In the 1980s, activists campaigned against anti-Catholic discrimination in private employment practices and highlighted state subsidies for large employers that perhaps engaged in discriminatory practices. These efforts coincided with 1980s preoccupations with discrimination as a cause of violence—in the metaconflict of academia and the everyday rhetoric of Sinn Féin as it embraced both "Armalite and ballot box."

In the mid-1980s, discrimination in employment against Catholics became a central focus of rights discourse, distinct from claims on state funds for welfare, job training, or enterprise. Although protests and campaigns to publicize unemployment had existed alongside the earlier welfare rights campaigns, in the early part of the decade such efforts were critical of broader economic decisions, rather than only discrimination.

In west Belfast, awareness of the unemployment gap was not new. Diarmuid remarked that, as a youth in the 1960s, he laughed while watching loyalists going to work, calling out to them, "There you are, knocking your pan in, to get the same wage I get on the dole!" Yet campaigns publicizing anti-Catholic discrimination had more at stake than simply recognizing this reality. They were also part of a more sophisticated approach to publicizing the local situation, with help from a international human rights figure, Seán MacBride.[9] In conjunction with an Irish American lobbying group, the Irish National

Caucus, MacBride developed a set of principles for international companies that invested in Northern Ireland. The nine MacBride Principles were affirmative action measures directed primarily at employee recruitment.[10]

In the early 1980s, alongside welfare rights activism, job training, and community enterprise projects, nationalist and loyalist activists attempted to articulate a broader case about the absence of work. In 1983, a public inquiry into unemployment was held at Conway Mill in west Belfast. Participants from loyalist and nationalist communities discussed unemployment as the consequence of how capitalism had worked in the region and the need for coalitions among working-class people of all communal origins. Critiques of government policies, church practices, and educational services surfaced. While concrete demands to address unemployment did not emerge, inquiry participants agreed that the Conservative government of the time was engaged in class warfare and that the working classes needed to unite to defend their interests.

Yet after that inquiry local employment campaigns coalesced around the matter of anti-Catholic discrimination and its role in the conflict, rather than treating systemic anti-Catholic discrimination as part of a broader economic critique. The most sophisticated campaign for employment was launched in nationalist west Belfast in 1987 and called Obair (Irish Gaelic for "work"). The campaign aimed to end both unemployment among and discrimination against area Catholics. Sponsored by community groups, political representatives, individuals (including Americans), and trade unionists, the campaign commissioned a study by two academics, who reviewed unemployment figures and state employment initiatives in nationalist west Belfast. The report (Rolston and Tomlinson 1988) argued that discrimination against Catholics, in west Belfast particularly, was manifested not just through employers but also through government initiatives. It was especially critical of the agencies that used state funds to attract inward investment from multinationals and to support small business development.

A key objective of Obair was to promote use of the MacBride Principles by international donors and multinational investors. Seán MacBride was in some ways an unlikely proponent of economic rights. In his career as a domestic politician in Ireland, he played a significant role in preventing Ireland from establishing comprehensive welfare entitlements in 1951, deferring to the Catholic Church's opposition to state provision of welfare. Nevertheless, in 1984 MacBride formulated nine principles that governments and corporations were urged to adopt to increase Catholic employment in the north. Britain rejected the principles, stating that its legal system treats affirmative policies as a form of discrimination. Nevertheless, many U.S. state governments adopted the principles, and in 1998 the U.S. Congress made IFI funds dependent on adherence to them.

Unlike the 1983 public inquiry and welfare rights campaigns, Obair and the MacBride Principles framed the matter of economic rights in terms of Catholic disadvantage, rather than as a challenge to the state's political-economic role. In the late 1980s, multiple policy changes attempted to make state agencies responsive to local demands, and employment law was further reformed. Some scholars argue that the MacBride Principles led to the Fair Employment (Northern Ireland) Act of 1989, which established a Fair Employment Commission to monitor public bodies and firms with more than twenty-five employees (Cochrane 2007). Darby and MacGinty (2000) take a different view, that these reforms were intended "to coopt the Catholic middle-class into the administration of Northern Ireland" (94). The efficacy of both local and international campaigns, then, is subject to debate.

What is less uncertain is that discourse regarding anti-Catholic discrimination both displaced and subsumed economic rights with ethnopolitics. As such, campaigns like the MacBride Principles had wider political consequences for how rights as a political tool were regarded. Shankill residents believed such campaigns ignored both their presence in west Belfast and their economic struggles. The campaign awakened not simply the rhetoric of civil rights but also prior animosities and suspicions that rights were being used for ideological ends. "Joe," a loyalist ex-prisoner and activist, told me, "But the benefits that they [Protestants] had from having their own government for seventy-odd years, discriminating against nationalists, I don't think there were any real benefits, to be honest. You'll get a slum quicker than somebody [else]. You could work for the same amount as the dole. I can remember as a kid, my da being unemployed, and I'm out getting food vouchers and clothing vouchers and being totally embarrassed. Going to buy clothes with vouchers, people were looking down their nose at ye. So I know what it feels like. It's not as if I did have anything."

"If You Can't Give Them Bread, Give Them a Circus"

> As your eye roams the city, . . . you see that there is indeed
> a division in the people here. Some call it religion, some
> call it politics. But the most reliable, the most ubiquitous

> division is money. Money is the division you can always put
> your money on. You see leafy streets and you see leafless
> streets. You can imagine leafy lives and leafless ones. In
> the plump suburbs and concrete districts your eyes see
> some truths, some real difference. The scars and marks of
> violence reside in only one place. Many of the populace
> seem to live well. Many prosper while many suffer.
>   —Robert McLiam Wilson, *Eureka Street*, 1996: 214–15

What, then, is the peace dividend? What was the price of peace, and who paid it? Although the settlement was about politics, not economics per se, these are not easily separable spheres. The usefulness of economic rights as a political instrument lies in recognition of the complex interdependence of political and economic structures. Just as politics and economics are entwined in how people understood paths to political violence in the 1980s, connections are still made in the postconflict era. Some of my research participants point to Catholic upward mobility as a benefit of peace—framed diplomas and photos of university graduations on the walls in public housing estates. Others point to increases in the number of wealthy nationalists living in the "leafy" Malone Road area—and subsequent disputes regarding Gaelic Athletic Association flags being flown in that neighborhood. A multiyear study of IFI and later European funding concluded that, although external funding did not alter structural economic conditions in Northern Ireland and the border regions, it did support the development of trust and good relationships among various groups and classes (Byrne 2011; Byrne, Skarlato, et al. 2009; Byrne, Standish, et al. 2009a, 2009b; Byrn, Thiessen,et al. 2008; Thiessen et al. 2010). Yet in areas like Ardoyne, young people continue to riot each summer. Communities that both endured and enacted the greatest violence remain disadvantaged, and "peace dividend" is a bitter joke. Meanwhile, in the devolved assembly of 2012, democratically elected politicians—even the former revolutionaries—enacted rather than challenged the Conservative British government's harsh cuts in welfare entitlements.

In the postconflict era, new rights groups, such as the Participation and the Practice of Rights project (PPR), echo the rhetoric of the 1970s and 1980s. For example, residents of the Seven Towers in New Lodge lobby for improvements in public housing, framing their activism as an innovative approach to rights yet continuing to cast their cause in terms of differential Catholic and Protestant access to public housing.[11] Nationalist and unionist communities in the city of Belfast continue to face different, long-standing social housing problems—shortages and poor conditions, respectively—and the broader issue of reduced social welfare expenditure remains subordinate to discussions of rights in communal terms.

"Pearce," a former PIRA member who remained dedicated to socialism throughout the movement's intermittent commitment to the Left, remains chagrined about ongoing poverty in his west Belfast community:[12]

> We're controlled. If you can't give them bread, give them the circus. So they give a certain amount of money, and allow us to rip the system off, because we're not really a threat to it in any case. . . . And it's almost as if the belief is that this [current political and economic conditions] is the best that we're ever gonna have, so don't really kick it too hard, because you ain't got any fucking thing else to put on your other foot.

Although unsatisfied by the mere promise of upward mobility, Pearce does not advocate a return to violence. Some former PIRA activists do, though, bringing technical expertise to so-called dissidents who oppose the settlement. Some republicans bristle as past colleagues enjoy material success and political power in the new structures; yet dismissing their discontent as pique is both inaccurate and perilous. The young people who riot each summer look around their neighborhoods and see that ex-prisoners enjoy esteem and respect that they have no way to achieve. Meanwhile, loyalist complaints are dismissed as grousing about the loss of unjust privileges. The potential for violence has not disappeared.

Anthropologist Richard Wilson urges caution regarding the contradictory consequences of rights: "they . . . facilitate social and political mobilization against maltreatment and may—insofar as human rights direct political aspirations toward the established legal process—normalize and legitimize unequal structures of power and authority" (2006: 78). In a similar fashion, rights discourse can normalize rather than challenge unequal economic structures. In the 1980s, struggles for economic rights strayed from demanding that the state fulfill its minimal responsibilities and returned to prior themes about inequality in terms of simple ethnopolitics. Funding and policies treating deprivation as a cause of conflict assisted the translation of economic rights into a familiar, and comfortable, domain of communal contest, and they made activists into state service providers struggling to critique a

broader system. Meanwhile, campaigns to challenge anti-Catholic discrimination addressed real injustices—but also limited economic critique to terms
of ethnopolitical gain or loss.

At the beginning of the 1980s, campaigns for welfare rights and economic
justice were a nascent political project, but their possibilities were not realized. Reform policies of the 1970s and 1980s produced gains for the Catholic middle class by the time of the peace process in the 1990s. Yet profound
stratification, as well as attendant social and political exclusions, remained.
The discourse of economic rights remained construed in terms of communal
gains and losses, and more robust, sustained claims for economic rights did
not materialize. In the 1980s, persistent rhetorical reductions of economic
rights to communal advantage helped establish an important human rights
domain as a theater for war by other means.

CHAPTER 4

The Politics We Deserve

"Do you think we get the politics we deserve?" a lawyer asked me over coffee on a gray morning in August 2011. She leaned back and answered her question before I could reply: "I do. It's nonsense to say that political representatives here don't speak for people—they do it well enough to keep getting votes!" Thirteen years after the Good Friday Agreement, and four years after devolved government became functional, "Yvonne" had a bleak view of post-conflict politics, as a kind of "cold peace." A specialist in human rights, she said politicians and the electorate remain preoccupied with collective identities of unionist and nationalist and endlessly contested injustices in those terms. Social and economic rights, her professional expertise, remained secondary in the political and legal culture. Yvonne saw power sharing not merely as a reflection of ethnopolitical divisions but also as an engine for their reproduction—and as a distraction from less newsworthy yet more pervasive failures of the state to safeguard fundamental rights to education or housing.

Her grim analysis of party politics saturated by sectarian struggle was bolstered almost a year later, in June 2012, when the Fair Employment Tribunal found that the former minister of regional development discriminated against a Protestant job applicant for a high-ranking position. Furthermore, the tribunal stated more broadly "that there was a material bias against candidates from a Protestant background within the DRD [Department of Regional Development]" (Fair Employment Tribunal 2012: 17).[1] Although the former minister (and former Sinn Féin MLA) will appeal, the decision affirmed the view of skeptics who suspect that the new political arrangements cannot fulfill the settlement's lofty aspirations. Indeed, the GFA's aspirations seem less noble in hindsight. The settlement's commitment to "parity of esteem" for two communities institutionalized the politics of collective rights.

Yet, fifteen years before, the peace process promised a transformed political future, far from the divisions of the Stormont era. Before the 1997–1998 negotiations, major shifts in the discourse and pursuit of political rights came from people whose lives had been enmeshed with the conflict. One of these shifts entailed a more expansive discourse about and exercise of freedom of association as a fundamental political right. Extending freedom of association as an everyday practice became a means for local activists to develop new discussions and relationships, and it facilitated a transition from paramilitarism to democratic politics. In the same period, however, the logic of "parity of esteem" for two political and religious traditions became increasingly prevalent.

The term "parity of esteem," a central premise of the GFA human rights provisions discussed in Chapter 1, originated with the Standing Advisory Commission on Human Rights Northern Ireland.[2] In 1990, the committee recommended legal recognition of two communities while, as Finlay (2010) notes, shirking the legal debate about individual versus collective rights (31). "Parity of esteem" as a state principle and practice was intended to resolve political grievances and produced the GFA's emphasis on human rights as collectively due to "both communities."[3] In the same period, intellectuals and peace advocates also popularized the term "civil society"; the term is drawn from political theory and designates a social sphere beyond economy and state, characterized by free and voluntary associations among citizens. Theoretically, both "civil society" and "parity of esteem" originated from Enlightenment understandings of political rights. In practice, the terms had profoundly divergent consequences for securing and exercising political rights. As community activists claimed the mantle of "civil society," "parity of esteem" operated in tension with associational practices. This theme of separate and equal was present even in the most innovative, promising practices of association and conflict transformation. The logic of collective entitlements to political rights subtly suffused grassroots work; and, in bitter and violent political conflicts surrounding parades, protests, and rights to assembly, parity of esteem overtook civil society as a dominant practical theory of rights.

In the 1990s, the conflict in Northern Ireland was dramatically transformed. In 1993, negotiations among local politicians and the British and Irish governments became increasingly public, with the Hume-Adams initiative and the Downing Street Declaration outlining a possible peace process (British and Irish Governments 1993).[4] In 1994, the IRA announced a ceasefire, followed by the Combined Loyalist Military Command on behalf of loyalist paramilitaries. In the years that followed, however, negotiations stalled. The

IRA resumed military operations in February 1996, with a massive bombing at Canary Wharf in London. During the next year, as the prospect of talks diminished, the IRA carried out major operations such as the Manchester city center bombing, and serious rioting occurred around Orange parades in the summer months. After a British general election returned a Labour Party government, the institutional process was reinvigorated, and multiparty talks resumed in September 1997, helped along by the reinstatement of the IRA ceasefire that summer. The GFA was unveiled on April 10, 1998, and ratified by a referendum on May 22.

Throughout the stalemates, breakthroughs, and returns to violence, grassroots activists and ex-prisoners worked toward reconciling local communities to changing politics and the prospect of a settlement. Innovative projects and initiatives emerged in the enclaves and interfaces where I conducted fieldwork. Everyday organizing transformed the way residents exercised their political rights to association, as well as how activists conceived their relationships with the existing state, political parties, and aspirational visions of an agreed Ireland. Yet, during the same period, freedom of assembly, a fundamental political right, was also a focus for conflict, as violence surrounding Orange Order parades became a recurrent and tragic summer ritual. Discourse regarding political rights had contradictory consequences during this period, offering a promise to end the conflict, as well as a vehicle to extend it. These patterns continue to determine contemporary rights talk, reproducing ethnopolitical antipathies and conflicts.

Civil Society, Political Rights, and Parity of Esteem

The argument was not that we must be free to talk,
the argument was that we are generally free to talk,
with exceptions, but what are we going to do with that
freedom? Are we gonna use it to change things? Not just
the values by which we would talk—the process values
of consultation and discussion—but the content and
substance of our arguments.
                    —Former NICVA employee, June 2000

Some analyses of the peace process emphasize the roles of elites, including political parties and British, Irish, and U.S. governments (e.g., Bew 2007;

Clancy 2010). Yet academics also acknowledge the importance of local actors, especially former combatants (e.g., Shirlow et al. 2010; McAuley et al. 2010; Shirlow and McEvoy 2008; McEvoy et al. 2004). A nongovernmental sphere of politics in Northern Ireland had become highly organized since the advent of the conflict. By 1990, community organizing was recognizable as a sector for both employment and political influence. Beyond paramilitarism, the self-help efforts originating in the 1970s and institutionalized in the 1980s came to be called "community development" in the 1970s and, later, "civil society" (McCready 2001; Cochrane and Dunn 2002). By 1996, community-based groups constituted 86 percent of an estimated 5,643 "voluntary organizations" in the region—4,909 groups (NICVA 1997: 12).

These conditions led some activists to promote their work as a grassroots peace process operating synergetically with elites and parties. They acknowledged that the *realpolitik* of party-based negotiations was necessary, but they argued that official peace processes are informed and supported by a range of interactions among other actors. They supported these arguments with reference to scholarship on conflict resolution. In this scholarship, grassroots work, as opposed to elite diplomacy, is variously denoted by terms such as "track two," "complementary diplomacy," and "conflict transformation" (Arthur 1990; Bloomfield 1995; Burgess and Burgess 2010; Lederach 1995a, b, 2001; Montville 1987).[5] Political rights of association are essential to this sphere of action and became crucial to rights discourse in Belfast.

In 1990s Belfast, where ethnopolitical divisions saturated daily life—in terms of residence, schooling, work, transportation, and leisure—developing associations among community-based NGOs appeared a promising route to strengthening a grassroots peace process. This rationale also echoed another strand of contemporaneous scholarship and global policy—a revival of the classical political theory of "civil society." As such, the "track two" approach to peace also implicated political rights—including, but not limited to, rights to association, assembly, expression, and conscience.

Although the Universal Declaration of Human Rights and the European Court of Human Rights recognize basic political rights, they are not definitive about how these rights should be expressed. Indeed, the expression, restriction, and denial of political rights to assembly and association, vary widely in place and time. Even civil rights that appear straightforward are not, such as the ECHR Article 6 guarantee of a fair trial. As Dickson (2010) notes, the lack of a jury tradition among many signatory states means that a jury is not part of the European legal requirements for fair trials, leaving intact the nonjury Diplock courts for terrorist offenses in Northern Ireland (206–7). This indeterminacy allows both legal definitions and talk of political rights to be malleable, convenient for justifying political actions that promote peace or conflict, sometimes simultaneously.

The 1990s revival of civil society theory was shaped by global political circumstances of the period. The idea of civil society, "a sphere of social interaction between economy and state," was developed in nineteenth-century liberal theory (Cohen and Arato 1994: ix).[6] The concept was resuscitated when the breakup of the Soviet Union and its satellites left academics scrambling to explain waves of popular protest in states presumed to deny political rights so absolutely that these associations could not occur. In a major intellectual history of the concept, Cohen and Arato define civil society as "composed above all of the intimate sphere (especially the family), the sphere of associations (especially voluntary associations), social movements, and forms of public communication" (ix). They describe the major contribution of civil society movements as "the democratization of values, norms, and institutions that are rooted ultimately in a political culture" (562). Political rights are therefore essential to civil society's curative power: "The rights to communication, assembly, and association, among others, constitute the public and associational spheres of civil society as spheres of positive freedom within which agents can collectively debate issues of common concern, act in concert, assert new rights and exercise influence on political (and potentially economic) society" (23).

In Northern Ireland, the idea that political associations within civil society could nurture the peace process had significant material ramifications. Many associations that became characterized as "civil society," originated within the mobilizations described in previous chapters. The 1990s discourse about "civil society" legitimated community activism as promoting both political rights and peace. As a peace process began to seem possible in the early 1990s, local NGOs embraced this associational discourse. One NGO poetically called local activism a form of "la vie associative" (NICVA 1993: 4). In the years before negotiations, larger NGOs made public arguments about the importance of a sphere of free association and proposed the equivalent of a "Marshall Plan" for the region (NICVA 1994: 1; see also NICVA 1995; NIVT 1995). Throughout the peace process, NGO representatives continued to argue for their work as a form of "civil society," "civic life," and "participatory democracy"—and, therefore, part of building peace (see NICVA 2004; McAleavey 2010).

Their arguments were successful, insofar as they secured significant European funding to support the peace process. The European Union Special Support Programme for Peace and Reconciliation in Northern Ireland and the Border Counties of Ireland (hereafter referred to as Peace I, Peace II, and Peace III) ran from 1995 to 2013 and directed massive international funding to these grassroots organizations.[7] In total, the three programs allocated €2.047 billion (approximately $2.42 billion) for peace building in Northern Ireland, with much of Peace I going to grassroots projects (see EU 2007).[8] Although the funding requirements and types of activities supported by international donors changed over time, the goal of funding grassroots efforts to support the peace process remained paramount.

In the same period, public discourse treated this work as indispensable to peace. For example, journalist Mary Holland called the work of nongovernmental actors "a parallel peace process."[9] Many people who had organized housing rights campaigns in the 1970s or economic development projects in the 1980s began to promote their work as necessary to create a peace process in communities where violence, poverty, and polarization cut most sharply.

Yet much common sense about civil society is aspirational rather than descriptive.[10] Scholarship on civil society in Northern Ireland is no exception. Contrasting their analyses with arguments that Northern Ireland has no "civil society," some scholars emphasize the role of community activism in making society less sectarian and contributing to a broader peace (Cochrane and Dunn 2002; Williamson et al. 2000; Couto 2001; Guelke 2003). They usually describe this contribution to peace in a nuanced way, recognizing the limitations on civil society's palliative force (e.g., Cochrane 2001, 2006; Farrington 2008). Other authors acknowledge that civil society's role in the peace process may be overstated, yet they argue for its potential to challenge identity politics in the future (e.g., Doran 2010). For example, Farrington (2004) points out that associational groupings do not necessarily diminish ethnopolitical divisions and may reinforce them, as in the case of the Gaelic Athletic Association and the Orange Order (4). Even the most optimistic analysis acknowledges that actually existing civil society is subject to the pervasive divisions and antagonisms that characterize society itself.

In practice, discourse about civil society and political rights recognized these divisions with the term "parity of esteem." Parity of esteem attempted to balance divisions—and in some ways surrendered to them. Finlay (2008, 2010) argues that parity of esteem was legitimated by essentialist understandings of culture and promoted in Ireland by revisionist historians who treated the island's turbulent history as the product of cultural conflicts. Parity of esteem also reflects the influence of liberal multiculturalism, which emphasizes collective rights (e.g., Taylor 1994; Kymlicka 2001). This form of liberalism, despite nods to "rights of exit," tends to underestimate the degree to which cultural groupings exercise compulsion over putative members (Cowan 2006).

In addition to driving consociational governance itself, Finlay (2010) cites parity of esteem as the force behind a new label for community organizing called "single-identity" work. As an alternative to cross-community projects, "single-identity" organizing claimed to contribute to peace by building confidence among people who feared the "other side." In this model, community-based NGOs that existed to serve homogeneous neighborhoods could, with a bit of tinkering, represent their work as promoting peace. Since the early days of conflict, contact exercises supported by governmental and nongovernmental bodies had failed to change relationships among nationalists and unionists. (Indeed, well-meaning efforts to take Catholic and Protestant children on holidays together were derided as "ghetto-aways" by my research participants.) By building confidence within residents of segregated communities, these groups could, perhaps, move toward practical collaborations on areas of mutual concern—for example, the matter of young people rioting during the parades season. As Bryan (2006b) notes, although many community groups continue to advocate this approach, their claims for reconciliation have not been substantiated. Ultimately, as Church et al. (2004) acknowledge, the rationale for single-identity work as peace promotion was as much about the practicality of ethnosectarian division as grassroots diplomacy.

Claims for the therapeutic effects of political rights were crucial to the changing global paradigm of human rights in the late twentieth century. Like the revival of civil society, this shift was related to changes in the global balance of power. Ignatieff (1999) notes that the Helsinki Accords marked global ascendance for the U.S. view of civil and political rights over the USSR's social and economic priorities. Moyn (2010) traces a rhetorical shift in human rights practices to popular anticommunist dissidents of the period and argues that this shift insidiously recast political issues as moral ones. A similar moralistic tenor is present in arguments for the importance of human rights in the Northern Irish peace process (e.g., Bell 2000; Harvey 2001, 2005). Yet local discourses about political rights, civil society, and parity of esteem simultaneously facilitated new political associations *and* new terrains of conflict.

These discourses of political rights worked in tension and in tandem to influence local understandings of political rights during the peace process. They drove the inclusive elections of peace negotiators, as well as increasingly violent conflicts about parades.[11] Ultimately, the logic of parity of esteem prevailed, and after the settlement the promise of association was usually subordinate to balancing acts and sectarian head counts.

Free Speech and Association: Challenging Common Sense in the 1990s

> The conflict is the defining principle of interpersonal and political relations. Thus, in this context, even talk, any kind of talk, of conflict resolution is deemed political, benefiting one side over the other. People live and die in warzones by these politics.
> —Carolyn Nordstrom, *A Different Kind of War Story*, 232

Following the announcement of an agreement on Good Friday 1998, my research participants were almost giddy. In offices, community centers, and pubs, they exchanged rumors about how the multiparty talks finally reached agreement and what the GFA's contents would actually entail. Talking in a café on the Falls, "Pádraig," a PIRA ex-prisoner turned community activist, sharply criticized the GFA's consociational arrangements and its alteration of the Republic's constitutional claim to the territory. Yet, when another activist asked how he would vote, he smoothly replied, "Oh, I'll vote yes. If it ends the war, it's magic. It's sectarian, but it's magic."[12]

Unionists were more divided than nationalists about the agreement, but most of my loyalist research participants in the Shankill area were resolutely for it. At a weekly pub quiz, the group at my table was triumphant. It was a victory for the foot soldiers of the war, not so much over their republican enemies but over the often derided "unionist governors" who had proclaimed "no surrender," while suffering little during the conflict. The deadline for an agreement had been April 9. On that night, anticipating an announcement, DUP leader Ian Paisley—whose party had boycotted the talks—led a group up the hill to Stormont to proclaim their opposition. He hoped to recreate the moment when loyalists brought down the Sunningdale settlement in 1974. This time, Paisley failed to rally working-class Protestants—indeed, he was met by a counterprotest of loyalists who jeered at him for his conduct during the conflict. "Chris," a housing activist since the 1970s, was delighted that working-class loyalists and politicians from the PUP and UDP challenged Paisley publicly. "He marched up the hill, and this time we didn't follow! We met him there."[13] Chris claimed one loyalist activist punched one of Paisley's group (I could not verify this). My companions laughed heartily at this rumor, delighted at the prospect of loyalists publicly confronting Paisley's leadership.

Both conversations reflected broader shifts that were taking place in community politics during the 1990s. These changes were vital to bringing paramilitary organizations into a political process. Although the peace talks took place over a relatively short time—September 1997 to April 1998—it took far longer to prepare rank-and-file paramilitaries and the wider communities to embrace nonviolent democratic politics. In the late 1980s and early 1990s, these shifts occurred alongside private talks among political leaders such as John Hume and Gerry Adams, as well as British and Irish ministers. A very different *realpolitik*, however, was at work in everyday political practice. Political association as a fundamental right enabled grassroots transformations— sometimes subtly, sometimes through confrontational claims.

Although ex-prisoners were leaders in this grassroots process, not all, or even most, community activists were sworn paramilitary members. As chapter 3 explains, though, a substantial number of activists in the late 1980s and early 1990s emerged from the ranks of ex-prisoners, having served full sentences for their activities during the early years of conflict. These individuals led significant changes in political consciousness and practice (see also Shirlow and McEvoy 2008; Shirlow et al. 2010). As noted earlier, for republicans, they pioneered tactics of engaging with the state. In loyalist areas, they were at the forefront of articulating working-class loyalists' ambivalence toward their more monied political representatives and the British state itself.

For ex-prisoners, the work of community organizing was a significant change from paramilitary operations. Some of their work involved developing alternative approaches to local problems—for example, focusing on youth education and training outside conventional schooling, or advocating local restorative justice rather than punishment attacks, to address antisocial behavior. Other projects were more abstract, involving "think tanks" on the Falls and Shankill, where local people began to imagine and discuss what a peace process might look like on the ground.

"Stephen," a republican ex-prisoner turned community organizer, describes what a change this was for many ex-prisoners: "You find that for most activists, former activists, that they are very impatient. Used to be in the old days, we did something [and] we could watch it on the six o'clock news. Now we do something and it takes a long time before it pans out, before it shows any sort of benefit. . . . Now it's a bit slower, not as glamorous, but at the end of the day it's about changing the society." These mundane engagements with the problems of housing, employment, and education depended on political rights to association—especially when ex-prisoners were involved. If groups and local communities were to draw on the skills of ex-prisoners, they had to be free to associate with these men and women—without state and security-force restrictions. Community groups' associations with ex-prisoners could be, and often was, construed as suspect, and in time produced a major conflict about political rights.

The increasingly bureaucratic work of engaging with state agencies also drew ex-prisoners and community organizers into tentative contact with their loyalist or republican counterparts. In some ways, the exercise of both free speech and association within and between communities worked subtly to allow both loyalists and republicans to contemplate politics that were previously unimaginable. Political transformations within republicanism were not simply caused by exhaustion with struggle or a stalemate with the security forces (Tonge et al. 2011). Stephen explained the transformation in this way: "After a long time, you come to a realization. I feel that removing the Brits from this country is very, very easy. That'd be a simple thing. Trying to convince 900,000 loyalists or whatever, unionists, that their destiny is a united Ireland is what the fight is all about. It's what the struggle is all about. That is the struggle." In short, republicans began to entertain the once unthinkable: that the right to national self-determination was best pursued not through armed struggle but by political means.

This approach required reflection and discussion—practices that can challenge paramilitary authority structures. In the 1990s, as ex-prisoners began to consider nonmilitarized politics, the broader republican community began to debate the future of the movement more publicly. Stephen was part of this change, and, although he was not a Sinn Féin leader, he was widely respected for his PIRA activities and time in prison during the blanket protests. He began to take part in a republican study group. His reflections on his life experiences help explain how many rank-and-file republicans, and the broader community, came to the peace process: "I believed that the armed struggle brought us as far as it could take us, and anything after that is just gratuitous violence. I don't believe at this point in time that violence serves any purpose. Strictly self-defense, if someone's going to shoot you, you shoot them; that's no problem there. I'm not a complete pacifist, but I just feel tactically we've gone as far as we can with the armed struggle."

Loyalists also began to interrogate their own political histories and practices. They began to complain about their client relation to unionist politicians. One community worker in the mid-Shankill area said, "They used to say, you could drape a donkey in a Union Jack and they'd vote for it on the Shankill." By the early 1990s, he said, that was changing: "We're starting to learn, you can fly a flag, but you can't fry it!" (Nationalist politician John Hume often expressed a similar sentiment.) More than economic and political exploitation, loyalist ex-prisoners began to challenge what they perceived as a division of labor within unionism—middle-class unionists were political representatives, while working-class loyalists fought the paramilitary war.

Loyalist ex-prisoners I met were especially resentful of Ian Paisley. They believed he incited conflict and encouraged loyalists to do the actual fighting, while he was safely insulated from violence and risk by wealth. They also believed he hypocritically disavowed loyalist violence when it was politically convenient to do so. "Robert," an ex-prisoner in his twenties, directly blamed Paisley for his imprisonment. At age fourteen, Robert said, he and a friend managed to obtain a rusty revolver. Paisley's rhetoric inspired them, he claimed; indeed, he and his friend were arrested with the gun after one of Paisley's rallies. He was held as a juvenile at the "Secretary of State's pleasure"—that is, for an indefinite period of incarceration.[14] "I believed Paisley," he said. "I believed we had to stop the republicans. But when you're 14, and it's Christmas Day, and you're in a cell, thinking about your family, it doesn't make sense anymore. I was still just a child, crying about the presents I was missing out on." As part of this growing challenge to past political leadership, members of the loyalist parties, the PUP and UDP, began to seek elected office. (These parties had some notable electoral successes, but the ambivalence of loyalists toward paramilitarism meant they became less successful in the years following the GFA.)

Challenges to how loyalists understood their history and Britishness became more widespread (see Graham and Shirlow 2002). For example, at one event at a community center in Woodvale, children dramatized the Battle of the Boyne. In writing their play, the young people studied the historical period and were surprised by the ambiguities absent from local folk history. Afterward, a community worker exclaimed to me, "I didn't know the Pope supported King Billy!"[15] Meanwhile, loyalist ex-prisoners began to think about recent history in critical terms. One Ulster Volunteer Force (UVF) ex-prisoner told me, "I think that people could have pulled the two working classes together to fight for civil rights. I mean, they managed to do it in the 1930s. There were hunger riots where people from the Falls and the Shankill rioted together down the town. . . . Now what actually happened then was that the unionist [party] . . . actually hired a gunman to fire off shots . . . so that they could say that protests were republican-oriented. So it was, again, any type of attempt at social change, it was a republican plot, you know." Even some of the most dedicated loyalists began to voice unthinkable thoughts, such as the possibility that they could be both Irish and British, like someone who is both Welsh and British. As Graham and Shirlow (2002) note, a key element of these reflections was the theme of betrayal—by unionist leaders and the British government.

Challenging armed struggle as the means to achieve Irish unification was a fundamental political transformation that people like Stephen began to promote in republican community politics. A right to armed struggle for national self-determination was fundamental to republicanism, immune to the vagaries of democratic practices like voting. Questioning British conduct toward the region, and unionism's internal loyalty, was a similar heresy for loyalism. Some loyalists went so far as to revive fantasies of an independent Ulster, which a group of reflective members of the UDA had mooted in the 1970s (New Ulster Political Research Group 1979). In the 1990s, the practical expression of rights to speech enabled important political shifts *within* loyalism and republicanism, which were as significant for the peace process as subsequent recognition of and associations with opponents.

Civil Society and Parity of Esteem in Practice

> Protestant and Catholic got together, they can make your life hell.
> —Loyalist community worker, February 1999

Shifts in local political consciousness were also fueled by rights discourse, which in turn spurred further public debates and discussions. A major campaign that transformed grassroots politics in the 1990s originated years earlier, with a parliamentarian's statement in 1985. On June 27, 1985, secretary of state for Northern Ireland Douglas Hurd claimed that certain community groups in Northern Ireland were too closely associated with paramilitaries and ex-prisoners and that their funding would be withdrawn (UK Parliament 1985: 879, col. 449). This policy (the "Hurd Principles") became infamous as "political vetting." Following these principles, government departments and the IFI withdrew funding from many groups. However, the most controversial revocations of funding were for the ACE "job training" programs described in the previous chapter. Vetting appeared to be mainly a weapon against republicans, and the Catholic Church replaced many community groups as an ACE provider (Mulrine et al. 1992). In the early 1990s, a coalition of nationalist and unionist NGOs successfully challenged the Hurd Principles, asserting their rights to freedom of association. One protagonist described this conflict as one of the first major "human rights track" battles that united large numbers of loyalists and republicans.

Although the policy's stated intent—not funding paramilitary groups—appeared reasonable, the principles were not neutral in effect. Virtually every resident of west Belfast, loyalist or nationalist, had, and has, what can be called paramilitary connections—through family, friends, and neighbors. In the 1980s, the main targets of vetting were groups perceived as republican. Conway Mill Community Development Projects was a frequent target of the policy. The group ran an education center and a nursery for children and was attempting to create an enterprise center.

Ironically, a government attempt at parity strengthened opposition to the policy. In 1989, the Glencairn Community Association (GCA), in a loyalist area, had fifty-three ACE posts withdrawn. Soon after that, a twenty-one-post ACE scheme was cut from Glór na nGael, a respected Irish language umbrella group with republican ex-prisoners on its board. The loyalist GCA reached out to Glór na nGael with a letter of support. Loyalists saw the GCA cuts as a preemptive gambit to justify cutting Glór na nGael—a transparent effort to appear even-handed. "'Well, we done it on a Protestant one,' was how they [the government] went," said "Jonathan," an activist in Glencairn.

Jonathan was frank about his situation: "Now, I know I had UDA members. I know I had UVF workers. And I know I had people who didn't belong to anything. I didn't have a right, nor did any committee, to ask anybody did they belong to a paramilitary organization." Nationalists took a similar approach to working with ex-prisoners or paramilitaries. One explained, "It wasn't saying that you were supporting shooting or that you were supporting violence; it was saying these people are part of the community."

After an initial outreach from Glencairn organizers to Glór na nGael, a more visible campaign swiftly materialized. The tit-for-tat logic of "doing it on a Protestant one" created loyalist opposition to the policy rather than the appearance of fairness. The Political Vetting of Community Work Working Group was formed, with representation from across Belfast and, indeed, Ireland as a whole. The Centre for Research and Documentation (a west Belfast poverty research center) compiled cases of political vetting—gathering official correspondence, documenting the type and governance of groups affected, and conducting interviews. The newly radicalized umbrella group for NGOs, the Northern Ireland Council for Voluntary Action (NICVA), joined the struggle.

In October 1990 NICVA published the proceedings of a conference on vetting, along with the documentation (Political Vetting of Community Work Working Group 1990). NICVA brought public relations skills, legal representation, and respectability to the campaign. With civil rights experts on board, the campaign publicly explored the legality of vetting under fair employment legislation and the ECHR. It also emphasized how vetting imposed sanctions without due process, counter to the putatively evidence-based system of justice in Britain. In the end, NICVA did not need to pursue legal action to win the argument. Disciplined and strategic publicity efforts were sufficient to get both groups' funding reinstated. The Hurd Principles remained in effect, but, since that campaign, they have been rarely applied.

NICVA workers supported the antivetting campaign because their new generation of staff embraced civil society arguments. Until 1986, the organization now known as NICVA had been called the Northern Ireland Council for Social Services. In this previous incarnation, it was an unlikely ally for community-based NGOs with suspected paramilitary members. Since 1938, its support had gone to genteel charities focused on disabilities or poverty. But, in the 1980s, the organization was restructured and renamed, and new employees took over. "Brian," one of these new employees, described the impetus to change in this way: "The organization got lost with the Troubles. It could not adjust and adapt to the conflict on the street, or the new ideas about society. It became an irrelevance—it was seen as middle-class, Protestant, and out of touch." Member NGOs and the board recognized this irrelevance and responded with changes to staff and the organization's ethos. Brian said, "The new values of the organization were being established. Younger, smaller, more radical CBOs [community-based organizations] were given a more prominent role and recognition that they were representative of what was happening on the streets, not the big, traditional, old, voluntary societies."

By 1990, NICVA was firmly committed to what Brian called "the new ideas about society"—that is, the new staff, he said, wanted to define "a third space, a neutral space between state and citizen, between state and market or private sector." Thus, NICVA's decision to join the antivetting campaign put these ideas into action. These "new ideas about society" were also inflected with the multiculturalism of the period. Brian said the group had to "attract traditional Protestant and Catholic groups, who were separate and separated by geography, into the same room to discuss housing, unemployment, disability." To do so, they drew upon multicultural politics and "the difference between nonracism and antiracism. . . . How do you move from a neutral, color-blind style in which nothing changes to a more proactive, challenging style toward racism and sectarianism, gender discrimination, disability discrimination?" NICVA achieved greater credibility among grassroots community organizations, becoming an influential umbrella organization. Furthermore, it developed a degree of authority for its own agenda—and became a strong advocate of associational politics in the 1990s and for civil society's role in the peace process.

Emboldened by success, NICVA undertook more ambitious initiatives. Some staff made common cause with grassroots organizers and created Initiative '92 to push for a peace process. The project morphed into a public citizens' inquiry, the Opsahl Commission, led by Norwegian academic Torkel Opsahl. In 1992 and 1993 the commission received more than 300 oral and written submissions on a settlement from more than 5,000 individuals and groups. Although the report itself (Pollak 1993) reiterated suggestions that had circulated for years—a bill of rights, devolution, power sharing, joint authority by the Republic and Britain—the greatest shift was one of process. Community organizers began to insert themselves into grander politics, and ordinary people began to entertain the idea that they could lead a resolution to the conflict. This shift emphasized inclusivity, irrespective of participants' past and present convictions (in both senses of the term).

Yet, as the Opsahl process solidified public recognition for nonparty political actors and free association, it also helped to entrench the principle of "parity of esteem." Indeed, Guelke (2003) argues that the GFA's use of the principle can be traced to the commission (71). In the longer term, associational politics gained credibility among both local NGOs and the broader public. NICVA swiftly coordinated and disseminated arguments for European peace subsidies to NGOs, the media, and policymakers. Meanwhile, the arguments for civil society, free association, and parity of esteem converged in more conscious efforts by community-based NGOs to build a grassroots peace process.

The Bleeding Edge: Freedom of Association as Conflict Transformation

On January 11, 1998, loyalists murdered twenty-eight-year-old Terry Enright while he was moonlighting as a nightclub bouncer, a retaliatory killing during the peace talks.[16] Enright was a community worker in the upper Springfield area who also coordinated activities for young people with a local interface group, the Springfield Inter-Community Development Project (SICDP). A husband and father of two, he was the son of a former trade union leader and community activist in the nationalist upper Springfield area. His father's leadership and his own cross-community work had created widespread respect for the family among both nationalists and loyalists. His murder was a visceral blow even for strangers, who saw in his life and work the promise of a new, peaceful future.

In the weeks following the murder, "Colm," a republican community organizer, somber with grief, encountered "Stephanie," a community worker from a loyalist interface area, at the SICDP. When Colm mentioned local grief over Terry's murder and their efforts to commemorate his life, Stephanie replied that Terry had been a "legitimate target" since Terry's wife was the niece of Gerry Adams. Colm was livid; later he told me he could not see how someone who had known Terry could say that.

This small, tense conversation between workplace colleagues highlights the volatility and precarious nature of intercommunity engagements during the peace process. The SICDP, with which Colm, Stephanie, and Terry all liaised, was a practical expression of 1990s ideas about civil society and parity of esteem. Situated on the Springfield Road, it was innovative in multiple respects. This intercommunity project differed from ubiquitous cross-community work in that it was based in the neighborhood it served, permanently located at an interface, what one activist called "the bleeding edge" of community organizing. In these areas, permanent security barriers, called peace lines or walls, divided nationalist and loyalist enclaves just a few feet apart. In the early 1990s, SICDP was founded to support groups in these areas as they struggled to develop local solutions to concrete problems such as poor housing, unemployment, health, and poor educational achievement. The project hoped its support of local "single-identity" development—community organizing within these homogeneous enclaves—would lead to practical cooperation and decreased antagonism among NGOs and residents of the area.[17] That is, its work could nurture a grassroots peace process. The project was designed in contrast to traditional community relations work—usually brief contact exercises for people who would never meet again. The first director was a loyalist ex-prisoner, who was soon joined by a republican ex-prisoner to support groups in nationalist areas.

SICDP hoped to encourage other forms of politics, accepting and to a degree sidelining the fundamental political division. Developing different relationships, even among professional community organizers, however, was a fraught process—as the bitter exchange between Colm and Stephanie demonstrates. Deep antipathies prevailed among residents, unchanged by ceasefires or peace talks, heightening tension even within civic associations. Staff, board members, and community organizers who liaised with SICDP harbored no illusions about developing lasting relationships or even about sustaining practical collaborations. One community organizer from Ballymurphy who worked with the group said, "Not that kids wanted . . . to throw their arms around each other across these barricades. I always tell people, there's people in Ballymurphy who'll not let their kids play with kids from the next street. . . . so this idea that kids from this area want to rush across and meet people from the Shankill or vice versa—it's unrealistic."

The SICDP was formally established in 1990 with IFI funding. The idea for the project originated in 1988, among community workers in the loyalist Ainsworth area, which backs onto the Springfield Road, a major thoroughfare that winds in a northwesterly loop from the lower Falls Road, between the Falls and Shankill Roads, and then returns southwest into nationalist west Belfast. The "upper" portion of the road divides westerly postwar estates such as the nationalist Ballymurphy, Springvale, and Newhill areas from loyalist Highfield, Ainsworth, and Springmartin areas. The Springfield area was an epicenter of conflict from 1969 onward, with neighborhoods becoming more ethnically homogeneous as riots and intimidation led to mass displacements. As a result, some areas along the Springfield Road are considered "nationalist" and others "loyalist." Recurrent violence led to the installation of a lengthy peace line dividing the area. The larger area is not so much a single interface as several interfaces between enclaves.

Progenitors of the project did not believe a single-identity approach would reinforce division between area nationalists and loyalists. "Seán," a republican ex-prisoner who worked with the Ainsworth group to design the project, felt they were being visionary. Collaborative projects among loyalists and nationalists would occur after confidence was built through single-identity work, he said. But the approach was controversial at the time:

> Community relations was this sort of generalized liberal view about, I don't know, sort of living together. And our argument was, yeah, we need to live together, but to do that we need to be who we are. . . . We needed to have a sense of confidence in our own identity before we could begin to share that. And much of that needed to be directed in the Protestant community because they had been through certainly a long period where the feeling was that they had lost the war, or their sense of identity was called into question. Their past had been, was under continuous criticism, and their present, well, they didn't know where the heck they were. . . . But to argue for single-identity work was almost to call into question the very essence of community relations as it was then perceived.

Project staff and board members saw its goals in practical rather than lofty terms. The work usually involved coping with the everyday conflict. In one case, residents of an interface area approached staff to discuss a section of the peace wall where kids congregated to throw bricks. In that instance, the group tried to help local organizations develop strategies to prevent fighting and vandalism. An SICDP worker said, "This is people from both sides of the community. With the same problem. And we say to them, you have the same problem. And you may be blaming each other for this, but there are other issues of concern to you both, which make life very difficult for you. And we could start off by getting some sort of idea of what those problems are." SICDP Staff supported local groups to survey residents about their views on solutions and guided their approach to the Northern Ireland Housing Executive (NIHE) with complaints. SICDP's method was open-ended about what the solution should be—whether residents wanted a larger barrier, more organized activities for young people, or actual meetings with their opposite number. In another instance, during the unrest surrounding Orange parades in the 1990s, the project helped loyalist estates develop community festivals in an attempt to divert young people from rioting.

Much of this work was a fraught, lengthy process. The project designers originally envisioned a standing conference to establish structured, ongoing discussions among residents of the upper Springfield, but that process began disastrously. Seán described the rationale in ambitious terms: "This idea was similar to the people's assemblies and councils we had set up in the '70s. But I thought it would have been much more professional—a continuous getting together to make a structured response to politics, based on social and economic conditions, a formal structure for meeting, outside conventional politics. . . . It would have been a continuous mechanism to work on the common issues along the interface." In 1993, the first attempt at a conference "blew up," as one participant put it, when campaigners against police use of plastic bullets during riots took the floor and discussion degenerated into recriminations and denunciations. Seán said, "A lot of people came away despondent and they didn't follow it through. I felt that was a mistake, because at least it got communities talking to each other, and . . . they should have continuously been working to build the standing conference."

The standing conference idea languished and the project established a more modest "think tank" initiative. Community activists from the Shankill and Falls areas held separate discussions in which residents talked about community identity, activism, and contemporary political events. A long-standing advocate of grassroots conflict resolution, Michael Hall published several reports from the think tanks (Shankill Think Tank 1994, 1995, 1998; Falls Think Tank 1996). As the discussions unfolded over time, participants increasingly complained that the peace process was steered from above, cosmetically incorporating grassroots concerns. Attempts at colloquia involving both think tanks did not proceed easily.

Project founders, staff, and board believed that mundane, everyday forms of community organizing—supporting women's groups, youth festivals, or appeals for traffic control in certain neighborhoods—had a larger value and was a form of "conflict transformation." Conflict transformation is both a theoretical and practical approach to peacemaking, whose key exponent is John Paul Lederach (1995a, b, 2005). The term "transformation" indicates an emphasis on changing social relationships that produce and are produced by violence—and differentiates the approach from the *telos* of conflict resolution, as well as the resignation of conflict management. Lederach visited Northern Ireland numerous times in the 1990s and addressed various groups of community activists, including the SICDP originators (1996, 1995a).[18]

By 1998 the project was in jeopardy. Its funding was ending, and the second phase of European peace funding, Peace II, was delayed. Many activists began to suspect that, since the peace talks had concluded, states and international donors would no longer deem their work as essential. Furthermore, both academics and funding bodies were critiquing the "single-identity" approach of the original project, and a stronger emphasis on "reconciliation," through cross-communal projects, had become a priority in the new Peace II funds.[19] Unlike many other projects, however, SICDP survived the first funding crunch that followed the settlement. The group published a new development plan in 2000 (SICDP 2000) and publicly launched it at City Hall. With reorganization, it secured funding from the Community Relations Council's core funding, Peace II, and the IFI, hired a new director and project workers, and renamed the project Inter-Action.

The most successful intervention in the project's postconflict incarnation revisited the problem that inspired its formation—the problem of intercommunal conflict, especially during the parades season. The group established a mobile phone network, in which twenty-eight community organizers along the interface, each armed with a mobile phone, monitored designated geographic areas. The phones facilitated communication when incidents of violence occurred. The most common incidents involved youth-led stone-throwing, often called "recreational rioting," which nevertheless could lead to full-scale rioting. The participants and SICDP staff acknowledged that they could not address orchestrated violence. But the network helped address common, ad hoc incidents; by communicating with counterparts on "the other side," phone holders could relay information about what had taken place, what was being done to restrain further actions on their side of the peace line, and, most importantly, dispel rumors about what had happened. History had shown that some of the most intense riots and mass displacements occurred when rumors about events or assaults led to violent conflicts at interfaces. During the parading disputes of the 1990s, I directly observed how rumors that loyalists were massing to assault the lower Falls led to patrols by local activists. Meanwhile, inflammatory rumors of nationalists being bused from the Falls to protest against contested parades in other areas circulated among loyalist research participants.

SICDP's mobile phone network was modeled on a north Belfast project that began in 1996 during the summer disturbances. The north Belfast effort was largely successful (Jarman 1997, 1999b), particularly given its cost: £3,000–4,000 (approximately $5,470) per year compared to the millions in damage—and state security expenditure—that one night of rioting can cost.

Through the mobile phone network, Inter-Action was able to establish a lasting forum for discussions among nationalist and loyalist community organizers. In 2001, as violence intensified at a flashpoint on the interface, phone holders met face to face. Although the initial, private meeting was reportedly tense, it gradually became a monthly, then weekly, meeting where they discussed broader problems their locales faced, as well as the resolution of a variety of incidents. Eventually, the discussion group took a name—the Springfield Inter-Community Forum.

In the Springfield area, the network and forum became a new, effective instrument for addressing violence during the annually contentious local Whiterock parade and for building civic associations among local community organizers. In the 2000s, however, funding cuts reduced the forum and phone network to a small, core group. Conflicts surrounding parades kept interethnic tensions alive, and, with decreased funding for interventions, serious violence returned. In September 2005, the annual Whiterock Lodge Orange parade was rerouted, and loyalists battled riot police at the interface. Rioting spread across the region, and bricks, blast bombs, and bullets flew. Parade-related violence, the initial impetus for the mobile phone project, had returned with a vengeance. The cost of policing alone was £3 million (approximately $5.46 million) in a single week.[20]

The peace process had depended on former combatants making a transition to democratic politics and local NGOs working at the grassroots level, yet funding for such groups decreased after the GFA. Although the SICDP's single-identity work followed a parity of esteem philosophy, it nevertheless promoted—through years of work—organizational, if not everyday, associations in some of the most violence-torn areas of the city. These associations were fragile and in conflict with a rights discourse of "parity of esteem." Throughout and after the peace process, this discourse intensified animosities; most notably, it became central to the conflicts surrounding parades and protests, through which political rights of assembly and expression were reinterpreted as entitlements of collective, communal subjects.

"Since This Trouble, the Protestant Workers Do Not Speak to the Catholics"

Throughout the 1990s, disputes about parades grew more violent. The bitterness of these conflicts seeped into even the most mundane interactions.

A research participant working at the Fair Employment Commission (FEC) said that, even in the agency established to combat workplace discrimination, office interactions became strained. During the 1997 dispute, employees were so tense, he said, that they moved their work to share tables with their coreligionists—effectively setting up two camps in the workplace.[21] His account of his stressful work environment echoed one mill owner's assessment of workplace relations after the communal violence of 1935: "Since this trouble, the Protestant workers do not speak to the Catholics" (Hepburn 1990: 83).

Since the eighteenth century, parades have been a means of social, political, and religious expression in Ireland, especially in the north. Loyal (Protestant) orders, the largest being the Orange Order, hold the most well-known and controversial parades.[22] The Ancient Order of Hibernians and the republican movement also commemorate significant events with parades (Jarman and Bryan 1998). Parades by nationalists, trade unions, and other groups, however, were historically more restricted than loyalist parades. That is, the state preferentially bestowed the right to assemble to loyalists (Jarman and Bryan 1996). Orange parades have changed in character over the centuries since the order's creation in 1795, shifting to manage the class and factional fissures within loyalism (Bryan 2000a). Furthermore, the state imposed a variety of limits on political rights during the conflict, giving police the authority to reroute parades. In the 1990s, limits on assembly became more institutionalized. A parades commission which regulated contentious parades and counterprotests was established in 1998. Both proponents and opponents of parades frequently took recourse to the language of parity.[23]

During the ceasefires and peace talks of the 1990s, the number of loyalist parades increased, as did protests against them. Jarman and Bryan (1996) record an increase in loyalist parades after the Anglo-Irish Agreement 1985. After the 1994 ceasefires, parades became an even more "prominent and highly visible means of displaying and mobilizing behind traditional political demands in an alternative site of conflict" (41). As loyalist parades increased, so, too, did nationalist protests. Orangemen invoked both tradition and a political right to free assembly to argue for unrestricted parading (Bryan 2006a). Meanwhile, protesters pointed to the parades' sectarian and triumphal dimensions, as well as the heavy-handed policing of local neighborhoods and protests. They, too, claimed a right to assembly. In the 1990s, opposition to parades in nationalist areas became more organized, as residents associations demanded restrictions on routes and music. In this way, various "rights"—to culture, to tradition, to assembly and expression—were blended into debates about parading. The Orange Order refused to meet residents groups directly, citing the number of former republican prisoners in the groups. This stance echoed unionist politicians who refused to enter direct peace talks with republicans in the early and mid-1990s. Neither nationalist nor loyalist mobilizations were wholly nonviolent; the parading season became an occasion for increasingly violent confrontations.

For both loyalists and nationalists, there was indeed a dimension of territoriality. One nationalist residents group organizer explained that, because the parades were perceived as triumphal, nationalists did not want any parade in "our areas." Meanwhile, loyalists argued for the right of British citizens to walk the "Queen's highway." Many also suspected that the growth of residents groups in the 1990s, often led by former prisoners, was a ruse directed by republicans. Some loyalists thought that, by encouraging the Orange Order to participate in the talks with these groups, republicans could amplify their claims of unionist intransigence in resisting peace talks when the Orangemen inevitably refused. In this analysis, invitations to talks were not a call to association and communication but a political weapon. Some nationalists held conspiratorial views of the residents groups as well. O'Doherty (1998), a political journalist, claims that residents groups were part of a republican strategy to reinvigorate legitimacy that the movement had lost during armed struggle. Thus, for a variety of reasons, the protest groups sometimes appeared to be a tactic of conflict instead of a genuine search for dialogue.

The Drumcree parade in Portadown was the most publicized parade conflict in the 1990s. Traditionally, the parade is held on the Sunday before the Twelfth (i.e., July 12, the celebration of King William's defeat of James II at the Battle of Boyne in 1690; see Glossary). Orangemen march from the town center to a church service and return. The parade's route had been contested in previous years and had already been rerouted away from one predominantly nationalist area of the town. In the 1990s, residents of the nationalist Garvaghy Road area organized a group to protest the parade's return route. This group displaced the Jesuit-fostered Drumcree Faith and Justice group that supported previous attempts to resolve disputes. The Orange Order, which originated in the area in 1795, vigorously opposed any change to the route.

In 1995, a stand-off occurred when police attempted to prevent the parade from proceeding along the Garvaghy Road. Orangemen and their supporters gathered at the point where the parade was stopped. Riots spread across the region, and supporters blocked routes to Larne, a major port. After two days, the police let the parade proceed. In 1996, another Drumcree standoff led to days of rioting, and loyalists murdered a Catholic taxi driver, Michael McGoldrick, on the night of July 7. Loyalists began to travel to Portadown, massing where the police lines blocked the Orangemen's route in Portadown. Supporters set up roadblocks across the region, the port of Larne was shut down again, and serious riots erupted in north Belfast. On Thursday, July 11, police announced that they and British troops could no longer contain the protests, and the parade was allowed to proceed along the Garvaghy Road. Nationalists in west Belfast and Derry reacted furiously: rioters threw petrol bombs, while police retaliated with plastic bullets. The disorder lasted until July 15.

The communal consensus depicted by antagonists was not absolute. Not all loyalists believed the right to assembly was absolute. One man said, "Them'uns at Drumcree should just turn around and go back the way they came. My grandfather was an Orangeman, and he would be ashamed. He would not want to go where he wasn't wanted." In contrast, one republican I knew argued repeatedly with his friends that the right to assembly was absolute, citing past bans on republican commemorations: "I remember when they wouldn't even let us walk down the Andersonstown Road [in the heart of nationalist west Belfast], for fuck's sake, because a few Prods [Protestants] in Suffolk might see us from their back windows and be offended! We don't need to do the same thing."

Minority perspectives like these were mostly drowned out by more vociferous proponents of parades or bans. In 1998, after the GFA ratification, the Drumcree conflict reached a horrifying climax, accompanied by the most severe civil disturbances since the early 1970s. On June 29, the new parades commission announced its decision on Drumcree: the parade could not return via the Garvaghy Road. Riots began to break out in loyalist areas following the announcement. Violence escalated when ten Catholic churches were petrol bombed on July 2. On Friday, July 3, before the scheduled parade on July 5, one thousand British soldiers and one thousand police personnel were deployed in the Garvaghy Road area. They dug a trench around the estate, strung barbed wire around the area, and built barricades across the Garvaghy Road and other roads leading into the area.

In Belfast, tensions were running high. Some of my research participants—loyalist and nationalist—told me of their plans to travel to Portadown to support their respective coreligionists. In the midst of the tension, I shared a laugh with "Mark," a community organizer from the nationalist Beechmount area, when we spied a tourist bus on the Falls Road with "The

Paddy Wagon" emblazoned on its sides. Mark said, "They need to get the fuck south [to the Republic]. They don't want to be trapped in that come Sunday. With that name, you won't know which side is hijacking you!" (Despite his laughter, he also took grave offense at what he saw as an ethnic slur.) "Michelle," another nationalist who worked in the Falls, seemed especially nervous after the announcement of the parade rerouting. Usually garrulous and witty, she became quiet, and a slight tremor in her hands betrayed her nerves. She lived with her family in Antrim—part of a minority community of Catholics in a predominantly Protestant town. They had left Belfast in the 1970s because of intimidation. She was worried loyalist violence would spread to Antrim.

On the day of the parade, when police stopped the Orangemen at the barricade, they refused to leave. Supporters from across the region descended to camp out in the fields. In the days that followed, these supporters began attacking the barricades and police lines. An Orange Order leader threatened to paralyze the region if their "civil and religious liberties" continued to be repressed.[24] By the end of the week, loyalists were hurling blast bombs at the security forces. In Belfast, a few days before the Twelfth, I was surprised as a group of loyalists from Tates Avenue moved into the street to block traffic on the Lisburn Road at about 3 p.m. On foot, I hurried back to my nearby flat, only to find the landlines were out of order. A neighbor darkly told me that "the boys" knew ways to shut down phone service.

Yet the Shankill Road was quiet; some recreational rioting went on at interfaces, but until the weekend the pro-agreement loyalists maintained calm. However, in other areas the high-profile clashes between men in riot gear and balaclavas in Portadown was matched by a more intimate intimidation campaign. Armed loyalist gangs targeted Catholic or "mixed marriage" households in predominantly Protestant areas—mainly outside Belfast, especially in County Antrim. Catholic businesses, homes, and schools were attacked with petrol bombs. One of these incidents left Michelle's family homeless a second time. The worst violence culminated in an incident in Ballymoney, when three brothers were brutally murdered in their home. Although the boys were raised as Protestants, their mother was Catholic. As the introductory chapter explains, when news of their deaths on the night of July 11 spread, Protestant ministers and politicians began to call for an end to the violence.

The violence did subside, and eventually an accounting became public. On July 11 and again on July 15, the Royal Ulster Constabulary (RUC) released figures on the disorder that gave a stark context to the anxiety and dismay I witnessed in this period. Between 6 a.m. on July 4 and 6 a.m. on July 14, there were 615 attacks on security forces; 76 RUC officers injured; 632 petrol bombings; 2,250 petrol bombs recovered; 178 hijackings; 144 homes and 165 other buildings damaged; 467 vehicles attacked; 837 plastic bullets fired.[25] Later figures showed that 141 Catholic or "mixed" families and the families of 50 RUC officers were resettled.[26] The bitterness of the Drumcree conflict also contributed to a more pervasive climate of sectarianism. Jarman (2005) found that between 1996 and 1999, housing intimidation increased to more than 1,700 reports annually (24), while twenty-seven interface barriers were constructed or augmented in Belfast between 1994 and 2005 (27).

A remnant of protesters remained at Drumcree several months. Harold Gracey, the Portadown Lodge district master, cut a forlorn figure as he remained in a caravan on the hill for 400 days. Dissident republicans attempted to bomb Newry and Armagh following the Twelfth, but the bombs were intercepted; in Omagh that August, however, they succeeded in detonating a bomb that killed twenty-nine people. While politicians vowed publicly that they would not be deterred from peace, in the summer of 1998, that peace felt much like the war.

A fourth annual Drumcree dispute did not materialize in 1999. As many loyalists predicted, the Orangemen have never walked that road again. Nevertheless, disorder intensified in 2000, and serious riots took place surrounding other parades in subsequent years—notably with riots in upper Springfield in 2005, north Belfast in 2010 and 2012, and east Belfast in 2011.

From 1995 to 1998, the Drumcree parade became a focal point for violence. Rights talk was appropriated to pursue ethnopolitical conflicts, as nationalists and unionists cited parity of esteem to argue for their positions on parades. The overwhelming dominance of the parades issue directed political violence during the peace process into a specific issue and the time frame of summer. As a result, ritualized and "recreational" rioting became annual events, and bitter legacies remain to this day. Rights discourse is not innocent here. The appropriation of rights in terms of collective political traditions worked against a discourse of political rights to association that enabled the peace process. These contradictions reproduced political subjectivities that privilege their collective, oppositional nature. This phenomenon continues within the structures of power sharing and cycles of everyday life—at the expense of other politics.

Contradictory Consequences of Political Rights

By elevating "cultural difference," the peace process
has unleashed a new round of sectarianism—driven
not by inequality and discrimination but by the idea
that Northern Ireland has two distinct communities
whose culture and interests are different, who must be
constantly policed and kept apart. Cultural diversity
is the new sectarianism—and in many ways, this new
sectarianism is even worse than the divisions of the past.
Stripped of any political content, today's conflicts in
Northern Ireland are now what many wrongly assumed
them to be during the Troubles: base, atavistic, sectarian
clashes.

—Brendan O'Neill, "How the Peace Process
Divided Ireland," *The Blanket*

On May 21, 1998, as voters debated the ratification of the GFA, divisions within loyalism were evident in the campaigning. Spring sunshine bathed the brick terraces of west Belfast, and the Shankill Road was buzzing with activity. Competing "yes" and "no" advocates broadcast their messages from cars with loudspeakers. Political parties associated with loyalist paramilitaries hired trailers to drive up and down the thoroughfare blasting dance music. City council representatives stood on street corners, smiling and greeting citizens, while the anti-agreement DUP had a small plane flying overhead with the banner "It's right to vote No." In contrast, the nationalist Falls area was quiet. Irish tricolors flapped gently in the breeze, while residents went about the everyday business of shopping, waiting for buses or taxis, and ferrying children school. The agreement needed little advocacy among nationalists and republicans. But for loyalists, the vote was highly contested. The DUP had boycotted the multiparty talks, and a large number of loyalists were uncomfortable with prisoner releases. Although the agreement was ratified by a 71.1 percent vote, exit polling found that 96 percent of Catholics but only 56 percent of Protestants voted "yes" (Elliott and Flackes 1999: 125).

There were complex reasons for nationalists' embrace of the GFA and unionists' ambivalence. Many nationalists I knew believed it replaced the discriminatory Northern Irish state with a partnership in which they were equals. This understanding of the agreement as a foundational document, ensuring equal rights for citizens with opposed national aspirations, developed into a ubiquitous political narrative that explained both the past and future of the conflict in terms of rights.

The political power of this narrative lies in its encapsulation of ordinary understandings of the conflict, rather more than its factual analysis of either historical events or the legal details of the GFA. The perspectives of loyalists were different and more fragmented. One research participant explained it this way:

> You've got a unionist community who believes its day has gone. . . . Before, unionism had it all. Or that's what they said. But they ran their own country, and they excluded the Catholic community as part of that. And they excluded a lot of Protestants too, in terms of voting rights, a quality of life. But that was part of a corrupt state. And it was a corrupt state. The problem is we're lumbered with that legacy of the past. And that's what unionism is now having to come to terms with.

Republican acceptance of the GFA was not unanimous, however, as dissident republican groupings have demonstrated. The quote at the beginning of this section was written by a republican critic of the peace process in *The Blanket*, an innovative online journal that published writing by republicans and some loyalists in 2001–2008. Its title refers to the prison protests for restoration of political status in the 1970s, when republican prisoners refused prison uniforms, draping themselves in blankets. The journal emerged from a study group of republican ex-prisoners organized in the 1990s, when a new politics appeared within reach. The journal facilitated dialogue and dissent among republicans and many articles were critical of Sinn Féin's peace strategy. However, the journal was not created to oppose the peace process. Rather, *The Blanket* attempted to use technology as a medium for broader dialogue and exchange. As such, it proclaimed a serious and sincere "commitment to freedom of speech."[27]

Some people at the forefront of these online discussions suffered for their forthright critiques of mainstream republicanism. Two ex-prisoners were driven from their homes by protesters in west Belfast when they criticized the PIRA killing of a dissident republican, Joseph O'Connor, in 2000. These critics were not intent on destroying the peace process or returning to armed struggle. Rather, they questioned the path taken by republican leadership, and their experiences underscore the complexity of viewpoints dismissed as "neanderthal" by leading figures such as Deputy First Minister Martin McGuinness.[28] The irony that advocates of the peace process engaged in a violent process of silencing opposition within their political movements was not limited to republicans. In 2000, the pro-GFA UVF and an anti-GFA company of the UDA divided the Shankill in a violent feud. Meanwhile, loyalist parties associated with paramilitarism declined and Sinn Féin's electoral support grew despite the IRA's approach to internal critiques.

The conviction of some *Blanket* authors that politics had been reduced to sectarian head counting has also appeared in academic literature. Notable critiques of an essentialist, two-cultures model of reconciliation include Butler (1994a,b), Burgess (2002), and Finlay (2008). Critics have also made compelling arguments against consociationalism and power sharing as a politically reductive, managerial approach to the conflict (e.g., Finlay 2010; Wilson 2010). Similarly, Dixon (1997) was an early critic who identified the tension between the associational politics of civil society and the liberal multiculturalism of consociationalism.

Disputes over decommissioning and ongoing paramilitary activity led to power sharing for two brief periods, from December 1999 to February 2000 and from May 2000 to October 2001. In the 2003 elections to the suspended assembly, the DUP and Sinn Féin became the two largest assembly parties. The parties that articulated their constitutional positions most vehemently eclipsed the UUP and SDLP, even though those parties' leaders shared a Nobel Peace Prize for their roles in the peace process. In subsequent years an inclusive process was attenuated, as the British negotiated with Sinn Féin and the DUP to reestablish the power-sharing government. In 2005, the PIRA decommissioned, and, after further negotiations, devolved governance was restored in 2007.

A peace process must bring along the opponents. But during the talks, inclusivity also brought broader perspectives on political rights to the negotiations, perspectives that are now subordinate to parity of esteem. Civil society advocates played a major role in a nonparty campaign for the agreement's ratification (Couto 2001; Guelke 2003). For example, NICVA's former director led "YES," a proagreement campaign. Cochrane and Dunn (2002) argue that the margin of ratification would have been smaller without this intervention (182). Alongside the assembly, the GFA proposed a "civic forum," with representatives of "business, trade union, and voluntary sectors" serving as consultants to politicians (*Agreement Reached* 1998: 9). The forum was intended to institutionalize a political role for NGOs and civil society actors. Some scholars praised the forum's brief and sporadic tenure or were at least optimistic about its potential (e.g., Bell 2004; Pålshaugen 2005). But the politics of direct rule continued for most of the subsequent nine years, and others argue that most community activists were content to pursue their interests through preexisting contacts with civil servants (Farrington 2004). Among many of my research participants, civil society itself became seen as an exercise for the "great and the good," legitimating new political elites. "Alex," a republican ex-prisoner and community activist, described it sharply: "I don't know what they mean by civil society. I mean, inherent in the phrase civil society there is this grouping which is divorced or is somehow unaligned to the existing condition of the state. . . . I think it's a nonsense, it cannot be. But people have been allowed to bandy this phrase about. And that's how we ended up with this civic assembly [sic], which is a quango. Civil society may be the end result of depoliticization."[29]

Despite public angst about Northern Ireland's "democratic deficit" under direct rule, in the long years of the assembly's suspension, many seemed unperturbed. As long as the ceasefires were reasonably secure, they could enjoy the benefits of "peace." Beyond the fundamental benefit of fewer people dying, my research participants were pleased with mundane shifts in everyday life—a revitalized city center nightlife and the end of manned border crossings or security screenings at shopping centers. The 2003 Northern Ireland Life and Times Survey bore out the extent of this sanguine attitude. Fifty percent of respondents said they would "not mind much either way" if the new assembly was abolished.[30] Forty-one percent of Catholics responded this way, despite the agreement having consistently strong support among nationalists; 56 percent of Protestant respondents felt the same. Three years after devolution was restored, the 2010 study found that only 1 percent of respondents were "very satisfied" with the work of the members of the legislative assembly; 22 percent "fairly satisfied"; 23 percent "neither satisfied nor dissatisfied," 29 percent "fairly dissatisfied," and 22 percent "very dissatisfied."[31]

Large-scale research projects about the EU Peace II funding and the IFI conclude that they contributed to the peace process through building civil society, while acknowledging that the approach of the funded work was seen by some as reproducing and entrenching communal oppositions (e.g., Byrne 2011). Many of the benefits are intangible, such as relationship building and creating "a sense of pride and hope" (Byrne 2011: 194). Meanwhile, the funds themselves generated the usual complaints that one group received more than their fair share—in this instance, that Catholics benefited disproportionately from the funds. Although reviews of awards concluded this was not the case, claims of bias continued (Haase and Pratschke 1999).[32]

Devolution offers plentiful examples that confirm public skepticism about transformed politics. The civic forum experiment was suspended with the assembly. With the restoration of devolution, the forum was subject to a lengthy public review. Years later, its fate remained undecided. With power sharing restored, multiple NGOs and public bodies were consulted on law and policy regarding human rights, parading, and community relations. The rare example of legislation that emerged was a draft Public Assemblies, Parades and Protests Bill (OFMDFM 2010b). The product of negotiations between Sinn Féin and the DUP, the draft bill modeled regulation of all political assembly on contentious Orange parades. That is, all public gatherings of fifty or more people were required to give the police thirty-seven days notice. Consultation responses by groups such as the Community Relations Council (2010) and public sector union (NIPSA 2010) were scathing and questioned the legality of the bill under the European Convention. After 410 submissions were received, the bill was quietly withdrawn in December 2010. One purpose of the GFA was to create functional local politics by setting aside the basic constitutional disagreement for referendum at an unspecified date. Yet neither violence nor antipathy was completely set aside, and, at many points after the GFA, the trajectory from violence to politics certainly did not seem inevitable. Functional local politics did not emerge, either.

The contradictory consequences of rights discourse in the 1990s are inseparable from the broader political landscape and from intensified divisions in everyday life since the ceasefires (see Shirlow and Murtagh 2006). Furthermore, division and fear remain concentrated among those living on what one research participant called the "bleeding edge"—interface neighborhoods. Jarman (2012) identifies ninety-nine different defensive barriers, that is, peace lines, in Belfast (11). The greatest increase in construction was in the 1990s—and one-third of the barriers "have been built since the ceasefires" (12–13). Byrne et al. (2012) note that every peace line is located in the "top 10 % of the most socially and economically deprived electoral wards" (4). Sixty-nine percent of residents in these interfaces believe they are "necessary because of the potential for violence" (13). Meanwhile, among the general population, 76 percent "would like to see peace walls come down now or in the near future" (27). Peace is differentially distributed, and part of this inequity and intensified division is traceable to how competing versions of political rights were appropriated during the peace process itself.

Political rights were appropriated as vehicles to both transform and perpetuate conflict. The *zeitgeist* of civil society and associational freedoms did facilitate changes, in grassroots and institutional politics and the transition from paramilitarism to democratic practices. At the same time, it was entangled with the imperatives of parity of esteem. In practice, parity of esteem treated rights as the entitlements of collective communal subjects. At its worst, rights talk justified violent mobilizations around marching, as well as the most intense wave of violence and displacements since the early 1970s. Thus, a discourse of competing collective rights prevailed, structuring future politics and nurturing past enmities in the present.

*

CHAPTER 5

No Justice, No Peace

Everyone's thought is forensic, everyone is simply putting
a "case" with deliberate suppression of his opponent's
point of view, and, what is more, with complete
insensitiveness to any sufferings except those of himself
and his friends. . . . One notices this in the case of people
one disagrees with, such as Fascists or pacifists, but in
fact everyone is the same, at least everyone who has
definite opinions.
                    —George Orwell, "Second War-Time Diary,"
                                              April 27, 1942

"At least I wasn't a traitor!" bellowed a Democratic Unionist Party councillor
in the September 1997 Belfast City Council meeting. He was enraged that
Progressive Unionist Party councillors David Ervine and Billy Hutchinson
did not vote to commemorate the Bloody Friday bombings of 1972. As if they
had rehearsed, the Sinn Féin delegates sarcastically hooted in unison, spectators to an entertaining intraunionist spat.

At that meeting, I received my first lesson in Northern Ireland's politics of
the past. "Lisa," a research participant and city councillor, had invited me to
the meeting. In those days, despite the ceasefires, security was strict at public
meetings. When I arrived at City Hall, I was screened and guided by an escort
to the upper gallery. I sat alone in the lofty area created for citizens to observe
their democracy at work.

After direct rule was imposed in 1972, local government had a restricted
set of responsibilities—sanitation, community, cemetery, leisure services, and

limited building regulation.[1] Within these parameters, council work veered between stultifying discussions about planning permission and arguments about commemoration and the peace process. That night, councillors vigorously debated a service to memorialize those killed and injured in the Bloody Friday bombings and a plaque in City Hall to their memory.

Bloody Friday was an especially shocking atrocity during the early years of the conflict. On Friday, July 21, 1972, the IRA detonated twenty-two bombs across Belfast in little more than an hour. Nine people were killed and 130 injured. McKittrick et al. (1999) report one policeman's account: "One victim had his arms and legs blown off and some of his body had been blown through the railings. One of the most horrendous memories for me was seeing a head stuck to a wall" (229). Although the IRA placed warning calls to press and public protection groups shortly before the bombs, they were interspersed with hoax calls. In that brief span of time, it was difficult for police to discern which calls were legitimate and to evacuate multiple locations. Later, rumors swirled as to why the operation took place: retaliation for Bloody Sunday six months earlier, a show of PIRA strength, or protest at the collapse of talks with the British government. Whatever the reasons, the atrocity damaged the republican movement's image across the world and led to internal recriminations.

The PUP's David Ervine often declared that Bloody Friday led him to join the Ulster Volunteer Force. Those bombings convinced him that the security forces could not protect the public from the PIRA, which was not subject to rule of law or rules of engagement. Loyalists, he explained, needed a force unfettered by legality or procedure to counter republican paramilitarism. Both he and Hutchinson had served sentences for paramilitary offenses.

To other unionists, Ervine and Hutchinson's paramilitary pasts and their abstention from the commemoration vote aligned them with Sinn Féin. To at least one fellow councillor, therefore, they were "traitors." The motion was not passed. As the meeting neared its end, councillors proposed several symbolic statements regarding peace talks—for example, that the council recommend release of political prisoners. These proposals were swiftly voted down, and the council's work, such as it was, ended for the day.

At the mayor's reception after the meeting, I innocently asked Lisa, "Why is it controversial to commemorate Bloody Friday?" She patiently explained that parties with paramilitary links, loyalist and republican, did not view the motion as a sincere commemoration of lost lives. Instead, she said, it was a point-scoring tactic to beat their opponents over the heads about the past. Lisa joined the point-scoring fray by adding that the commemoration was one-sided, with no acknowledgment of police and security force violence. She pointed out that both Sinn Féin and the Social Democratic and Labour Party shared this sentiment and voted against the motion. A future peace, she said, could not be found by endlessly apportioning blame for the past.

The following month, supporters of the measure found enough votes, and abstentions, to pass it. In spring 2000, the plaque was unveiled in City Hall. It reads, "Erected by Belfast City Council on 18th April, 2000 / in memory of those / who were killed and injured in the IRA's bombing of the City / on Bloody Friday, 21st July, 1972 / and also / all those innocent victims of terrorism over the last 28 years."[2] Sinn Féin councillors did not attend the unveiling ceremony because the plaque does not acknowledge the victims of state violence.

Blame for past violence saturates contemporary political discourse in Northern Ireland. The Bloody Friday debate I observed was part of a long-standing discursive pattern in which recriminations are interjected in the least-contentious debates of the postconflict assembly. For example, in June 2011 DUP legislator Pam Lewis proposed a debate regarding domestic violence policy. When Caitríona Ruane, Sinn Féin MLA, spoke in support of the proposal, Gregory Campbell, Lewis's party colleague, interrupted to ask Ruane, "Does the Member understand the difficulty that some people might have with her talking about the trauma of victims?" (Northern Ireland Assembly 2011: 96). Campbell continued speaking out of turn, criticizing Sinn Féin's appointment of an ex-prisoner to an advisory post in the Department of Culture, Arts, and Leisure. Such exchanges are not unusual; any political debate may become an opportunity for bitter accusations regarding completely unrelated grievances.

Political contests regarding victimization, harm, and responsibility have continued throughout the peace process and postconflict decade. The lack of a formal, inclusive approach to past violence, through a retributive justice or public truth process, leaves gaps in postconflict institutions and society within which these contests flourish. Politicians, NGOs, and campaigners have appropriated human and victims' rights in various ways to discuss past violence. Often these appropriations objectify victim experiences to legitimate or critique past violence, as well as the present political positions of different actors. Human rights advocates highlight state violence and collusion allegations, and victims' rights are invoked to designate "innocent" victims and exclude others. In this case, rights talk is entangled in contests about victimization because, in this unusual civil conflict, nonstate actors killed the largest number of people. Although evidence has demonstrated state collusion with loyalist paramilitaries during the conflict, investigations have increased rather than diminished contention surrounding human and victims' rights (e.g., Police Ombudsman 2007; Stevens 2003). Some victims of nonstate actors argue that collusion investigations privilege state victims and diminish resources for investigating nonstate actors. Marie Smyth (2007) neatly summarizes the risks of discursively perpetuating the conflict: "A political culture based on competing claims to victimhood will support and legitimize violence, and fail to foster political responsibility and maturity" (80). Past violence casts a long shadow over the region's political future.

Justice Is Negotiable: Gaps in the Settlement

> Most political players demand truth from those they
> perceive as the other side or sides, but seem unwilling to
> offer the truth from their side, or acknowledge and take
> responsibility for their actions. This is mostly due to fear
> that such acknowledgement (public or otherwise) will
> weaken their position as parties vie for power in the new
> dispensation and that the truth may be used against them
> within the context of the delicate peace that prevails.
> —Brandon Hamber, *Past Imperfect*, 80–81

The Good Friday Agreement did not establish a formal transitional justice process or a truth-recovery process, an unusual feature of the settlement, given current conflict resolution practices. Following ratification in 1998, the settlement took years to implement. During implementation, conflicting understandings of the past, particularly the role of state violence, continued to shape the political disagreements. During negotiations in the 2000s, nationalist parties demanded investigations of state violence and collusion with loyalist paramilitaries (Powell 2008).

Human rights discourse in Northern Ireland has emphasized state violence and violations of law. As such, the broader public perceives this talk as partial—incompletely describing the conflict and supporting a political analysis that treats state deficiencies as the direct cause of the conflict. Therefore, human rights talk is inextricable from the larger discursive context of politics. McEvoy (1999, 2001) defends local NGO focus on state actors, arguing they kept human rights above the fray of victim hierarchies. In contrast, Dickson

(2010), cofounder of one of the region's first human rights NGOs in 1981, is brutally self-critical of local human rights advocacy:

> One of the unfortunate features of the time was the refusal of many of those who continued to campaign for better human rights protection to recognize that what the paramilitaries were doing (the so-called loyalists just as much as the republicans) was denying the very human rights the campaigners (quite rightly) were calling on the government to uphold. It is hard now to remember that, in those relatively early days of human rights work, most activists believed that breaches of human rights were things only governments could commit; atrocities perpetrated by paramilitaries were simply breaches of criminal law. . . . This was the position adopted by . . . the Committee on the Administration of Justice (CAJ). (21)

Thus, human rights talk and mobilizations are ensnared in ethnopolitical conflict. In popular perception, human rights took on ethnopolitical associations, particularly for unionists. Meanwhile, nationalist victims of state violence and their advocates asserted that a hierarchy of victims prevailed in Northern Ireland, with nationalist lives valued least (see Lundy and McGovern 2008a; Bell and Keenan 2005). Human rights advocacy and lawsuits provided a tool to assert the value of lives lost through state violence. To unionists, however, decisions of the European Court of Human Rights appeared to privilege the victims of state violence, creating a different hierarchy of victims. The problem under power sharing, however, is not that unionists have the power to undermine basic human rights principles, as in the Stormont era. Rather, it is how human rights talk can function as an inclusive instrument for reconciliation, especially because historic appropriations of human rights have been received as extensions of local ethnopolitics.

In the postconflict era, these circumstances hamper efforts to create either legal accountability or an inclusive account of past violence—that is, they hamper the establishment of formal transitional justice or truth recovery. Hamber's (1998, 2003) research on violence, human rights, and victims' rights in Northern Ireland concludes that an official truth-recovery process is not politically possible. His observation that "the debate and intricacies of dealing with the past have certainly gained political and public momentum" was borne out exponentially in the ensuing decade (2003: 1088). Debates about past violence are directly linked to the way human and victims' rights discourse has functioned politically—as well as the way this violence was handled during peace negotiations. In the talks, parties and the government treated investigations of past crimes as demands or concessions. Making justice part of the negotiations heightened the public sense that human rights talk served political aims rather than justice and the rule of law.

The settlement's lacuna regarding past violence was a consequence of this rhetorical contest. The political tactic of expressing outrage about opponents' violence partly led to the inability of the parties to accept de jure amnesty for their opponents. Certainly, the local political culture is heavily reliant on rhetorical expressions of grievance, sometimes called a "culture of victimhood" (Morrissey and Smyth 2002; Smyth 2006). Another reason for this gap was that the political legitimacy of new institutions, as well as new political elites, would be hampered by full disclosure of the past. Instead, antagonists tacitly accepted that some admissions of responsibility and some prosecutions would occur, but that a comprehensive accounting could be avoided.

In the absence of a uniform approach to past violence, various victims' groups and political parties have filled the gap with demands for investigations of specific incidents. New grievances and disputes seem to follow each investigation. The resultant piecemeal approach to justice offers daily fodder for political recrimination, as politicians interpret various reports and inquiries in a fashion that supports their party positions. Some of my research participants alleged that the devolution talks at St. Andrews in 2006 considered a formal amnesty but that neither Sinn Féin nor the DUP were willing to abandon their pursuit of prosecutions for opponents.

Beneath the political rhetoric of victimhood lie lost lives and serious injuries. The Cost of the Troubles survey, an extensive statistical survey of the conflict, estimates that 3,585 people died from direct violence between 1966 and 1998 (Morrissey et al. 1999: 37). Of these victims, 53 percent were civilians unaffiliated with state or nonstate forces; approximately 28 percent were members of state security forces; and 15.5 percent were members of paramilitary organizations (37). In addition to almost 3,600 deaths, forty to fifty thousand people were injured (Ferguson et al. 2010: 858), and at least thirty thousand were seriously maimed (Mesev et al. 2009: 894). In terms of responsibility, the Cost of the Troubles survey concludes, "Republican paramilitaries have killed almost 59% of the total killed, 704 of whom were civilians. Loyalist paramilitaries have killed almost 28% of whom 818 were civilians, and the security forces have killed just over 11%, 204 of whom were civilians" (Morrissey et al. 1999: 37).

Statistical research frequently considers the conflict as having three groups of armed combatants—republicans, loyalists, and the British state. Hayes and McAllister (2001) differentiate "dimensions" of violence for a more nuanced analysis—between PIRA and security forces, from loyalists toward nationalist civilians, and from PIRA toward the broader civilian population. Another significant dimension of violence was directed from paramilitaries against individuals within their own ranks or local areas—punishing alleged antisocial behavior, spying, or political disloyalty.

Violence and intimidation were widespread. One in five people experienced intimidation; one in seven were victims of direct violence; one in five lost a family member; and more than half the population knew someone killed or injured (Hayes and McAllister 2001: 908). Hayes and McAllister assert that, since World War II, no industrial society "has experienced political violence at a remotely comparable level to that of Northern Ireland" (908). The violence, however, was not evenly distributed across the populace. Instead, it was most intense among those living in segregated and economically deprived areas; north and west Belfast were a geographic epicenter of violence (Mesev et al. 2009). Furthermore, Catholics were twice as likely to experience direct violence or intimidation and, to a lesser extent, experienced more indirect violence (Hayes and McAllister 2001: 909). However, statistical and geographic analysis by Mesev et al. (2009) reveals that "a greater number of fatalities were caused by members of a victim's own group than the opposition" (902).

The origins of transitional justice, like international human rights law, lie with the post–World War II political arrangements. In the late twentieth century, however, transitional justice processes have proliferated alongside the increasing number of violent intrastate conflicts and political transitions (see Hinton 2010; Hayner 2010). Transitional justice usually focuses on dealing with patterns of human rights violations rather than individual cases. The rationales for transitional justice tend to be that conventional criminal justice is inappropriate to the needs of a given postconflict society. This is because new institutions are not established or credible enough to produce retributive justice, or retributive justice will undermine a fragile peace. Transitional justice processes balance familiar and competing imperatives such as ensuring accountability for past crimes and broader institutional abuses, creating political legitimacy for new states, reconciling the political demands of various actors, fulfilling individual and collective needs for acknowledgment and information, and developing inclusive accounts of past violence. Despite the fact that transitional justice faces similar concerns in different locales, the particular circumstances of conflicts have created widely varying approaches (see Shaw et al. 2010; Hinton 2010; Hayner 2010).

Truth commissions or truth and reconciliation commissions (TRCs) are the best-known form of transitional justice process. Hayner (2010) has documented forty truth commissions around the world since 1974. These commissions have had varying relationships to criminal justice, sometimes giving truth recovery a higher priority. The South African TRC, for example, offered amnesty in exchange for full disclosure from perpetrators. However, some scholarship on postconflict justice concludes that retributive justice is crucial for establishing legitimate postconflict institutions and preventing future violence (e.g., Wilson 2001; Borneman 1997, 2002).

A different critique of transitional justice highlights the importance of grassroots processes, in contrast to imposed or imported legal models. This work echoes a long-standing strand of research in anthropology that examines the role of traditional conflict resolution practices (see Nordstrom 1997). For example, Theidon (2010) contrasts microlevel conciliation processes in Peru with the nationally constituted TRC. Northern Irish scholars offer similar critiques of transitional justice for privileging national, legalist processes over local efforts. McEvoy (2007) and Smyth (2007) argue that the legalistic emphasis of contemporary transitional justice overlooks grassroots NGO work in Northern Ireland—and that it privileges legal institutions, retributive justice, and state legitimacy over restorative justice and social relationships.

In Northern Ireland, both state agencies and community groups have struggled to address legal and social gaps in the settlement. The state's piecemeal approach to investigations and victim support has become fodder for the rhetorical contest about victims and perpetrators, responsibility and harm. Grassroots efforts to commemorate and record experiences, as well as to campaign for investigations of past violence, have proliferated. Sometimes these efforts have helped individuals and groups accept the settlement; at other times, they sustain the political contest about past rights and wrongs.

Selective Accountability

The global proliferation of TRCs in postconflict situations has underscored the conflicts between human rights principles and the *realpolitik* of conflict resolution. For example, in the South African case, the TRC faced competing imperatives to publicly recognize victim experiences and create legitimacy for the new state (Wilson 2001; Hamber 2003). In Northern Ireland, the absence of a TRC did not allow either society or the new institutions to avoid these competing demands. Additionally, this absence aggravated contemporary political debates about past violence. Political parties and victims groups called for investigations as part of the peace process, but through selective inquiries rather than a single process. An early use of investigation as a negotiating tool was the Saville Inquiry into Bloody Sunday, announced during the 1998 negotiations. Occurring early in the peace process, the inquiry hinted at the selective approach to investigation that would follow.

Bloody Sunday was a momentous atrocity that occurred on January 30, 1972, in Derry. Members of the British Army Parachute Regiment shot and killed thirteen protest marchers, wounding seventeen others, one of whom died later from his injuries. Outrage swept Ireland, and protesters in Dublin burned the British Embassy to the ground. Following the killings, the British government swiftly organized a judicial inquiry. This inquiry, the Widgery Tribunal, accepted soldiers' claims that their actions were justified and placed a shadow of guilt on the unarmed victims by alleging some had fired weapons earlier (Widgery 1972). These findings widely were denounced as slanderously false, and even officials within the process disputed the Widgery account.[3] As Chapter 2 explained, Bloody Sunday reverberated in local and international consciousness for decades and had immediate consequences in terms of violence and political polarization. During the 1998 peace talks, British prime minister Tony Blair announced a new inquiry into Bloody Sunday, the Saville Inquiry, treating the proposed investigation as "a confidence-building measure" (Bell and Keenan 2005: 78).

The Widgery Tribunal also established what is often called a "hierarchy of victims" (see Hamber 2003; Bell and Keenan 2005). This hierarchy elevates those construed as innocent victims, while placing lesser value on victims who are seen as contributing to their own deaths in some way. Critics assert that victims of state violence—some of whom were engaging in illegal activity during the conflict—are placed at the bottom of this hierarchy (e.g., Hegarty 2005; Lundy and McGovern 2008a). Since the early 1970s, human rights discourse has worked against this hierarchy and, to an extent, inverts it to privilege victims of state violence. Therefore, many people perceived human rights talk as rooted in politics rather than principles, even in obvious instances of state wrongdoing, such as Bloody Sunday.

The new Saville Inquiry vindicated the Bloody Sunday victims, calling the shootings "unjustified" (Saville et al. 2010: 90). When the report was finally published in June 2010, Conservative Prime Minister David Cameron publicly apologized on behalf of the state.[4] On its face, the new inquiry seemed a reasonable effort to resolve a long-standing injustice while avoiding an inconvenient criminal investigation. The Saville Inquiry took ten years and cost £190.3 million (approximately $327 million) between 2000 and 2010.[5] By its conclusion, however, the inquiry seemed more a bureaucratic correction than a political bombshell, since few people, in political rhetoric or everyday conversations, justified the killings. Yet more than one research participant remarked that the inquiry did more for lawyers' bank balances than truth or justice.

While the assembly remained suspended and the inquiry's cost rose exponentially, debates about past violence escalated. Other inquiries were established and more families of victims called for investigations of their cases. When police announced a criminal investigation of the soldiers based on the Saville report, antagonism about Bloody Sunday erupted once more. Victims of other atrocities complained that the police had no resources for investigating their cases. First Minister Peter Robinson suggested that his colleague, Deputy First Minister Martin McGuinness, should also be investigated for his actions in Derry on the day of the killings.[6] Investigating Bloody Sunday was not only part of the settlement—it also inspired new grievances in contemporary debates about past violence.

The peace negotiations produced other special investigations into state violence, particularly collusion between state intelligence agents and loyalist paramilitaries. In 1999, an inquiry was established to investigate the 1989 murder of defense lawyer Patrick Finucane. Finucane's family and other campaigners had long alleged state collusion in his murder by loyalist paramilitaries. Loyalists claimed that he was a member of the IRA and that this was the reason for his murder. Multiple investigations established that Finucane was not a member of the IRA; his law practice had simply defended paramilitary clients, both republican and loyalist. A particularly controversial element of the situation was that a few weeks before Finucane's murder a government minister, Douglas Hogg, publicly denounced some Northern Irish lawyers as "unduly sympathetic" to the IRA.[7] Nationalists believed his remarks were spurred by police briefings against local lawyers—implicating people in high levels of government in the murder.

The1999 inquiry was led by Sir John Stevens, a Metropolitan (London) police officer who had conducted two prior investigations into security force collusion with paramilitaries. In Stevens's report (2003), he describes how his previous collusion inquiries had been blatantly obstructed and concludes that there was substantial evidence of state collusion in the Finucane case. He also stated that Douglas Hogg, the MP whose statements about defense lawyers caused such controversy, "was compromised" by police briefings against solicitors (11). When Stevens's report on Finucane was published, his three inquiries had resulted in 144 arrests and ninety-four convictions (15). One man was convicted of murder in the Finucane killing in 2004. However, Finucane's family was dissatisfied with Stevens's investigation and continued to request a full public inquiry in the manner of Saville.

In 2002, the British government established several other collusion inquiries to satisfy SDLP demands during negotiations to implement the GFA (see McGrattan 2012; Powell 2008: 216–17). It appointed retired Canadian judge Peter Cory to investigate six allegations of state collusion in violence. The selected cases were "balanced," with three incidents in which Catholics were killed and three incidents in which unionist figures were killed. Cory investigated the murder of Pat Finucane once more, as well as the deaths of Rosemary Nelson and Catholic civilian Robert Hamill. Inquiries into the deaths of loyalist prisoner Billy Wright; RUC chief superintendent Harry Breen and Superintendent Bob Buchanan; and Lord Justice Maurice Gibson and Lady Cecily Gibson addressed unionist concerns. Cory established that there was sufficient evidence to warrant public inquiries in the Breen/Buchanan, Finucane, Hamill, Nelson, and Wright cases (Cory 2003a,b,d,e,f).

In the midst of growing public complaints about the Saville Inquiry's cost, Cory (2003a) made an extended case for his inquiries, arguing that costs could be controlled. The British government had committed to carry out Cory's recommendations, but the subsequent Inquiries Act 2005 allowed ministers to impose many restrictions on inquiries—in effect, keeping many of their details private. Phythian (2011) argues that the act was an apparent effort to limit political damage that a Finucane inquiry might produce. Human rights NGOs and Cory himself protested against the law (Phythian 2011: 56–57). The Hamill, Nelson, and Wright inquiries did not yield solid evidence of systematic police collusion, although serious negligence was outlined in the Nelson report (Morland et al. 2011; Jowitt et al. 2010; MacLean et al. 2010).[8] In October 2011, the British government established another review of the Finucane killing, rather than a public inquiry, led by Sir Desmond de Silva. His report, released in December 2012, further documented a shocking degree of state collusion in the murder (de Silva 2012). Prime Minister David Cameron publicly apologized to the Finucane family for the scale of state malpractice, but the family was not satisfied. Indeed, many of the families of these victims remain unsatisfied.

Other institutional mechanisms for investigation emerged from the peace process, but it would be an overstatement to claim that these various mechanisms work together in a systematic fashion. One such mechanism, the Police Ombudsman's office, was established as part of police reform. Its purpose is to investigate complaints of police misconduct or mismanagement independently of police influence. In design, this office is more oriented to current or future policing; nevertheless, the ombudsman has pursued several historical investigations—for example, the loyalist bombing of McGurk's in 1971 and the PIRA bombing of Claudy village in 1972 (Police Ombudsman 2011, 2010). In 2007, a major Police Ombudsman report into police intelligence activities, called Operation Ballast, documented the involvement of police informants in murder, attempted murder, punishment attacks, and drug-dealing between 1991 and 2003 (Police Ombudsman 2007).

In 2006, police established a special unit called the Historical Enquiries Team (HET) to investigate more than 3,000 conflict-related deaths between 1968 and 1998. Some of HET's work has been well received by campaign groups, but others have criticized its approach. Sinn Féin denounced HET's 2011 report on the Loughgall massacre.[9] HET concluded that the eight IRA men killed by the British Army in 1987 had fired first in the engagement.[10] Additionally, a PUP leader accused HET of bias and of disproportionately arresting loyalists.[11] A broader critique, voiced by Relatives for Justice and others, is that HET's case-by-case approach obscures systematic, institutionally sanctioned state violence (e.g., Lundy 2011). Lundy's (2011) review of HET critiqued its approach to investigating violence by state actors, and the Northern Ireland police chief requested a review of HET procedures from Her Majesty's Inspector of Constabulary. HET was initially scheduled to operate until 2011 but now plans to continue at least until 2013 (Lundy 2011).

The Independent Commission for the Location of Victims' Remains, created in 1999, is yet another investigating body. The commission's investigations cannot result in criminal proceedings and effectively offers immunity from prosecution to those who provide information to the commission.[12] The commission's brief is to locate and repatriate the remains of sixteen victims known as the Disappeared because their burials were hidden. PIRA has acknowledged killing thirteen of the Disappeared, and INLA one.[13] Although paramilitary groups cooperated with the commission, only nine bodies have been recovered.

Security force collusion with paramilitaries remains the most contentious issue investigated by these agencies and inquiries. Many of these investigations are ongoing. For example, the Police Ombudsman's inquiry into collusion in north Belfast, Operation Ballast, was passed to HET, which charged more than twelve people with crimes. The investigation has continued, renamed Operation Stafford, and was passed on to the police's serious crime branch in 2009. In 2012, the Ombudsman opened an additional historical inquiry into collusion between police and the UVF in the Shankill area. Some investigations have substantiated collusion allegations; other revelations have complicated these claims in terms of both the nature of collusion and the nature of its harm to specific victims and the broader populace. For example, in 2003 many newspapers reported that the head of internal security for PIRA had been a paid informer for the British army's intelligence unit.[14] Papers named the man and alleged that he was a paid agent for more than two decades, during which time he carried out several killings of alleged "touts" or informers—earth-shattering allegations in west Belfast. Immediately, some of my own research participants wondered if people whose deaths they had dismissed because they were touts were actually the victims of state collusion.

Some of my research participants see HET investigations of past paramilitary violence as a continuation of the security forces war against paramilitaries. They believe the GFA created a de facto amnesty that HET willfully disregards. Meanwhile, a new group was formed in 2012, the Irish Centre on Wrongful Convictions, to help ex-prisoners overturn their convictions. The group is considering civil actions against former and current police officers. An end is not in sight in the struggles between security forces and paramilitaries regarding the legitimacy of past violence, as well as individual and collective culpability. In the absence of a structured process, this array of investigations and agencies sustains bitter debates.

Political bargaining about these issues continued throughout the negotiations that finally restored devolution in 2007. In 2005, PIRA decommissioned its weapons and disbanded in 2006: the organization had finally succumbed to international pressure during the years after 9/11, pressure that intensified following a large PIRA bank robbery and the highly publicized murder of a civilian by PIRA personnel in 2005 (see Clancy 2010). A final matter of dispute was amnesty for IRA members who were "on the run" (OTRs)—that is, members who were avoiding investigation or charges for past actions—but the British government and Sinn Féin finally agreed on a de facto amnesty for OTRs. After the IRA decommissioning in 2005, the government proposed the Northern Ireland (Offences) Bill, which granted immunity to both OTRs and state actors.[15] The inclusion of state actors was a response to former police officers who, angered by previous collusion inquiries, threatened to name publicly more republican informers if further investigations or prosecutions occurred. The SDLP opposed amnesty for state actors, Sinn Féin withdrew support for the bill, and it was abandoned. Finally in 2006, movement toward restoring devolution resumed. Sinn Féin recognized the new police service in 2007, and plans to prosecute OTRs were shelved.[16] Devolution was restored May 8, 2007.

In the absence of a transitional justice process, some section of the public may be offended by any given investigation or inquiry. Investigative efforts often inflame rather than resolve public debates about violence and responsibility. Indeed, they appear to enable what one ex-prisoner described to me as a generalized political tendency to "Waking up each morning and asking, 'What am I offended by today?'" Even Senator George Mitchell (1999), who led the multiparty peace talks, commented on this "highly developed sense of grievance," reporting that a talks participant told him, "To understand us, Senator, you must realize that we in Northern Ireland would drive 100 miles out of our way to receive an insult" (13). No doubt these speakers did not intend to diminish the experience of victims; instead, their humor is aimed at the perennial outrage that surrounds past violence. The outrage is self-reproducing, in that it stymies any proposal for a consistent institutional approach—creating new opportunities for public acrimony

In Northern Ireland, investigations of past violence have been influenced by political concerns and have been treated tactically as demands or concessions in the negotiations. Wilson (2001) warns that such politicization profoundly damages the credibility of human rights claims, pointing to the South African example: "Human rights talk has become the language of pragmatic political compromise rather than the language of principle and accountability. This is the main obstacle to the popular acceptance of human rights as the new ideology of constitutional states" (228). In postconflict Northern Ireland, human rights discourse is embedded in broader debates about the legitimacy of violence and the culpability of different actors in the conflict. These debates simplify experiences and practices of violence and, indeed, the multiple roles a single person may inhabit. They also reinforce public perceptions of human rights talk as a selective and partial form of politics. Yet neither the peace process nor global human rights discourse autonomously produced this differentiation of victims and score keeping; these discursive practices reflect and reproduce ordinary people's understandings of their experiences.

Settling Scores

> Everyone is dishonest, everyone is utterly heartless
> towards people who are outside the immediate range of
> his own interests. What is most striking of all is the way
> sympathy can be turned on and off like a tap according
> to political expediency. I am not thinking of lying for
> political ends, but of actual changes in subjective feeling.
> —George Orwell, "Second War-Time Diary,"
> April 27, 1942

One reason human rights discourse has been so politically powerful—either for expressing grievances or provoking anger—is the way it resonates with people's subjective understandings of their experiences. This is particularly true for those who both enacted and suffered most of the violence. Throughout the conflict, everyday explanations of and responses to violence were linked to assertions of victimization. Smyth (2007) writes that "Victimhood is deployed as a legitimization for further violence, which is cast as retaliation for the initial victimization, and ultimately blamed on the original perpetrator" (80). The roles of perpetrator and victim are blurred in both actuality and in rhetoric, and local understandings of victimhood apportion responsibility for the conflict. Unsurprisingly, then, people differentially express sympathy for suffering and loss, usually depending on their own ethnocommunal origins and allegiances. In these circumstances, the politics of human rights depend on the local context of reception. As a consequence, human rights discourse about past violence often reproduces prior grievances and justifications for violence.

"Gail," a community organizer in the Shankill area, frequently expressed frustration to me about the postconflict politics of victimhood in Northern Ireland. Her family was intimidated from their home in a mixed area in the early 1970s; this experience was not unusual in west Belfast. In both the Falls and Shankill areas, many residents experienced such displacement. What is unusual about Gail is her capacity for discussing the complex dimensions of her experiences of violence. She is keenly critical of ongoing rhetoric about past violence, as well as the use of human rights discourse in victims' advocacy. She believes that victims, consciously or not, contribute to the rhetorical contest about past violence and responsibility, making it impossible to develop inclusive historical accounts of or legal accountability for the conflict. "It's probably not the right thing to say, but in Northern Ireland, for victims, a grieving process has become a grievance."

One criticism that Gail and other victims voice is that human rights advocacy, state investigations, and victims' advocates treat the roles of victim and perpetrator as static, failing to recognize the fluidity of these experiences. In May 2010, she rhetorically asked me, "Who am I the victim of?" She pointed out that, "I was burned out of my home by Protestants. . . . My brother-in-law was shot dead by the British Army, and my best friend, who was in the police, was shot by the IRA." Underneath the specific complexities of her life is the broader fact that paramilitaries could also be victims and that victims of violence may eventually support paramilitarism (Hayes and McAllister 2001). Similarly, anthropological scholarship on human rights practices has noted that claims for objectivity risk oversimplifying the complex social dimensions of violent conflicts. For example, Wilson (2003) observes that the "forensic truth" of InfoComm, a categorical tool for human rights documentation, permits only three categories of person—victim, perpetrator, and witness. These rigid classifications of *victim* and *perpetrator* simplify experiences that do not fit either positivist or politically useful accounts of the violence (see Ross 2002).

In Northern Ireland human rights talk not only fails to capture important subjective dimensions of violence; conditions of reception also sustain subjective orientations to the conflict. Claims of collective victimization are integral to justifications for violence in Northern Ireland. Therefore, when human rights discourse is appropriated into the politics of victimhood, its focus on certain victims has inverted, yet reproduced, another subjective dimension of violence: the differential value that people attached on a daily basis to the suffering and death of others. Postconflict inquiries and investigations have rightly attempted to expose state collusion and make visible the suffering of state victims. But these efforts have also at times created new exclusions and hierarchies of victims. For "Sam," a victims' campaigner who lost close family members in a PIRA bombing of a civilian site, the inquiry process is particularly pernicious in this regard: "Pat Finucane, Rosemary Nelson, Robert Hamill, Billy Wright—I mean, you know, these killings, they were all high-profile cases that have a big campaign team behind them, but if you happen to be just some guy killed . . . with no community support or any political support, no one is going to order an inquiry. It's not the fairest way to do it, to be honest with you."

The differential and politicized values attached to victims' experiences did not emerge autonomously from human rights discourse. Some research participants acknowledged an ugly type of "scoring"—one point for each opponent killed—that took place privately and sometimes publicly. The best-known public incident was during an Orange parade along the Ormeau Road in 1992. As paraders passed the lower Ormeau, they taunted spectators, making a hand gesture of five fingers followed by a fist while chanting "Five-nil," in the manner of a sports score. Their actions referred to five civilians shot and killed in a betting shop by loyalist paramilitaries earlier in the year. That attack was part of a series of killings in the early '90s, as the IRA, UVF, and UDA/UFF engaged in so-called tit-for-tat shootings. The betting shop shooting—where gunmen shouted "Remember Teebane"—was presumably in retaliation for an IRA bomb attack at Teebane Crossroads in rural County Tyrone the previous month (McKittrick et al. 1999: 1277).

Privately, some ex-prisoners I met were frank about "score-keeping" during the conflict. Some called the nightly news the "shooting results," watching to review the results of operations. Concern for the deaths of core-ligionists was accompanied by devaluing the deaths of "others." One loyalist ex-prisoner was the most blunt: "In the '80s we watched it [television], and we seen there's somebody been shot dead. 'Shit, me, shot in the Shankill, oh shit, it's a Prod.' Next there's a news flash, it was a Catholic who was driving down the Shankill. 'Ah well, that's nothing to get bothered about.'" He suggested that people from these enclaves who claimed they had genuine sympathy for communal others were being dishonest. Similarly, "Séamus," the nationalist taxi driver discussed in chapter 1, admitted that, despite now recognizing the horror of the Shankill bombing, "I wouldn't have said that twenty years ago. Twenty years ago I'd have been, like, 'Fuck them.'" When Orwell wrote in his war diary that "sympathy can be turned on and off like a tap according to political expediency," he added, "I am not thinking of lying for political ends, but of actual changes in subjective feeling" (Orwell 2012 [1942]: 376). Post-conflict objectifications of victim experience into political points reverberate against these darker, yet genuine, responses to past violence, even when campaigns are intended to correct past dismissals of particular deaths.

Distinctions in genuine sympathy became apparent to me in the early days of my research in Northern Ireland. During fieldwork in 1997, I stayed with a nationalist family in Portadown until my Belfast flat was available. In those few weeks, I was stunned by the local antipathies. Robert Hamill, a Catholic civilian, had been beaten to death by a loyalist mob in April, a few weeks before I arrived. A commemoration of flowers, candles, and mass cards where he died on the main street was repeatedly vandalized during the weeks I stayed there. One day my host and I passed Hamill's mother in the street, and my companion spoke to her in sympathy. Mrs. Hamill was still wan with grief for her son and could barely speak. I stood awkwardly to the side, an uncomfortable intruder in the presence of her grief and my host's sympathy. Yet having briefly glimpsed Mrs. Hamill's suffering firsthand, the murder of Robert Hamill, followed by cruel vandalism of those modest commemorations to his life, seemed even more shocking to me.

Fourteen years later, I reflected upon these distinctions in sympathy with "Gerard," a community organizer who has worked with both victims and ex-prisoners in Belfast for decades. Despite his years of experience, he continued, like myself, to grapple at a visceral level with people's absence of sympathy for some victims. He explained that people who make these distinctions are not cold-hearted but rather are shaped by sharp ethnocommunal divisions. He recalled a discussion he had at a nationalist community organization in March 1996. Everyone arrived at a meeting that day shaken by news from Dunblane in Scotland. At Dunblane, distant in place and significance from Northern Ireland, a gunman had murdered sixteen children and one teacher at the Dunblane Primary School. Gerard reported that "Some of the women were near tears, and even one of the ex-IRA men who was there was shaking his head, saying it was terrible, horrendous. So within the room there was a sense of horror, genuine empathy" for the victims. The meeting was scheduled to discuss the violence of the past, one of many such discussions during the peace process. The Dunblane massacre conversation led to a discussion of so-called legitimate targets. As the conversation turned to Patsy Gillespie, the first human proxy bomb used by the IRA, Gerard asked if Patsy was a legitimate target.[17] Many people said that he should not have been working at the army base, and the killing was part of the war. Gerard said,

> I was stunned. And if I had walked into that room just then, and heard those responses, I would have thought these are all callous, cold-hearted people. . . . But I knew that twenty minutes previously, they'd been nearly in tears about what happened in Scotland. And that's what hit me, the fact that humane people can still . . . can still *suppress*

those emotions because of the identity of their community. You know what I'm saying? "They were the enemy, they shouldn't [have] done this, they shouldn't have been here, they shouldn't have been caught on that street, they shouldn't have done that," . . . and it showed me that it's not black and white, it's not callous versus kind.

My research participants were deeply conscious of how sympathy is differentially bestowed, and this awareness often intensified stress and fear in their everyday lives. The experience of "Laura," a nationalist working for an economic development project in a loyalist area, demonstrates this phenomenon. During the sectarian murder campaign that loyalists carried out after Billy Wright's murder (described in the previous chapter), Laura tried to continue at work. But she felt estranged from her colleagues. She was certain they could not understand and sympathize with the anxieties she felt as nationalist working in a loyalist community: "people here, in the office, the activists, were all going, 'Oh, that's awful'—but they didn't have the same feeling as me, they weren't having to look around their shoulders." Anxiety overwhelmed Laura: "one night I woke up having a nightmare that the LVF got into my house and they were beating me to death. So I woke up freaking about that, and I was sleeping with the light on. And that's when I knew it was time out for a while. . . . That time it was so bad, you know, like, feelings were so high that—. . . that it was nearly like back in the '70s. You know, when things were really bad." She took a leave of absence from her job.

Despite the way sympathy is saturated with communal associations, withholding sympathy also serves as a survival mechanism; too much sensitivity can leave people vulnerable to depression or even suicide. "Ian," a youth worker from one of the loyalist estates in the Upper Springfield, was overwhelmed when sympathy converged with fears he had managed his entire life. In his childhood, rioting had been common in his neighborhood, and his friends became involved in paramilitarism. Ian avoided paramilitarism himself, although his best friend served a life sentence. By the early 1990s, he worked as a taxi driver and youth organizer. Several incidents in these years just before the ceasefires, combined with his longer exposure to violence, made life unbearable. One of his closest friends was shot dead. During this period, he also had a close brush with his own mortality: "I was taxiing, and a car stopped ahead of me, with four guys with rifles. At that time they were shooting taxi drivers on both sides, and I thought it was me. And they shot a fellow who was coming across the road. Right in front of me. And that was it there. I put my head down, and thought it was all over for me." A few weeks later, he was driving up the Shankill Road at the time the Shankill bomb went off. He says, "I run up and I took people out. You know, arms and legs missing, dead. And I actually lifted the bomber out. I didn't know it was him. The skin was just completely off his face. And it was a terrible experience." Later, he offered condolences to the family of one of the children killed by the bomb: "Seeing her out in the coffin, it was horrific. . . . And it just cracked me up. I had a breakdown. . . . And that was it. I must have cried for about two days. Getting flashes of, of horrific scenes, you know." He was able to return to work only after medical treatment.

Although a degree of desensitization may be necessary for people to function, distinctions in sympathy are also related to the way everyday explanations of violence incorporate assertions of victimization; sympathy is differentially felt because responsibility for the conflict is at stake. Republicans frame their campaign as a response to a state that was irredeemable in its anti-Catholicism. Loyalist paramilitaries frame their violence as reactive, as a response to republican provocations. My research participants often attributed responsibility and guilt beyond security forces and paramilitaries. One Sinn Féin activist compared Protestants' attitudes to the pervasive German anti-Semitism described in Goldhagen's (1996) book *Hitler's Willing Executioners*.[18] Many loyalists argued that Sinn Féin's electoral successes from the 1990s onward were a tacit endorsement of armed struggle by nationalists. (This was despite the fact that Sinn Féin achieved greater electoral success when republicanism moved away from armed struggle.) Still others claim the entire society bears collective responsibility for the violence. One loyalist said, "Every one of us bears responsibility. Because every one of us in Northern Ireland is very, very guilty."

Although some victims understand combatants' motivations, they refuse to accept blanket responsibility. Sam says, "I don't think the conflict was inevitable. I think it was hugely preventable. I respect them [former combatants], but I don't agree with their position in the conflict. I don't agree with them getting involved, but I do accept them as good people. I don't see them as devils or as demons, you know? They, absolutely, they were caught up in something that was beyond their control, and this is how they responded. I think they could have probably chosen a better way. They didn't."

In the postconflict decade, the deeper consequences of widespread exposure to violence over a long period have become apparent. Tomlinson (2012) finds that, since the GFA, suicide rates have nearly doubled among the generation that grew up in the 1970s, the worst years of the conflict. He also notes other indications of poor mental health: "The transition to peace has involved mass medication with anti-depressants, alcohol and non-prescription drugs" (477). These lingering consequences work at both individual and collective levels. Harm and responsibility are differentially distributed across the populace, and these experiences are objectified in both political rhetoric and everyday rationalizations. In the absence of a formal truth recovery process, accounting of and accountability for past violence occurs selectively at the individual level and remains elusive in the collective sense. Alongside selective investigations, commemorations of the past and campaigns for different victims have proliferated. Although these efforts have allowed political movements and individuals to accept difficult elements of the peace process, in the absence of official truth recovery these accounts have also sustained sentiments of grievance and located responsibility for past violence in a partial fashion.

Selective Accounts

> They all had stories. But they weren't short stories. They
> shouldn't have been short stories. They should each have
> been novels, profound, delightful novels, eight hundred
> pages or more. And not just the lives of the victims but
> the lives they touched, the networks of friendship and
> intimacy and relation that tied them to those they loved
> and who loved them, those they knew and who knew
> them. What great complexity. What richness. . . . The
> pages that follow are light with their loss. The text is less
> dense, the city is smaller.
> —Robert McLiam Wilson, *Eureka Street*, 231

In the summer of 2003, people enjoying a walk at a remote beach in County Louth, Ireland, discovered decomposed human remains. DNA tests revealed they were the remains of Jean McConville, one of sixteen people who had become known as the Disappeared. In 1994, the families of these victims formed a group to lobby for the return of the victims' remains—Families of the Disappeared. Jean McConville's family became the best known, partly because of the circumstances of her death and partly because her daughter,

Helen McKendry, was a vocal advocate. As a result of this campaign, a commission was established to locate the victims' remains. For several years, the commission's search teams had intermittently scoured the Louth coastal area with the assistance of PIRA contacts, yet did not find Jean McConville's body. The ongoing controversy surrounding her death demonstrates starkly how victims, and the past more generally, are objectified into points to score in contemporary political struggles.

Jean McConville lived with her ten children in the Divis flats. She had been widowed ten months before she was abducted and murdered by the PIRA in December 1972. She was christened a Protestant but converted to Catholicism when she married. Because they were a "mixed" family, in 1969 the McConvilles were driven from Avoniel in east Belfast and moved to Divis in the lower Falls. Rumors abound about the reasons for her murder. Some republicans insist she was an informer. However, the Police Ombudsman's report about the inadequate police investigation of her death concludes that "There is no evidence, information or intelligence of any kind which refers to or emanated from Mrs. Jean McConville prior to January 2, 1973. She is not recorded as having been an agent at any time. She was an innocent woman who was abducted and murdered" (Police Ombudsman 2006: 15).

The discovery of Jean McConville's remains did not end controversies surrounding her death. McConville's plight became a bitter point of contention in struggles within republicanism about the peace process—and the subject of an international legal battle. The legal controversy began with a 2011 subpoena for oral history interviews held by Boston College in the United States. The college had funded an oral history project to record interviews with loyalist and republican paramilitaries, and archived the recordings. Researchers conducted the interviews during 2001–2006, to preserve combatants' perspectives for future research on the conflict. The project assured participants that their interviews, including recordings and transcripts, would be held securely until after their deaths. Ed Moloney (2010), the veteran Irish journalist who organized the project, waited until the death of two interview subjects to publish some of their interviews in the book *Voices from the Grave*. In the book, the late Brendan Hughes implicates Gerry Adams in McConville's abduction and murder (128). Hughes was a widely respected republican figure, serving as commanding officer in the Maze/Long Kesh Prison during the first republican hunger strike of 1980.

In 2011, the British government, at the request of the Police Service of Northern Ireland (PSNI), asked the U.S. Department of Justice to subpoena some of the interviews. The UK invoked the *Mutual Legal Assistance Treaty* with the United States to request interviews that the PSNI claimed would assist investigation of McConville's murder. Resisting the subpoena, researchers and their advocates publicized the proceedings as widely as possible.[19] Believing that Boston College's response to the subpoena failed their research participants, the researchers also contested the subpoena independently. The case raises serious legal issues concerning confidentiality assurances for research participants (see Palys and Lowman 2012).[20] Beyond this legal dispute, the case publicized debates within republicanism about past violence and underscore how history and storytelling are used to legitimate political practices.

The GFA has not been welcomed by all republicans. Some republicans are critical of the current leadership's characterizations of the PIRA campaign as a battle for Catholic equality. Former volunteers argue that they fought for Irish sovereignty and that this new account of republican history, described in Chapter 1, is a ruse to legitimate Sinn Féin's acceptance of the GFA and elevation to conventional political power. Republicans who support the current leadership, such as Danny Morrison, claim the oral history project was created to challenge the current leadership and undermine the peace process, rather than for archival purposes.[21] The researchers vigorously deny this accusation. Meanwhile, HET claims its investigation was spurred by one of the project's interview subjects, Dolours Price, an ex-prisoner who helped organize an IRA bombing campaign in England in 1973. Before her death in January 2013, Price made several public comments that illustrate the political complexity surrounding the peace process and past violence.

In the February 18, 2010, edition of the *Irish News*, a Belfast paper, Dolours Price alleged that Gerry Adams was her "officer commanding" in PIRA. Price also claimed to have information regarding the Disappeared and implied that Adams oversaw the kidnapping, killing, and concealment of the bodies of people who were troublesome for the movement. As the legal and political battle over the subpoena continued, Price gave further interviews to a U.S. television news show and to the UK *Sunday Telegraph*, in which she repeated the allegations.[22] For Price, the public furor regarding the subpoena and the McConville investigation had profoundly political importance: "I think the [peace] process should be undermined, I think the process should be destroyed in some way and I think Gerry Adams deserves to admit to his part, in all of the things that happened."[23] Other republicans are less categorically opposed to the peace process, but believe the oral history project will prevent an official account of the conflict from erasing dissenting perspectives and experiences from history. For example, Hughes's interview in Moloney (2010) makes assertions about the two hunger strikes that are profoundly different from the mainstream account (see also O'Rawe 2005).

Debate about the case also underscored the continuing politicization of the past and ongoing struggles between paramilitaries and security personnel about past violence. Journalist Eamonn McCann argued that the subpoena results from grudges held by former police officers against republicans generally and Adams particularly.[24] Former police officers have expressed "healthy appreciation" for the debate; one claimed in the *Belfast Telegraph* that some of the archive's loyalist interview recordings might resolve other unsolved murders of Catholic civilians.[25] Meanwhile, members of the Commission for the Location of Victims' Remains worried that the subpoena undermines the commission's legal pledge of confidentiality, and the case will discourage people from disclosing information.[26] Some loyalists who took part in the project requested that their interviews be withdrawn from the archive. Yet Adams himself remained publicly untroubled and repeatedly expressed sympathy for Dolours Price, noting that she had been treated for PTSD.[27]

The Boston College case and the campaigning by families of the Disappeared also highlight problematic postconflict arguments for "storytelling" as a way to record history and promote truth recovery. Commemorations of victims have become intertwined with campaigns for inquiries into specific events. Neighborhoods, different victim groupings, and individuals have created a plethora of projects to commemorate and record historical experiences, including oral history projects, memorials, and campaigns. Yet these projects are as fragmented as postconflict investigations. For some participants, narrative projects may produce a sort of catharsis, and for others, retraumatization (see Hayner 2010). In such projects, representations of experience may also emerge partially and selectively and, in the political culture of victimhood, appear as attempts to score political points. Mesev et al. (2009) observe that "a common understanding of this term, *victimhood,* is that the community a person belonged to is composed of bona fide victims . . . placing those [other] victims on an equal plane would weaken political legitimacy" (902).

Many projects use storytelling to record and commemorate the conflict. Some projects are area-based, such as an archive in the Falls area (since 2000) and a more recent project in Protestant east Belfast. In 2005, twenty-nine oral history projects were operating (HTR 2005). Undoubtedly, the number of these projects has increased since that time. Academics and journalists have also attempted to record and commemorate the loss of life. McKittrick et al. (1999) combed public records and newspaper accounts to create *Lost Lives*, a book containing narrative accounts of deaths during the conflict (see Sloan 2010). The Conflict Archive on the Internet (CAIN) and archives at the Linenhall Library maintain large collections of material related to the conflict and commemoration. In 2011, the European Peace III fund awarded €643,542 ($826,276) to the Pat Finucane Centre to create the Recovery of Living Memory Archive. The archive will combine personal and family testimonies with records from the Historical Enquiries Team and Police Ombudsman.

Regarding the proliferation of oral history projects, one victims' campaigner told me that "There is a common assumption that storytelling is a good thing—virtually imperative." A common refrain is that oral history allows ordinary people to act as authors of their own history. In the postconflict era, efforts to establish local truth recovery processes and justice campaigns for specific episodes of violence have incorporated storytelling in their work.

One local truth recovery project that gathered oral histories was organized in the Ardoyne area of Belfast. The project commemorated the lives of the ninety-nine area residents who died between 1968 and 1998. In 1998–2000, local residents conducted more than 300 oral history interviews. Two scholars who conducted participatory research with the project present it as a reactive effort because Ardoyne residents believed that unionists used the victims of nonstate violence to make political points (Lundy and McGovern 2006, 2008a). Thus, the purpose of the project was to commemorate lost lives through storytelling and to highlight the state's responsibility for violence that killed twenty-six people in Ardoyne during the conflict (Lundy and McGovern 2006).

Deaths caused by republican paramilitaries, however, swiftly became problematic for the project (Lundy and McGovern 2006, 2008a). Over the course of four years, the project established an informal truth recovery process with republicans, which allowed some families to learn the truth about their loved ones' deaths. Although Lundy and McGovern argue that the project allowed local people to reconcile relationships within the community and gain clarity about the circumstances of some deaths, they acknowledge several weaknesses in a grassroots process. First, the project did not have access to information from state agencies, leaving large gaps in knowledge regarding deaths caused by security forces. Furthermore, the project's single-identity focus was interpreted in political terms by neighboring loyalist communities (Lundy and McGovern 2008b). Local oral history projects can lead to intracommunity reconciliation but are only a partial contribution to developing an inclusive record of victims' experiences.

The proliferation of storytelling—and the public contest for recognition of victims' stories—has also become part of victims' campaigning. For example, the campaign to investigate Bloody Sunday emerged from commemorative storytelling. Hegarty (2005) writes that those who witnessed the atrocity began "telling the truth" in a variety of commemorative contexts—written and performative—and that "communal story-telling—itself important in the Irish cultural tradition—is one way in which a form of truth was agreed" (225). Although the Bloody Sunday campaign was in some ways emblematic of competing unionist and nationalist understandings of the conflict, Conway (2010) argues that the campaign also involved internal struggles for ownership. As early as 1978, Conway writes, one victim's family was protesting republican "appropriation . . . of the event for narrow propaganda purposes" (2). The process of truth telling that Hegarty (2005) traces to the twentieth anniversary in 1992 was tied to this internal struggle. Conway (2010) argues that, although republicans monopolized Bloody Sunday commemorations to depict Catholic victimization from the 1970s into the 1990s, during the peace process this narrative was challenged by other actors, especially victims' families, and the debate was resituated in terms of human rights and justice rather than victimization.

The Bloody Sunday Justice Campaign was only one of the victims' campaigns formed in the 1990s. Many of the groups that formed in this period are seen as exclusive, in some sense, because they direct their efforts to victims of particular actors. For example, Relatives for Justice (RFJ) was founded in 1991, bringing together several families whose relations died at the hands of security forces. The group now offers many support services and receives European peace funds. In the 1990s, however, RFJ was seen as partisan by many unionists, promoting a biased account of violence during the conflict (see Relatives for Justice 1995). Conversely, Families of the Disappeared was seen by some republicans as a critique of the armed struggle and an attempt to discredit ex-prisoners who moved into politics.

After the GFA, unionist anger at prisoner releases coalesced around a belief that campaigns for victims of state violence elevated these victims above the more numerous victims of nonstate actors—with the complicity of local discourses about human rights. Groups such as Families Acting for Innocent Relatives (FAIR) lobbied for victim recognition but only for "innocent" victims of nonstate actors. FAIR grew out of the frustrations of the minority Protestant community living near the border, many members of which served in the security forces. When conflict erupted, they found themselves the enemies of former friends and neighbors (see Donnan 2005; Donnan and Simpson 2007).

Another transitional justice practice, commemoration, has also incorporated partial accounts of history and storytelling. Of course, commemoration practices, particularly murals and parades, have long been a significant form of social and political expression in Belfast (Jarman 1999a, 1993). In the postconflict era, memorials to the dead have been treated as part of the peace process. Some scholars argue that these commemorations actually "symbolize the enduring importance of ethnonationalist and sectarian politics and the continuation of the conflict by other means" (Graham and Whelan 2007: 492). Yet this characterization overlooks two important contributions that commemoration practices have made to the peace process. In the period after the GFA, recognition of PIRA veterans' sacrifices and deaths was vital to demobilizing the organization. For example, republicans published *Tírghrá*, a book of photos and descriptions of PIRA personnel who died during the conflict. Permanent memorials were erected across west Belfast, with the names of those who died in the conflict and space for the addition of veterans' names when they die. The book and the memorials aided the transition from armed struggle by recognizing these losses, rather than treating this history as obsolete in the postconflict environment.

Furthermore, in the years following the GFA, some nationalist and republican politicians used their offices to make symbolic gestures of generosity toward unionists. In 2002, the first Sinn Féin lord mayor, Alex Maskey, laid a wreath at the City Hall Cenotaph to commemorate the Battle of the Somme. Despite the significance of the gesture—republicans traditionally boycotted such commemorations for their association with the British military— unionists claimed it was an empty political gesture because Maskey did not attend the official remembrance ceremony. Later that year, the BBC aired a film documenting a journey by David Ervine of the PUP and Tom Hartley of Sinn Féin to the graveyards of the Somme. Each reflected on the other's political tradition and acknowledged the scale of Irish loss in the battle.[28] In the 1990s, the Republic began to recognize casualties of World War I, north and south—departing from national policy that excluded the dead who fought for Britain from collective commemoration (see McCarthy 2005).

Some NGOs and state initiatives have attempted to use commemoration to produce an inclusive account of the past. Although their efforts have been earnest, they have been hampered by a lack of authority to implement recommendations and plagued by the persistent politicization of the victim experiences. One of these NGOs is a group called Healing Through Remembering (HTR), formed after the GFA to develop an inclusive set of recommendations for truth recovery. Following public consultation and the review of 108 submissions, in 2002 the group published multiple recommendations: a network of commemorative projects, an annual day of remembering, a collective archive of oral histories, a memorial museum, and the creation of a truth recovery process (HTR 2002). The report called for both the British and Irish states and all paramilitary actors to acknowledge responsibility for the conflict, to pave the way toward an official truth recovery process. It did not, however, recommend a single TRC, suggesting that multiple bodies, local and international, be established to create an account of the past. Furthermore, HTR recommended that truth recovery be divorced from legal processes (see Hamber 2003: 1089). HTR continues to bring together diverse NGO actors to discuss and produce reports on truth recovery and commemoration, but lacks authority to implement policy.

State efforts at inclusivity in both victims' services and commemoration have been undermined by contentious claims about human and victims' rights. In 1997, the British government appointed Sir Kenneth Bloomfield, former head of the Northern Irish Civil Service, as victim commissioner and asked him to write a report on state policy regarding victims. Like other reports, Bloomfield's (1998) did not recommend a truth commission, emphasizing instead victim support services and state compensation. Nationalist groups condemned the report for reinforcing a hierarchy of victims and privileging the losses of security force members (Ardoyne Commemoration Project 2003). Cox et al. (2006) write that this backlash against Bloomfield's attempt at neutrality fueled unionists' politicization of victimization (16). As a result, state victim and survivor support services remained controversial. When the widow of an RUC reserve officer was appointed to the post of victim commissioner, groups representing victims of state violence protested that she could not represent all victims, and one individual lodged a High Court challenge against the appointment. The matter was eventually resolved in 2008 when the post was replaced with a corporate body led by multiple commissioners.[29] In 2012, the commission returned to the original model with one commissioner.

In 2009 unionist victims' campaigners frustrated another state initiative. The Consultative Group on the Past (2009) released a comprehensive set of recommendations, recommending the establishment of a truth commission. But its report was leaked shortly before completion, and, with advance knowledge of its recommendations, unionist campaign groups disrupted the report's launch on January 28, 2009. These groups, particularly FAIR, took umbrage at the report's compensation recommendations, which suggested that all surviving relatives, whether victims were civilians, state combatants, or nonstate combatants, be given a single payment of £12,000 ($18,788). The campaigners swiftly mobilized against the report, arguing that families of paramilitaries should not be compensated. The report's other recommendations were overshadowed by the compensation controversy. Although the government said it endorsed other provisions, a truth commission has not been established.

Victims' advocates treat the leaking of the report conspiratorially. Gail believes the civil service leaked it to undermine the recommendations because implementation would cost more than £300 million ($486.2 million). Others argue that it was leaked because no party to the conflict is completely willing to engage with a truth commission; the compensation issue was easily appropriated by campaigners and could be quickly publicized to discredit the truth commission recommendations. Some research participants argue that many recommendations were sound and that some opponents regret their actions. In academic literature, the report is considered significant for incorporating "some of the emerging soft-law standards pertaining to a state's duties under international human rights law," including victims' rights to information, reparations, and state accountability (Duffy 2010: 39).

Against this contention, there are glimmers of consensus. Victim commissioners created a victims' forum, bringing together campaigners from a diverse array of NGOs. One member, although initially skeptical, sees progress: "They picked people who would not expect to sit down together on a forum and to debate issues, and we stayed together. . . . We agreed [to] a set of principles for truth recovery. And this is everybody, I mean unanimous. So people like Willie Frazer [from FAIR] and Mark Thompson [from Relatives for Justice] signing up to the same set of principles of truth recovery is a huge step forward." Nevertheless, both a truth commission and an inclusive account of the past remain elusive. Although some politicians have expressed willingness to accept a truth commission, achieving broad cooperation from state and nonstate actors is unlikely.

Some scholars argue that loyalist opposition will prevent a truth-recovery process (Lawther 2011). Yet willingness to engage in such a process is not a given within republicanism, either. In 2010, I broached the subject with a republican activist I had known for thirteen years. He had no expectations that a formal truth-recovery process would ever take place. He also had no doubt that other former combatants shared his attitude, which was simply, "I will not engage with a truth commission. I cannot relive—I cannot even think about some of the things I've done." In 2012, the British secretary of state consulted parties regarding a truth process, and in 2013 all-party talks were convened to discuss, once more, dealing with the past. Richard Haass, former U.S. envoy to Northern Ireland, returned to convene the negotiations. Despite these initiatives, a consensual approach to past violence remains elusive. Investigations taper off and commemorations continue to proliferate. Meanwhile, the legal battle regarding the Boston College archive will likely make recording the past more difficult for both academics and grassroots NGOs. One research project with former security personnel was put on hold in 2012 because the case raised concerns about criminal charges among possible participants.[30] This is a serious loss to the historical record; and given the magnitude of collusion allegations, such a project might have revealed some truths, at least to future generations.

Is Another Politics of the Dead Possible?

> Nothing is new or radical in Irish politics. . . . Northern
> Irish politics are the politics of the dead.
> —Belfast Libertarian Group, *Ireland: Dead or Alive?* 23–24

Political institutions in Northern Ireland underwent tremendous changes in recent years, with devolution, power sharing, and reforms in policing and justice. But the settlement left an institutional gap regarding transitional justice. Within this gap, political bargaining, multiple inquiries, commemorative projects, and victims' campaigns sustain the politics of victimhood. The rhetoric of human and victims' rights has been incorporated into local practices that differentiate victim experiences. These practices are also enmeshed with arguments about the legitimacy of past violence. The fault lines that run throughout both society and the new power-sharing government ultimately prevent an inclusive approach to the violent past. These divisions are engrained in everyday understandings of past violence. As this chapter has shown, "the way sympathy can be turned on and off like a tap" is not, as Orwell (2012) explained, simply political dishonesty but "actual changes in subjective feeling" (376). Furthermore, in the midst of contests about past harm and responsibility, many NGOs and grassroots groups do contribute to reconciliation, particularly within communities, if not between them.

Critiquing contemporary global politics and rhetoric, as well as academic theory, anthropologist and physician Didier Fassin (2009) asserts that "another politics of life is possible." He argues that a different politics of life would reveal and counter the political and economic processes that create inequalities in "the value they [contemporary societies] attach to life in general and on the worth they attach to lives in particular" (57). Fassin's insights, when applied to Northern Ireland, underscore how debates about truth recovery, or the lack thereof, reproduce and contest distinctions among lives and deaths, rather than moving toward an inclusive legal or social account. In Northern Ireland, human rights talk fell prey to local contests about distinctions such as legitimate targets or innocent victims. Commemorative practices and political rhetoric are also enmeshed in this broader politics of the dead, differentially valuing forms of suffering. In a political culture dominated by such distinctions, perhaps only minimal generosity and recognition of others' suffering is possible. Yet another politics of the dead can be discerned in quieter, subtler efforts to support reconciliation among residents of these deeply divided communities.

One of these subtler efforts is the Island Pamphlets series, which works with grassroots organizations to encourage discussions of past experiences, as well as hopes for the future. Each series of discussions is recorded and then summarized in a pamphlet. The widespread dissemination of these pamphlets across many communities in Belfast (185,000 have been distributed to date) also allows those who rarely meet people from different backgrounds to read about the experiences of others—and to some extent, they develop understanding, if not sympathy, for their ethnopolitical opponents.

Michael Hall began publishing the series in 1993, reporting on a conference for community organizers working in west Belfast interface areas. In 2012, he published the hundredth pamphlet, the fifth in a series about internal debates within republicanism. The pamphlets record a range of views from republican and loyalist ex-prisoners, the families of prisoners (Hall 2000a,b; 2010), the Loughgall victims of state violence, and victims of republican violence (Hall 2001a,b). Although many of the pamphlets are available online, through the CAIN website, the discussions take place in real space, and the pamphlets are widely read in printed form. The pamphlets' aims of promoting grassroots reconciliation are fulfilled as much through their production—the processes of collaborative discussion and editing—as their distribution.

Michael Hall's background helps explain the origins of the pamphlet series and their popularity with local people. Hall grew up in a family of dedicated socialists and communists who were faithful to these movements' ideals of internationalism and antisectarianism. Growing up, he says, he began to learn the "hidden history" of life under communism and began to question official political histories, searching out the experiences of individuals that are hidden or silenced by authorized narratives. In the 1960s, he became a student radical, as a cofounder of People's Democracy (PD), and eventually a pamphleteer. Hall said in an interview with me in 2011,

> I realized that, in all the periods of radical social upheaval and revolution which I studied, there was invariably a vehicle for popular expression which wasn't controlled by the powers-that-be. For example, in the English revolution, there was a pamphleteering explosion. Similarly in the French revolution. And in Spain prior to 1936, there were the *casas del pueblo*, where industrial or rural workers endlessly discussed their vision of a new society. And in the States [during the U.S. revolution]. Or in Czechoslovakia before the Russian tanks moved in [1968], where a widespread café debate had blossomed during the Prague Spring. So there were vehicles for people to talk about themselves and discuss alternatives. Whether it was pamphleteering, "houses of the people" in Spain, cafés in Prague, or whatever. And I thought, what is there here?

I first met Hall in 1996, on a prefieldwork visit to the city; he graciously introduced me to many different community organizers. Over the years of my fieldwork, I saw the importance of his pamphlets to working-class people across Belfast. Often when I first met activists, they would offer me an Island Pamphlet that addressed their particular interests; later, as I developed relationships with them, they would ask if I had seen the latest publication. The pamphlets offered people a way to represent themselves internally and externally. Activists also avidly sought out pamphlets about the "other side."

Hall's trajectory from PD to publisher of the people began with an early pamphlet that is now well known in the history of Irish anarchism (see Ó Catháin 2004). Hall says he published *Ireland: Dead or Alive?* in frustration, when violence had engulfed the city (see Belfast Libertarian Group 1973). He says he thought no one would even read his pamphlet, with its critiques of anti-Catholic discrimination as well as IRA violence. Yet two weeks later, "Word was sent through a friend of mine from the Provos saying, 'Tell your mate if he writes anything like that again, he'll get his knees ventilated.'" Later, Hall says, a loyalist told him, "We're watching you, you bastard; we're gonna get you." Hall's earlier denunciation by paramilitaries from both sides and his family background give him unusual antisectarian credibility. He happily told of one meeting where a woman counting the numbers of nationalist and loyalist participants told him she was counting him as "nothing." "That's good," he jokingly replied, "I don't want to be anything."

Although Island Pamphlets has little in common with that early pamphlet, written with the naïvety of youth and anger of the early conflict, Hall learned from the experience that pamphlets have great communicative potential. He began publishing Island Pamphlets with Shankill and Falls think tank projects in the 1990s, and soon local groups began to ask him to organize pamphlets for their areas or interests (Hall 1995, 1996). His work is like that of a native ethnographer, recording and reflecting people's experiences so that they may engage in a process of self-representation. Overall, he says, the pamphlets "are not just a way of giving people a vehicle, but helping a process. . . . Obviously, when the pamphlets are distributed around the community network, they serve to inform a sizeable number of people. But even before then, the actual participants to the small-group discussions are engaged in their own process of learning. They're hearing things from other people that they may not have heard before, even in their own community."

The process of transcription and editing is itself an ethical act. Hall says of victims' accounts,

People would be very courageous in telling . . . their personal stories. And even though these stories could be heartbreaking, it was also evident that many people found it actually therapeutic to be able to talk openly about what they had gone through. And when I would be transcribing my recordings later, I would sometimes find myself actually crying, even to the extent that I couldn't see my keyboard. But

I realized that the best way to honor the courage of a person who has been prepared to disclose all this to me was to try and get their story onto the page in such a way that anyone who reads it starts to cry as well. . . . I wanted to convey it to the reader in all its intensity.

Once a transcription is complete, he works with participants to edit the pamphlets collaboratively.

The Island process protects anonymity to allow participants the liberty to speak frankly, a need that is particularly relevant with the most recent series, *Republicanism in Transition*. Throughout the peace process, some republicans became uneasy with Sinn Féin's resistance to internal critique. My own research participants complain that the party stifles discussion by dismissing all critics as "dissidents" who wish to return to war. Michael Hall took up the project at the request of republican community workers, who feared that silencing criticism and discussion makes people more likely to return to armed struggle (Hall 2011a,b,c; 2012a,b). The discussions included current and former members of the Official Republican Movement, éirígí, the Republican Network for Unity, Irish Republican Socialist Party, Republican Sinn Féin, and 32 County Sovereignty Movement members. Participants discussed their different positions on armed struggle and shared the sacrifices they made during the conflict. The fifth pamphlet in this series grew from the group's desire to engage loyalists in the discussion (Hall 2012b).

After nineteen years of facilitating dialogue and recording, Hall has developed skepticism about the usefulness of an official truth-recovery process. He is concerned about the broader political tendency to sanction some accounts of experience and marginalize others, as well as the lack of support that victims and perpetrators may receive after participating. As time goes on, small initiatives like Island Pamphlets may be the only kind of projects that continue to allow people to confront the past collectively. This is simply a matter of economics. In 2010, Gail, the loyalist community organizer, voiced another harsh truth: "You no longer have the money. . . . That's all drying up, and many, many people who've spent their lives within the peace and reconciliation industry are going to find that the money's not there because people, especially Americans, are moving on to other parts of the world, and maybe rightly so." She concluded sadly that few people recognize the conflict's diminished international significance: "I done a program recently with a woman from Rwanda . . . and I said to the producer, 'There's no way you could compare me with a woman from Rwanda.' I mean, they were massacred there by the thousands on a daily basis. There's no way you could compare me to her experience. . . . You know, Northern Ireland was only a tiny wee thing." Few people in Northern Ireland are ready to critique the distinctions that have given their experiences greater international prominence than conflicts on a massive scale in the developing world. Yet this other, critical politics of life—and death—may be necessary for local rights discourse to shift from privileging ethnocommunal subjects toward the broader liberatory project articulated by human rights principles.

CHAPTER 6

"Love Is a Human Right"

There can be no viler act, apart from homosexuality and
sodomy, than sexually abusing innocent children.
—Iris Robinson, remarks in UK Parliament, June 17, 2008

"Over the years, the way she has treated my community, I have opposed her
at every turn. I can't tell you the number of waiters I've told to spit in her
food." "Daniel," a young civil servant from a nationalist background, was
relaxing with a pint as we enjoyed late evening sunshine in May 2010. Like
many pub conversations in Belfast that year, ours had turned into a gleeful
dissection of the most recent Iris Robinson scandal. The wife of first minister Peter Robinson had been "outed" that winter for having an affair with a
nineteen-year-old family friend. Her infidelity was compounded by their age
difference (she was in her fifties), assistance to the young man with a business
license, and a £50,000 (approximately $92,000) "loan." The affair was a source
of joking *schadenfreude*, since Iris Robinson was a devout evangelical and
established politician in her own right (at the time she was an MP, MLA, and
local councillor).

Although the Robinsons are members of the intensely loyalist DUP, Daniel was not talking about nationalists as his "community." He was alluding
to an earlier Robinson scandal and his own response as a gay man. In 2008,
Robinson had inspired outrage with a series of antigay remarks to the media
and in both the assembly and the House of Commons. She praised reparative
therapy and invoked the biblical death sentence of Leviticus for the incur-
able. Gay activists were livid, and complaints led police to investigate her for
incitement to hatred.[1] Daniel decided to register his anger through activism,

working undercover to reveal how reparative therapy practitioners operated. Nevertheless, "community" was an unusual term for Daniel—he claimed to hate "community" politics in Northern Ireland. I teased him about this, and he laughed: "Fair enough. But this is different—it's not the sectarian bullshit; it's my community of choice that's been put down and oppressed by the 'right' kind of community for years."

The Robinson incident, despite the harshness of her rhetoric, actually underscores the effectiveness of lesbian, gay, bisexual, and transgender (LGBT) rights mobilization in the post-Good Friday Agreement years. Activists astutely seized on Robinson's remarks and pushed representatives of other political parties to condemn them. With the Belfast Pride Festival taking place at the end of July, her comments in June gave organizers time to recruit new support for that year's parade. The number of parade participants doubled to 6,000 that year and continued to grow to 17,000 in 2011. Trade unions, churches, and all political parties save the DUP were represented at the parade. "Calum," a volunteer with Belfast Pride for twenty years, explained, "Her timing was great. It was perfect. Far enough in advance to allow us to build up the publicity. She kept bringing it up, and that then is what brought along the unions and politicians and church leaders and so on, out to say, 'Well, we wouldn't previously have supported [Belfast] Pride, but we're not being seen to take sides with that witch!'" Individuals were also galvanized. "Adam," a teacher, said, "It was absolute rage on my part. I thought, I've got to *do something* about this. I can write a letter, I can sign a petition. Or I can give her what I thought was the ultimate two fingers: I can actually get involved with the gay community again."

Daniel's perspective on community, Robinson's remarks, and the public responses to her comments indicate long-standing tensions surrounding sexuality, as well as an emerging social rapprochement between queer and straight people in the post-agreement years. This rapprochement resulted from a synergy between gay rights activism and the GFA legal mandate for equality. The alliances that have accompanied gay rights activism contrast to the GFA "semi-benign apartheid" regarding nationalism and unionism, and they demonstrate how rights discourse can work quite differently within the same context (McAuley et al. 2010: 36). Postconflict gay rights mobilizations provide a clear—and rare—example of rights discourse that is focused on practical outcomes and choice, rather than ascription, regarding collective identity. Using legal rationales drawn from the GFA and European policy, these campaigns have altered social relationships and law. A primary example of these efforts and their effects is the Belfast Pride Festival. In a city whose parade cultures are often fraught, the festival brings together gay and straight groups and individuals and offers a new perspective on the changed city and political culture. Through a weeklong schedule of events each year, the festival also creates spaces where rapprochements have begun to unfold. This chapter considers how gay rights campaigners have created new politics in the postconflict years, in contrast to more prevalent forms of rights discourse.

Gay Rights Activism and Opposition in Belfast

> Homosexuality in Ulster remains a precarious pursuit,
> clandestine through circumstances rather than choice.
> —G. D. Ingoldby, "You've Got a Friend," 13

In 2010, as I joined the crowd for Belfast's twentieth pride parade, the sky shifted between sunshine and cloud, a typical summer day of contrasts. As the crowd grew in Custom House Square, well-known political allies and adversaries appeared, constitutional disagreements set aside for the occasion. Bairbre de Brún, Sinn Féin member of the European Parliament, embraced friends. Unsurprisingly, Jeff Dudgeon appeared, a former plaintiff in a case with the European Court of Human Rights regarding the criminalization of homosexuality.[2] A Unitarian minister and liaison to loyalist paramilitaries arrived wearing his clerical collar. Eamonn McCann, no longer the curly-mopped militant of his youthful civil rights activism, helped young Socialist Workers Party members prepare placards denouncing homophobia and capitalism. Less-famous politicians, trade unionists, and human rights advocates mingled with drag queens and parents pushing strollers under "Love is a Human Right" signs provided by Amnesty International.

Since the GFA, the Belfast Pride Festival has allowed LGBT rights discourse to facilitate broader debates about the shape of postconflict society. The festival became a focal point for religious opposition in the 2000s, and in the aftermath of the Robinson uproar, organizers have embraced that debate. At the same time, the Belfast Pride Festival organization acts as a focal point for LGBT activism, with monthly public meetings and participation from various LGBT NGOs. In Belfast, it is far more than a one-day parade:

during the week before the parade, it holds dozens of events, including public debates, plays, exhibitions, cabarets, and church services. State agencies such as the Northern Ireland Housing Executive (NIHE) and the police sponsor events and send representatives, as do trade unions and churches.

The festival only began in 1991, but Northern Ireland's gay activists have taken recourse to human rights law since the 1970s. The case *Dudgeon v. UK* that came before the European Court of Human Rights led to the decriminalization of sodomy in 1982. More recently, activists have used elements of the GFA to influence legislation. At the same time, they have used the spirit of the GFA to engage in social and religious debates about sexuality. Local queer activism originated from LGBT social networks that, until 1981, were outside the law—and are sustained by a contemporary "community." Especially since the GFA, this form of activism has recognized that legal rights must be socially embedded. The social and legal reconciliations they pursue are intertwined in everyday life and hint at possibilities for sustained and productive political engagements among people with very different national aspirations. LGBT activism creates alternative political spaces and remakes city spaces in ways other movements have failed to do. Furthermore, it demonstrates that rights discourse need not inevitably serve as war by other means.

Literally and conceptually, LGBT rights in Northern Ireland locate individuals in different social and political fields than do rights allocated to the two communities of the GFA's human rights section (see Chapter 1). This discourse draws on existing rights in the European convention and the more recent GFA, as well as a more inclusive conception of political subjectivity. In this way, this discourse echoes the Yogyakarta Principles, which, rather than claiming new rights for gay people, simply demand that existing rights be extended without discrimination (O'Flaherty and Fisher 2008).[3] Both rights discourse and the legal frameworks it invokes allow gay activists to build political associations beyond dominant ethnopolitics. Queer activism, deeply transgressive though it may seem in terms of local religious beliefs, has succeeded in creating new communicative spaces for politics in Belfast. New political spaces are crucial to rebuilding postconflict societies, as Nordstrom (1997) observes in her work on the aftermath of the Mozambique conflict. She writes that, if "citizens cannot forge a space of action outside lethal political scenarios, power politics is reproduced in every action, no matter how mundane and everyday" (232). "Without a space *outside* these politics," she argues, "people cannot critique them" (emphasis original).

Although the GFA created an institutional space for nonviolent politics, the power-sharing arrangements and human rights provisions of the settlement are not securely beyond the politics that were once lethal. Queer activists outside these politics, however, have developed a critique of how parties operate in the new institutions. This critique supports the analysis of Finlay (2010), a persuasive critic of consociationalism, who recalls his own experience of counterculture in Belfast to argue for the value of identities and politics outside normative ethnic categories. Although Finlay accepts Rolston's (2001) dismissal of counterculture's political impact in Belfast, gay rights activism emerged from a queer counterculture that established social spaces outside ethnocommunalism—and has been increasingly visible because of the GFA. In this instance, rights discourse did not become a proxy for ethnopolitical conflict, and demonstrates how broader discourses of human rights can play a role in creating postconflict social and political reconciliation—though perhaps not in a predictable fashion.

LGBT activism in Belfast dates back to the 1970s, when a broad range of organizations, campaigns, and legal battles produced a transnational social movement—and rights discourse—of the *soixante-huitard* variety. That is, LGBT rights struggles since the early 1970s were informed by what was then called gay, now queer consciousness. Their actions are aimed at what Touraine (1988) calls "historicity"—socially situated struggles to produce both social change and political subjectivity. Touraine's classic understanding of the new social movements, however, excludes efforts to change state institutions; in Northern Ireland, this broad movement is more similar to his student Mellucci's (1989) analysis, which recognizes efforts to change both state and society.

Contemporary analyses of Belfast LGBT advocacy frequently use a more constrained analysis, like Touraine's. For example, Conrad (2006) asserts that Belfast's queer activism functions politically as a "counterpublic," in that it moves beyond state-focused identity politics (597). Although this characterization draws on Warner's (2002) counterpublic, it echoes Touraine's limits on what a social movement must address. Yet this distinction is not descriptive of the actual dynamic of state and society in either the past or present for gay activists. Gay activists in Belfast work to change *both* law and society, recognizing their complex interplay in daily life. LGBT movements in Northern Ireland originated in, are sustained by, and reproduce everyday practices of sociality; therefore, these efforts underscore the consequences of law in everyday life. As such, exploring the ramifications of this rights discourse locally and how the settlement's legal provisions worked synergistically to nurture postconflict alternatives in society and politics is a classic anthropological effort to understand "the complexity of . . . embedding rights in social life" (Wilson 2004: 242).

The claims on physical space made by the Belfast Pride Festival are immediately apparent in a city where Orange parades are annually contested (Jarman 2003, 2007). The significance of the parade is heightened by what social geographers call Belfast's uniquely heterosexist geography (e.g., Kitchin and Lysaght 2003). The festival's status as Ireland's largest annual cross-communal public gathering has been produced by and is productive of new postconflict relationships. Furthermore, the queer rights discourse that animates Belfast Pride and other LGBT NGOs poses more profound social challenges to traditional ethnopolitical approaches. For example, evangelical Protestantism and orthodox Catholicism have globalized their opposition to gay rights. Some Irish nationalists have claimed that homosexuality is not an authentically Irish phenomenon (see Marston 2002; Conrad 2001).

Homophobia is a longstanding feature of Northern Irish society; it is as commonplace, perhaps even more engrained, than sectarianism. Iris Robinson's 2008 outbursts regarding homosexuality began as a commentary on the brutal assault of a young gay man in Newtonabbey, just north of Belfast. Quantitative evidence indicates continuing, and perhaps escalating, incidents of homophobic violence, harassment, and hate crime since the GFA (McDermott 2011; Equality Commission 2009; Jarman and Tennant 2003). (However, increased reporting may be a factor in this rise.) Furthermore, since the agreement, several homophobic murders have been committed. Ian Flanagan and William McAuley were beaten to death in separate incidents in Belfast in 2002, and Shaun Fitzpatrick was murdered in Dungannon in 2008. Trials for the Flanagan and Fitzpatrick cases resulted in convictions, but the McAuley murder remains unsolved. Homophobic violence occurred throughout the conflict years, as well. Before the settlement, paramilitary policing of communities also involved regulation and punishment of deviant sexualities, including prostitution and homosexuality. For example, Presbyterian minister David Templeton was brutally attacked and killed by loyalists after a newspaper outed him; his murder is widely believed to have been instigated by a UVF man who is now imprisoned and faces other murder charges. In the early years of conflict, republican paramilitaries attacked gay clubs, with PIRA bombing the Casanova, a popular 1970s venue. The less mainstream INLA fire bombed the Dunbar Arms in the 1990s, almost killing one transvestite patron; its successor, the Parliament Bar, was the site of the Bradshaw murder (see Chapter 1). During the conflict, criminalization of sodomy effectively sanctioned police harassment of gay people; Jeff Dudgeon's European case was spurred by a series of police raids on homes of gay activists. Over time, sectarianism, homophobia, and both state and paramilitary authoritarianism combined to create a profoundly dangerous city for gay people.

Gay rights discourse in Northern Ireland traces its origins to the 1960s. Just as 1968 was an important year for student and democracy movements, 1969 was a turning point for an international gay rights movement. The genesis of that movement occurred at a gay bar, the Stonewall Inn, in New York City (see Humphreys 1972). In June 1969, riots took place over several nights in New York, when patrons of the Stonewall Inn spontaneously resisted a police raid, and Stonewall became a catalytic event for queer consciousness. Similarly, Belfast's gay rights movement was rooted in the city's nightlife. Gay men and women socialized semi-secretly in bars, cafes, and discos, establishing a "scene" that became a movement. Indeed, the first significant extension of international human rights law to sexual orientation—*Dudgeon v. UK*—grew from these social connections.[4] Dudgeon's suit was a response to police raids on members of a new group that organized both social activities and law reform in the 1970s, the Northern Ireland Gay Rights Association (NIGRA).[5]

Rhetoric like Iris Robinson's also has historical roots from this period. As the decriminalization of sodomy was widely discussed in the 1970s, the DUP, and especially Ian Paisley, were highly visible and vocal in opposing gay rights. During the Northern Ireland Office's public consultation on reforming the antisodomy law, Paisley began a "Save Ulster from Sodomy" campaign, which claimed to have gathered 70,000 signatures in opposition to reform. Paisley declared that "The crime of sodomy is a crime against God and man, and its practice is a terrible step to[ward] the total demoralisation of any country and must inevitably lead to the breakdown of all decency within the province" (cited in O'Leary 2009: 136).

Gay activism and oppositional religious rhetoric of the 1970s provide context for understanding how local gay rights discourse reappropriated human rights discourse in the post-settlement period. After the success of *Dudgeon v. UK*, local activism seemed to enter a lull in the 1980s. In the 1990s, a new generation of activists and the broader peace process revitalized LGBT advocacy. Gay rights activism in the 2000s created new visions of politics, building on both the GFA's legal provisions and the earlier synergy of social practices and rights discourse.

Activism and Legal Equality Since the Good Friday Agreement

On the morning of the launch of the Belfast Pride Festival in 2011, Calum, a volunteer since the first parade in 1991, arrived at the LGBT center Saturday morning to finalize preparations for the week. At the door, he found a young man who thought it was parade day. In fact, he and his family were so thrilled about his first pride parade that his father had driven him into the city and dropped him off outside the Kremlin nightclub at nine that morning. After waiting outside the shuttered club for an hour, the youth phoned his father, who looked online to discover that the parade was a week later. He also located the LGBT center address, so the youth wandered over to the center, where Calum introduced him to members of the LGBT youth group, Gay and Lesbian Youth Northern Ireland (GLYNI). The young man spoke with organizers, picked up some brochures, and, by the time his father picked him up, had made plans to attend several Pride events.

"This," said Calum, "is why I do it. Because of kids like that, like I was." Thirteen years after the GFA, and twenty after the first pride parade, this story underscores substantial changes in Belfast. In a society where parents sometimes reject their gay children, this father's acceptance and support are striking. The youth's confidence in coming from the suburbs to a gay club in the city (albeit during the day), as well as his desire to be visibly out, reflects a broader trend in which more young people recognize their sexuality and feel safe acknowledging it. Furthermore, the existence of an established LGBT center is a physical change to the social space of the city. Many of the city's LGBT NGOs operate from the offices that opened in 2009, in the former War Memorial Building. Cara-Friend, the first group set up in 1974, when sodomy remained a criminal offense, shares the space with newer groups such as the Lesbian Advocacy Service, Rainbow Men's Health Project, GLYNI, QueerSpace, and Belfast Pride.

The GFA inclusion of sexual orientation as an equal protection category created several openings for legal advocacy that did not exist in the past, and advocates are candid about their tactical approach to legal and social equality. Although the GFA emphasizes parity of esteem for two traditions, its post-conflict guarantee of liberties for LGBT persons also hints at new possibilities for political practices where "ethnic identity is not the highest virtue" (Finlay 2010: xiii). Yet as years passed during the prolonged implementation of the GFA, uncertainty surrounded efforts for LGBT legal equality. Some scholars concluded that devolution would be necessary to fulfill the settlement's promise (e.g., Conrad 2001: 135). Other scholars argued that the communal politics practiced by parties—and institutionalized in the GFA—actually fostered attitudes that prevent LGBT equality (e.g., Duggan 2010: 174; Livingston 2003: 1211). The latter analysis appears more sound: since the GFA, rights for LGBT people have been secured more often by gay rights advocates than local politicians, who remain captive to some of their most conservative constituencies.

Legally, the relevant rationale for gay rights advocacy is drawn from section 6 of the GFA, "Rights, Safeguards and Equality of Opportunity," which charges government to "promote equality of opportunity in relation to religion and political opinion; gender; race; disability; age; marital status; dependants; and sexual orientation." Many attribute the GFA's progressive elements to the Women's Coalition and its collection of academics and activists who were committed to feminist principles.[6] Calum expressed a common view, stating that sexual orientation "was slipped in by the Women's Coalition" while everybody else was concentrating on ethnic politics. Including sexual orientation in equality law, he continued, became a catalyst for a flourishing gay rights movement: "That created the Equality Commission [for Northern Ireland], and they got the remit to cover sexual orientation. There was a rights process, and it gave us legitimacy for getting involved in all of these processes." After the GFA, its principles were established in law. The Government of Northern Ireland Act 1998 enacted the GFA, reformulating state responsibilities from passive nondiscrimination to active promotion of equality. The most cogent statement of this responsibility is section 75 of the act, which came into force on January 1, 2000.

Section 75 of the act created the new Equality Commission in 1999, which combined several other quangos—the Commission for Racial Equality for Northern Ireland, the Equal Opportunities Commission for Northern Ireland, the Fair Employment Commission, and the Northern Ireland Disability Council—to implement affirmative equality policies. The Equality Commission requires that each public authority monitor their promotion of equality ("equality schemes")—in policy, training, delivery of services, and so on. The Equality Commission must approve these plans and can refer inadequate schemes or outcomes to the secretary of state. Individuals and groups may file complaints about state practice to the commission, and it may initiate its own investigations. The commission is also responsible for promoting awareness of antidiscrimination regulations.

In 1998, section 75 appeared to be simply about discrimination in state policy and services. Queer activists extended these protections into other domains as they claimed their place in rights processes during the 2000s. Legal changes since 1998 include bans on discrimination in services and employment, freedom from victimization, equalization of the age of consent, and recognition of same-sex domestic partnerships.[7] However, prolonged periods of direct rule after the GFA meant that Westminster or civil servants implemented these changes, rather than local politicians. Because current MPs from Northern Ireland are members of local parties rather than the primary British parties (Labour, Conservative, and Liberal Democrat), activists often lobbied MPs from Britain rather than local representatives to change law. These legal changes directly affected how gays and lesbians could fully exercise civil, political, and economic rights. Comparisons with the past illustrate the significance of these changes—and the complexity of subjectivity and legality at stake in these struggles.[8] In the 1970s, criminalization created multiple limits on the capacity of gay men and women to exercise their political rights. As noted earlier, police raids on the homes of gay activists set in motion *Dudgeon v. UK*. Furthermore, while criminalization of homosexuality applied to consensual relationships among adult men, lesbians were also subject to legal and social opprobrium.[9] Men and women of this generation often married and had children, coming to terms with their sexuality only after attempts at sexual conformity. During divorce proceedings, legal inequality often combined with social prejudice to cut especially sharply for gay women. For example, one early activist, "Margaret," lost her four-year-old daughter in a custody battle because a judge disapproved of her sexuality and her activism. In Margaret's case, recent legal changes are especially poignant. In 2004, she was married in a civil partnership ceremony; the daughter she had lost served as her matron of honor.

Several other important social and political factors created a very different context for activism since the 1990s. The political discourse of equality was interpreted by a new generation of activists influenced more by AIDS activism and alternative rock than by the events of 1968. The 1993 ceasefires offered hope for a settlement, and the city center was gradually redeveloped. In this context, the queer community developed the literal and rhetorical space to create a new, more public self-consciousness.

For example, during the 1990s, one sexual health group, the Rainbow Project, began to offer more wide-ranging support services. Rainbow was originally formed in 1993 to provide sexual health testing and education to gay and bisexual men. It quickly expanded its agenda, and in the 1990s, along with Cara-Friend, supported gay men and their families with other issues, such as the challenges of coming out. In the 2000s, Rainbow sponsored a range of policy research projects, and employed an advocate who supported clients through civil and criminal complaints processes (e.g., McDermott 2011). Although the Rainbow Project continues to provide sexual health testing and safer sex education, its overall work bridges the literal and social distances between many gay men, their families, and wider communities.

"May," a community worker from the Shankill, reminded me of this poignant, subjective dimension of Rainbow's work. She lived in a fiercely loyalist estate where many residents were aligned with the UVF. Although her older children were rambunctious, her youngest son, she said, "was always different." She struggled against her intuitions and eventually even took him to a child psychologist. As he neared eighteen, he became withdrawn, and she became increasingly anxious. Finally, unable to bear watching him slide into depression, she confronted him:

> I says to him, "Josh,[10] have you got anything you want to tell me, son?" "No." Now the whole time he kept his hand over his eyes. I says, "Look, if you have a problem, come out with it, and talk to me, because that's what I'm here for." "Mommy, I've nothing wrong with me, I'm okay, I'm all right; just go on out and turn the light out." Now, it was either I walked out of the room and closed me eyes to what was going on, or laid the cards on the table here. And I just turned and I says to Josh, I says, "Right son, I'm going to ask you something. You can tell me whether I'm right or wrong, and then I will leave your room." "What?" he says, and still the arm, like this, over his eyes. I says, "Are you gay?" And I saw his lip starting to go, and I seen the tears starting to drop off the side of the chin. And still the arm is up. And I put me arms around him, just lied down on top of him, and I says, "Son, if you think for one minute that I'm going to be any different with you because of this, then you're up the wrong street." But he turned and he says to me, "But I don't want to be."

She knew that Josh's depression partly stemmed from fears about how his family and community would treat him if he were "out." In their neighborhood, as she put it, "There's some bad fellows who would have a field day with this." Along with fears of rejection, he also felt loss—loss of a heterosexual future with a wife and children. May realized that they both needed support and advice. She turned to the Rainbow Project and joined their family support group. Her son received support as well and began to socialize with gay peers, meeting young people from very different backgrounds. May was amused and amazed that his new best friend came from Lenadoon, a nationalist neighborhood. Despite his mother's easing his way to family acceptance, Josh eventually decided to move away from their neighborhood, finding acceptance in his new community.

Another organization that emerged in the late 1990s was called Queer-Space. Like Rainbow, QueerSpace reflected changes in queer politics, but from the outset it was not focused on a particular issue (sexual health) or population (gay and bisexual men). Instead, it began as a cultural resource center where men and women could develop collective forms of expression outside conventional politics. QueerSpace members also wanted to change how gay people were represented in broader society, media, and politics. "Anna," a founding member, said, "For many of us, culture is as important as politics—it *is* politics." By "culture," she meant a broad range of queer historicity, artistic forms, and the everyday attitudes and practices of different queer subcultures. Yet QueerSpace also had a practical goal: to develop concrete strategies regarding the challenges and opportunities presented by the peace process. Rather than use the premises of existing groups or meet in the LGBT bar, the group rented a flat as an alternative to the gay nightlife that some found intimidating. QueerSpace was an open collective: anyone could join, and each member was expected to share rent and utilities on the flat "according to his or her abilities." This collectivist orientation led to an emphasis on process, with a fluid model of membership rather than conventional boards or officeholders. They were trying, "Caitríona," another founding member, said, to reach people who had not been activists before.

Caitríona recalled early QueerSpace discussions with a wry smile for the passions of youth: "We had all the usual rows, about whether you had to be out to be a member, or if using the term 'queer' was an act of empowerment." Yet having these arguments soberly and face to face, rather than on the Internet, in bars, or in cultural studies journals, became a chance to meet and develop empathy for people with divergent experiences. For example, the pain older people described from being labeled "queer" in their youth tempered the transgressive thrill some young people took in the term. Once their first principles had been somewhat established, the collective took up other questions. Is marriage an intrinsically partriarchal, heteronormative institution, or an important legal recognition of queer relationships? Is lobbying political parties antithetical to radical democratic practice?

This account of lofty aspirations and open-ended goals could foreshadow a series of worthy but tedious salons, ending in schism. The result was actually less predictable—during a decade of weekly collective meetings on Wednesdays and a drop-in coffee lounge on Saturdays, members held political discussions and created a social hub. They organized a variety of activities such as bowling nights, literary clubs, dancing lessons, and sign language classes. During the 2000s, QueerSpace sponsored multiple weekly social and educational gatherings. The open-ended definition of the collective's purpose meant that a drama workshop, a club night for "bears," or an art installation was a politically valid form of expression.[11] A less ephemeral result of the collective was Outburst, a queer arts festival begun in November 2006 that hosts films, plays, and exhibitions exploring queer experiences. QueerSpace continues to meet twice monthly, rather than weekly, and is now located in the LGBT center. Given the contingent nature of the project, its activities are changeable, depending on ebbs and flows among members' interests. Or another project could arise entirely—the possibility of redundancy is present within any such endeavor.

The founding principles of the collective and its focus on culture and representation echo a 1960s approach to cultural politics, but the group's practices were shaped by the 1990s. These influences came from changes in local politics during the peace process, changes in the local scene, and in international popular culture. Regarding politics, Caitríona said that QueerSpace's formation at the time of the 1998 agreement was "no accident." If the general populace were unaware that something like section 75 would emerge from the peace process, gay activists were not. They were astute about the possibility of equal protection incorporating sexual orientation, which led them to combine interests in culture and representation with pragmatic policy. Organizational innovations grew from the collective's discussions, such as the Coalition on Sexual Orientation (COSO), which formally provided feedback and policy consultation to government. Although COSO no longer exists, a forum grew up in its place, and efforts continue to formalize political influence .

In this period, political activism often meant working with local civil servants charged with monitoring and promoting equality, as well as British lords and MPs. Since the agreement, activists have used section 75 to assert rights, but to a large extent legal change has been the result of lobbying national lawmakers and policymakers, rather than local representatives. For example, when the Sexual Offences Act 2003 was debated in Westminster, the local assembly was in a prolonged suspension. The act was a significant reform of criminal law regarding rape, reformulating the parameters of consent, and eliminating differences between sexual offences based on gay and straight distinctions. These changes were not extended to Northern Ireland, however, until members of the House of Lords intervened. The same was true regarding civil partnerships: MPs from other regions pushed its extension to Northern Ireland.

Alongside changing political conditions, both the "scene" and political organizing were changing. Women took up more prominent leadership roles. Here, too, the everyday social life of the queer community drove changes in political activity. A younger generation of lesbians had become dissatisfied with a lack of venues or activities exclusively for women. Some of these women embraced the ethos of "riot grrrl," an underground feminist punk movement that originated in the U.S. Pacific Northwest.[12] Applying the DIY (do-it-yourself) ethic of riot grrrl, they began by organizing women's discos, such as Giros, an anarchist punk collective. Belfast became one site in the "scattered cartographies of rebellion" inspired by the riot grrrl movement (Marcus 2010: 275). The discos were held in a variety of venues—flats, leisure centers, and clubs. The woman-oriented ethic of this punk movement also drove attempts to unite, bridging social gaps such as those between "crunchy" granola lesbians and a younger, "alternative" generation. Eventually women's clubs, such as Howl and the Black Box, were established, bringing over American acts such as Gossip. The development of this new lesbian scene was another important shift in this resurgent LGBT advocacy.

Although the suspensions of devolution in the 2000s forced some political efforts into a background role, the broader aim of LGBT visibility nurtured a more potent challenge to this conservative society. For activists involved with both new and existing NGOs, the Belfast Pride Festival became a focal point in the postconflict city. Anna pointed to the first parade in 1991 as a key moment in her own consciousness. She described it as a white-knuckle race down a route lined by police. That terrifying journey now seems long ago. Two decades later, despite seeing herself as a cynic, she was nearly moved to tears by the size of the parade and the sight of sixty schoolchildren carrying a huge rainbow flag. Alongside other groups that emerged in the 1990s, Belfast Pride has become a unifying project for LGBT NGOs and individuals, while bringing political, legal, social, and religious debates about sexuality out of the closet. Through this expansion of public debate, Belfast Pride uses rights discourse to build alternative spaces for political exchange—and reconciliation.

"You Won't Reroute This Fruit"

The freedom to make and remake our cities and ourselves
is . . . one of the most precious yet most neglected of our
human rights.

—David Harvey, "The Right to the City," 23

Belfast's Pride parade was first held in 1991, funded with the remnant of Jeff Dudgeon's legal fund (organizers say they spent the money mostly on pink balloons). It is now the largest cross-community organization in the region, with an all-volunteer staff that strives for inclusivity. The parade also reflects its more conservative context; it might seem sedate by comparison to larger city parades where Dykes on Bikes parade alongside men in backless chaps. Drag queens feature here, of course, but often participants walk with their children. It is recognizably a pride parade, with costumes, floats, and dance music. However, it also includes a children's carnival, to promote a family-friendly image.

The first parade in 1991 was hastily organized, in June on the traditional Stonewall anniversary. After a quick walk through the city center, approximately 100 participants boarded a bus at City Hall, changing their route to avoid protesters. The parade continued and grew annually. As disputes over Orange parades in June and July caused violent disruptions in the 1990s, the parade was moved to the last week of July. By 2000, as LGBT organizing increased and more groups formed, the parade expanded into a festival with multiple events. In 2001, the first street party was held in Barrow Square with about 500 people. As the event grew, the free public after-party was moved from Writers' Square to the larger Custom House Square in 2007. In 2012, organizers estimated that 35,000 people celebrated in the square. The size of the festival requires year-round labor and management (all unpaid), and a committee, elected annually, holds open monthly meetings throughout the year.

As the festival grew, protests against the parade became more organized. In turn, the protests catalyzed support for the parade. Calum said, "There were lots of my gay friends who said, 'Oh, I would never walk in a parade.

I wouldn't want to be like that, it's not needed. It's all in your face, all drag queens." But protests changed that: "There was an attitude. . . . 'Well, I'm not having somebody else telling me what I can and cannot do. So if they say I can't, well, I'm gonna walk.'" The protests also brought publicity to Belfast Pride, partially because reporters were anxious to find news in the post-conflict environment. Adam said, "The protesters, they've got their publicity machine, and they get into the media, and they say to the media, 'The parade's gonna be stopped.' And people go, 'Oh! Parade's on tomorrow. I forgot about that!' So, thank God, they reminded everybody."

With the legal expansion of LGBT rights and increased queer visibility, reactionary religious opposition became more heated. In the early 2000s, a group called Stop the Parade Coalition began organizing evangelicals, calling for a ban. In 2005, the parade was referred to the Parades Commission, which usually regulates contentious loyalist parades. Belfast Pride was allowed to proceed, but the commission placed restrictions on both the parade and the protest.

Stop the Parade used a range of tactics to undermine the event, such as protests at the parade, advertising in print and on mobile street signs, and an anti-parade website with an address similar to the festival's.[13] Nevertheless, parade participation continuously increased.[14] One obvious indication of broader support is the increasing number of rainbow flags around the city during Pride Week. In 2011, I was surprised to see a display of ten rainbow flags over the entrance to Lavery's, a well-known "gin palace" where counter-cultural types gather in the back bar and flirtatious Queens University students congregate on upper floors. More commonly, these flags are flown in the city center. While much has been made of Orange parades, St. Patrick's Day parades, tricolors, and Union Jacks over the past fifty years, rainbow flags signal changes in the city.

The queer politics of Belfast Pride are international ones, of course. Since the late 1960s, pride celebrations endorse a common political theme: queer "invisibility," due to law or the closet, enables and perpetuates harassment and discrimination. Therefore, gay pride parades are a way to oppose and neutralize stigma and inequality, making gay people visible. As Bunzl (2004) observed of Vienna's gay pride parade, "it emerged as not only the principal vehicle for the public articulation of lesbian/gay existence, but as the main site of collective subjectification" (119). In Belfast, public assertions of queer subjectivity and rights challenge local associations of persons and places, as well as the associations of religious orthodoxies and political identifications.

This broader message—that shame oppresses—has particular resonance in Belfast, given the secrecy, shame, and violence of the city's past, as well as its intersections of politics and conservative Christianity. In a city where the sidewalks rolled up in the evening, people "up to no good" frequented the area where the parade begins and ends, an area near the docks where prostitutes and homosexuals historically gathered. After the ceasefires, the louche haunts and the alleys of the rebranded Cathedral Quarter were redeveloped. Venues and retail outlets now vie for the "pink pound" by asserting their "gay-friendliness." Today Belfast's gay residents, at least those who are old enough, laugh when they recall the days of slipping down alleys to the Parliament Bar. I first visited the city in 1996, and the physical changes in the docks and cathedral areas north of the city center are striking. At that time, the Parliament, the only gay bar, still had a furtive air. Now the revamped venue is one of several gay or gay-friendly venues in the quarter, where discount shops are interspersed with galleries, restaurants, and shops. Although there are still many empty storefronts, the redevelopment of existing properties and new developments like the Victoria Square mall have created a lively area by day and night.

Conflicts surrounding the parade are, in a sense, struggles for "rights to the city," another conception of rights that emerged from 1968 (Lefebvre 1996; Harvey 2008). Here, struggles to socially construct space in the city take place through assertion of recognized rights to assembly and speech. Unlike conflicts about Orange parades, these struggles do not reiterate communal politics in space. Although Pride does not challenge the political economy of urban renewal—indeed, Pride organizers emphasize the power of the neoliberal pink pound—it does provide a different perspective on the complex intersection of politics, place, and persons which has captivated politics in Northern Ireland.

Iris Robinson's 2008 remarks created a furor partly because in both politics and social space queer sociality had become gradually more visible and accepted. Soon after her remarks aired, a planned reception at Stormont for LGBT groups was moved up in the calendar from September to June. At the reception, members of other parties publicly distanced themselves from the DUP and expressed support for gay rights. Belfast Pride organizers, meanwhile, actively solicited more participation in the festival. But opponents were also galvanized. On August 1, the day before the parade, Sandown Free

Presbyterian Church placed a full-page advertisement in the *Belfast News Letter* condemning the parade. The ad quoted Leviticus 18:22 and called homosexuality a perversion and an abomination. The ad also linked homophobic attacks that summer to Belfast Pride itself, stating "It is a cause for regret that a section of the community desire[s] to be known for a perverted form of sexuality, which in certain incidences has provoked the unacceptable and totally unjustifiable response of violence." After multiple complaints, the Advertising Standards Authority ruled in December 2008 that the ad breached Clause 5.1 of the CAP Code (Decency). Eventually, however, a judge overturned the ruling, and David McIlveen, minister of the Sandown church, declared that the church had scored a victory for religious liberty, but they did not wish to run the ad again. That summer, the parade doubled in size, to an estimated six thousand people.

Since the high-profile conflict of 2008, the protests have continued, but police and spectators render them largely invisible from the route; indeed, one must now go to City Hall before the parade to glimpse the protests. Meanwhile, McIlveen disassociated his church from the original counterdemonstrations. A qualitative shift has occurred since the Robinson incident in 2008, partly because of the alliances that Belfast Pride created with churches and civil society groups. Although organizers robustly asserted their right to assemble, they also began to reach out to opponents with their newfound allies, and both the tone and content of debate have changed, in sharp contrast to disputes about Orange parades, which continue to result in annual riots.

Is Hate a Human Right, Too?

Belfast Pride creates spaces where the legal and social consequences of gay rights are debated civilly. Although street conflict provides spectacle, albeit mild by local standards, a more significant dialogue has emerged between gay rights opponents and advocates during Belfast Pride events. Social and political disagreements about sexuality are resituated at diverse festival activities during the week of the parade.

Iris Robinson's remarks, as noted earlier, had both contemporary correlates in the anti-parade protests and historical ones in the "Save Ulster from Sodomy" campaign.[15] As civil society groups began actively to support the festival, however, religious supporters also took a prominent role. These supporters walked in the parade as "Changing Attitude Ireland" for the first time in 2008, and one minister was actually accosted on the route (Curtis and Spencer 2012). Since then, church services have become part of the festival roster. At the same time, organizers made concerted efforts to open discussions with opponents. For example, at the 2010 Amnesty International-sponsored "Pride Talks Back" event, David McIlveen served as a panelist.

McIlveen's appearance at that event was a coup for Belfast Pride, held in what had been the poshest hotel in Belfast for decades, the Europa. (Holding events at the Europa "shows we've made it," Adam told me.) The discussion followed a lecture by David Norris, the Irish senator who successfully challenged the Republic's sodomy laws in 1988. McIlveen was welcomed warmly, despite his opposition to gay rights. As at other Belfast Pride events, the audience strove to appear reasonable while disagreeing, politely thanking him for appearing before posing questions or challenges. McIlveen distanced himself from protesters motivated by homophobia, and condemned violence.

After the event, one longtime activist remarked waspishly that McIlveen had merely modernized his language, not his attitude: "He talks about lesbian, gay, bisexual, and transgendered people. He very laboriously goes through the list—he doesn't use the letters." But others were less skeptical. "Owen," a festival volunteer, recalled sitting next to McIlveen on a flight to Malaga. Despite his traveling companion's discomfort, he cheerfully confronted McIlveen about Belfast Pride. McIlveen responded pleasantly, and they had a polite discussion about whether McIlveen's religious beliefs should restrict Owen's right to free assembly. This, Owen said, is the way politics works in small places: you can't avoid your opponents completely. Furthermore, he argued, McIlveen's civility on the flight and his appearance at the discussion were part of broader political gains for gay rights: "Look, the guy showed up for the talk, at the Europa ballroom, one of three big venues in this city. . . . They are being forced to talk to us, just like in the peace process." His sense of inevitability echoes the claims of peace process advocates. Unionist parties refused to enter talks with Sinn Féin for years before the GFA was negotiated; the DUP maintained opposition until 2007, when the party took the leadership of the power-sharing government. Unionists only gradually engaged with the process. Like GFA proponents, gay activists feel that they have a political cause that will eventually, inexorably compel opponents to engage.

Such engagements are still surprising, though, when they occur. As McIlveen consented to pose with other panelists beneath the festival's rainbow logo, he laughed when festival organizers pointed out the scene's incongruity.

Adam, surprised by McIlveen's humor, remarked to him, "You know, this is the first time I've met you when you weren't shouting at me in the street. I like you a lot better when you're not shouting at me."

For Adam, the significance of this exchange extended well beyond the ballroom. His experience introduces two other issues where advocacy is changing relationships: with unions and within schools. As a teacher, Adam's reengagement with gay activism had heightened tensions at his workplace. The chair of his school's board was a prominent parade opponent. Adam said he encountered resistance to his involvement and was told to keep it out of the school. Upset by Iris Robinson's remarks in 2008, he asked his union to support the parade by marching. The trade unionists readily agreed, but only one representative arrived on the day. A friend who was not a teacher carried the other end of the union's banner. Frustration overcame Adam's anxieties about being out in the workplace, and he came out publicly at his union's 2009 conference. From the floor of the conference, he declared that he was gay and strongly critiqued the union's failure to support gay rights. Inspired by what Adam calls his "big coming-out moment," his union sponsored a Belfast Pride event that year and more than a dozen union representatives walked with the union banner in the parade. Since 2010, the union has sponsored a major festival event each year in the Europa Hotel. That year, in an elegant—and full—conference room, a panel discussed the challenges of being out for both teachers and students and what role the union should play. The trade union's engagement has opened other debates—state-sponsored religious education, bullying in schools, and the legal anomalies that prevented an extension of section 75 to schools—subjects that are now receiving a much wider hearing both at Belfast Pride events and across society.

In Northern Ireland, 95 percent of students attend schools that are predominantly Catholic or Protestant (Lundy and Gallagher 2006). Although most Protestant schools joined the state system after partition, they did so with protections for their denominational character. Catholic schools retained control over religious instruction and ethos, with state funding. Only 5 percent of students attend schools that are termed "integrated." Schools are exempt from equality legislation at multiple levels. The religious character of education in Northern Ireland received an exemption from the European Council 2000/78/EC framework for equal treatment (Article 15 (2)), which allows faith schools to exercise religious preferences in hiring. Furthermore, the Equality Commission did not designate schools as "public authorities" for the purpose of section 75 monitoring. These exemptions for schools mean that Employment Equality (Sexual Orientation) Regulations (Northern Ireland) 2003 offer flimsy protections for teachers.

Gay people from a variety of backgrounds say that legal protection for religious education effectively sanctions church doctrines—in other words, that homosexuality is a sin. Campaigners argue that religious protections reinforce schools' reluctance to acknowledge homophobic bullying or the role of theology in justifying it. Additionally, some religious leaders in the educational system endorse reparative therapy, which leads some gay parents to fight for schools *not* to teach their children that they are sinners.

NGOs such as Rainbow Project and Cara-Friend have taken up the matter of how religious education adversely affects LGBT teachers and students. Belfast Pride publicizes their campaigns, and the intimidation of young people who are gay or perceived to be gay. During the 2011 festival, organizers screened a public service announcement made by a young Derry filmmaker, which won first prize for film from the Public Health Agency. The film briefly and starkly dramatizes the internalization of a homophobic culture. The piece intercuts scenes of a young man with his girlfriend, his sexual encounter with another youth, and his eventual despair. The film ends with the statement that "70 percent of teenage suicides are because of being gay." Of course, the message is not that homosexuality causes suicide, but rather that the fear of exposure and rejection lead many young people to take their lives.

"Alison," a young NGO worker who conducts school workshops on sexual orientation and gender bias, explained to me the subtler consequences of the school environment even for young people. Seventy-five percent of LGBT students who are bullied do not report it (Boyd 2011: 2). Alison points out that acknowledging harassment can be as difficult for young people as coming out. A climate of denial about homophobic bullying and schools' failures to respond often deny gay students' right to education. International NGOs, such as Human Rights Watch (2001), have documented how such bullying diminishes the educational achievement of gay students. Locally, Alison estimates that more than half of bullied gay students leave school at the age of sixteen. These students often have lowered exam results and diminished life chances. One bright student she worked with deliberately failed all her General Certificate of Secondary Education exams so she could leave school. Furthermore, Alison claims that a heterosexist curriculum damages the educational experience of gay students. Campaigners decry the absence of LGBT history in the state curriculum, particularly since *Dudgeon v. UK* was an internationally significant ruling with a local history. The curriculum emphasizes cultural awareness with regard to religion, race, and politics, while other dimensions of experience are excluded because of religious sensibilities. Alison argues that the result is a systematic invisibility.

"Trevor," an education analyst, argues that these circumstances fail to protect young people's rights under European Convention Articles 2 (right to education) and 14 (nondiscrimination) as well as the Human Rights Act, which incorporated the convention into UK law. Although he argues that section 75 is more aspirational than enforceable, he still passionately believes it is "one of the most important pieces of human rights legislation in the world." Thus, the Equality Commission's refusal to apply section 75 to education is profoundly frustrating. For Trevor, the failure of schools to address homophobia and their reluctance to discuss sexual orientation are related. The combination creates systematic failures to observe responsibilities under the European Convention on Human Rights and the UK Human Rights Act 1998. Furthermore, Trevor says these practices breach local law, including the Equality Act (Sexual Orientation) Regulations (Northern Ireland) 2006 and the Education and Libraries Order (Northern Ireland) 2003, through which schools and their governors are responsible for the welfare of pupils. (The commission has argued that section 75 would cause an undue administrative burden on schools. Activists say the commission fears challenging religious tenets that saturate education, framing a conflict between religious rights and LGBT rights, rather than a denial of some people's fundamental rights to education.)

With legal remedies reaching an impasse, students and teachers have begun to explore other solutions focused on social attitudes. "Shana" became the faculty sponsor for Northern Ireland's first gay-straight alliance (GSA) in a state school, an integrated secondary. She was moved to start the group by a student reaction to a guest speaker. A performance artist visited the school with a program about undergoing seventeen years of reparative therapy, and Shana noticed that one student began to cry during the program. When she spoke to the eleven-year-old privately, he explained that the performance was upsetting because his best friend had committed suicide, plagued by homophobic bullying. He had never had a chance to talk about his grief. She realized that, even in a relatively progressive school, homophobic bullying was a problem that staff did not acknowledge. Her empathy for the child, she said, left her with a profound "urgency" about the issue. She and a small group of students set up a GSA. They organized school assemblies to explain what LGBT orientations actually are but with lighter touches, such as videos from musicians like Katy Perry and clips from the "It Gets Better" project. Students launched a poster campaign in the school promoting acceptance and went through courses on becoming "allies" to gay friends. They created a website and Facebook page and recently received a national award for their efforts to change the school's culture.[16] Shana has seen changes in attitudes at the school, saying students report decreased bullying and homophobic language. This is congruent with U.S. research indicating that gay-straight alliances reduce bullying in schools (Kosciw 2004).

Shana's experiences illustrate one local attempt to change the cultures of schools. But as a teaching union representative told me, it remains difficult to oppose homophobia in schools if teachers are prevented from coming out or speaking openly about the problem. "Erin," a straight union member who takes part in Belfast Pride events, said, "Look, schools are workplaces as well. And they aren't safe, and they aren't protected by the Fair Employment Act. Staff and students cannot legally harass, on one hand, but on the other, where are the adults who are accepted, are respected, are models in schools showing that adults can live visibly and be accepted? They are teachers, and they need to be accepted as they are by colleagues and students." Her union has always endorsed LGBT equality, but, when Adam brought the local's attention to the risks, hypocrisies, and idiosyncrasies attached to the teaching profession in Northern Ireland, she realized how unusual the local situation is. Now, in addition to supporting the parade and sponsoring events, her union is reaching out to other unions to build a stronger, unified front.

Of course, harassment and intimidation occur even more frequently outside schools and workplaces. Police report that most assaults and homophobic incidents take place in public, at night, outside social venues. Broader stigmatization of homosexuality, and the point at which stigma becomes a crime, has also become a subject for Belfast Pride, especially in light of the murders of gay men that have taken place in recent years. Pride annually schedules discussion events with state agencies. Through these events, queer citizens have begun to develop more trusting relationships with state agencies, and one of the most active agencies in this work is the old enemy of gay activists, the police. The new Police Service of Northern Ireland (PSNI) has sponsored Belfast Pride events since the early 2000s. Its public events are designed to underscore the service's serious approach to hate crimes. Unlike initiatives that "place the onus of avoiding crime . . . squarely on the shoulders of individual victims," the PSNI emphasizes prosecuting offenders, as well as social initiatives to decrease the prevalence of hate crimes (Stanko 2000: 25). Of course PSNI's events are oriented toward the reformed service's goals of promoting itself as a truly reformed body and establishing relationships with the communities it serves. But for Belfast Pride participants, PSNI involvement allows a rare opportunity for a marginalized community to engage with the state directly.

During Belfast Pride 2011, I attended a police-sponsored production of *The Laramie Project*, performed by a local company in the Lyric Theater. The play dramatizes the 1998 homophobic murder of Matthew Shepard, a University of Wyoming student, and its aftermath. Soon after the murder, members of New York's Tectonic Theater Project traveled to Laramie, Wyoming, and interviewed townspeople, building a script from their multiple voices and perspectives. The play has been filmed and performed by companies across the Anglophone world. After the Belfast performance, a panel of police officers, lawyers, actors, and local activists assembled at the front of the theater. Before the moderator opened the floor to questions, there was a collective pause, as if the suffering of Matthew Shepard, beaten, alone, and waiting for death in a frozen field, had robbed the audience of breath.

As the discussion unfolded, people spoke of fear and rejection by peers, pastors, and friends. The weight of loss became heavier when a Rainbow Project worker spoke of a friend's murder in Dungannon and the BBC moderator spoke of the murder of a close friend from seminary. Both homophobic murders were widely publicized. Yet frustration accompanied the outpouring of sorrow among both the audience and panelists. Questioners struggled with the inadequacy of "hate crime" as both a legal and social category—frustrated by the ubiquity of hatreds, bound up not just with sexuality but also the past conflict.[17] While the audience thanked the police representative for the PSNI's seriousness about hate crime, the stark fact remained that harassment and violence remain endemic and underreported. After the event, one panelist, a lawyer, told me that "hate crime" is an attractive term to identify malice as a motivation for crime and the extra experience of humiliation that accompanies these crimes, but does little substantively. The unfortunate reality, she said, was that, although recognition of hate crimes allows judges to consider aggravating factors in sentencing, the category itself does not alter the fact that this society punishes people for their sexuality. Legal recognition of hate crimes has not changed social practices or attitudes.

Historically, the RUC, precursor to the PSNI, had a confrontational relationship with the gay community. In contrast, the reformed policing service was one of the first state agencies to liaise with gay activists and NGOs to address homophobic violence. One duty of the police hate crime unit is to track homophobic incidents, whether the actions constitute offenses or not. The new service documents and identifies areas for interventions such as community policing. Hate incidents are classified by five categories: ethnicity, sexual orientation, transgender status, disability, sectarian/political, and religion. At Pride events, police officers promote the anonymous phone line and an online reporting form for such incidents, emphasizing that they maintain confidentiality. All these efforts notwithstanding, one police representative I met was almost apologetic about levels of homophobia in Northern Ireland. He said that the service is "acutely" aware of underreporting. He was especially exasperated by media reports that police do not take reports seriously or that they discourage prosecution, which, he said, is demonstrably untrue. Even if current procedures have not changed the attitudes of individual officers, he argued that the intensively rationalized nature of policing since reform has made such behavior a thing of the past. Furthermore, he concluded, individual officers are far more likely to be personally sympathetic to the victims of racist, homophobic, or sectarian harassment—not just because of training but because the makeup of the service is more balanced in terms of religion, gender, and sexual orientation.

The ease with which activists now engage with police and other state representatives is a sharp contrast to past raids and harassment in the 1970s, more recent use of surveillance to arrest men for cruising, and even early Belfast Pride appearances by the PSNI.[18] At early PSNI events, audiences publicly challenged officers for not investigating hate crimes (Conrad 2009). But familiarity and rapport emerged over time. At one event in 2010, officers and audience members addressed one another by first names. When challenged about prosecuting hate crimes, an inspector frankly stated that he and his colleagues were unhappy with outcomes. Beyond the law's imperfections, he said that, as an investigator, "of course" he thought there were an inadequate number of prosecutions. An audience member then asked, "You say that the legislation isn't perfect. Is that in how it is drafted or in how it is applied?" He replied, "Look, there have only been *thirteen* cases prosecuted since the introduction of [hate crime] legislation in 2004. I think PPS [Public Prosecution Service] may not be applying it well. The hate crimes dimension does apply more to sentencing than prosecution, but it is an actual dimension of more cases than *that*." The audience chimed in with critiques of prosecutors as a shared opponent; one participant said, "The PPS claims that the legislation is actually not strong enough. But my experience is that it is the actual PPS practice of applying it. The PPS simply won't invoke it, or a judge won't allow it to go through, and victims are exhausted from the retelling by the time the PPS has backed down on the hate crime dimension." As they develop more cordial relationships, campaigners and police appear to have found common causes and enemies.

Gay activists' relationships with church and state are only partially repaired. But Belfast Pride creates spaces where rapprochements and reconciliations can be acknowledged and where conflicts can be discussed. As one woman explained to me, the serious debates and discussions organized by Belfast Pride "are how you build bridges. It's not pissed [drunk] people on a float." These bridges between the gay community and society are *tenuous* signs of rapprochement. After McIlveen's 2010 appearance at the festival, the LGBT community's most famous opponent agreed to appear the following year at a discussion organized by young people. He withdrew on the day of the event. Rumors circulated that his church had forced him to withdraw because he was softening his antigay stance, and these seemed substantiated when, despite distancing itself from the contentious 2008 advertisement, the church ran the ad again on July 31, 2011.

The Belfast Pride parade is a very public claim on the contested space of Belfast. But the organization's greater significance is its expanding range of interlocuters and spaces for discussion. In the longer view, conflict in Northern Ireland created greater political cohesion for queer activism. Queer people have found common causes and presented them to broader society. The movement's increasing emphasis on family and respectability may cause discomfort for older activists who pursued sexual liberty and transgression, but this new approach has yielded results. Antidiscrimination legislation and the insistent, persistent work of gay rights activists have produced gradual change and extended equality debates far beyond decriminalization or marriage rights. In contrast to dominant discourses of collective rights, their advocacy concerns the practical ramifications of equality in law for individual queer people at work, in school, in housing, and in everyday safety—not equality claims for their community's ethos or aspirations. The role of political parties in these legal and social changes, however, remains ambiguous. Despite the peace process's successes, reconciliation appears more distant in the new assembly. Belfast Pride demonstrates that alternative political spaces may have greater potential for creating social and political rapprochement than the institutions of consociationalism.

Stormont's Return

In July 2010, Jeff Dudgeon made a sharp accusation standing outside Stormont, home to both the past parliament and the new power-sharing government: "No reform legislation has ever happened in this building or is likely to happen." Jeff was speaking to a group of festival participants, including myself, on a QueerSpace gay history bus tour. Other participants shared his cynicism regarding the capacity of politicians. Although informed by history, this view is also a comment on governance since devolution in 2007. LGBT rights remained a source of contention after devolution, and a religiously oriented party, the DUP, led the Northern Irish coalition government. Soon after taking office in 2007, First Minister Ian Paisley attempted to freeze funds allocated for LGBT NGOs and stalled legislation to bring Northern Ireland into compliance with the European Union's nondiscrimination framework. Paisley's denomination, the Free Presbyterians, insisted that he should not oversee funding of gay groups, even though £230,000 (approximately $460,300) had been allocated for them earlier under direct rule. Ultimately, Westminster interceded and the funds were released.

This local political paralysis continues. In July 2010, the First and Deputy First Ministers' Office published draft plans for community relations, including the issues of sectarianism and racism—but said it would release recommendations regarding sexual orientation at a later date (OFMDFM 2010a). One straight community activist from the Shankill was incredulous: "A shared future was one of the big policies that came out of the Good Friday Agreement. We now have a draft document twelve years later. The thing about the draft is, it doesn't mention anywhere how they're going to deal with the gay and lesbian community. Are they not part of the shared future? And you know, Northern Ireland is still at that, still slicing off who doesn't come into a shared future."

In 2011, the Pride Talks Back political debate—an annual event—was held for the first time at Stormont. The building's parquet floors, tall windows, and chandeliers lent gravitas to the local parliament, when it was constructed after partition. At the event, a BBC presenter moderated before a crowd of more than fifty people, admitted with special passes. Politicians from the SDLP, Sinn Féin, UUP, and the Alliance, Green, and Conservative Parties attended. The DUP refused to participate, although it did actually RSVP for the first time. When declining, the DUP MLA who responded called the Belfast Pride march "totally repugnant," causing another brief media storm.

Moments of levity were rare at the event, and a pattern quickly emerged. From the first question about how they would characterize parties' relationships with the gay community, politicians complained about the DUP. Meanwhile, questioners persistently dragged them back to their own parties' policies. When would parties nominate openly gay candidates for the assembly? Why are schools exempt from section 75? Given levels of homophobic attacks, why isn't this issue brought to the Policing Board by the political representatives who serve on it? Some questioners were visibly frustrated: "I am angry, and you are sitting there complacent!" said one audience member. Several politicians appeared surprised by the questions—the Sinn Féin MLA was amazed that section 75 did not apply to schools. He was even more baffled that the exemption was granted when a member of his party led the Department of Education. Primary school teachers, parents, and students described hostile school environments and their frustrations with religious education. Finally, in disgust, an NGO worker said, "Each party here says they support the extension of section 75 to the schools. You could *all* do something now. You could raise it, but it doesn't happen."

But the politicians' refrain was the same: power sharing requires consensus, the DUP is the biggest party, they are unreasonable, and we can do nothing but listen to your concerns. After the discussion, I spoke with an MLA about education, and received the standard reply about DUP dominance, but with a bit more self-critique. She said that, theoretically, the other parties could stand together to meet the consociational voting requirements. In practice, though, she said, these coalitions are easily fragmented, with different parties leaving when offered deals on issues—often ethnopolitical ones—that are a higher priority for them. In reality, the assembly's work is straitened on substantial issues, and this explains why LGBT groups are now focused on taking matters to the courts. LGBT advocates also have a new ally for making gay rights central rather than marginal to policy. The new chair of the Human Rights Commission (HRC) is Michael O'Flaherty, a respected scholar and lawyer who was influential in framing the Yogyakarta Principles (O'Flaherty and Fisher 2008). Although caveats about bypassing the local democratic process apply, outstanding matters such as blood donation restrictions and full marriage rights will likely be settled not by power sharing but by judges or Westminster politicians.[19] For example, in 2011 the HRC applied for a judicial review of Northern Ireland's ban on adoption by gay couples. In October 2012, a judge ruled that the ban illegally discriminated on the basis of sexual orientation, violating the European convention and the Human Rights Act (1998). The judge ordered the HRC and the Department of Health to amend adoption procedures to comply with human rights law.[20] The Court of Appeals rejected the department's challenge to the ruling in 2013.

Political parties' support for gay rights is often superficial at best or nonexistent, as with the DUP. The UUP is internally fragmented on the issue, with two straight, high-profile members walking in the Belfast Pride parade annually—although one reports that a colleague sarcastically congratulated him on coming out. The SDLP and Sinn Féin are supportive of gay rights in principle, but, as Conrad (1999) has noted, nationalist parties do not make these policies a priority since they do not wish to alienate conservative Catholic supporters. The Alliance Party has had electoral gains recently, as the broader unionist population becomes less devout, most notably with Naomi Long's defeat of first minister Peter Robinson for the Westminster seat in Belfast East.

Since 1998, gay activists have influenced how human rights aspirations in the GFA were translated into law and policy. More recently, when Iris Robinson publicly denounced homosexuality, LGBT activists galvanized support across society. Often the objectives of gay rights advocates have been pursued through international instruments like the European convention, now enshrined in British law, or through lobbying MPs in London. Bypassing local democracy is not a political ideal, nor, usually, is recourse to the judiciary. Yet the contemporary law and practice of human rights emerged from situations where individuals and groups had little protection from local or national institutions. Thus, the case of gay rights discourse in Belfast underscores that rights discourse can be an effective tool for securing basic rights in the face of resistant local politics. At the same time, gay rights discourse has nurtured the creation of alternative political practices and alliances. Owen's faith that gay rights will force engagement with adversaries has been gradually borne out: in 2012, for the first time, the DUP relented and sent a political representative to the Pride Talks Back debate. Acknowledging these engagements and changes is a key step for developing broader insights about the contradictory roles that rights discourse plays in postconflict reconciliation. As conflict and its legacy are cemented in structures of governance, appeals to humanity—including sexual orientation—as a basis for equal treatment have other consequences, notably the opportunity to recognize and mobilize political subjectivity beyond reductive ethnopolitical allegiances.

Changing the Subject: Gay Rights as Human Rights

We feel that gay people are their own best witnesses
and that the case is doomed if the judges see the
applicant using the terms of reference of the government/
oppressor, . . . seeing the issue in terms of morals/
medicine rather than human rights.
—Jeff Dudgeon, in a letter to his solicitor, 1978[21]

On December 19, 2005, "Aiofe" and "Andrea" walked out of Belfast City Hall as the first couple publicly to exchange civil partnership vows in the United Kingdom. Friends holding flowers lined their path to a taxi. They had gathered to celebrate the event and to shield the couple from ubiquitous religious protesters. In a cheeky mockery of the religious protesters not planned by the couple's friends, two diapered men stood to the side with signs reading "Earth Is Still Flat" and "Bring Back Slavery." Photographs of the couple appeared in media across the world, and the mass of flowers framing the couple gave the effect of a meticulously planned wedding photo. It also, said Andrea, felt as if they were walking out on "a wave of love." Before the ceremony, they were met by a flurry of reporters, and Aiofe found herself flustered, repeating that their union was "for protection." At the time, she was uncertain what she meant. Three years later, though, they discovered what "protection" entailed, when Andrea became critically ill. A U.S. citizen, she was too ill to countermand her panicked family's attempt to bring her back to the States. Aiofe exercised her partnership rights, and Andrea remained in Northern Ireland, where she made a full recovery.

When friends shielded the couple from protesters, when images of the celebration were broadcast internationally, and when gay pride parades marched through the city center, different forms of political subjectivity were asserted. The "us" created by queer community is not merely a matter of lifestyle. It is an "us" that is assaulted to the extent that nine children commit suicide in Minnesota.[22] It is an "us" that eventually throws bottles at Stonewall or gathers with candles in Laramie, instead of submitting to another assault. In the last forty years, it is also an "us" that has begun to lawyer up, seeking relief in the form of human rights principles. In Northern Ireland, this "us" has become a powerful, meaningful alternative formulation of political priorities and rights discourse. It has situated the experiences of queer people not within the entrenched politics of nation, but within a larger, global community that shares similar experiences across time and distance.

The globalization of gay rights as human rights is a historical process distinct from the local role of gay rights discourse in postconflict reconciliation. Yet these processes are not unrelated, since the efficacy of gay rights as a political project in Belfast is linked to the legitimacy accorded to human rights claims internationally. Although the UN Human Rights Council narrowly voted to affirm LGBT rights as human rights for the first time in 2011, international consensus remains elusive. Nevertheless, there are increasing efforts to recognize that widespread denials of rights due to perceived or actual sexual orientation are human rights violations. The Yogyakarta Principles are such a project, developed in response to the ways that LGBT people suffer human rights violations daily, "from denials of the rights to life, freedom from torture, and security of the person, to discrimination in accessing economic, social and cultural rights such as health, housing, education and the right to work, from non-recognition of personal and family relationships to pervasive interferences with personal dignity" (O'Flaherty and Fisher 2008: 208).

Michael O'Flaherty's appointment in 2011 as the chair of the Human Rights Commission had a poetic resonance in Belfast. Jeff Dudgeon's successful challenge to sodomy laws thirty years earlier was the first international recognition of a connection between gay rights and universal human rights; it was cited, for example, by the U.S. Supreme Court in *Lawrence v. Texas*.[23] The appointment of an influential proponent of gay rights as human rights, three decades after Dudgeon's case, marked a historic moment for the local movement. Dudgeon's case did not establish sexual orientation or gender identity as categories that qualified under the nondiscrimination clause of the European convention (Article 14); that recognition came only in 1999, in *Salguiero da Silva Mouta v. Portugal*.[24] As part of the legal domain of human rights, gay rights only gradually became a concern for human rights NGOs. The NIGRA archive in Belfast contains many documents that describe early campaigns for Amnesty International to recognize people imprisoned for their sexual orientation as prisoners of conscience. During this period, NIGRA activists worked with the new International Gay Association to highlight the sodomy laws in Northern Ireland and other countries, as an organized international movement grew from the sexual liberation protests of the 1960s. In 1991, Amnesty finally broadened its advocacy to recognize LGBT victims of human rights violations, at the same fractious meeting where the organization recognized the abuses of nonstate actors. Human Rights Watch took up the issue in 1996.

The relation of international law and discourse to domestic laws and discourse has been theorized in various ways. Political scientists Keck and Sikkink (1998) describe a "boomerang" model, through which domestic activists appeal to transnational NGOs to work against the policies and practices of national governments. Risse and Sikkink (1999) outline a "spiral model," through which national human rights norms change over time through the interactions among international NGOs, intergovernmental organizations, domestic actors, and national governments. Kollman (2007) criticizes these models for insufficiently considering the way national or local values influence these processes. Northern Irish gay activists sometimes appeal to international instruments and courts, but the potent influence of gay rights discourse is best understood qualitatively, in the particular circumstances of the region. Yet rather than contorting human rights to the demands of local ethnocommunal politics, gay activists resituate their local struggles in the broader transnational discourse of both human rights and gay activism. Seen this way, the case of gay rights advocacy complicates recent common sense about the role of human rights in peacemaking. It becomes evident that the politicization of human rights does not necessarily introduce a fatal weakness into legal principles. Instead, appropriations of human rights discourse can produce liberatory political projects. In Northern Ireland, political subjects seized the opportunities offered by that global discourse to confront local oppressions, rather than appropriating that discourse to reiterate them.[25]

This project introduces new limits, of course. As noted earlier, older activists in Belfast who came of age seeking sexual liberation are sometimes uneasy with younger people's desire for respectability and (relatively) conventional domestic arrangements. Dave's (2010) research on lesbian activism in India explores similar losses that occur with political mobilization—subjectivity may become regulated for authenticity or the unruliness of sexual desire displaced by respectable activism. A similar sacrifice is required to translate sexual orientation into the language of human rights, argue Kollman and Waites (2009): "human rights norms limit sexual diversity and the positive recognition of sexual difference" (13). In this vein, Mertus (2007) advocates moving away from sexual orientation toward sexual rights, emphasizing actions over identity. Theoretical concerns about the fluidity of sexuality, however, do not always easily translate into practice. Dave (2010) has observed that "Political communities always form through disparate needs, agents, and agendas.

More important, they form by bringing together people who feel (and are educated to feel) under siege, inadequately recognized, and politically impotent" (617). If a society regards queer people as less than human, then promoting recognition of their humanity is an obvious and effective strategy. Yet struggles to exercise political agency do not blaze direct paths to liberation, just as efforts to develop nonviolent politics are often fitful and flawed. Adopting the language of human rights to pursue these journeys is as much a matter of politics as universal ethics. With these caveats, by appropriating human rights talk, gay activists in Belfast have created political possibilities that sharply contrast with the role of rights discourse in the postconflict politics of unionism and nationalism. Here we see intimations of peace, rather than war, by other means.

CHAPTER 7

Ethnopolitics and Human Rights

In the twenty-first century, Northern Ireland's inclusive peace process was attenuated; many negotiations about the Good Friday Agreement's (GFA) implementation took place between the British government and one or two political parties. Senior British advisers such as Jonathan Powell (2008) frame this as *realpolitik*, recognizing that extreme factions in a conflict require more accommodation, and wield greater power, than centrists. Against triumphal accounts of the peace process, academics have documented increasing communal and class-based divisions (e.g., Shirlow and Murtagh 2006), and critiqued how the agreement institutionalizes sectarian politics (Finlay 2010). Social, political, and economic data indicate a fragile peace; uncertainties stem from the power-sharing government's failure to develop reconciliation and equality policies, and polarized public understandings of both political and economic conditions (Nolan 2013: 7, 2012). Since devolution in 2007, republican dissidents have killed police and soldiers and pursued a bombing campaign; loyalist paramilitaries assassinated one of their own in broad daylight on a busy street; and riots surrounding parades and symbolic matters like flags have become dangerous and costly year-round events, intimating, for some, a return to conflict. Many of the poorest residents of Belfast, formerly the conflict's most ardent foot soldiers, fail to see a peace dividend. Global recession has curtailed investment in the region, while uprisings in North Africa and the Middle East preoccupy both geopolitical strategists and transnational activists. Northern Ireland is "settled," and the continuing anxieties of local residents no longer capture distant imaginations. These conditions of "cold peace" challenge commonsensical accounts of human rights and conflict (see Taylor 1991). Human rights and conflict resolution have been definitionally and practically debated and circulated over time. Rights

politics in Northern Ireland's case demonstrate that these debates and journeys produce fraught, contradictory consequences, rather than foregone
conclusions.

The hidden history of rights discourse in Northern Ireland reveals a more
complex relationship between human rights and peace. As Northern Ireland
was transformed into an exemplar of conflict resolution, a popular history
emerged that establishes a central role for human rights—as cause and cure of
the conflict. This narrative legitimizes both the settlement and prior violence,
rather than serving as a neutral description of events. Closer historical analysis demonstrates that the appropriation of rights talk in the everyday work
of local activism created new terms and terrains for the conflict, at the same
time as it supported campaigns for social justice and peace. These contradictory consequences were as much to do with public reception of rights talk as
the intentions of rights advocates.

In the 1960s, civil rights became a vehicle for challenging political injustices in the post-partition state. As violence erupted, rights entered the 1970s
vernacular, in housing rights campaigns that were suffused with ethnocommunal territoriality. In the 1980s, community organizers claimed economic
and welfare rights, and these claims often devolved into debates about relative
Catholic and Protestant deprivation. In the 1990s, claims to rights of association supported the transformation of paramilitaries into democratic political
actors—while claims for rights to assembly intensified division and violence.
In the post-GFA period, debates regarding human rights and victims' rights
have created competing valuations of victim experiences and stymied truth
recovery regarding past violence. Rights talk simultaneously furthered liberatory projects and reproduced, even exacerbated, profound ethnopolitical
divisions. Over the years, rights talk subsumed international politics and policies into the local conflict. However, gay rights advocacy in the postconflict
era, hints at new possibilities for rights discourse—as a tool to resituate local
conflicts within international norms, rather than deploying these norms for
local political contests.

The Enlightenment in Ireland

When I finished Carlyle's French Revolution in 1871, I
was a Girondist; every time I have read it since, I have
read it differently—being influenced and changed, little by

little, by life and environment (and Taine and St. Simon):
and now I lay the book down once more, and recognize
that I am a Sansculotte! And not a pale, characterless
Sansculotte, but a Marat. Carlyle teaches no such gospel,
so the change is in me—in my vision of the evidences.
            —Mark Twain, letter to William Dean Howells, 1887[1]

In the 1790s, the Enlightenment came to Ireland, and would-be revolutionaries, following France and the United States, attempted to liberate the island
from British rule and the local Protestant Ascendancy. In 1798, the republican
United Irishmen led a violent revolt that left thousands dead. That the principles of the Enlightenment are implicated in the bloodiest episode of Irish
history is both tragic and ironic. Grand ideas about the rights of man were
transformed in the Irish context and inspired political movements that fractured in intense sectarian violence. Foster (1988) writes, "The 1798 rising was
probably the most concentrated episode of violence in Irish history"; he estimates that thirty thousand people died during the rebellion, including British
forces, Irish rebels and their French allies, and civilians (280).[2] Contemporary critics of human rights discourse would no doubt greet these unintended
effects with world-weary aplomb—for, indeed, the story of the United Irishmen goes to the core of current debates about the validity of laudatory histories of human rights. The contentious history of universal rights and national
rights in Ireland does not determine the present. It does, however, serve as
a useful rhetorical resource in contemporary debates. It also underscores
the profound ethnopolitical divisions that have pervaded rights discourse
over time. Irish history, recent and distant, demonstrates that rights-based
philosophies do not inevitably produce liberty. The Irish Enlightenment is
a warning that remains salient today—a caution against elevating "inchoate
domestic failures into clear-cut moral victories" (Foster 1988: 286).
    How the United Irishmen traveled from Enlightenment ideals to brutal
sectarian atrocities is a contested history, much like the contemporary story
of conflict and its resolution. Stewart (1998) writes that "Though the principles of the original United Irishmen had inculcated a brotherhood of affection
among Irishmen, the effect of 1798 in the North was to painfully empha-
sise divisions which already existed in religion and society. Catholic soldiers
fought with Protestant rebels, and sometimes Orange yeomanry. Neighbour
hunted down neighbour, the Church of Ireland was set against Presbyterian,
landlord against tenant, engendering feuds among families which have lasted

almost to the present. . . . Republicanism which was intended to free the Irish people from sectarianism became in the nineteenth century part of the dispute" (38). As with the contemporary conflict, arguments about causality and political value—that is, was the rebellion due to the politicization of the Irish people or ethnic antipathy?—surround assessments of this history. For some, the rebellion's horrors, such as a massacre in Wexford in June 1798, ought not to overshadow "the living principles of democracy and pluralism which the United Irishmen created" (Whelan 1996: 35; see also Dunne 2010). Other historians acknowledge the sectarian violence that occurred during the uprising, yet still characterize the movement as a positive force for politicization in eighteenth-century Ireland, particularly among Catholics and the poor (e.g., Elliott 1982; O'Donnell 1998; Chambers 1998). Commemorations of the rebellion's bicentennial in 1998 constructed a direct line of descent from the 1798 coalition of Catholic, Protestant, and Dissenter to the present Irish state (Foster 2001).[3]

The Society of United Irishmen (UI) formed in Belfast in October 1791. In November, Dubliners formed their own branch. Bew (2007) notes that the northern UI were mostly bourgeois dissenters, as Ulster became increasingly urban and industrial, while, in Dublin, the middle-class revolutionaries had "a sprinkling of gentry and aristocracy" and an even membership of Catholic and Protestant (10). Despite the eloquent pamphleteering and revolutionary fervor of the Dublin leader, Theobald Wolfe Tone, Belfast, rather than the capital, Dublin, was the locus of UI Enlightenment thought.[4] McBride (1997) argues that "Presbyterian radicals . . . constituted the backbone of organized republicanism for most of that pivotal decade" (63). Their ministers gave sermons "wherein the nature of civil liberty and civil government were explained" (66). Thompson (1991) notes, "In the years before and after '98, the Dissenters of Ulster, the most industrialized province, were not the most loyal but the most 'Jacobinical' of the Irish" (470).

In the eighteenth century, Catholics and members of nonestablishment faiths like Presbyterianism (Dissenters) were subject to Penal Laws limiting their property rights, voting and political participation, and religious expression. By 1791, the Anglo-Irish establishment was gradually reforming these laws, and the issue of Catholic emancipation had begun to pose challenges to the ambiguous constitutional relationship between Britain and Ireland.[5] Alongside these challenges to the political order were challenges to the economic order that the Penal Laws had created by transferring land from the Catholic aristocracy to Anglican members of Britain's established church.[6]

In Belfast, republican ideas found a receptive audience. The newly bourgeois dissenters, like their fellow radicals in Dublin and Cork, were overtly sympathetic to the U.S. revolution, drawing parallels to their own condition. Republicans in Belfast, Dublin, and Cork were also inspired by the French revolution (see Elliott 1982; Gargett and Sheridan 1999; Bew 2007). The Ulster radicals were heavily influenced by the liberationist ideals of Presbyterian New Light theology and Scottish Enlightenment thought (McBride 1998; see also Foster 1988: 264–67). These radical and libertarian ideas were disseminated throughout the city of Belfast. The *Belfast News Letter* (still published as the *News Letter*, albeit now with a unionist editorial policy) reflected these radical views. It was the first European paper to publish the U.S. Declaration of Independence in 1776. In 1789, it published a translation of the Declaration of the Rights of Man. Foster (1988) writes that the appetite for "Enlightenment debate [was] diffused through Belfast 'society' . . . [with] seven Irish editions of the *Rights of Man* between 1791 and 1792" (265).

In rural areas, secret societies—Protestant, Catholic, and mixed—proliferated, mobilizing a series of violent agrarian revolts in protest of rates of taxation, rents, and the tithes demanded by the Catholic Church. Secret societies varied in region and causes, and, by the 1790s, they had produced a larger movement called the Catholic Defenders. This group was centered in mid-Ulster, where sectarian animosities and divisions were profound. While Belfast dissenters began to embrace common cause with Catholics (remaining reserved about Catholicism generally), in Armagh, rival Protestant and Catholic secret societies engaged in bitter violence. In September 1795, members of a Protestant secret society attacked a group of mostly unarmed Catholic Defenders at the Battle of the Diamond, leaving several Catholics dead. Following the battle, the Orange Order was established.

Ireland in the 1790s was home to multiple violent political movements and areas of extreme sectarian violence. In this local context, where mass movements were a dominant cultural practice, Enlightenment ideas became a force for further mobilization. During the mid-1790s the UI sent the Ulster radical Henry Joy McCracken around the island under cover of his textile business, strengthening coalition with the Catholic Defenders. Yet the Defenders and the UI had very different political ideologies and, in these incompatibilities, were the seeds of the violence that was to follow. Like the UI, the Catholic Defenders advocated republicanism and national rights, but, as Foster (1988) argues, their ideology also "went back to the Limerick Treaty and the Battle of the Boyne, in a way that divided them from their radical Presbyterian allies" (273). Unlike the

Defenders, the UI were little interested in history; Foster notes, "they appealed, as they themselves put it, to posterity, not ancestors" (270).[7]

Eventually, the Anglo-Irish establishment and Britain could not ignore the UI's subversive aims. Wolfe Tone was exiled in 1795, and several leaders were tried for treason. From his French base, Tone enlisted French military support, which resulted in an aborted French naval invasion in December 1796. In 1797, a harsh military crackdown was executed, most viciously against radicals in Ulster with the assistance of the new Orange Order. Foster (2001) notes, however, that despite these measures, "in February 1798, there were still about 500,000 sworn United Irishmen, with perhaps 280,000 in possession of arms" (70). In March, the state extended repressions across the island, but this did not prevent the rebellion, which began in May. The insurrection unfolded in phases, which contributed to its failure. In Dublin, the May rebellion was quickly stifled by the military. In June, UI uprisings took place in the southeast, and rapidly became Catholic peasant revolts. In July, the Presbyterians of Ulster rebelled, but British forces and loyalists easily put down that rising. A brief, failed French invasion of Mayo took place in September, but it too was defeated.

Leaders of the movement were imprisoned, tried, and executed. In years to come, sectarian violence in Wexford was widely publicized in Ulster and fueled communal enmity. In 1800, the Act of Union officially incorporated Ireland in the United Kingdom and abolished the Irish Parliament. Ireland was given one hundred seats in the British House of Commons, yet Catholics were not allowed to hold office until twenty-nine years later. Many radicals escaped execution, emigrated to the United States and, following in Thomas Paine's footsteps, became influential activists and journalists in the new republic (Durey 1997). Ultimately, the loyalty of dissenters was secured, through both the stratagems of British governance and reactions against the rising's bloodshed. A striking outcome of imported Enlightenment ideals was that Irish Presbyterians were transformed from the most subversive elements in Ireland to British loyalists.

Rose (1971) observes that "Ireland is almost a land without history, because the troubles of the past are relived as contemporary events" (70). Although contemporary republicanism reveres Tone and the United Irishmen, reverence for their failed revolution extends beyond republicanism. On the eve of the GFA, public intellectuals at the local political journal *Fortnight* bemoaned how repeatedly "reason has shattered on the rocks of ethnicity."[8]

They noted that Enlightenment ideals of the United Irishmen of 1798 and the People's Democracy of 1968 were both swiftly superseded by movements advocating communalized rights. The *Fortnight* editorial claimed,

> Equality, the international touchstone of thirty years ago, has been dumbed down to a sectarian balancing act, where parity of insulted feelings outweighs any sense of the common good. . . . The equality agenda, ghettoized as a Sinn Féin demand, is now part of the British government spin service. . . . Have things not come to a pretty pass when equality is assumed to be purely defined along lines of national identity? Women, Travellers, the long-term unemployed, the homeless and the swathe of groups and individuals referred to as "socially excluded" might have something to say about such a narrow definition. This society is rotten with inequality. It blights hope, and disfigures any talk of distributing democracy in this province. . . . The Enlightenment cannot be allowed to wither on the vine of whatever sectarian deal emerges from the Castle Buildings. Our best future still depends on the best ideals of two centuries ago. (5)

A Bill of Rights for Northern Ireland

Debates regarding fundamental rights remain susceptible to ethnopolitical appropriation, as demonstrated by public consultations on the GFA's proposed bill of rights. The responses of political parties and NGOs to proposals often split along lines of unionism and nationalism. The Northern Ireland Human Rights Commission (HRC), created by human rights provisions in the GFA, was primarily charged with monitoring equality policies. It was also charged to develop a bill of rights containing "rights supplementary to those in the European Convention on Human Rights, to reflect the particular circumstances of Northern Ireland" (*Agreement Reached* 1998: 20–21). This bill of rights was to define the obligations of public bodies "to respect, on the basis of equality of treatment, the identity and ethos of both communities in Northern Ireland" (21). That very specific brief—to identify human rights that are particular to Northern Ireland—runs counter to the universalism of instruments like the European convention. The brief goes further in its particularism, privileging equality for "both communities." These brief phrases indicate the profound degree to which human rights discourse has been suffused with local political concerns. Thus, it is unsurprising that the process of consultation became captive to local ethnopolitics.

The call for a bill of rights is not new. Brice Dickson (2010) describes proposals by a Liberal Catholic MP in the Stormont parliament in 1964 (16), as well as subsequent proposals in 1966, 1967, and 1968 (17). Throughout the 1970s, the Standing Advisory Commission on Human Rights in Northern Ireland considered a bill of rights, but discussions did not yield results (Dickson 2010). In the 1990s, the local human rights NGO Committee on the Administration of Justice (CAJ) revived the bill of rights idea (CAJ 1990, 1993, 1997). Human rights advocates gave the idea new momentum as talks opened. Dickson, a cofounder of CAJ and first head of the HRC, recalls that, by the time the HRC began consultations on a bill, the incorporation of the European convention into domestic law by the Human Rights Act 1998 "slightly took the shine off the Bill of Rights concept" (2010: 366). Nevertheless, following consultations, the HRC published draft proposals in 2001 (NIHRC 2001). Political parties, grassroots campaigners, and some academics were critical of the proposals (Dickson 2010; Whitaker 2010); others saw merit in them. For example, Hamber (2003) argues that the proposals incorporated victims' rights and called for a process to examine the conduct of both state and nonstate actors during the conflict (1090–91).

Revised suggestions did not satisfy the British and Irish governments or local unionist parties (NIHRC 2004; Dickson 2010). After a third draft in 2005 (NIHRC 2005) and reorganization, the HRC created the Bill of Rights Forum in 2006. The forum invited fourteen members from political parties, fourteen representatives of civil society organizations, and an international chair to produce yet another proposal (Whitaker 2010; Dickson 2010). Whitaker (2010) conducted fieldwork during the forum process, and she argues that the process facilitated substantive discussions of rights beyond the communal logics of unionism and nationalism. Although the process was inclusive, the forum's final report indicates deep dissension (Bill of Rights Forum 2008). In a 2009 submission to Parliament, a disillusioned Dickson wrote, "Those attending the Forum did not work in a spirit of give and take. The Forum's report is, as a result, a most disappointing document. The only positive thing that can be said of it is that it makes explicit, if crudely at times, the vast differences of opinion that exist on this topic between the political parties in Northern Ireland (and in civil society too)."[9] The HRC produced its own set of formal recommendations for a bill of rights (NIHRC 2008), but more public debate greeted these recommendations, and the government held yet another public consultation in 2010.

Conflicts about human rights throughout this process reveal and reproduce local political values. The communal character of these debates has been obvious from the outset, with unionist parties treating human rights as a nationalist issue (see Whitaker 2010). Other debates along a Left-Right axis, however, are more related to the curious politics of human rights after the GFA. For example, the 2008 recommendations included a "right to health" and a right to "an adequate standard of living" (NIHRC 2008: 45–46). The revised 1996 European Social Charter was the source for many of these suggestions; the charter expands basic economic and social rights that are complementary to those in the European convention. Although the UK is a signatory to the revised charter, the charter has not been ratified. Chong (2010) writes that Northern Irish HRC commissioners believed their proposals would create "the strongest national legal document to protect [social and economic] rights in the world" (44).

For many human rights campaigners, the foregrounding of social and economic rights was a welcome development. Nevertheless, the recommendations demonstrate a more recent phenomenon of the postconflict era—that is, nonpartisans resorted to the human rights process, rather than political channels, to pursue social democratic goals. Meanwhile, the right mobilized through unionist political parties to oppose the establishment of social and economic rights in law. Jeff Dudgeon, now a Conservative decades after his early radicalism and successful European challenge to the Northern Irish sodomy law, wrote scathingly that the bill showed that "The industry [of human rights advocates] simply cannot stop itself doing politics through human rights."[10] The spectacle of one of the most well-known human rights plaintiffs in the world condemning the proposals is merely one of the many ironies produced by the quest for a bill of rights. Meanwhile, Brice Dickson expressed profound disappointment that "some of the most prominent and respected NGOs and individuals working in the human rights field in the UK . . . have played the political game, arguing that a Bill of Rights is not required because we already have the Human Rights Act 1998."[11]

Whitaker (2010) argues that the diverse debates and positions taken by a variety of actors in the consultations themselves disprove a "communalization of rights" analysis. She concedes, however, that the final recommendations contained "scant rapprochement between unionists on the one hand and nationalists and most civil society representatives on the other" (32).

Even Left-Right discussions of the proposals, in the last analysis, degenerated to communal contest. For example, at the McCluskey Civil Rights Summer School in 2009, the PUP representative reversed the party's earlier support for economic rights, arguing that the proposals were antithetical to Protestant self-reliance and individualism.

Unionists are not alone in objecting to postconflict human rights discourse. Some republican critics regard the rights-based account of the conflict as a political fable. They are skeptical of the story of a state compromised by human rights violations and replaced by new institutions that promote a culture of human rights. Instead, they see this rights discourse as a tool that legitimizes Sinn Féin's newfound political power and upward mobility for some nationalists. For example, Barra McGrory, a lawyer from a nationalist background, was appointed director of public prosecutions in 2011. His father P. J. McGrory was a well-known attorney who represented the families of IRA members killed by security forces before the European Court of Human Rights.[12] The *Irish Times* called Barra McGrory's appointment "revolutionary" because in the Stormont era nationalists simply did not hold such high state offices.[13] Nonetheless, his job—prosecuting alleged offenders on behalf of a state that remains part of the UK—has led some republicans to deride him as "Barra the Brit." These, then, are the existing human rights politics in Northern Ireland: the various arguments voiced in these debates are not reducible to unionism and nationalism, yet somehow arguments predictably coalesce around these categories.

Under the new leadership of Michael O'Flaherty, the HRC produced a rebuttal to critiques of its bill of rights recommendations (NIHRC 2012). Consultations are now underway for a UK-wide bill of rights, and the HRC remains hopeful that its recommendations for Northern Ireland could be part of broader human rights protections in the context of devolution. Yet in practical terms, any British government, Tory or Labour, is unlikely to approve of a local bill of rights in the absence of cross-party consensus. In 2011, the Human Rights Consortium, a local NGO that lobbies for a bill of rights, commissioned a public opinion poll (Human Rights Consortium 2011; Ipsos Mori 2011), which found that more than 83 percent of unionists and 86 percent of nationalists support a bill of rights. However, Dickson was scathing about the poll:

> That is just sophistry, because it is based on survey results where the questions asked were of the motherhood-and-apple-pie variety. Do

you think you should have a right to an adequate standard of living? Do you want the right to the highest attainable standard of physical and mental health (not just health *care*)? Do you want the right to work? Who would answer no to such questions? But who would answer yes if the question was, would you like a group of rich white elderly men to decide on whether your standard of living was adequate or your accommodation was appropriate to your needs? That would be the result of allowing the extent of socio-economic rights in Northern Ireland to be determined by Northern Ireland's Court of Appeal and, on appeal, by the UK's Supreme Court.[14]

Who Is the Subject of the Good Friday Agreement?

Another example of the slow trudge to equality policy is the story of "A Shared Future," the long-awaited community relations policy, now called "Programme for Cohesion, Sharing and Integration." Following the GFA, the power-sharing government pledged to create a comprehensive strategy to promote equality and community relations. In 2001–2002, the government consulted hundreds of organizations, and Jeremy Harbison presented a report in January 2002 (Harbison 2002a,b), yet no legislation emerged. The government launched another consultation in 2003, issued another report in 2004, and published a policy framework in 2005; full implementation was deferred until devolution was restored (Community Relations Unit 2003, 2005; Darby and Knox 2004). After devolution in 2007, Sinn Féin and the DUP disagreed about how to approach the issue, and the policy languished until David Ford of the Alliance Party demanded action in exchange for serving in the executive. In July 2010, the First and Deputy First Ministers Office opened a new consultation; in May 2013 it published a strategy for combating sectarianism, racism, and hate crime (OFMDFM 2010a, 2013); and, as noted in Chapter 6, it promised to release recommendations regarding sexual orientation at a later date. During consultations and debates lasting more than a decade, smaller parties such as the Alliance Party and the now dissolved Women's Coalition criticized the Executive's communalized approach to equality; a frustrated Alliance party withdrew from the policy working group in 2012, two years after it had demanded action. More than fifteen years after the settlement, these policy discussions remained an arena for major parties to contest national emblems, parades, and past violence. In September 2013,

Richard Haass, former U.S. envoy to Northern Ireland, returned to chair more talks on these issues. Inaction in this area is yet another example of how the "parity of esteem" logic prevails in postconflict governance, privileging communalized rights—and paralyzing decision-making. Rights discourse continues to work in synergy with communal political subjectivity, and has failed to displace contested national identities with universal individual subjects sharing common humanity.

Local gay rights advocacy offers a sharp contrast to the way in which human rights have been absorbed into local communal contests. Comparing local and global gay rights activism to this dominant rights discourse is instructive. Unlike the GFA brief to identify rights that fit the particular circumstances of Northern Ireland, the Yogyakarta Principles use existing international law to recognize how rights are denied to individuals on the basis of sexual orientation or gender identity (O'Flaherty and Fisher 2008). Local gay rights advocacy concerns the practical ramifications of equality in law for individual queer people at work, in school, in housing, and in everyday safety—rather than issuing equality claims for their community's ethos or aspirations. Both rights discourse and existing legal frameworks have enabled gay activists to build political associations beyond dominant ethnopolitics. Queer activists have succeeded in establishing alliances across communal blocs. Simply put, rights discourse resituated and transformed local debates concerning gay rights, rather than absorbing rights talk into ethnopolitics. Marginalized political subjects transformed local political debates.

The potential of rights discourse to produce new subjects and subjectivities is its greatest advantage for those who view it as a tool for progressive politics (see Goodale 2009b; Speed 2008). Recent critics of the proliferation of human rights discourse, however, are uneasy with indeterminate subjects of rights (see Balfour and Cadava 2004). Dissatisfaction with contemporary human rights politics has led some scholars to revisit the work of political theorist Hannah Arendt ([1951] 2004; e.g., Moyn 2010). Arendt forcefully asserted the primacy of national rights in the wake of World War II, arguing that rights were dependent on citizenship—indeed, that human rights were the rights of last resort, the rights of the stateless and displaced who had no other effective rights. However, in Northern Ireland rights of citizenship are at the core of ethnopolitical battles; rather than offering a release from conflict, national rights sustain it, and serve tactical purposes in a variety of situations.

In privileging "two communities," postconflict human rights talk and practice actually limit potential transformations of political subjectivity and action while privileging communal, collective subjects. Indeed, Finlay (2008) argues that community activists "have tended to manufacture and objectify difference and to dig in behind it. After the GFA, such reification has not been checked or mitigated even by a tenuous notion of a common culture—all there is, is the constitutional right to hold simultaneously both a British and an Irish passport" (288). As Finlay observes, the ubiquity of opportunistic arguments about political rights to nationality trivializes these rights into a tactical resource, restricting and steering other politics into these terms. For example, in 2012, while contesting an Irish judgment of bankruptcy against him, former IRA prisoner Thomas McFeely declared, "As a British citizen I have always objected to being forced into bankruptcy in a foreign jurisdiction purely on the basis that I have a judgment liability in that state. . . . I maintain this is a breach of my human rights and that it is objectionable to expose me as a British citizen to the punitive bankruptcy laws of another country."[15] McFeely, like some other well-known Irish property developers, had declared bankruptcy in the UK, claiming residency in the north. The reasoning was simple: Irish bankruptcy law is stringent, and debts may not be discharged for up to twelve years. In contrast, the UK process may last as little as a year. What made his case most remarkable is that McFeely was formerly so dedicated to his Irish citizenship that he endured imprisonment for IRA activity.

As the McFeely example demonstrates, specifying a national basis for rights does not correct the excesses of rights talk. Indeed, just as the GFA's communal logic reproduces limited political subjectivities, disciplining human rights talk in this fashion also restricts political subjectivity and its expression. In this regard, theoretical considerations of human rights and subjectivity offer important insights. Rancière (2004) asks, "Who is the subject of the rights of man?" He answers his own question by linking political subjectivity and subjectivization. Human rights, he writes, "are not the rights of a single subject that would be at once the source and the bearer of the rights and would only use the rights that she or he possesses. If this was the case, indeed, it would be easy to prove, as Arendt does, that such a subject does not exist. . . . The subject of rights is the subject, or more accurately the process of subjectivization" (302). This is a clear rejection of the "suspicion that the 'man' of the Rights of Man was a mere abstraction because the only real rights were the rights of citizens, the rights attached to a national community as such" (298).

In Rancière's formulation, political subjects—in the sense of both the agents of politics and the governed—are not abstractions, but persons produced in particular historical circumstances. Because subjects emerge differently, in different contexts, the subject of the rights of man is indeterminate rather than abstract. Therefore, "Political subjects are not definite collectivities. They . . . set out a question or a dispute (*litige*) about who is included in their count. Correspondingly, freedom and equality are not predicates belonging to definite subjects. Political predicates are open predicates: they open up a dispute about what they exactly entail and whom they concern in which cases" (2004: 303).

Rather than Althusser's (1971) "interpellation," whereby states create subordinate subjects, Rancière's definition of subjectivization establishes rights as instruments for political agency. Althusser's Stalinist Marxism was inadequate for analyzing either the subjects or politics that emerged in the international protests of 1968 or the new social movements they produced pursuing feminism, sexual liberation, and environmentalism (Wolin 2010). Butler (1993) suggests that the inadequacies of Althusser's theory of interpellation stem from not recognizing disobedience and from assuming that power is totally effective. She argues that "The law might not only be refused, but it might also be ruptured, forced into a rearticulation that calls into question the monotheistic force of its own unilateral operation" (122). A more robust theory of subjectivization recognizes that political agency emerges when rights are claimed, when subjectivity is mobilized to produce subjects as agents who exercise rights, rather than servile clients of the state (Rancière 2004: 302).

Since the 1960s, rights have become a lingua franca for producing disobedient subjects. Ignatieff (1999) argues, "Rights language has been central not simply to the protection, but also to the production of modern individuals" (323). Recent empirical studies of rights claims support the analysis of Ignatieff and Rancière. These studies demonstrate that the subjects of rights cannot be assumed and are not the abstract product of subjection to a state, but instead are produced through processes of subjectivity that include the state as a "field of relational power" (see essays in Cowan et al. 2001; Wilson and Mitchell 2003; Wilson 1997b). As Cowan (2006) notes, rights claims may produce subjectivities and subjects, just as subjects may produce claims. Often, a synergetic process takes place, and rights claims and subjectivity are mutually productive. Subjects are not conjured from thin air by rights claims, of course, but may transform existing subjectivities, with the language and logic of rights acting as a catalyst.

This processual rather than definite understanding of "subject" directs us to empirical questions. How rights discourse became an instrument of both war and peace in Northern Ireland is one such question, and central to it is the way rights discourse simultaneously reflects, reproduces, and restricts the protagonists of the conflict: the actual subjects of political action. The early 1970s was a key period when these patterns and processes were established. Rights discourse and its subjects established both liberatory and communalized politics over time, and this history lingers into the present. Recognizing this legacy is necessary for understanding the contemporary contradictions of human rights politics in Northern Ireland. It is simultaneously part of the peace process and a form of war by other means. These historical origins also underscore how rights discourse became an ambiguous political practice, rather than a direct journey to either conflict or peace.

Unionist minimalism regarding human rights is congruent with recent critiques of human rights politics globally. Such critiques often treat human rights discourse as responsible for a politicization of human rights, straying far from legal principles, individual subjects, and universal themes. In this vein, Wilson (2007) writes, "Human rights have gone from a general list of what governments should not do to their citizens in the 1940s to a full blown moral-theological-political vision of the good life" (349). Unionist opposition to a bill of rights, however, does not originate from this principled critique of global human rights advocacy. It stems from the political uses of rights discourse locally. Dickson (2010) argues, "The reality is that human rights, like so many concepts, had by 1981 become a propaganda tool in the war of words between all sides to the conflict in Northern Ireland" (22).

As this book explains, even liberatory appropriations of human rights talk at the grassroots level repeatedly fractured on the blocs of nationalism and unionism. This hidden history indicates that the problem with treating human rights as a vehicle for peace is not about a unionist veto on human rights. If a large group of people who are party to the peace process do not accept human rights as a peace-promoting vehicle, it is extremely difficult to imagine a way for human rights, in law or discourse, to overcome these perceptions and functionally promote peace. This is an unfortunate legacy of rights talk's incorporation in the conflict. Over a long period, in everyday advocacy and NGO campaigning, basic rights have been appropriated, even diminished, to fit the local conflict. As such, they have been frequently transformed into resources for conflict. Advocates of human rights in the postconflict era fail to recognize this nuance at the peril of their larger liberatory project.

Yet the solution to counterproductive or even disingenuous appropriations of rights discourse is not a return to legal authority. Human rights will no doubt continue to be used for war by other means in Northern Ireland, rather than as a straightforward instrument of peace. Yet human rights discourse has also promoted progressive politics and social rapprochements. The rhetoric and practice of freedom of association helped paramilitaries' transition to democratic politics; gay rights advocacy secured legal equality and promotes social change.

Historical contexts shape the production, reception, and practical consequences of rights discourse. Therefore, allocating rights to conflicting political collectivities, unsurprisingly, reproduces them. Yet using human rights discourse to resituate local conflicts within broader terms of reference has the potential to transform conflicts and allow new political subjects to mobilize. Persuading activists to approach human rights in a narrow, legal fashion will foreclose those possibilities. A measured critique will empirically analyze the politics that direct or suffuse rights discourse and its reception, rather than scrutinize and dismiss rights discourse for hints of politicization.

In Greek myth, after Pandora released tremendous suffering into the world, hope was last to leave the box. Disciplining human rights talk is a bit like returning hope to the box, while all the ills of the world remain at large.

NOTES

Chapter 1. Whose Rights and Whose Peace?

1. Pseudonyms—indicated by quotation marks on first occurrence—are used throughout the book because research was conducted on the understanding that anonymity would be protected. When more contextual information would make a person more recognizable, such as the neighborhood where he or she lives and works, I omit this information. I have altered pseudonyms each chapter to prevent cumulative recognition. Actual names are used by mutual agreement only.

2. IRA and PIRA are often used interchangeably. PIRA is the main republican paramilitary grouping that was active during the conflict, advocating a united Ireland. PIRA distinguishes the mainstream group from smaller factions like the RIRA, and the Official IRA, from which PIRA split in 1969. See the glossary entry for PIRA for more information.

3. Since 1997, when severe disorder and intimidation surrounding Orange parades displaced many families, mobile phones have been distributed to local leaders to monitor the community tensions. Using the phones, they contact leaders in neighboring communities and attempt to defuse situations. Jarman 1999b, an anthropologist who has worked extensively with grassroots conflict resolution groups, worked with the establishment of the first mobile phone network and describes its rationale, formation, and effects.

4. For published accounts of respective republican and unionist critiques, see McIntyre 2008 and Vance 2008.

5. Following the Irish War of Independence, the island of Ireland was partitioned into two jurisdictions, the Irish Free State in twenty-six southern counties and Northern Ireland in six northern counties. Northern Ireland remained part of the United Kingdom. See glossary entries for "Partition" and "Republic."

6. Funding for research in Belfast was provided by the UK Economic and Social Research Council, the Wenner-Gren Foundation for Anthropological Research, and the U.S. Institute of Peace.

7. Special precautions regarding my travel, notes, and recordings were necessary to protect the identities of research participants. The legitimate anxiety, mistrust, and outright fear people felt after years of violence required conducting myself so as not to exacerbate fear. I resided in the city center and organized my schedule so as not to cross

peace lines. Crisscrossing the lines between areas in west Belfast can be highly suspicious, if not downright dangerous, even in relatively "peaceful" times.

8. I have never engaged in a study of paramilitarism, and, although I met and worked with people who had paramilitary connections, I was not concerned with past or current paramilitary affiliations and did not inquire into or gather information about these activities.

9. See Meehan and Murphy 2008; Hart and Hanley 2005; Ryan, Meehan, and O'Riordan 2005; Hart 2005; Boldt and Ó Ceilleachair 2005; Ryan 2005.

10. See Bourgois 2001, 2003 for a review of how different types of violence have been categorized and the embedding of violence in everyday life after conflict.

11. Full text available online at the Cain Web Service, cain.ulst.ac.uk/. Adams was speaking during a suspension of power sharing, at a time when unionists were pressing for decommissioning.

12. "Spectacular" is a term used by paramilitaries to refer to major bombs that cause tremendous property damage and often human casualties.

13. Members of the legislature created by the GFA are called MLAs. See glossary entry.

14. "Provo" and "provie" are colloquial terms for members of the Provisional Irish Republican Army. See glossary entry for "PIRA."

15. Henry McDonald, "Opinion: How the Provos 'Sold Out,'" November 19, 2008, BelfastTelegraph.co.uk.

16. Internment without trial of suspected paramilitaries was introduced in the early years of the conflict. See glossary entry for "Internment."

17. Called the Twelfth, it commemorates the Battle of the Boyne, where forces for a Protestant claimant to the British throne, William of Orange, defeated armies for his rival Catholic claimant, James. The battle took place in eastern Ireland. See glossary entries for "Twelfth" and "Orange Order."

18. Named for U.S. senator George Mitchell, who facilitated the peace talks, these were undertakings to use nonviolent tactics for political change. For some republicans, this was a renunciation of the moral authority of the armed struggle for Irish sovereignty.

19. The UK voted in the UN for adoption in 1948. It signed both covenants in 1968 and ratified them in 1976. Ireland signed the covenants in 1973 and ratified them in 1989.

20. UK residents' right of individual petition was not established until 1966.

21. The UK signed the charter in 1961 and ratified it in 1962. Ireland signed the charter in 1961 and ratified it in 1964.

22. The UK signed the revised social charter in 1997 but has not yet ratified some elements. Ireland signed and ratified the revised charter in 2000.

23. See Jean-Klein and Riles 2005 for a discussion of how the globalized character of human rights discourse is often assumed in research.

24. In 1996, a police officer on the security detail of unionist politician Nigel Dodds was shot by the IRA while the politician visited his son in the children's hospital at the Royal. Opposition to the closure of the unit was not limited to loyalists; constitutional

nationalist legislators and women's party legislators for the south Belfast constituency also opposed the closure in the interests of serving the area they represented.

25. In the UK, Remembrance Day honors armed forces members who died in the line of duty; it was first commemorated in 1919, and wearing a red poppy in the lapel has traditionally signified one's recognition of the day. Veterans Day in the United States shares an origin and traditions with Remembrance Day.

26. The proceedings of the debate are available at the Northern Ireland Assembly website, niassembly.gov.uk.

27. *Donaldson v. the United Kingdom*-56975/09 [2011] ECHR 210.

28. Quoted in Mary Holland, "A Very Good Friday," *Observer*, April 11, 1998.

29. See Botes 2003 for an overview of debates about conflict transformation.

30. European Court of Human Rights, "Fourth Section Decision as to the Admissibility of Application no. 28326/0 by P. F. and E. F. against the United Kingdom," at British and Irish Legal Information Institute (BAILII) web site, www.bailii.org/.

31. Information about this work over the past decade can be viewed and downloaded at the Northern Ireland Human Rights Commission website, www.nihrc.org.

32. Unfortunately, arterial damage is a real risk in such shootings, in addition to loss of limbs and other permanent disabilities; Andrew Kearney's death on July 18, 1998, was a highly publicized incident of arterial injury, a year to the day after the 1997 ceasefire (see McKittrick et al. 1999: 1436–37).

33. The new policing service has combined previous statistics and publishes them annually. There was a rise in both loyalist and republican shootings and beatings following the ceasefires and again after the GFA. A decline occurred in 2004–2005, with a sharp upswing in 2010, followed by decreases in 2011 and 2012. These statistics are aggregated, but breakdowns by paramilitary group and type of assault are located in the statistical reports (see PSNI 2004, 2012a); see appendix to this chapter.

34. Air date August 13, 1996. The title was a reference to republican hero James Connolly's *Labour in Irish History*.

35. For detailed discussion of these projects and their role in conflict transformation, see Shirlow and McEvoy 2008, McAuley et al. 2010, and McEvoy 1999.

36. Indeed, this legal reality was reflected in Northern Ireland in a minimal system for state compensation to victims during the conflict. Nevertheless, the proposal of a larger scheme for compensation became intensely contentious in early 2009; see Chapter 5 for a longer discussion.

37. See Dickson 2010 for a comprehensive account of legal challenges.

38. The remaining 214 deaths are attributed to "others."

39. McKittrick et al. attributes eighty deaths to "unknown/other" actors.

40. Multiple state inquiries have been conducted over the years, including several since the settlement, discussed at greater length in Chapter 5. NGOs and international bodies have also conducted inquiries. For a list of inquiries with associated reports, see "Collusion Between Security Forces and Paramilitaries," Cain Web Service, "Key Issues." For discussion of collusion in the killings of two lawyers, see McEvoy 2011.

41. Bradshaw himself was not closeted (see McKittrick et al. 1999: 1407).

42. Political geographers especially have documented and analyzed these processes over time. See Boal 1969, 1978, 1982; more recently, see Shirlow and Murtagh 2006.

43. Explaining the circumstances in which his phone number became known would compromise his anonymity.

44. Speech to the Northern Ireland Human Rights Commission annual conference in Belfast, September 16, 2010, http://www.attorneygeneralni.gov.uk/hrc_speech.pdf.

45. See "Board Shoots Itself in the Foot" (Editorial), *PoliceBeat*, February 2011.

Chapter 2. The Usual Suspects

1. Patrick Rooney was killed by police machine-gun fire as he and his family attempted to hide in their flat from the fighting. The Scarman Report on the 1969 violence found that the police had fired into the flats without justification (Government of Northern Ireland 1972).

2. From 1949 to 1967, the rate of British sterling to the U.S. dollar was fixed at £1 = $2.80. I used this rate, given the time period in question. See Feinstein 1994: 103. The practice of linking property, and property value, to enfranchisement ended in 1969.

3. The practice of internment was used only in certain periods, however. Its reintroduction in the early 1970s accelerated the descent into conflict. The Republic of Ireland had a similar special powers act, Offences Against the State (Amendment) Act 1940, and, like its northern counterpart, practiced censorship during the conflict.

4. The Easter Rising was the initial Irish rebellion in 1916 against British rule; eventually, it began a war that led to Irish independence. The 1916 anniversary of the Battle of the Somme is significant in Ireland, especially for unionists, because many Irishmen died fighting for the British Army in that battle; see Graham and Shirlow 2002.

5. See Devlin 1988, McCluskey 1989, Purdie 1990, Dooley 1998, Prince 2007, O'Dochartaigh 1994. The success of comparisons to the U.S. movement is apparent in their staying power; it became a central theme not just of rhetoric but of several later books, for example, Dooley 1998 and O'Dochartaigh 1994.

6. July 9, 1969, Gogarty Papers, Public Record Office of Northern Ireland (PRONI) D3253/1/3/5 A and B.

7. For a detailed account of the movement's organization and these events, see Purdie 1990.

8. "Communication Regarding Violations of Human Rights in Northern Ireland," submitted to the Secretary-General of the United Nations by Northern Ireland Civil Rights Association, Association for Legal Justice, and National Council for Civil Liberties, 1973, Boyle Papers, PRONI D3297/10.

9. McCann became less sympathetic over time and became critical of PIRA strategies and actions.

10. The phrase is taken from taken from Eoin McNamee's 1994 novel about the Shankill butchers, the colloquial name for a loyalist murder gang in the 1970s (13).

11. The term "two-up, two-down" refers to the number of rooms on each story of the house—a sitting room and kitchen on the ground floor and two bedrooms upstairs. They were also called "kitchen" houses to distinguish them from the somewhat larger "parlor houses," which were also terraced but had a third, larger sitting room on the ground floor.

12. Hepburn 1990 notes that, for both Catholics and Protestants, "dependence on female labour" was a reality for generations, since well before the Great Depression of the 1930s, due to low wages for men in the dominant industry of shipbuilding (76).

13. The split in the IRA did not occur until December 1969, when PIRA was formed; the experiences of IRA members like Andrew in Clonard were a large factor in their rejection of what became known as the Official IRA and their alignment with PIRA.

14. In October 1969, when the Hunt Report recommended disbandment of the B-Specials and disarming of the RUC, among other reforms, loyalists protested on the Shankill Road. In a brutal irony, since the protest was putatively in defense of the police, a riot broke out, and Victor Arbuckle was shot dead—the first police officer to die in the conflict, at the hands of loyalists.

15. NICRC 1974. This report was prepared by John Darby and Geoffrey Morris, but, in its original edition, the NICRC is the corporate author.

16. Military and police control were more firmly reestablished over these areas until July 31, 1972. Operation Motorman involved thousands of troops entering Free Derry and west Belfast with bulldozers and armored cars, tearing down barricades and asserting state presence.

17. After the attack on the Long March in January, Derry residents of the Bogside area had put up barricades and declared the area "Free Derry." This lasted for about a week, when police were allowed back into the area. After the August 1969 riots, "Free Belfast" was established in the nationalist areas of the Falls and Ardoyne but lasted about one month (Arthur 1974). Free Derry was reintroduced, lasting from August until October of that year. Two years later, in August 1971, with the reintroduction of internment, the most intense rioting since 1969 took place, barricades went up, and the police were expelled once more across nationalist areas of Northern Ireland. After the Bloody Sunday shootings of civil rights marchers in Derry on January 30, 1972, Free Derry was reinstated, although Free Belfast was not reestablished.

18. The UK did not ratify the International Covenant on Economic, Social and Cultural Rights until 1976. Article 11 recognizes housing rights as part of a basic standard of living.

19. Articles describing Shankill people's belief in a conspiracy of systematic depopulation appeared in the *Sunday News*, March 6, 1977, 3 and December 4, 1977, 7; *Irish Times*, September 30, 1978, 5; and notably an article entitled "Save the Shankill?" endorsed this explanation in *Fortnight*, December 1977, written by Jonathan Stephenson 1977 of the Northern Ireland Council of Social Services. *Fortnight* is a journal concerned with Northern Irish politics.

20. The phrase "Armalite and ballot box" became shorthand to describe republicans' combination of armed struggle and contesting political elections. "Armalite" is a reference to PIRA, "ballot box" to the political party Sinn Féin. See Glossary.

Chapter 3. Peace Sells—Who's Buying?

1. This was based on Robson et al. 1994. Robson's research using 1991 census data was a significant analysis of the spatial distribution of deprivation. It was the basis for new policy initiatives like Targeting Social Need and Making Belfast Work, an urban regeneration agency focused on human needs and skills rather than simply the built environment.

2. This convergence is in terms of straightforward economic analysis, not the more complex workings of class as a social relationship, although the social and cultural expansion of the Catholic middle class is undeniable. See Thompson (1991 [1963]) on class as a social, historical happening.

3. Local human rights work by groups such as the Committee for the Administration of Justice became more influential in the 1980s, advocating policing and justice reforms to ensure basic civil rights, but this chapter concentrates on economic concerns as a driver of grassroots rights discourse and economic development efforts in the western areas of the city where violence was intense.

4. BBC broadcast by Harold Wilson, May 25, 1974, at www.cain.ulst.ac.uk. The Ulster Workers' Council strike in 1974 was a series of loyalist protests that brought down the short-lived Sunningdale settlement. See the glossary entry for Sunningdale.

5. There are 890 areas measured in this study. The geographic units are called "Super Output Areas" and constitute about 2,000 people each. They are usually based on electoral wards and subdivisions of electoral wards. The statistics also use a smaller unit, output areas, of which there are 5,022, with roughly 350 people in each.

6. Cited in Brett 1990: 432.

7. Article 10 of November 15, 1985, Anglo-Irish Agreement: an international fund for "the economic and social development of those areas of both parts of Ireland which have suffered most severely from the consequences of the instability of recent years," Supplemental Treaty, September 18, 1986, International Fund for Ireland constituted.

8. To calculate the historical exchange rate, I used the web tool at http://fxtop.com/en/historical-exchange-rates.php.

9. Seán MacBride was an Irish politician who served in the IRA during the Irish War of Independence. He was an international human rights campaigner who was awarded both the Nobel Peace Prize and the Lenin Peace Prize. However, his legacy and commitment to human rights principles are contested in Ireland. For veneration of McBride, see Tolley 2009. For an alternative view, hear Senator David Norris's lecture, part of the "Speaking Ill of the Dead" series, recorded by the RTÉ, at the National Museum in Dublin in March 2006: http://itunes.apple.com/us/podcast/rte-speaking-ill-of-the-dead/id207348624 (last accessed February 5, 2012).

10. For a list of the principles, see Cochrane 2007: 219.

11. See, for example, the PPR response to a proposal for integrated public housing in 2012, titled "Equality Can't Wait—Implement the Law," PPR web site, http://www .pprproject.org.

12. For a journalistic account of PIRA's on-off, sometimes instrumental, engagement with Left politics, see Moloney 2007.

Chapter 4. The Politics We Deserve

1.Fair Employment Tribunal 2012, case ref. 75/11 FET). The full decision was made available by the Equality Commission at equalityni.org.

2. See Finlay 2010 for the historical origins of parity of esteem with the commission.

3. See especially section 6 of the GFA, "Rights, Safeguards and Equality of Opportunity," which emphasizes "the identity and ethos of both communities and parity of esteem."

4. Gerry Adams was the leader of Sinn Féin and John Hume of the SDLP.

5. "Track two" is differentiated from "track one," diplomacy by operating outside state and party systems.

6. Some scholars trace the idea farther back, to the Scottish Enlightenment; see Seligman 1992.

7. The program was delivered in a series of three phases, with different priorities in each phase.

8. Although the money was administered under the European Structural Funds, which are administered from the EU to poorer regions, it was theoretically additional to Northern Ireland's existing share of the fund.

9. "Latest Plan to Tackle Inequality Crucial to the North Peace," *Irish Times*, March 12, 1998, 16.

10. Critiques include its moralistic roots (Seligman 1992); specificity to Western modernity (Comaroff and Comaroff 1999; Hann 1996; Hearn 1997; Medeiros 2001; Verdury 1996); descriptive inadequacy and imprecision (Gellner 1994; Dunn 1996; Spulbeck 1996; Buchowski 1996; Sampson 1996); and its political deployment to foster neoliberalism and undermine fragile democratization processes and states (Elyachar 2005; Paley 2001).

11. Elections of negotiating parties were held on May 30, 1996, and they followed stipulations laid out in the Northern Ireland (Entry to Negotiations) Act of 1996. These stipulations used proportional representation to bring the ten most successful parties to the table. The rules were constructed with the small loyalist parties in mind (PUP, UDP), since these parties, associated with paramilitaries, did not have electoral support as large as the four main parties.

12. "Magic" here is a term used by older Belfast people to mean wonderful, in the same fashion that some people in the United States use "awesome."

13. Chris's comment was a reference to the Grand Old Duke of York, a loyalist nickname for Ian Paisley, derived from a nursery rhyme. In the rhyme, the Duke marched 10,000 men up the hill but did not go over it, instead marching them back down. It refers

to the widespread loyalist sentiment that unionist politicians, especially Paisley, encouraged their violent campaigns and then publicly condemned violence when it reflected badly on themselves. The 1974 and 1977 strikes were key moments that cemented this loyalist resentment.

14. The relevant law is Children and Young Persons (Northern Ireland) Act 1968.

15. The largest Orange parade on July 12 commemorates Protestant King William's 1690 defeat of Catholic King James's forces at the River Boyne in eastern Ireland. The pope at the time supported the Protestant king in the interests of European stability.

16. In late 1997, a member of the INLA murdered antipeace process loyalist Billy Wright. This murder, carried out in a high security prison, led to allegations of state collusion and will be discussed further in the next chapter. In the dark days of January 1998, loyalists killed eight Catholic civilians, working men such as bouncers and taxi drivers, in a retaliatory series of sectarian assassinations, including Terry Enright. Peace talks, nevertheless, continued, with a brief suspension of the loyalist parties for associated paramilitaries' involvement in the killings and a later suspension of Sinn Féin for PIRA activity.

17. See Cochrane 2001, Cochrane and Dunn 2002 for extensive discussion of types and tactics of community-based NGOs—cross-community, intercommunity, single-identity, and more.

18. Even Lederach encountered the tension between the two sides. At one SICDP event, some nationalists withdrew at short notice, feeling that the conference excluded Sinn Féin. The influence of conflict transformation has endured in the region, especially after prisoner releases; see McAuley et al. 2010; Shirlow et al. 2010; Shirlow and McEvoy 2008; McEvoy et al. 2004.

19. Peace II added the caveat that, to meet the criteria of reconciliation, groups "should at least be ready to participate in cross-community initiatives" (Special European Union Programmes Body 2003: 41).

20. "Policing Parade Trouble Cost £3m," news.bbc.co.uk, October 31, 2005.

21. Indeed, in 1997, the FEC was under Baroness Denton, a British minister whose private aide was determined to have harassed, in a sectarian fashion, a Catholic civil servant during the 1995 Drumcree standoff. This incident occurred in the Department of Agriculture, not the FEC, but Denton's decision to transfer the victim of the harassment rather than her aide intensified the ill feelings. The FEC employee was acutely aware of this recent scandal.

22. For historical background to the order, see Bew 2007. Analyses of parade disputes are plentiful, e.g., Jarman and Bryan 1996 and Bryan 2000a,b, 2006a.

23. Limits on assembly and expression were usually legally justified by the European Commission's 1961 decision in *Lawless v. Ireland* which permitted the suspension of basic civil and political rights, even due process, when "there was a public emergency threatening the life of the nation" (Dickson 2010: 70). Dickson characterizes this decision as "regrettable" because it held that Ireland's internment without trial of Gerard Lawless, suspected IRA member, did not breach the European convention. The parades

commission has been challenged on human rights grounds for its restrictions on assembly, but it remains in place, with the devolved government failing to devise an alternative. For fuller discussion see Dickson (2010: chap. 11, "Freedom of Expression, Belief, and Assembly," 300–339).

24. See "Orange Threat to 'Paralyse' the North Is Condemned," *Irish Times*, July 10, 1998.

25. See "Violent Incidents," *Irish Times*, July 15, 1998.

26. See "Executive Must Find Housing for 141 Catholic Families," *Irish Times*, July 24, 1998.

27. The journal is no longer published but is held in archive form by the Indiana University-Purdue University Program of Digital Scholarship.

28. Henry McDonald, "Martin McGuinness Condemns Real IRA's Derry Bomb," *theguardian.com*, October 5, 2010.

29. Quangos are appointed bodies to which some state responsibility or authority has been devolved. See Glossary.

30. Northern Ireland Life and Times Survey—2003, Political Attitudes module.

31. Northern Ireland Life and Times Survey—2010, Political Attitudes module.

32. Haase and Pratschke 1999 studied Peace I uptake for the Northern Ireland Statistics and Research Agency to reach this conclusion.

Chapter 5. No Justice, No Peace

1. Local councils no longer oversaw major public services, such as housing; the reasons for these restrictions, past discriminatory practices, are discussed in Chapter 2. For a full discussion of direct rule, see Birrell 2009.

2. A photograph of the plaque is online on the Cain website, cain.ulst.ac.uk.

3. For example, the coroner, Major Hubert O'Neill said, "They were shooting innocent people. These people may have been taking part in a march that was banned but that does not justify the troops coming in and firing live rounds indiscriminately. I would say without hesitation it was sheer unadulterated murder" (McKittrick et al. 1999: 145).

4. David Cameron, "Statement to the House on the Saville Inquiry," *London Telegraph*, June 15, 2010.

5. See "The Bloody Sunday Inquiry," at the website for the National Archives, http://webarchive.nationalarchives.gov.uk.

6. Michael McHugh and Derek Henderson, "Bloody Sunday Probe 'Should Include Martin McGuinness," *Belfast Telegraph*, July 6, 2012.

7. *Hansard*, House of Commons, Standing Committee B., January 17, 1989, at col. 508.

8. See "Pat Finucane's Family Anger [*sic*] After PM Rules Out Inquiry," *BBC News*, Northern Ireland, October 11, 2011.

9. See "Loughgall Was Shoot-to-Kill," December 2, 2011, at http://www.sinnfein.ie.

10. In 2001, the European Court of Human Rights had found that the IRA men's Article 2 rights were violated by an inadequate investigation but did not rule the killings unlawful. Case of *Kelly and Others v. UK*; *Application no. 30054/96*.

11. "Progressive Unionist Party Accuses HET of Arrest 'Bias,'" *BBC News*, Northern Ireland, March 15, 2011.

12. Established by the Northern Ireland (Location of Victims' Remains) Act 1999 (http://www.legislation.gov.uk) and Criminal Justice (Location of Victims' Remains) Act 1999, *Irish Statute Book* (http://www.irishstatutebook.ie).

13. See "The Disappeared" at the website of the Independent Commission for the Location of Victims' Remains, http://www.iclvr.ie.

14. See Rosie Cowan, Stuart Millar, and Richard Norton-Taylor, "This Man Says He Isn't Stakeknife, and Has Never Left Ulster. Just What Is Going On?" *The Guardian*, May 15, 2003.

15. Full text at http://www.publications.parliament.uk

16. Henry McDonald, "Prosecuting IRA Fugitives 'Not in Public Interest,'" *The Guardian*, February 10, 2007.

17. In October 1990, Gillespie was forced to drive a van packed with explosives into an army installation, while the IRA held his family hostage in their home; he and five soldiers died in the explosion.

18. Similarly, in 2005 Irish president Mary McAleese managed to compare Protestant sectarianism in Ireland to Nazi anti-Semitism while she attended Holocaust commemorations. President McAleese grew up in Ardoyne in north Belfast; she was attending events where international leaders recognized the sixtieth anniversary of the Auschwitz liberation. She later apologized for not mentioning anti-Protestant sectarianism among Catholics—but did not acknowledge the implicit slight posed to Holocaust survivors by comparing sectarianism to that systematic genocide. News coverage of the furor and apology is available online; see "McAleese Rowe over Nazi Comments," January 28, 2005, and "McAleese 'Sorry' over Nazi Remark," January 29, 2005, http://news.bbc.co.uk.

19. Moloney, researcher Anthony McIntyre, and a supporter, Chris Bray, highlighted the case in various publications, including the *Boston Globe*, *Irish Times*, and *Chronicle of Higher Education*; see Ed Moloney and Anthony McIntyre, "Fishing in BC's Archives," *Boston Globe*, August 23, 2001; Chris Bray, "The Whole Story Behind the Boston College Subpoenas," *Chronicle Review*, July 5, 2011; and "Boston College Saga Shows How the State Has Failed," *Irish Times*, January 10, 2012.

20. In April 2013, researchers' legal struggles to resist the subpoena effectively ended when the U.S. Supreme Court refused to review the First Circuit's decision upholding the subpoena. In response to Boston College's separate actions, the U.S. Court of Appeals for the First Circuit restricted the number of interviews produced in response to the subpoena but did not support arguments that First Amendment rights were at stake in the process.

21. See [Danny Morrison], "Foot in the Mouth," June 16, 2011, at his blog *Danny Morrison, Writer*, http://www.dannymorrison.com.

22. See Mark Philips, "Former IRA Member Admits Role in Killings, Says Peacemaker Politician Should Do the Same," *CBS Evening News with Scott Pelley*, September

24, 2012; and Patrick Sawer and Bob Graham, "'Republicanism Is Part of Our DNA,' Says IRA Bomber Delours Price," *The Telegraph*, September 23, 2012.

23. Ibid.

24. See Éamonn McCann, "Norman Baxter's Long Crusade," *Counterpunch*, February 13, 2012.

25. See "Dark Truths from Our Past Lie Silent in Boston College," *Belfast Telegraph*, January 25, 2012.

26. See Henry McDonald, "Hunt for Northern Ireland Disappeared Could Be Disrupted, Warn Investigators," *The Guardian*, July 4, 2011.

27. See "Gerry Adams Rejects Delours Price Allegations," *RTÉ News*, September 28, 2012.

28. Although both Catholics and Protestants, particularly working-class Protestants, served in the British Army during World War I, the Battle of the Somme is traditionally commemorated as a demonstration of the depth of Ulster Protestant loyalty to Britain. As the new loyalist parties emerged in the 1990s, they often pointed out that Britain's lack of reciprocity is evident in the fact that Ulster Protestants were the first troops sent on this suicidal mission.

29. Commission for Victims and Survivors Act (Northern Ireland) 2008, www .legislation.gov.uk.

30. This project involves a London university's plan to conduct oral history interviews with former police and army intelligence officers; see Henry McDonald, "US Court Says IRA Member's Secret Testimony Can Be Handed over to Police," *The Guardian*, July 8, 2012.

Chapter 6. "Love Is a Human Right"

1. The relevant law here is the Prevention of Incitement to Hatred Act (Northern Ireland) 1970.

2. European Court of Human Rights 1981, *Dudgeon v. United Kingdom Judgment* (Application no. 7525/76), Strasbourg: European Council. Dudgeon's case challenged the criminalization of sodomy in Northern Ireland, contained in the Offences Against the Person Act 1861—which prescribed the death penalty for homosexual activity—and the Criminal Law Amendment Act 1865, which lowered the penalty to life imprisonment. This law had been rescinded in England and Wales in 1967, but civil servants, governing the region directly since the suspension of the local Stormont parliament in 1974, were unwilling to extend this change to Northern Ireland. The reformed law is the Homosexual Offenses (Northern Ireland) Order 1982.

3. In 2006, a group of human rights experts met in Yogyakarta, Indonesia, to formulate what became the principles. These do not suggest new rights but instead outline how internationally recognized rights are being denied or violated on the basis of sexual orientation and gender identity and make recommendations for interpreting international law. They are comprehensive, covering rights to human and personal security, nondiscrimination, association, and legal redress, among others. Although the UN high

commissioner for human rights has not endorsed the principles, O'Flaherty and Fisher 2008 report that field office heads "welcomed the Principles as a useful tool for bringing greater coherence to their efforts" (241). The full title is "The Yogyakarta Principles: Principles on the Application of International Human Rights Law in Relation to Sexual Orientation and Gender Identity," and the full text is available at www.yogyakartaprin ciples.org.

4. The Republic of Ireland counterpart to *Dudgeon v. UK* came when Senator David Norris successfully challenged the Republic's sodomy law in 1988, which was eventually repealed in 1993. European Court of Human Rights, 1988, *Norris v. Ireland Judgment* (Application no. 10581/83), Strasbourg: European Council.

5. The Northern Ireland Gay Rights Association was established in 1975 to coordinate a growing number of LGBT organizations. The acronym NIGRA referenced NICRA, the Northern Ireland Civil Rights Association. Organizers were also conscious that the acronym was a derogatory term for African Americans in the U.S. South, but they saw it as a sideways jibe at local civil rights campaigners' self-image in comparison to the U.S. civil rights movement. That is, being Catholic was not a criminal offense, but physical expression of one's sexual orientation was.

6. Similarly, the work of scholar Kimberlé Crenshaw is said to have influenced the equality clause of South Africa's new constitution (Constitution of Republic of South Africa, 1996, Section 9).

7. Sexual Offences (Amendment) Act 2000; Employment Equality (Sexual Orientation) Regulations (Northern Ireland) 2003; Sexual Offences Act 2003; Civil Partnership Act 2004; Criminal Justice (No 2) (Northern Ireland) Act 2004; Equality Act (Sexual Orientation) Regulations (NI) 2006; Sexual Offences (Northern Ireland) Order 2008.

8. As in earlier chapters, the definition of subjectivity used here is "the felt interior experience of the person that includes his or her positions in a field of relational power" (Das and Kleinman 2000: 1).

9. In 1921, the House of Commons tried to extend gross indecency to lesbian women, but the House of Lords stopped the change.

10. "Josh" is a pseudonym. Research was not conducted with minors due to ethical concerns, so work here is based on the views of adults working in schools and NGOs, as well as young people over eighteen.

11. "Bears" are part of a gay male subculture. Part of the bear aesthetic includes cultivating a large or muscular physique and facial hair.

12. See a reprint of the Riot Grrrl Manifesto, originally published in the fanzine for Bikini Kill, a female punk band, in 1991: http://onewarart.org/riot_grrrl_manifesto.htm.

13. The address they used was www.belfastpride.co.uk. Pride's address is www .belfastpride.com.

14. This section's title was drawn from a sign a parade participant carried at the 2005 parade, in response to attempts to ban it.

15. O'Leary 2009 asserts that evangelicals increased their anti-LGBT activism in the postagreement years, as they shifted from anti-Catholicism to homophobia.

Historical perspective indicates that this is not the case. Rather, this activism continues a long-standing position and a style of expressing that position.

16. The award was part of a program established by the UK government to commemorate the late Princess Diana and recognizes young people who have demonstrated active citizenship.

17. In Northern Ireland, the Protection from Harassment (Northern Ireland) Order 1987 mandated increased sentencing for crimes aggravated by hostility to a racial or religious group. The Criminal Justice (No 2) (Northern Ireland) Act 2004 added sexual orientation, or presumed sexual orientation, and disability to the legal definition of hate crimes.

18. Public sexual activity is an offense under the Sexual Offences Act 2003.

19. The current British government, a coalition of Conservatives and Liberal Democrats, plans to extend marriage rights to gay people before 2015. Extension of the bill to Northern Ireland was rejected by the Northern Ireland Assembly in 2013, but this decision is susceptible to challenge on human rights grounds. See the Marriage (Same Sex Couples) Bill 2012–13 to 2013–14.

20. Judicial Review taken by Northern Ireland Human Rights Commission [Compatibility of the Adoption Order NI 1987 with the ECHR].

21. PRONI D/3762/3/1; 1978 letter from Jeff Dudgeon to his solicitor during his European challenge to the sodomy law in Northern Ireland.

22. For a compelling journalistic account of these circumstances, see Sabrina Ruben Erdely, "One Town's War on Gay Teens," *Rolling Stone*, February 2, 2012.

23. *Lawrence v. Texas*, 539 U.S. 558 (2003), which struck down the Texas sodomy law.

24. App. No. 33290/96, 1999-IX Eur. Ct. H.R. 309, 31 Eur. H.R. Rep. 47 (2001).

25. This movement does not transcend real political differences regarding sovereignty, nor does it attempt to. Instead, it focuses on political struggles in the present rather than deferring them and treating them as subordinate to a future change in sovereignty. There have been fractures, of course. For example, in the 1980s, gay men were often perceived as more unionist, and many lesbians as "politically correct," anti-imperialist republicans. More recently, though, the GFA's deferral of the constitutional issue to allow other politics to flourish has actually been realized in gay rights politics, and perhaps only in gay rights politics.

Chapter 7. Ethnopolitics and Human Rights

1. Quoted in Masters 1938: 193.

2. Estimates vary, of course. Pakenham 1972 suggests 50,000 dead (392); Bartlett (in Smyth 1992: 100) says 10,000 is more reasonable.

3. See Dunne 2010 for critique of the complex mingling of contemporary politics and history involved in remembering 1798, and Foster 2001: 87–88 for discussion of popular and political reactions to Dunne's book.

4. See Bew 2007 for the extent to which Tone and some republicans were more inclined to Burkean sentiments of the organic nation than to radical democracy. For a

postcolonial reading of Burkean thought and the Enlightenment in Ireland, see Gibbons 2003.

5. The most notable reform of the century, however, was the Catholic Relief Act of 1793, which removed most restrictions but did not allow membership of the Irish Parliament.

6. For detailed discussion of how regional, class, and communal interests formed under the penal laws, see Foster 1988.

7. Foster continues "(Given the way that the ancestors of Belfast radicals had treated the Gaelic Irish, this was just as well)."

8. Leader [Editorial], "Enlightenment's Wake." *Fortnight* 369 (March–April 1998): 5.

9. Written evidence from Brice Dickson, April 15, 2009, www.publications.parlia ment.uk.

10. See "Platform," *News Letter*, April 29, 2012.

11. Brice Dickson, "Comments on Second Consultation Paper from UK Bill of Rights Commission," *RightsNI*, September 6, 2012, http://rightsni.org.

12. See *Case of McCann and Others v. United Kingdom* (21 ECHR 97 GC). The case was significant for establishing a procedural dimension to the European convention's Article 2 right to life.

13. See "Revolutionary Appointment Reflects 'Transformation' in Northern Society," *Irish Times*, December 3, 2011.

14. Dickson, "Comments on Second Consultation Paper."

15. Official transcript unavailable at this time; the witness statement was reported in Mark Hennessey,"Developer McFeely Bankruptcy Overturned Following Challenge," *Irish Times*, June 16, 2012.

GLOSSARY

Agreement See GFA.

Alliance A moderate cross-confessional political party in Northern Ireland associated with the liberal bloc European parties.

Anglo-Irish Agreement An agreement between the governments of the UK and Ireland in 1985. The agreement stated that the constitutional status of Northern Ireland would not change without the consent of its residents, while establishing a consultative role for the Republic of Ireland in the governance of Northern Ireland. The agreement was part of a shift to cooperative relations between the two governments and was intended to move toward a peace process. Unionists objected to the consultative role of the Republic in northern affairs, and republicans rejected making Irish unification dependent on consent.

Armalite and ballot box The republican strategy combining armed struggle and electoral politics, which was developed after the hunger strikes. The phrase is drawn from a 1981 speech by Sinn Féin publicity director Danny Morrison to the party conference after the hunger strikes. In the speech, he asked, "Who here really believes we can win the war through the ballot box? But will anyone here object if, with a ballot paper in one hand and an Armalite in the other, we take power in Ireland?" (see Hannigan 1985: 34). Arguably this strategy led to the peace process and mainstream republicanism's renunciation of armed struggle. Some committed republicans who were part of the prison protests argue that the hunger strikes were a military, not a political tactic, and should not be subsumed into the narrative of republicanism's transition to democratic politics. ArmaLite is a small arms manufacturer whose brand has been vernacularized.

Assembly The Northern Ireland Assembly, the regional legislative body created by the peace settlement and the Northern Ireland Act (1998). The implementation of the GFA took several years, and the assembly was suspended on several occasions, notably from 2002 to 2007. Elections are held at four-year intervals, and seats are allocated on the basis of proportional representation—voters rank candidates rather than choosing only one. The assembly has 108 members, which will be reduced to 96 in the 2015 elections. They are called MLAs—Members of the Legislative Assembly. Members must designate themselves as "unionist," "nationalist," or "other" on entrance. "Key decisions" must be ratified on a "cross-community" basis—with either a majority of nationalists and of unionists voting in favor or a "weighted" majority with 60 percent overall approval and 40 percent of these designations (see *Agreement Reached* 1998). Key decisions are identified by the Office of the First and Deputy First Minister (OFDFM) or by petition from a "significant minority." The assembly has devolved legislative powers on matters such as health, social development, economic development, and education. It elects a power-sharing Executive, within which members of the different parties are elected as ministers of these different governmental departments. Ministers implement policy and legislation in these departments, with a staff of nonpolitical civil servants, as well as some politically appointed advisors. This model differs from the UK model, in which a government is formed from Parliament's majority party or a coalition of parties. Roughly equivalent to the Northern Irish Executive is the UK government cabinet of ministers overseeing departments. However, rather than being drawn from different parties according to their size in the assembly, which is the power-sharing dimension of governance, in the UK, the cabinet is appointed by the prime minister of the majority party. One important consequence for the Northern Ireland Assembly is that there is no official opposition party—all parties are expected to participate in a consensual governing model.

CBO   Community-based organization. A CBO is a type of nongovernmental organization (NGO). These are formally constituted, nonprofit groups that serve a local area. Sometimes called community organizations or community groups, they usually emphasize self-help and skills or capacity building, rather than direct aid. In this fashion, their grassroots emphasis and modes of practice differentiate them from large international charitable or development NGOs. As conflict in Northern Ireland led to massive mobilizations of people in political or violent actions, it also led to the proliferation of CBOs as a vehicle of rights advocacy, as well as self-help. In Belfast, CBO issues range from political and economic development to basic entitlements, including education, housing, health services, child care, and gender equality.

Celtic Tiger   The economy of the Republic of Ireland during a period of rapid expansion from 1995–2007. Unemployment fell dramatically, while wages and inflation grew. Growth was heavily dependent on credit for property sales and development, and, during the financial crisis of 2008, fundamental economic vulnerabilities were exposed. The crash was severe, property prices collapsed, unemployment rose, and emigration increased. Ireland's deeply indebted government received a bailout package from the International Monetary Fund, European Union, and European Central Bank in 2010; the terms of the bailout dictate severe state austerity in welfare and stimulus spending.

Civic forum   Along with the assembly, the GFA created the Civic Forum, which would allow representatives of "business, trade union, and voluntary sectors" to advise on legislation. The forum was intended to institutionalize a political role for NGOs and other civil society actors. The Civic Forum was suspended with the assembly.

When the assembly was restored, the Forum was not, and it became the subject of a public review.

Devolution   Devolution is a political system of governance in which a central state grants powers of administration and legislation to a regional body. Unlike federalism, in which states are constitutionally guaranteed, devolved bodies are part of a unitary governing system, and their powers may be withdrawn by central government. In Northern Ireland, the Stormont legislature after partition, and the new Northern Ireland Assembly are devolved governing bodies.

Direct rule   Those periods when Northern Ireland was directly governed by Westminster, that is, the British central government, rather than a local, devolved legislature. Northern Ireland did elect members of Parliament to the House of Commons, but they had little influence on policy. Local councils continued to operate but with a restricted set of responsibilities—sanitation, community, cemetery, leisure services, and limited building regulation. Direct rule was introduced in 1972 as the conflict became intractable (see Stormont). Brief attempts to restore a local parliament took place in 1973–1974 (see Sunningdale), and in 1982. Under the GFA, a local assembly operated intermittently from 1999–2001, with direct rule being periodically reintroduced. Direct rule was imposed from 2002 until 2007, when the parties reached a new accommodation and the assembly was restored.

Dissident   A designation for republicans who oppose the Good Friday Agreement (GFA). A dissident is usually associated with violent opponents of the peace process, such as the RIRA. The term is also applied pejoratively to some GFA opponents who condemn the use of force, often to discredit their views.

DUP   Democratic Unionist Party. The DUP is an extreme unionist party founded by Ian Paisley; its forerunner was his Protestant Unionist Party (PUP), which opposed local reform efforts to end anti-Catholic discrimination, from 1966 to 1971. The DUP was the second largest unionist party during the peace process and boycotted the multiparty peace talks. The party originally opposed the GFA but took its seats in the local assembly that followed. After negotiations with the British government and Sinn Féin and after PIRA decommissioning, the DUP entered the devolved power-sharing government in 2007, and Ian Paisley became the first minister. Its policies include anti-LGBT (lesbian-gay-bisexual-transexual) legislation, and its members are often fervent religionists.

Easter Rising   An insurrection during Easter Week 1916 by Irish republicans to establish Irish independence from Britain. The rebellion was suppressed, and its leaders were publicly executed. Outrage at the executions increased public support for republicanism, and in 1918 republicans won 73 of the 105 Irish seats in elections to the British Parliament. They declared an independent Irish republic, and the British and northern unionists resisted this move. The Irish War of Independence followed. This was largely a guerrilla war, fought by the IRA against unionists and British representatives in Ireland. The Government of Ireland Act 1920 established two territories on the island, and the conflict ended with the Anglo-Irish Treaty in

1921. This reinforced partition, allowing twenty-six southern counties of Ireland to leave the UK, while six northern counties became Northern Ireland, remaining part of the UK. This division of the island is known as partition. Following partition, pro- and antitreaty republicans clashed in the Irish Civil War, 1922–1923. This war claimed more casualties than the war for independence and left an enduring legacy of bitterness after the pro-treaty side prevailed.

Executive   The power-sharing committee that administers the post-GFA devolved government, which was most recently restored on May 8, 2007. It is made up of the Office of the First and Deputy First Ministers (OFMDFM), as well as ministers of eleven departments (e.g., Department of Regional Development, Department for Social Development). The ministers heading these departments are nominated and confirmed according their parties' size in the assembly. The Executive Committee is responsible for developing governmental plans and budgets and for collective decision making on issues that cut across ministerial areas.

Falls Road   A major road running in a southwestern direction from the city center of Belfast. In everyday talk, "the Falls" also refers to the broader district around the road, composed of multiple smaller neighborhoods and housing estates. Residents of this area are predominantly nationalist, Catholic, and Irish. Sinn Féin's headquarters are located on the road itself, so the area has historically been associated with republicanism. Defined most broadly, nationalist west Belfast has a population of approximately 80,000. The Falls Road is approximately parallel to the Shankill Road when both begin west of the city center. Residents of the Falls area are traditionally working class and have suffered from multiple forms of deprivation and poverty. In the 1960s, riots and attacks from Shankill Road residents—who are predominantly loyalist and Protestant—led to greater cohesion in the area and the construction of a famous "peace wall" between the districts. The areas nearest the city center are called the "lower" Falls. See maps.

GCSE   General Certificate of Secondary Education. Certificates in specific subjects, e.g., English or mathematics, granted to students in secondary schools in England, Wales, and Northern Ireland. Students take a range of GCSE courses for two years, usually during the equivalent of the U.S. freshman and sophomore years of high school, followed by exams. Students who wish to attend university usually complete a further two years of "A-level" courses and must achieve a certain number and standard of both GCSEs and A-levels.

GFA   Good Friday Agreement or Belfast Agreement. The GFA is the agreement that emerged from negotiations among eight parties during fall 1997 and winter 1998 and is known as the peace settlement. It was accompanied by an agreement between the UK and Ireland governments and approved by a Northern Ireland referendum in May 1998. At the same time, voters in the south voted to amend the Irish constitution to give up a territorial claim to the north, replaced by an affirmation of northern residents' rights to Irish citizenship. It was enacted in law by the Northern Ireland Act 1998 and came into force in December 1999. It is officially called the

Agreement Reached Through Multi-Party Negotiations. This unwieldy title reflects attempts at neutrality, avoiding mention of contested designations for the region like "Northern Ireland." Part of not recognizing the legitimacy of partition involves republicans referring to the "six counties," the "occupied six counties," or simply "the North." Such linguistic marking of difference is ubiquitous. Unionists tend to prefer the "Belfast Agreement," avoiding reference to the Easter holiday that marks the 1916 uprising that led to independence in the southern twenty-six counties.

HET   Historical Enquiries Team. A unit established by the PSNI in 2006 to investigate more than 3,000 deaths during the conflict, approximately 2,000 of which were unsolved, between 1968 and 1998. HET's stated goal is "to provide as many answers as possible for families seeking information about their loved ones." HET was initially scheduled to operate until 2011 but now is scheduled to continue at least until 2013.

Hunger strikes   The British government introduced new security strategies in Northern Ireland in 1976. One of these was "criminalization." Paramilitary prisoners, who previously had special category (i.e., political) status, were criminalized, and this status was revoked. In the late 1970s, republican prisoners protested, holding a "blanket" protest (refusing to wear prison uniforms) and a "no wash/no work" protest. Protests escalated, and two hunger strikes were held, in 1980 and 1981, demanding five rights related to political status: to wear civilian clothes, to associate freely within cell blocks, to be exempt from prison work requirements, to education and recreation, and to restoration of sentence remissions. In 1980, the strike was called off because the British appeared ready to compromise. However, a resolution did not take place, and a new strike began in March 1981. Ultimately, ten men died. The strike ended in October when it appeared that families of the six remaining strikers would request medical intervention to stop their starvation. The government soon announced revised measures that met many of the strikers' demands. The hunger strikes raised global consciousness of the conflict and increased grassroots support for republicanism. Indeed, while on hunger strike, Bobby Sands was elected an MP for the Fermanagh/South Tyrone seat. Following the hunger strikes, Sinn Féin began to contest elections and eventually ended the policy of abstention from the Irish, but not the British Parliament. The strike transformed Sinn Féin's position in politics, but recently some republicans have alleged that the leadership refused the eventual deal earlier during the strikes, allowing several of the men to die needlessly (see O'Rawe 2005). These claims have become part of broader critiques of Sinn Féin's political strategies and tactics.

IFI   International Fund for Ireland. An international aid body formed in the 1980s to fund economic development for the northern and border regions of Ireland affected by the conflict. The 1985 Anglo-Irish Agreement established the IFI, funded by the United States, Canada, Australia, New Zealand, and some of the European Community. The U.S. Congress mandated that its initial $120 million contribution be used to promote industry in the private sector and not replicate or replace statutory development funds.

INLA   Irish National Liberation Army. The INLA was a paramilitary group formed in 1974 by members of the Official Irish Republican Army, who were driven from the organization when it renounced armed struggle in 1972. The new group attracted some members of the Provisional Irish Republican Army (PIRA) by more explicitly advocating a socialist united Ireland than the Provisionals. The organization engaged in feuds, internally and with other groupings. Three of its members died during the 1981 hunger strike, and it was responsible for some high-profile killings, e.g., Billy Wright. It initially opposed the GFA but declared a ceasefire after the Omagh bombing solidified support for the agreement and decommissioned and renounced armed struggle.

Interface   A term used to indicate a geographic area where two segregated communities meet. Interfaces are often marked by official boundaries or defensive architecture, such as peace lines or peace walls, to deter vandalism or attacks. Unofficial markers may also denote interfaces, such as roads that are closed to cars or specific bridges or streets. Interface areas are frequent sites of intimidation and violence and are often blighted, with houses or storefronts nearer to peace lines having been abandoned.

Internment   Arrest and confinement without trial. It was used in both Northern Ireland and the Republic of Ireland to counter republican paramilitarism at different times in the twentieth century. The reintroduction of internment in Northern Ireland had a dramatic impact in the conflict, when from 1971 to 1975 the government detained almost 2,000 people on suspicion of paramilitary activity. The policy was introduced by the Stormont government, and the vast majority of internees were nationalists/republicans. Civil rights groups, and nationalists generally, were outraged by the practice. Some informants said internment became one of the republican movement's best recruitment strategies. Interrogation techniques in the internment camps were classified as torture by the European Commission of Human Rights.

Inward investment   An economic term to describe external or foreign companies investing in a region to develop a sales or manufacturing presence. During the Celtic Tiger years, for example, the Irish state courted call centers to locate their European operations in Ireland, emphasizing low wages and taxation, as well as a relatively well-educated, English-speaking workforce. Inward investment is often criticized as a national economic strategy because it is usually depends on promises of local subsidies, as well as a low-wage workforce. Furthermore, foreign investors often relocate when other regions or states promise more favorable conditions. Meanwhile, critics argue that inward investment strategies neglect the development of indigenous business creation.

IRSP   Irish Republican Socialist Party. A political party associated with the INLA.

Loyalist   Political term indicating British, usually Protestant, identity and a desire to maintain Northern Ireland's status in the United Kingdom. A loyalist usually has working-class origins but does not necessarily support violence. However, Protestant paramilitaries are almost invariably loyalists, as distinct from "unionists." The distinction is primarily one of class, with unionists having middle-class origins. Some of my informants saw, resentfully, the historical participation of loyalists in paramilitarism, and unionists in political parties, as a structured division of political labor.

LVF   Loyalist Volunteer Force. The LVF is the mid-Ulster brigade of the Ulster Volunteer Force (UVF) that split from the organization in 1996 in reaction against the peace process.

MLA   Member of Legislation Assembly, that is, representatives in the Northern Ireland Assembly, the regional legislative body established by the GFA.

Nationalist   Political term indicating Irish, usually Catholic, identity with an aspiration for a united Ireland. "Nationalist" is a broad category for a political orientation: all republicans are nationalists, but the reverse is not true. A more specific use of the term indicates constitutional nationalism, emphasizing the use of democratic means—rather than armed struggle—to pursue national unity.

NHRI   National Human Rights Institution. An NHRI is a relatively new model for institutions that monitor states' human rights policies and promote social understanding of human rights principles. Part of a network created by the Paris Principles (UN General Assembly 1994), accredited NHRIs are coordinated in the UN human rights system by the ICC (International Coordinating Committee of National Institutions for the Promotion and Protection of Human Rights.)

NICRA   Northern Ireland Civil Rights Association. NICRA was formed in the 1960s to advocate civil rights, particularly for Catholics, in opposition to discriminatory practices in housing, voting, employment, and policing. Although the group was originally more middle class and Catholic in composition, some working-class Protestants, also disenfranchised under the Stormont electoral arrangements, became part of the movement. When violence became widespread in the region in the late 1960s and early 1970s internal splits regarding leftist and republican politics became intense.

NIHE   Northern Ireland Housing Executive. As part of reforms to the Stormont regime, control of public housing was removed from Unionist-dominated local councils in 1971. Public housing administration and maintenance were taken over by a central regional body, run by civil servants and an appointed board rather than politicians. The move was intended to correct anti-Catholic bias in the allocation of public housing. NIHE also attempted to modernize and upgrade the poor quality of public housing.

OFMDFM[NI]   Office of the First Minister and Deputy First Minister of Northern Ireland. The leaders of the new devolved government, they are nominated by the largest and second largest parties in the new legislative assembly respectively.

OIRA   Official Irish Republican Army. The OIRA emerged from a split in the IRA in 1969. The group no longer embraces physical force republicanism. Members are often called "stickies" or "sticks" because traditionally members use sticky tape to fix paper Easter lapel lilies when commemorating the 1916 Easter rising. (Provisionals use pins to attach the lilies to their lapels.)

Orange Order   A Protestant fraternal organization founded in 1795 in County Armagh, following sectarian clashes between Catholics and Protestants. It was originally called the Loyal Orange Institution, commemorating the Protestant king William of Orange. William's forces battled King James, a Catholic rival for the throne of England, Scotland, and Ireland, in 1690 at the River Boyne in eastern Ireland. This battle was crucial to William's eventual defeat of James and succession to the monarchy. The Orange Order views William's reign as a victory for British sovereignty, not only in Ireland but in terms of British governance being independent of the Catholic Church. The Orange Order is known primarily for its tradition of parading, particularly on the Twelfth. Its parades are seen by many nationalists as sectarian and triumphalist and have been the occasion for serious violence and rioting. The order also has a formal role in Ulster Unionist Party (UUP) governance and, as such, was seen as part of the institutional favoring of Protestants in Northern Ireland after partition.

Parades Commission   A public body that regulates contentious parades and protests in Northern Ireland. It was established in 1998 after political parades, especially loyalist parades, became increasingly contested, leading to serious protests and violence. It has the authority to designate parades as contentious and to ban or reroute them. It may also place restrictions on parades, such as forbidding music in certain parts of a route or banning particular bands from participating in a parade. It is authorized by the Public Processions Act (Northern Ireland) 1998, and members are appointed by the secretary of state for Northern Ireland, who is a minister of the UK, rather than the local, government.

Partition   The division of the island of Ireland into two jurisdictions. Partition was originally enacted by the Government of Ireland Act 1920, establishing two territories on the island of Ireland. Partition was reasserted by the Anglo-Irish Treaty in 1921, which ended the Irish War of Independence, with twenty-six southern counties forming the Irish Free State and six northern counties remaining part of the UK as Northern Ireland. Internal conflicts among republicans about partition led to a bloody civil war in 1922–1923, in which pro-treaty (partitionist) forces prevailed, and partition was reinforced.

PD   People's Democracy. A now-dissolved, radical organization formed at Queens University in 1968. Leftist students and lecturers formed the group to agitate for civil rights in the context of a thirty-two-county, socialist Irish Republic. Well-known public figures and scholars who later embraced a range of political positions were part of the group, including Bernadette Devlin McAliskey, Paul Bew, Eamonn McCann, Kevin Boyle, and Jeff Dudgeon. The group should not be confused with the Progressive Democrats in Ireland, an economically neoliberal political party.

PIRA   The Provisional Irish Republican Army. PIRA is the largest paramilitary organization associated with republicanism, a movement dedicated to the unification of the jurisdictions of Ireland. The IRA split in 1969, into the "Official" and "Provisional" IRA (see OIRA). Both groups had military and political wings. The split was

driven by the emergence of conflict. When loyalists attacked nationalist neighborhoods in 1969, the IRA offered little defense. Frustrated by this, some members of
the republican movement split, forming the PIRA. It soon became the most lethal
paramilitary organization in the region, with a strong base of support in west Belfast. It also became the most politically effective republican organization, especially
after the 1981 hunger strikes, electing candidates to local and national government
through its associated political party, Sinn Féin. The group declared a ceasefire in
1994. Many of its military leaders in the 1970s and 1980s later led the organization
into ceasefires, peace talks, and a settlement in the 1990s and 2000s. After the GFA,
PIRA initially resisted decommissioning and demobilization but completed the
process in 2005. Sometimes colloquially called "provisionals," "provos" or "provies."

Police Ombudsman [for Northern Ireland] As part of police reform after the GFA, the
Office of the Police Ombudsman was established through the Police (Northern
Ireland) Acts of 1998 and 2000. This body provides an independent complaints
system to monitor and investigate the conduct of the reformed PSNI. The Police
Ombudsman investigates historical complaints regarding the RUC as well and has
conducted inquiries into allegations of police collusion with loyalist paramilitaries.

Provisional   See PIRA.

PSNI   Police Service of Northern Ireland, the police service that succeeded the Royal
Ulster Constabulary. The service was restructured and reformed following recommendations from the Patten Commission as part of the peace settlement. Importantly, PSNI pursued affirmative recruitment policies to increase the proportion of
nationalist officers. In 2007, Sinn Féin recognized the PSNI and took up seats on its
policing board, a crucial step in legitimizing the new institutions.

PUP   Progressive Unionist Party, a loyalist political party associated with the Ulster
Volunteer Force. The PUP became prominent during the 1990s peace process, as its
leaders stewarded the paramilitary group's participation in the peace process. The
PUP supports union with Britain but advocates more leftist and secular politics than
the DUP or UUP. The party aims to provide working-class Protestants with political
representatives drawn from their own communities, unlike the DUP and UUP who
often sponsor candidates from outside loyalist districts. Associated with loyalist
paramilitarism, the party also sought to imitate Sinn Féin's success in supporting a
transition from violence to democratic politics. Although several ex-prisoners were
charismatic party leaders during the peace process, Protestant reluctance to vote for
ex-prisoners, as well as deep splits within unionism regarding the GFA, prevented
the party from achieving the electoral successes of Sinn Féin.

Quango   Quasi-autonomous nongovernmental organization. Quangos are bodies,
such as the Human Rights Commission and the Equality Commission, to which
some state responsibility or authority has been devolved. They are designed to work
outside the government departments and ministers to create some independence
from political calculations. The official term for these groups in the UK is "non-
departmental public body." Because they are composed of appointed, rather than

elected, commissioners, they are open to charges of being simultaneously politically designed and undemocratic.

Republic The Republic of Ireland. From 1921 to 1937, the twenty-six southern counties that constituted the Irish Free State, following the Irish War of Independence and partition, were a British dominion. In 1937, a public referendum was held, and the state became fully independent and constituted as Ireland. In 1949, the state declared itself the Republic of Ireland, severing all ties with the British monarchy.

Republican Political designation indicating an aspiration for a united Ireland. Republicanism has traditionally been notable for its fierce insistence on the legitimacy of armed struggle to achieve this aim. While republicans often have more working-class origins than constitutional nationalists, this position on political violence was historically the strongest axis of difference between republicans and nationalists.

RIRA Real IRA, a group of dissidents who split from the PIRA in 1997 when the group affirmed Sinn Féin's participation in the peace negotiations. The RIRA opposed the GFA and set off a bomb in Omagh in 1998. In 2012, it merged with two other dissident groups in an attempt to revive armed struggle for a united Ireland.

RUC Royal Ulster Constabulary. RUC was the police force for Northern Ireland from 1922 to 2000. Personnel were overwhelmingly unionist, and the force was frequently accused of human rights violations and collusion with loyalist paramilitaries. More than 300 RUC officers were killed during the conflict. As part of the GFA, a policing review recommended reform of the RUC, which was reorganized as the Police Service of Northern Ireland (PSNI).

SDLP Social Democratic and Labour Party, a moderate constitutional nationalist party; that is, it supports the reunification of Ireland by political means rather than armed struggle. The SDLP is aligned with other social democratic parties in Europe but is not a straightforward heir to the labor movement in Northern Ireland. After partition, the Northern Ireland Labour Party drew support from the working classes and attempted to avoid splits between nationalism and unionism. After conflict broke out, this neutrality became electorally unsustainable and support for the Labour party dramatically decreased. In 1971, the SDLP was formed to support civil rights reforms alongside labor goals and was part of the short-lived Sunningdale executive. In the 1970s, the party struggled internally with reconciling its socialist and nationalist principles, and its founding leader left the party in 1979, arguing that nationalism had eclipsed its socialism. From the 1980s onward, the party competed with Sinn Féin for nationalist voters, advocating a democratic resolution of the constitutional conflict. During peace talks, the SDLP took a moderate nationalist position and was a primary influence on the final settlement. For example, "the principle of consent"—that Ireland must be unified with majority consent in both jurisdictions—was a longstanding SDLP position. In the post-GFA years, Sinn Féin eclipsed the SDLP electorally, although the SDLP continues to receive the third largest vote share and is part of the power-sharing executive.

Shankill Road   A major road running in a northwestern direction from the city center of Belfast. In everyday talk, "the Shankill" also refers to the broader district around the road, composed of multiple smaller neighborhoods and housing estates. Residents are predominantly loyalist, Protestant, and British. The area was at one time a thriving commercial and industrial center, but redevelopment and deindustrialization since the 1970s diminished the population from about 76,000 to 26,000. The remaining residents usually have long-standing ties to the area. After redevelopment, local activists began to define the spatial district of the Shankill more broadly to include estates such as Glencairn, west of where the Shankill Road ends. Areas nearest the city center are called the "lower" Shankill. See maps.

Sinn Féin   The largest republican political party in Northern Ireland. It is associated with the political wing of PIRA and was originally called "Provisional Sinn Féin" after the IRA split in 1969. Sinn Féin began to contest elections after the 1981 hunger strikes, and in the next decade elected representatives to Westminster and local government. Sinn Féin was one of the most important parties within the peace process, representing physical force republicanism in the multiparty talks. In the 2001 assembly and Westminster elections, Sinn Féin became the largest nationalist political party in Northern Ireland and now is a senior partner in the power-sharing government. Despite criticisms by republican opponents of the peace process, Sinn Féin's electoral support has almost doubled since the ceasefires. Many of its high-profile leaders and candidates are former republican prisoners. Sinn Féin's success represents political legitimacy and equality for many republicans and, as such, is a major political consequence of the peace process.

Stormont   Literally, Stormont is a woodland park in east Belfast where Stormont Castle and the Parliament buildings are located. In everyday usage, "Stormont" refers to both the parliament that governed from these buildings from 1921 to 1972, and sometimes to the new assembly created by the GFA. In the 1960s, attempts to reform the state and end anti-Catholic discrimination led to internal dissent among unionists, who had effectively controlled the local Parliament since 1921. As political disagreements descended into violence, the local government refused to surrender control of policing and justice to Westminster. In 1972, Stormont was abolished by the British government following multiple failures to manage the security situation, notably the Bloody Sunday atrocity, and was replaced by direct rule. During direct rule, civil servants worked from administrative buildings on the Stormont estate. Despite the troubled history of the previous parliament, the new Northern Ireland Assembly convenes in the original stately building constructed to house the post-partition parliament. Today, "Stormont" sometimes refers to the contemporary local assembly, but, for republicans, the term continues to carry troubling associations with the previous regime and its discriminatory practices.

Sunningdale   An agreement that established a power-sharing government and cross-border bodies for Northern Ireland, in an attempt to establish consensual local governance in the region. The power-sharing executive functioned from December 1973 to May 1974. The outlines of the agreement were similar to what was contained later in the GFA, with a local assembly, and governing ministries drawn from the assembly on a power-sharing, rather than majoritarian, basis. However, unionists opposed the plan, especially its attempt to recognize an Irish dimension to governance in the North. In May 1974, this opposition was mobilized in a massive series of strikes and disturbances sponsored by the Ulster Workers' Council, a group formed specifically for this purpose. Protestant workers in major industrial sectors went on strike. Loyalist paramilitaries strengthened the protests, sabotaging electricity supply, forcing closure of factories, and organizing roadblocks and vehicle hijackings across the region. Many workers were intimidated into withholding their labor, and major public services, such as the mail, were suspended. Large demonstrations were organized against the agreement, and riots occurred. After two weeks, the head of the power-sharing executive resigned along with his unionist colleagues. The attempt at a consensual resolution ended, and direct rule was restored.

Twelfth   The Twelfth of July holiday. This annual holiday marks William of Orange's victory at the Battle of the Boyne and is celebrated with a large Orange Order parade and community bonfires in loyalist areas. For many loyalists, the holiday brings together the disparate factions within Protestant religious and political groupings, reinforcing and celebrating a distinctive British identity. Many nationalists regard the celebration as sectarian and anti-Catholic. Since the 1990s, contentious parading has led to widespread disorder during the summer months.

UDA   Ulster Defence Association, the largest loyalist paramilitary organization, created in 1971 from a loose coalition of informal vigilante and defense associations in loyalist areas. In 1974, it was a critical force behind the massive loyalist demonstrations against the Sunningdale Agreement. Throughout the conflict, most of its victims were civilians, and it was regarded as less organized and effective than either UVF or PIRA. Despite internal disputes regarding the GFA, the group was largely supportive of the peace process and benefited from prisoner releases. It demobilized in 2007 and completed decommissioning in 2010.

UDP   Ulster Democratic Party. Now defunct, the UDP was a political party associated with the UDA and UFF. Although politically unionist, in the 1980s, it supported the idea of an independent Ulster and later supported a less radical scheme for devolved local governance. Like the PUP, it was part of the peace negotiations and supported the transition from paramilitarism to nonviolent politics. The party was weakened by UDA feuds and a violent campaign against UVF supporters in the lower Shankill in 2000. Ultimately, internal disagreements about the peace process led to the party's dissolution in 2001. Its role of internal mediation and political research has been taken up by the Ulster Political Research Group.

UFF   Ulster Freedom Fighters, a cover name used by the UDA to claim responsibility for its most violent actions during the conflict. The UFF was banned by the British government in 1973, while the UDA remained legal until 1992. The fiction of the

UFF as a distinct entity helped maintain the UDA's legality, although in reality the UFF was not a separate or autonomous group.

Unionist   Political term indicating British, usually Protestant, identity and a desire to maintain Northern Ireland's status within the United Kingdom. Like nationalist, unionist is a broad category and also has more specific class connotations. For the most part, unionist indicates a middle-class background—in contrast to loyalist, which has a working-class one.

UVF   Ulster Volunteer Force, a loyalist paramilitary group. The contemporary UVF formed in 1966, taking its name from a group formed in 1912 to oppose Home Rule in Ireland. The current group grew from opposition to proposed political reforms to combat anti-Catholic discrimination in the 1960s and 1970s. Its aim was to ensure Northern Ireland's constitutional status in the UK. Many of its actions were sectarian assassinations of Catholic civilians. The UVF campaign began before the outbreak of widespread violence in 1969, with the 1966 murder of Peter Ward, an eighteen-year-old Catholic working in the Shankill area. The UVF supported the peace process, and its imprisoned members benefited from the prisoner release program. In 1996, its mid-Ulster brigade split off to form the LVF in protest at its peace strategy. The group demobilized in 2007 and decommissioned in 2009.

UUP   Ulster Unionist Party, the contemporary incarnation of a unionist party that was formally constituted in 1905. As the Unionist Party, it dominated the Stormont parliament from 1921 to 1972. During this period, most of its leadership was drawn from the landed gentry, and the Orange Order had a significant, formal role in its governing council. Following partition, the northern party became the Ulster Unionist Party, although it was usually called simply the Unionist Party. During the 1960s and 1970s, unionism was in internal turmoil regarding local state reforms. Several splits took place within the party, Ian Paisley's hardline party grew in power, and some moderate unionists left to form the Alliance party. During the 1970s, it was often called the Official Unionist Party because it was led by the remaining members of the previous governing party. As the largest party in Northern Ireland, the UUP had a leading role in the multiparty talks, rejecting proposals that appeared to give the Republic too much influence in governance. Following the GFA's ratification, the UUP became locked in another intraunionist struggle with the anti-Agreement DUP, and its own anti-Agreement members. Its leader at the time, David Trimble, shared a Nobel Prize with John Hume of the SDLP for his role in the peace process. However, in the post-Agreement years, several members defected to the DUP, and ultimately his party lost its electoral advantage as the largest unionist party to the DUP in 2005 elections. It remains a part of the power-sharing executive, but after the party renewed its ties with the British Conservative Party (officially the British Conservative and Unionist Party) its only remaining MP at Westminster, Sylvia Hermon, left the party and continues to represent North Down as an Independent.

Victims Commission   Commission for Victims and Survivors. In 2008, ministers in the power-sharing executive agreed to appoint a commission to promote the interests of victims and survivors of the conflict. The four-member appointed commission was created to monitor and advise government regarding policy and legislation affecting victims. In 2012, the commission was replaced by a single victims commissioner.

Victims' Forum   Victims and Survivors Forum, established by the Victims Commission as a vehicle for victims and survivors to be consulted regarding policy and legislation. A pilot forum held discussions in 2009–2010, followed by a transition group that continued until the formal establishment of the body in 2012. The forum will meet on a monthly basis until 2014. It has twenty-five members, including two associates who are not victims. Creating the forum was a monumental task, given the vast range of victim experiences, at the hands of paramilitary and state forces and the different, often opposed political convictions of victims. Nevertheless, some members found the discussions productive. For example, despite very different experiences and viewpoints, the group reached consensus about a set of principles to guide an official truth recovery process. However, the establishment of such a process does not appear to be a political priority either for the assembly or the UK government.

Westminster   The Parliament of the United Kingdom, the House of Commons and the House of Lords, located in the Palace of Westminster in central London. Often in Northern Ireland, "Westminster" is an abbreviated term for referring to the UK Parliament, as well as the central government of the UK more generally.

Women's Coalition   A small cross-community political party formed in 1996 to take part in elections to the multiparty talks. It did not declare a position regarding the constitutional status of the region and was focused on supporting an inclusive peace process and increasing women's participation in public life. The group made significant contributions to the process regarding human rights and civil society but did not succeed electorally in the following decade and was wound down in 2006. Officially called the Northern Ireland Women's Coalition.

BIBLIOGRAPHY

The Agreement Reached in the Multi-Party Negotiations. 1998. Belfast: Government of the United Kingdom of Great Britain and Northern Ireland.

Althusser, Louis. 1971. "Ideology and Ideological State Apparatuses (Notes Towards an Investigation)." In *Lenin and Philosophy and Other Essays*, trans. Ben Brewster, 121–73. New York: Monthly Review Press.

Alston, Philip. 2005. "The 'Not-a-Cat Syndrome: Can the International Human Rights Regime Accommodate Non-State Actors?" In *Non-State Actors and Human Rights*, ed. Philip Alston, 3–36. Oxford: Oxford University Press.

Amnesty International. 1994. *Political Killings in Northern Ireland*. London: Amnesty International

Appiah, Anthony. 1994. "Identity, Authenticity, Survival: Multicultural Societies and Social Reproduction." In *Multiculturalism: Examining the Politics of Recognition*, ed. Amy Gutmann, 149–63. Princeton, N.J.: Princeton University Press.

Ardoyne Commemoration Project. 2003. *Ardoyne: The Untold Truth*. Belfast: Beyond the Pale.

Arendt, Hannah. (1951) 2004. *The Origins of Totalitarianism*. New York: Schocken.

Arthur, Paul. 1974. *The People's Democracy 1968–73*. Belfast: Blackstaff.

———. 1990. "Negotiating the Northern Ireland Problem: Track One or Track Two Diplomacy?" *Government and Opposition* 25 (4). 403–18.

Baker, Pauline. 2001. "Conflict Resolution versus Democratic Governance: Divergent Paths to Peace?" In *Turbulent Peace: The Challenges of Managing International Conflict*, ed. Chester Crocker, 753–64. Washington, D.C.: U.S. Institute of Peace.

Balfour, Ian and Eduardo Cadava. 2004. "The Claims of Human Rights: An Introduction." *South Atlantic Quarterly* 103 (2/3): 277–96.

BAN Project Team. 1976. *Belfast Areas of Special Social Need*. Belfast: HMSO.

Bardon, Jonathan. 1982. *Belfast, an Illustrated History*. Belfast: Blackstaff.

Bartlett, Thomas. 1998. *The Life of Theobald Wolfe Tone*. Dublin: Lilliput.

Belfast Libertarian Group. 1973. *Ireland: Dead or Alive?* Belfast: Belfast Libertarian Group.

Bell, Christine. 2000. *Peace Agreements and Human Rights*. Oxford: Oxford University Press.

———. 2003. "Dealing with the Past in Northern Ireland." *Fordham International Law Journal* 26 (4): 1095–1147.

——. 2006. "Human Rights, Peace Agreements and Conflict Resolution: Negotiating Justice in Northern Ireland." In *Human Rights and Conflict: Exploring Links Between Rights, Law and Peacebuilding*, ed. Julie Mertus and Jeffrey Helsing, 345–76. Washington, D.C.: U.S. Institute of Peace.

Bell, Christine and Johanna Keenan. 2004. "Human Rights, Nongovernmental Organizations, and the Problems of Transition." *Human Rights Quarterly* 26 (2): 330–74.

——. 2005. "Lost on the Way Home? The Right to Life in Northern Ireland." *Journal of Law and Society* 32 (1): 68–89.

Bell, Vikki. 2004. "In Pursuit of Civic Participation: The Early Experiences of the Northern Ireland Civic Forum, 2000–2004." *Political Studies* 52 (3): 565–84.

Bew, Paul. 2007. *Ireland: The Politics of Enmity*. Oxford: Oxford University Press.

Bill of Rights Forum. 2008. *Final Report: Recommendations to the Northern Ireland Human Rights Commission on a Bill of Rights for Northern Ireland*. Belfast: NIHRC.

Birrell, Derek. 2009. *Direct Rule and the Governance of Northern Ireland*. Manchester: Manchester University Press.

Bloomfield, David. 1995. "Towards Complementarity in Conflict Management: Resolution and Settlement in Northern Ireland." *Journal of Peace Research* 32 (2): 151–64.

Bloomfield, Sir Kenneth. 1998. *We Will Remember Them*. Belfast: Stationery Office.

Boal, Fredrick W. 1969. "Territoriality on the Shankill-Falls Divide, Belfast." *Irish Geography* 6 (1): 30–50.

——. 1978. "Territoriality on the Shankill-Falls Divide, Belfast: The Perspective from 1976." In *An Invitation to Geography*, ed. David A. Lanegran and Risa Palm, 58–77. New York: McGraw-Hill.

——. 1982. "Segregating and Mixing: Space and Residence in Belfast." In *Integration and Division: Geographical Perspectives on the Northern Ireland Problem*, ed. Frederick W. Boal and J. Neville H. Douglas, 249–80. London: Academic Press.

Boal, Frederick W., Paul Doherty, and Dennis G. Pringle. 1973. *The Spatial Distribution of Some Social Problems in the Belfast Urban Area*. Belfast: Northern Ireland Community Relations Commission.

Boldt, Andreas and Seán Ó Ceilleachair. 2005. "Peter Hart and His Enemies." *History Ireland* 13 (5): 12–14.

Borneman, John. 1997. *Settling Accounts: Violence, Justice and Accountability in Postsocialist Europe*. Princeton, N.J.: Princeton University Press.

——. 2002. "Reconciliation After Ethnic Cleansing: Listening, Retribution, and Affiliation." *Public Culture* 14 (2): 281–304.

Botes, Johannes. 2003. "Conflict Transformation: A Debate over Semantics or a Crucial Shift in the Practice of Peace and Conflict Studies?" *International Journal of Peace Studies* 8 (2): 1–27.

Bourgois, Philippe. 2001. "The Power of Violence in War and Peace: Post-Cold War Lessons from El Salvador." *Ethnography* 2 (1): 5–34.

———. 2003. "Introduction: Making Sense of Violence." In *Violence in War and Peace: An Anthology*, ed. Nancy Scheper-Hughes and Philippe Bourgois, 1–27. Oxford: Blackwell.

Boyd, Gavin. 2011. *Left Out of the Equation: The Experiences of Lesbian, Gay and Bisexual Young People at School*. Belfast: Cara-Friend and the Rainbow Project.

Breen, Richard. 2000. "Class Inequality and Social Mobility in Northern Ireland, 1973–1996." *American Sociological Review* 65 (3): 392–406.

Breen, Richard and B. Miller. 1993. *A Socio-Economic Profile of the Making Belfast Work Area*. Belfast: MBW.

Brett, C. E. B. 1986. *Housing a Divided Community*. Dublin: Institute of Public Administration in Association with Institute of Irish Studies, Queen's University of Belfast.

———. 1990. "The International Fund for Ireland, 1986–1989." *Political Quarterly* 61 (4): 431–40.

British and Irish Governments. 1993. "Joint Declaration on Peace: The Downing Street Declaration, Wednesday 15 December 1993." Cain Web Service, http://cain .ulst.ac.uk/.

Brown, James Larry and Hank Pizer. 1987. *Living Hungry in America*. New York: Macmillan.

Brown, Wendy. 2004. "'The Most We Can Hope For . . .' : Human Rights and the Politics of Fatalism." *South Atlantic Quarterly* 103 (2/3): 451–63.

Bryan, Dominic. 2000a. *Orange Parades: The Politics of Ritual, Tradition and Control*. London: Pluto Press.

———. 2000b. "Drumcree and 'The Right to March': Orangeism, Ritual and Politics in Northern Ireland." In *The Irish Parading Tradition: Following the Drum*, ed. T. G. Fraser, 191–207. Basingstoke: Macmillan.

———. 2006a. "'Traditional' Parades, Conflict and Change: Orange Parades and Other Rituals in Northern Ireland, 1960–2000." In *Political Rituals in Great Britain: 1700–2000*, ed. Jorg Neuheiser and Michael Schaich, 123–38. Augsburg: Wisner-Verlag.

———. 2006b. "The Politics of Community." *Critical Review of International Social and Political Philosophy* 9 (4): 603–17.

Buchowski, Michal. 1996. "The Shifting Meanings of Civil and Civic Society in Poland." In *Civil Society: Challenging Western Models*, ed. Chris Hann and Elizabeth Dunn, 79–98. London: Routledge.

Bunzl, Matti. 2004. *Symptoms of Modernity: Jews and Queers in Late-Twentieth-Century Vienna*. Berkeley: University of California Press.

Burgess, Heidi and Guy Burgess. 2010. *Conducting Track II Peacemaking*. Washington, D.C.: U.S. Institute of Peace.

Burgess, Thomas Paul. 2002. *Community Relations, Community Identity, and Social Policy in Northern Ireland*. Lewiston, N.Y.: Edwin Mellen.

Buss, Doris and Didi Herman. 2003. *Globalizing Family Values: The Christian Right in International Politics*. Minneapolis: University of Minnesota Press.

Butler, David. 1994a. "The Study of Culture in Northern Ireland or 'What's So Bad About Peace, Love and Understanding?' Part I." *Causeway* 1 (2): 27–33.

———. 1994b. "The Study of Culture in Northern Ireland or 'What's So Bad About Peace, Love and Understanding?' Part II." *Causeway* 1 (3): 50–55.

Butler, Judith. 1993. *Bodies That Matter: On the Discursive Limits of "Sex".* New York: Routledge.

Byrne, Jonny, Cathy Gormley Heenan, and Gillian Robinson. 2012. *Attitudes to Peace Walls: Research Report to Office of First Minister and Deputy First Minister.* Belfast: University of Ulster.

Byrne, Sean. 2011. *Economic Assistance and Conflict Transformation.* Abingdon: Routledge.

Byrne, Sean, Olga Skarlato, Eyob Fissuh, and Cynthia Irvin. 2009. "Building Trust and Goodwill in Northern Ireland and the Border Counties: The Impact of Economic Aid on the Peace Process." *Irish Political Studies* 24 (3): 337–63.

Byrne, Sean, Katerina Standish, Eyob Fissuh, Jobb Arnold, and Pauline Tennent. 2009a. "Building the Peace Dividend in Northern Ireland: People's Perceptions of Self and Country." *Nationalism and Ethnic Politics* 15 (2): 160–88.

———. 2009b. "The EU Peace II Fund and the International Fund for Ireland: Nurturing Cross-Community Contact and Reconciliation in Northern Ireland." *Geopolitics* 14 (4): 630–52.

Byrne, Sean, Chuck Thiessen, Eyob Fissuh, Cynthia Irvin, and Marcie Hawranik. 2008. "Economic Assistance, Development and Peacebuilding: The Role of the IFI and EU Peace II Fund in Northern Ireland." *Civil Wars* 10 (2): 106–24.

CAJ (Committee on the Administration of Justice). 1990. *Making Rights Count: Includes a Proposed Bill of Rights for Northern Ireland.* Belfast: CAJ.

———. 1993. *A Bill of Rights for Northern Ireland.* Belfast: CAJ.

———. 1997. *Making a Bill of Rights Stick: Options for Implementation in Northern Ireland, a Discussion Paper, September 1997.* Belfast: CAJ.

Chambers, Liam. 1998. *Rebellion in Kildare, 1790–1803.* Dublin: Four Courts Press.

Chong, Daniel P. 2010. *Freedom from Poverty: NGOs and Human Rights Praxis.* Philadelphia: University of Pennsylvania Press.

Church, Cheyanne, Anna Visser, and Laurie Shepherd Johnson. 2004. "A Path to Peace or Persistence? The 'Single Identity' Approach to Conflict Resolution in Northern Ireland." *Conflict Resolution Quarterly* 21 (3): 269–93.

Clancy, Mary-Alice. 2010. *Peace Without Consensus: Power Sharing Politics in Northern Ireland.* Burlington, Vt.: Ashgate.

Cochrane, Feargal. 2001. "Unsung Heroes or Muddle-Headed Peaceniks? A Profile and Assessment of NGO Conflict Resolution Activity in the Northern Ireland 'Peace Process.'" *Irish Studies in International Affairs* 12: 97–112.

———. 2006. "Two Cheers for the NGOs: Building Peace from Below in Northern Ireland." In *A Farewell to Arms? Beyond the Good Friday Agreement,* ed. Michael Cox, Adrien Guelke, and Fiona Stephen, 253–66. Manchester: Manchester University Press.

———. 2007. "Irish-America, the End of the IRA's Armed Struggle and the Utility of 'Soft Power.'" *Journal of Peace Research* 44 (2): 215–31.

Cochrane, Feargal and Seamus Dunn. 2002. *People Power? The Role of the Voluntary and Community Sector in the Northern Ireland Conflict*. Cork: Cork University Press.

Cohen, Jean L. and Andrew Arato. 1994. *Civil Society and Political Theory*. Cambridge, Mass.: MIT Press.

Comaroff, John L. and Jean Comaroff. 1999. "Introduction." In *Civil Society and the Political Imagination in Africa: Critical Perspectives*, ed. John L. Comaroff and Jean Comaroff, 1–43. Chicago: University of Chicago Press.

Community Relations Council. 2010. *Consultation on Public Assemblies, Parades & Protest Bill (Northern Ireland)*. Belfast: Community Relations Council.

Community Relations Unit. 2003. *A Shared Future: A Consultation Paper on Improving Relations in Northern Ireland*. Belfast: Community Relations Unit, Office of the First Minister and Deputy First Minister.

———. 2005. *A Shared Future: Policy and Strategic Framework for Good Relations in Northern Ireland*. Belfast: Community Relations Unit, Office of the First Minister and Deputy First Minister.

Conrad, Kathryn. 1999. "Women Troubles, Queer Troubles: Gender, Sexuality and the Politics of Selfhood in the Construction of the Irish State." In *Reclaiming Gender: Transgressive Identities in Modern Ireland*, ed. Marilyn Cohen and Nancy Curtin, 53–68. New York: St. Martin's.

———. 2001. "Queer Treasons: Homosexuality and Irish National Identity." *Cultural Studies* 15 (1): 127–37.

———. 2006. "Queering Community: Reimagining the Public Sphere in Northern Ireland." *Critical Review of International Social and Political Philosophy* 9 (4): 589–602.

———. 2009. "'Nothing to Hide . . . Nothing to Fear': Discriminatory Surveillance and Queer Visibility in Great Britain and Northern Ireland." In *Ashgate Research Companion to Queer Theory*, ed. Noreen Giffney and Michael O'Rourke, 329–46. Surrey: Ashgate.

Consultative Group on the Past. 2009. *Report of Consultative Group on the Past*. Belfast: CGPNI.

Conway, Brian. 2010. *Commemoration and Bloody Sunday: Pathways of Memory*. Basingstoke: Palgrave Macmillan.

Cory, Peter. 2003a. *Cory Collusion Inquiry Report: Chief Superintendent Breen and Superintendent Buchanan*. Dublin: Department for Justice, Equality and Law Reform.

———. 2003b. *Cory Collusion Inquiry Report: Patrick Finucane*. London: HMSO/ Stationery Office (TSO).

———. 2003c. *Cory Collusion Inquiry Report: Lord Justice Gibson and Lady Gibson*. Dublin: Department for Justice, Equality and Law Reform.

———. 2003d. *Cory Collusion Inquiry Report: Robert Hamill*. London: HMSO/Stationery Office (TSO).

——. 2003e. *Cory Collusion Inquiry Report: Rosemary Nelson.* London: HMSO/ Stationery Office (TSO).

——. 2003f. *Cory Collusion Inquiry Report: Billy Wright.* London: HMSO/ Stationery Office (TSO).

Coulter, Colin. 1999. *Contemporary Northern Irish Society: An Introduction.* London: Pluto Press.

Couto, Richard. 2001. "The Third Sector and Civil Society: The Case of the 'YES' Campaign in Northern Ireland." *Voluntas* 12 (3): 221–38.

Cowan, Jane K. 2006. "Culture and Rights After Culture and Rights." *American Anthropologist* 108 (1): 9–24.

Cowan, Jane K., Marie-Bénédicte Dembour, and Richard Ashby Wilson, eds. 2001. *Culture and Rights: Anthropological Perspectives.* Cambridge: Cambridge University Press.

Cox, Michael, Adrian Guelke, and Fiona Stephen. 2006. "Introduction: A Farewell to Arms? Beyond the Good Friday Agreement." In *A Farewell to Arms? Beyond the Good Friday Agreement*, ed. Michael Cox, Adrian Guelke, and Fiona Stephens, 1–23. Manchester: Manchester University Press.

CSJ (Campaign for Social Justice). 1964. *Northern Ireland: The Plain Truth.* Dungannon: CSJ.

——. 1966. *Northern Ireland: Legal Aid to Oppose Discrimination—Not Likely!* Dungannon: CSJ. Cullen, Holly. 2009. "The Collective Complaints System of the European Social Charter: Interpretative Methods of the European Committee of Social Rights." *Human Rights Law Review* 9 (1): 61–93.

Cullen, Louis. 1986. "Catholics Under the Penal Laws." *Eighteenth-Century Ireland/Iris an dá chultúr* 1: 23–36.

Curle, Adam. 1990. *Tools for Transformation.* Stroud: Hawthorn Press.

Curtis, Jennifer. 2008. "'Community' and the Re-Making of 1970s Belfast." *Ethnos* 73 (3): 399–426.

——. 2010. "'Profoundly Ungrateful': The Paradoxes of Thatcherism in Northern Ireland." *PoLAR: Political and Legal Anthropology Review* 33 (2): 201–24.

Curtis, Jennifer and Jonathan Spencer. 2012. "Anthropology and the Political." In *Sage Handbook of Anthropology*, vol. 1, ed. Richard Fardon and Richard Ashby Wilson, 134–45. London: Sage.

Darby, John. 1976. *Conflict in Northern Ireland: The Development of a Polarised Community.* Dublin: Gill and Macmillan.

Darby, John and Colin Knox. 2004. *"A Shared Future": A Consultation Paper on Improving Relations in Northern Ireland, Final Report [An Analysis of the Responses to the Shared Future Consultation].* Belfast: Community Relations Unit, Office of the First Minister and Deputy First Minister.

Darby, John and Roger MacGinty. 2000. "Northern Ireland: Long, Cold Peace." In *The Management of Peace Processes*, ed. John Darby and Roger MacGinty, 61–106. Basingstoke: Palgrave.

Das, Veena and Arthur Kleinman. 2000. "Introduction." In *Violence and Subjectivity*, ed. Veena Das, Arthur Kleinman, Mamphela Ramphele, and Pamela Reynolds, 1–18. Berkeley: University of California Press.

Dave, Naisargi. 2010. "To Render Real the Imagined: An Ethnographic History of Lesbian Community in India." *Signs: Journal of Women in Culture and Society* 35 (3): 595–619.

De Baróid, Ciarán. 1989. *Ballymurphy and the Irish War*. Báile atha Clíath (Dublin): Aisling.

de Silva, Sir Desmond. 2012. *Pat Finucane Review*. London: HMSO/Stationery Office.

Dean, Séamus. 1988. *Selected Poems*. Loughcrew: Gallery Press.

Dembour, Marie-Bénédicte. 2010. "What Are Human Rights? Four Schools of Thought." *Human Rights Quarterly* 32 (1): 1–20.

Devlin [McAliskey], Bernadette. 1988. "A Peasant in the Halls of the Great." In *Twenty Years On*, ed. Michael Farrell, 75–88. Dingle: Brandon Books.

Dickson, Brice. 2010. *The European Convention on Human Rights and the Conflict in Northern Ireland*. Oxford: Oxford University Press.

Divis Residents Association. 1986. *The Divis Report: Set Them Free!* Belfast: Divis Residents Association.

Dixon, Paul. 1997. "Paths to Peace in Northern Ireland (I): Civil Society and Consociational Approaches." *Democratization* 4 (2): 1–27.

———. 2001. *Northern Ireland: The Politics of War and Peace*. Basingstoke: Palgrave Macmillan.

Donnan, Hastings. 2005. "Material Identities: Fixing Ethnicity in the Irish Borderlands." *Identities: Global Studies in Culture and Power* 12 (1): 69–105.

Donnan, Hastings and Kirk Simpson. 2007. "Silence and Violence Among Northern Ireland Border Protestants." *Ethnos* 72 (1): 5–28.

Donnelly, Jack. 2003. *Universal Human Rights in Theory and Practice*. Ithaca, N.Y.: Cornell University Press.

———. 2006. "Peace as a Human Right: Commentary." In *Human Rights and Conflict: Exploring Links Between Rights, Law and Peacebuilding*, ed. Julie Mertus and Jeffrey Helsing, 151–56. Washington, D.C.: U.S. Institute of Peace.

Dooley, Brian. 1998. *Black and Green: Civil Rights Struggles in Northern Ireland and Black America*. London: Pluto Press.

Doran, Peter. 2010. "Can Civil Society Succeed Where Elites Have Failed in the War on Sectarianism? Towards an Infinitely Demanding Politics for the North." *Irish Journal of Sociology* 18 (2): 126–50.

Duffy, Aoife. 2010. "A Truth Commission for Northern Ireland?" *International Journal of Transitional Justice* 4 (1): 26–46.

Duggan, Marian. 2010. "The Politics of Pride: Representing Relegated Sexual Identities in Northern Ireland." *Northern Ireland Legal Quarterly* 61 (2): 163–78.

Dunn, Elizabeth. 1996. "Money, Morality and Modes of Civil Society Among American Mormons." In *Civil Society: Challenging Western Models*, ed. Chris Hann and Elizabeth Dunn, 27–49. London: Routledge.

Dunne, Tom. 2010. *Rebellions: Memoir, Memory and 1798.* Dublin: Lilliput.

Durey, Michael. 1997. *Transatlantic Radicals and the Early American Republic.* Lawrence: University of Kansas Press.

Elias, Robert and Jennifer Turpin. 1994. "Introduction: Thinking About Peace." In *Rethinking Peace,* ed. Robert Elias and Jennifer Turpin, 1–12. Boulder, Colo.: Lynne Rienner.

Elliott, Marianne. 1982. *Partners in Revolution: The United Irishmen and France.* New Haven, Conn.: Yale University Press.

Elliott, Sydney and W. D. Flackes. 1999. *Conflict in Northern Ireland: An Encyclopedia.* Santa Barbara, Calif.: ABC-CLIO.

Elyachar, Julia. 2005. *Markets of Dispossession: NGOs, Economic Development, and the State in Cairo.* Durham, N.C.: Duke University Press.

Equality Commission for Northern Ireland. 2009. *Equality Awareness Survey 2008.* Belfast: Equality Commission.

———. 2010. *Monitoring Report No. 21: A Profile of the Monitored Northern Ireland Workforce.* Belfast: Equality Commission.

European Union. 2007. *Peace III: EU Programme for Peace and Reconciliation 2007–2013 Northern Ireland and the Border Region of Ireland Operational Programme.* Belfast: Special EU Programmes Body.

Fair Employment Tribunal. 2012. CASE REF: 75/11FET.

Falls Think Tank. 1996. *Ourselves Alone? Voices from Belfast's Nationalist Working Class.* Comp. Michael Hall. Island Pamphlets 15. Newtownabbey: Island Publications.

Farrington, Christopher, ed. 2004. *Models of Civil Society and Their Implications for the Northern Ireland Peace Process.* Dublin: Institute for British-Irish Studies University College Dublin.

———. 2008. *Global Change, Civil Society and the Peace Process in Northern Ireland: Implementing the Political Settlement.* Basingstoke: Palgrave Macmillan.

Fassin, Didier. 2009. "Another Politics of Life Is Possible." *Theory Culture Society* 26 (5): 44–60.

Feher, Michel. 1999. "Terms of Reconciliation." In *Human Rights in Political Transitions: Gettysburg to Bosnia,* ed. Carla Hesse and Robert Post, 325–38. New York: Zone Books.

Feinstein, Charles. 1994. "Success and Failure: British Economic Growth Since 1948." In *The Economic History of Britain Since 1700,* vol. 3, ed. Roderick Floud and Deirdre McCloskey, 95–122. Cambridge: Cambridge University Press.

Feldman, Allen. 1991. *Formations of Violence: The Narrative of the Body and Political Terror in Northern Ireland.* Chicago: University of Chicago Press.

Ferguson, Niall, Mark Burgess and Ian Hollywood. 2010. "Who Are the Victims? Victimhood Experiences in Postagreement Northern Ireland." *Political Psychology* 31 (6): 857–86.

Finlay, Andrew. 2008. "The Persistence of the 'Old' Idea of Culture and the Peace Process in Ireland." *Critique of Anthropology* 28 (3): 279–96.

———. 2010. *Governing Ethnic Conflict: Consociation, Identity and the Price of Peace*. Abingdon: Routledge.

Foster, Roy. 1988. *Modern Ireland: 1600–1972*. London: Penguin.

———. 2001. "Remembering 1798." In *History and Memory in Modern Ireland*, ed. Ian McBride, 67–94. Cambridge: Cambridge University Press.

———. 2007. "Partnership of Loss." *London Review of Books* 29 (24): 21–23.

France, Anatole. 1910. *The Red Lily*. New York: Current Publishing.

Gaffiken, Frank and Mike Morrissey. 1989. "Community Enterprise in Northern Ireland: Privatising Poverty?" In *Lost Horizons, New Horizons: Community Development in Northern Ireland (Conference Proceedings)*. Belfast: Workers' Educational Association and Community Development Review Group.

Galant, Ghalib and Michelle Parlevliet. 2005. "Using Rights to Address Conflict: A Valuable Synergy." In *Reinventing Development: Translating Rights-Based Approaches from Theory into Practice*, ed. Paul Gready and Jonathan Ensor, 108–28. London: Zed.

Gamble, Andrew. 1988. *The Free Economy and the Strong State: The Politics of Thatcherism*. Basingstoke: Macmillan Education.

Gargett, Graham and Geraldine Sheridan, eds. 1999. *Ireland and the French Enlightenment, 1700–1800*. New York: St. Martin's.

Gellner, Ernest. 1994. *Conditions of Liberty: Civil Society and Its Rivals*. London: Hamish Hamilton.

Gibbons, Luke. 2003. *Edmund Burke and Ireland*. Cambridge: Cambridge University Press.

Gidron, Benjamin, Stanley N. Katz, and Yeheskel Hasenfeld. 2002. *Mobilizing for Peace: Conflict Resolution in Northern Ireland, Israel/Palestine and South Africa*. Oxford: Oxford University Press.

Gledhill, John. 2003. "Rights and the Poor." In *Human Rights in Global Perspective: Anthropological Studies of Rights, Claims, and Entitlements*, ed. Richard Ashby Wilson and Jon P. Mitchell, 209–28. London: Routledge.

Goldhagen, Daniel Jonah. 1996. *Hitler's Willing Executioners: Ordinary Germans and the Holocaust*. New York: Knopf.

Goldstein, Joshua S. 2011. *Winning the War on War: The Decline of Armed Conflict Worldwide*. New York: Dutton.

Goodale, Mark. 2009a. *Dilemmas of Modernity: Bolivian Encounters with Law and Liberalism*. Stanford, Calif.: Stanford University Press.

———. 2009b. *Surrendering to Utopia: An Anthropology of Human Rights*. Stanford, Calif.: Stanford University Press.

Goodale, Mark and Sally Engle Merry, eds. 2007. *The Practice of Human Rights*. Cambridge: Cambridge University Press.

Government of Northern Ireland. 1972. *Violence and Civil Disturbances in Northern Ireland in 1969*. Belfast: HMSO.

Graham, Brian and Peter Shirlow. 2002. "The Battle of the Somme in Ulster Memory and Identity." *Political Geography* 21 (7): 881–904.

Graham, Brian and Yvonne Whelan. 2007. "The Legacies of the Dead: Commemorating the Troubles in Northern Ireland." *Environment and Planning D: Society and Space* 25 (3): 476–95.

Griffiths, Hywel. 1974. *Community Development in Northern Ireland: A Case-Study in Agency Conflict*. Belfast: Hywel Griffiths.

———. 1975a. "Paramilitary Groups and Other Community Action Groups in Northern Ireland Today." *Centro Sociale* 22 (Winter): 189–206.

———. 1975b. "Community Development: Some More Lessons from the Recent Past in Northern Ireland." *Community Development Journal* 10 (1): 2–13.

———. 1978. "Community Reaction and Voluntary Involvement." In *Violence and the Social Services in Northern Ireland*, ed. John P. Darby and Arthur P. Williamson, 165–94. London: Heinemann.

Guelke, Adrian. 2003. "Civil Society and the Northern Irish Peace Process." *Voluntas* 14 (1): 61–78.

Gurr, Ted. 1970. *Why Men Rebel*. Princeton, N.J.: Princeton University Press.

Haase, Trutz and Jonathan Pratschke. 1999. *European Union Special Support Programme for Peace and Reconciliation: Analysis of Community Uptake*. Belfast: NISRA.

Hall, Michael, comp. 1993. *Life on the Interface*. Belfast: Island Pamphlets.

———. 1995. *A New Beginning*. Belfast: Island Pamphlets.

———. 1996. *Ourselves Alone?* Belfast: Island Pamphlets.

———. 2000a. *Seeds of Hope*. Belfast: Island Pamphlets.

———. 2000b. *Left in Limbo*. Belfast: Island Pamphlets.

———. 2001a. *The Forgotten Victims*. Belfast: Island Pamphlets.

———. 2001b. *The Unequal Victims*. Belfast: Island Pamphlets.

———. 2010. *Time Stands Still*. Belfast: Island Pamphlets.

———. 2011a. *Republicanism in Transition (1): The Need for a Debate*. Belfast: Island Pamphlets.

———. 2011b. *Republicanism in Transition (2): Beginning a Debate*. Belfast: Island Pamphlets.

———. 2011c. *Republicanism in Transition (3): Irish Republicanism Today*. Belfast: Island Pamphlets.

———. 2012a. *Republicanism in Transition (4): The Question of "Armed Struggle."* Belfast: Island Pamphlets.

———. 2012b. *Republicanism in Transition (5): An Engagement with Loyalists*. Belfast: Island Pamphlets.

Hall, Stuart. 1988. *The Hard Road to Renewal*. London: Verso

Hamber, Brandon. 1998. "Conclusion: A Truth Commission for Northern Ireland?" In *Past Imperfect: Dealing with the Past in Northern Ireland and Societies in Transition*, ed. Brandon Hamber, 78–79. Derry/Londonderry: University of Ulster/ INCORE.

———. 2003. "Rights and Reasons: Challenges for Truth Recovery in South Africa and Northern Ireland." *Fordham International Law Journal* 26 (4): 1074–94.

Hamill, Heather. 2011. *The Hoods: Crime and Punishment in Belfast.* Princeton, N.J.: Princeton University Press.

Hann, Chris. 1996. "Introduction: Political Society and Civil Anthropology." In *Civil Society: Challenging Western Models,* ed. Chris Hann and Elizabeth Dunn, 1–26. London: Routledge.

Hannigan, John A. 1985. "The Armalite and the Ballot Box: Dilemmas of Strategy and Ideology in the Provisional IRA." *Social Problems* 33 (1): 31–40.

Harbison, Jeremy. 2002a. *Review of Community Relations Policy: Annexes 1 to 10.* Belfast: Community Relations Unit, Office of the First Minister and Deputy First Minister.

———. 2002b. *Review of Community Relations Policy: Main Report.* Belfast: Community Relations Unit, Office of the First Minister and Deputy First Minister.

Harrington Kilbride PLC. 1989. *Employment Gazette* 5 (May). London: Employment Department.

Hart, Peter. 1998. *The I.R.A. and Its Enemies: Violence and Community in Cork, 1916–1923.* Oxford: Clarendon.

———. 2003. *The IRA at War 1916–1923.* Oxford: Oxford University Press.

———. 2005. "Peter Hart and His Enemies." *History Ireland* 13 (4): 16–19.

Hart, Peter and Brian Hanley. 2005. "Interview: Hart to Heart." *History Ireland* 13 (2): 48–51.

Harvey, Colin J. 2001. "Building a Human Rights Culture in a Political Democracy: The Role of the Northern Ireland Human Rights Commission." In *Human Rights, Equality and Democratic Renewal in Northern Ireland,* ed. Colin J. Harvey, 113–130. Oxford: Hart.

———. 2003. "Stick to the Terms of the Agreement." *Fortnight* 416: 9.

———. 2005. "Creating a Culture of Respect for Human Rights." In *Human Rights in the Community: Rights as Agents for Change,* ed. Colin J. Harvey, 1–5. Oxford: Hart.

Harvey, David. 2008. "The Right to the City." *New Left Review* 53: 23–40.

Hayes, Bernadette C. and Ian McAllister. 2001. "Sowing Dragon's Teeth: Public Support for Political Violence and Paramilitarism in Northern Ireland." *Political Studies* 49 (5): 901–22.

Hayner, Priscilla B. 2010. *Unspeakable Truths: Transitional Justice and the Challenge of Truth Commissions.* New York: Routledge.

Healing Through Remembering (HTR). 2002. *The Report of the Healing Through Remembering Project.* Belfast: HTR

Hearn, Jonathan. 1997. "Scottish Nationalism and the Civil Society Concept: Should Auld Acquaintance Be Forgot?" *PoLAR: Political and Legal Anthropology Review* 20 (1): 32–39.

Hegarty, Angela. 2005. "Truth, Law and Official Denial: The Case of Bloody Sunday." In *Truth Commissions and Courts,* ed. William A. Schabas and Shane Darcy, 199–246. Dordrecht: Kluwer Academic.

Helsing, Jeffrey and Julie Mertus, eds. 2006. *Human Rights and Conflict: Exploring Links Between Rights, Law and Peacebuilding.* Washington, D.C.: U.S. Institute of Peace.

Helsinki Watch. 1991. *Human Rights in Northern Ireland.* New York: Human Rights Watch.

Hepburn, A. C. 1990. "The Belfast Riots of 1935." *Social History* 15 (1): 75–96.

Hewitt, Christopher. 1981. "Catholic Grievances, Catholic Nationalism and Violence in Northern Ireland During the Civil Rights Period: A Reconsideration." *British Journal of Sociology* 32 (3): 362–80.

———. 1983. "Discrimination in Northern Ireland: A Rejoinder." *British Journal of Sociology* 34 (3): 446–51.

———. 1985. "Catholic Grievances and Violence in Northern Ireland." *British Journal of Sociology* 36 (1): 101–5.

———. 1987. "Explaining Violence in Northern Ireland." *British Journal of Sociology* 38 (1): 88–93.

Hinton, Alexander Laban. 2010. "Toward an Anthropology of Transitional Justice." In *Transitional Justice: Global Mechanisms and Local Realities After Genocide and Mass Violence*, ed. Alexander Hinton Laban, 1–22. New Brunswick, N.J.: Rutgers University Press.

———, ed. 2010. *Transitional Justice: Global Mechanisms and Local Realities after Genocide and Mass Violence.* New Brunswick, N.J.: Rutgers University Press.

Holland, Jack. 2001. *The American Connection: U.S. Guns, Money and Influence in Northern Ireland.* Boulder, Colo.: Roberts Rinehart.

Howard, Michael. 2000. *The Invention of Peace: Reflections on War and International Order.* London: Profile Books.

———. 2005. *'Storytelling' Audit: An Audit of Personal Story, Narrative, and Testimony Initiatives Related to the Conflict in and About Northern Ireland.* Belfast: HTR.

Human Rights Consortium. 2011. *Bill of Rights for Northern Ireland: OVERDUE!* Belfast: Human Rights Consortium.

Human Rights Watch. 2001. *Hatred in the Hallways: Violence and Discrimination Against Lesbian, Gay, Bisexual, and Transgender Students in U.S. Schools.* New York: Human Rights Watch.

Humphreys, Laud. 1972. *Out of the Closets: The Sociology of Homosexual Liberation.* Englewood Cliffs N.J.: Prentice Hall.

Hunt, Lynn. 2007. *Inventing Human Rights: A History.* New York: Norton.

Ignatieff, Michael. 1999. "Human Rights." In *Human Rights in Political Transitions: Gettysburg to Bosnia*, ed. Carla Hesse and Robert Post, 313–24. New York: Zone Books.

———. 2001. *Human Rights as Politics and Idolatry.* Princeton, N.J.: Princeton University Press.

Ingoldby, G. D. 1976. "You've Got a Friend." *Fortnight* 125: 8, 13.

Ipsos Mori. 2011. *Attitudes Towards the Bill of Rights in Northern Ireland: Summary of Findings.* Belfast: Ipsos Mori.

Ishay, Micheline. 2008. *The History of Human Rights: From Ancient Times to the Global-ization Era*. Berkeley: University of California Press.

Jacobson, Matthew Frye. 2006. *Roots Too: White Ethnic Revival in Post-Civil Rights America*. Cambridge, Mass.: Harvard University Press.

Jarman, Neil. 1993. "Intersecting Belfast." In *Landscape: Politics and Perspectives*, ed. Barbara Bender, 107–38. Oxford: Berg.

———. 1997. *On the Edge: Community Perspectives on the Civil Disturbances in North Belfast, June–September 1996*. Belfast: Community Development Centre.

———. 1999a. "Commemorating 1916, Celebrating Difference: Parading and Painting in Belfast." In *The Art of Forgetting*, ed. Adrian Forty and Susanne Kuchler, 171–95. Oxford: Berg.

———. 1999b. *Drawing Back from the Edge: Community-Based Response to Violence in North Belfast*. Belfast: Community Development Centre: North Belfast.

———. 2003. "From Outrage to Apathy: The Disputes over Parades, 1995–2003." *Global Review of Ethnopolitics* 3 (1): 92–105.

———. 2005. *No Longer a Problem? Sectarian Violence in Northern Ireland*. Belfast: Institute for Conflict Research.

———. 2007. "Another Form of Troubles: Parades, Protests and the Northern Ireland Peace Process, 1995–2004." In *The Street as Stage: Protest Marches and Public Rallies Since the Nineteenth Century*, ed. Matthias Reiss, 255–72. Oxford: Oxford University Press.

———. 2012. *Belfast Interfaces: Security Barriers and Defensive Use of Space*. Belfast: Belfast Interface Project.

Jarman, Neil and Dominic Bryan. 1996. *Parade and Protest: A Discussion of Parading Disputes in Northern Ireland*. Coleraine: Center for the Study of Conflict, University of Ulster.

———. 1998. *From Riots to Rights: Nationalist Parades in the North of Ireland*. Coleraine: Center for the Study of Conflict, University of Ulster.

Jarman, Neil and Alex Tennant. 2003. *An Acceptable Prejudice? Homophobic Violence and Harassment in Northern Ireland*. Belfast: Institute for Conflict Research.

Jean-Klein, Jean and Annelise Riles. 2005. "Anthropology and Human Rights Admin-istrations: Expert Observation and Representation After the Fact." *PoLAR: Political and Legal Anthropology Review* 28 (2): 173–202.

Jowitt, Edwin, Kathleen Richardson, and John Evans. 2010. *Interim Report by the Rob-ert Hamill Inquiry to the Secretary of State for Northern Ireland* (dated January 28, released March 12). Belfast: Robert Hamill Inquiry.

Kang, Susan L. 2009. "The Unsettled Relationship of Economic and Social Rights and the West: A Response to Whelan and Donnelly." *Human Rights Quarterly* 31 (4): 1006–29.

Keck, Margaret and Kathryn Sikkink. 1998. *Activists Beyond Borders: Advocacy Net-works in International Politics*. Ithaca N.Y.: Cornell University Press.

Keenan, Alan. 2006. "Building a Democratic Middle-Ground: Professional Civil Society and the Politics of Human Rights in Sri Lanka's Peace Process. In *Human Rights and Conflict: New Actors, Strategies and Ethical Dilemmas*, ed. Jeff Helsing and Julie Mertus, 459–505. Washington, D.C.: U.S. Institute of Peace.

———. 2007. "The Temptations of Evenhandedness: On the Politics of Human Rights and Peace Advocacy in Sri Lanka." In *Nongovernmental Politics*, ed. Michel Feher, 88–117. New York: Zone Books.

Kennedy, Kieran A., Thomas Giblin, and Deirdre McHugh. 1988. *The Economic Development of Ireland in the Twentieth Century*. London: Routledge.

Kennedy, Liam. 2001. *They Shoot Children, Don't They? An Analysis of the Age and Gender of Victims of Paramilitary "Punishments" in Northern Ireland*. Report Prepared for the Northern Ireland Committee Against Terror (NICAT) and the Northern Ireland Affairs Committee of the House of Commons.

Kennedy, Richard K. 1976. "Letter." *Fortnight* 126: 18.

Kerr, Michael. 2006. *Imposing Power-Sharing: Conflict and Consensus in Northern Ireland and Lebanon*. Dublin: Irish Academic Press.

Kipnis, Andrew B. 2007. "Neoliberalism Reified: Suzhi Discourse and Tropes of Neoliberalism in the People's Republic of China." *Journal of the Royal Anthropological Institute (N.S.)* 13 (2): 383–400.

———. 2008. "Audit Cultures: Neoliberal Governmentality, Socialist Legacy, or Technologies of Governing?" *American Ethnologist* 35 (2): 275–89.

Kirkup, Alex and Tony Evans. 2009. "The Myth of Western Opposition to Economic, Social, and Cultural Rights? A Reply to Whelan and Donnelly." *Human Rights Quarterly* 31 (1): 221–38.

Kitchin, Rob and Karen Lysaght. 2003. "Heterosexism and the Geographies of Everyday Life in Belfast, Northern Ireland." *Environment and Planning A* 35 (3): 489–510.

Kodras, Janet E. 1997. "The Changing Map of American Poverty in an Era of Economic Restructuring and Political Realignment." *Economic Geography* 73 (1): 67–93.

Kollman, Kelly. 2007. "Same-Sex Unions: The Globalization of an Idea." *International Studies Quarterly* 51 (2): 329–57.

Kollman, Kelly and Matthew Waites. 2009. "The Global Politics of Lesbian, Gay, Bisexual and Transgender Human Rights: An Introduction." *Contemporary Politics* 15 (1): 1–17.

Kosciw, Joseph G. 2004. *The 2003 National School Climate Survey: The School-Related Experiences of Our Nation's Lesbian, Gay, Bisexual, and Transgender Youth*. New York: GLSEN.

Kymlicka, Will. 2001. *Politics in the Vernacular: Nationalism, Multiculturalism, and Citizenship*. Oxford: Oxford University Press.

Lauren, Paul Gordon. 2011. *The Evolution of International Human Rights: Visions Seen*. 3d ed. Philadelphia: University of Pennsylvania Press.

Lawther, Cheryl. 2011. "Unionism, Truth Recovery and the Fearful Past." *Irish Political Studies* 26 (3): 361–82.

Lederach, John Paul. 1995a. "Beyond Violence: Building Sustainable Peace." In *Beyond Violence: The Role of Voluntary and Community Action in Building a Sustainable Peace in Northern Ireland*, ed. Arthur Williamson, 11–22. Belfast: Community Relations Council.

———. 1995b. *Preparing for Peace: Conflict Transformation Across Cultures*. Syracuse, N.Y.: Syracuse University Press.

———. 1996. "Remember and Change." Paper presented at Peace and Reconciliation Conference, Fermanagh District Partnership, Enniskillen, Northern Ireland, July 1996.

———. 1997. *Building Peace: Sustainable Reconciliation in Divided Societies*. Washington, D.C.: U.S. Institute of Peace.

———. 2001. "Civil Society and Reconciliation." In *Turbulent Peace: The Challenges of Managing International Conflict*, ed. Chester A. Crocker, Fen Osler Hampson, and Pamela R. Aall, 841–54. Washington, D.C.: U.S. Institute of Peace.

———. 2005. *The Moral Imagination: The Art and Soul of Building Peace*. Oxford: Oxford University Press.

Lefebvre, Henri. 1996. *Writings on Cities*. Oxford: Blackwell.

Leonard, Madeleine. 1994. *Informal Economic Activity in Belfast*. Aldershot: Avebury.

LeSueur, Meridel. (1934) 1990. "Women Are Hungry." In *Ripening: Selected Work*, ed. Elaine Hedges, 144–57. New York: Feminist Press at City University of New York.

Lijphart, Arendt. 1977. *Democracy in Plural Societies: A Comparative Exploration*. New Haven, Conn.: Yale University Press.

———. 1999. *Patterns of Democracy*. New Haven, Conn.: Yale University Press.

———. 2002. "The Wave of Power-Sharing Democracy." In *Architecture of Democracy: Constitutional Design, Conflict Management, and Democracy*, ed. Andrew Reynolds, 37–54. Oxford: Oxford University Press.

Livingston, McKenzie A. 2003. "Out of the Troubles and into Rights: Protection for Gays, Lesbians, and Bisexuals in Northern Ireland Through Equality Legislation in the Good Friday Agreement." *Fordham International Law Journal* 27 (3): 1207–63.

Livingstone, Stephen and Rachel Murray. 2004. "The Effectiveness of National Human Rights Institutions." In *Human Rights Brought Home: Socio-Legal Perspectives of Human Rights in the National Context*, ed. Simon Halliday and Patrick Schmidt, 137–64. Oxford: Hart.

Lovett, Tom and Robin Percival. 1978. "Politics, Conflict and Community Action in Northern Ireland." In *Political Issues and Community Work*, ed. Paul Cuano, 174–95. London: Routledge and Kegan Paul.

Lundy, Laura and Tony Gallagher. 2006. "Religion, Education, and the Law in Northern Ireland." In *Religious Education in Public Schools: Study of Comparative Law*, ed.

José Luis Martínez López-Muniz, Jan de Groof, and Gracienne Lauwers, 171–95. Dordrecht: Springer.

Lundy, Patricia. 2011. "Paradoxes and Challenges of Transitional Justice at the 'Local' Level: Historical Enquiries in Northern Ireland." *Contemporary Social Science: Journal of the Academy of Social Sciences* 6 (1): 89–105.

Lundy, Patricia and Mark McGovern. 2006. "Participation, Truth and Partiality: Participatory Action Research, Community-Based Truth-Telling and Post-Conflict Transition in Northern Ireland." *Sociology* 40 (1): 71–88.

———. 2008a. "Whose Justice? Rethinking Transitional Justice from the Bottom Up." *Journal of Law and Society* 35 (2): 265–92.

———. 2008b. "A Trojan Horse? Unionism, Trust and Truth-Telling in Northern Ireland." *International Journal of Transitional Justice* 2 (1): 42–62.

MacLean, Lord, Andrew Coyle, and John Oliver. 2010. *The Billy Wright Inquiry—Report.* HC 431, September 14 . London: Stationery Office (TSO).

Mageean, Paul, and Martin O'Brien. 1999. "From the Margins to the Mainstream: Human Rights and the Good Friday Agreement." *Fordham International Law Journal* 22 (4): 1499–1538.

Maney, Gregory M. 2000. "Transnational Mobilization and Civil Rights in Northern Ireland." *Social Problems* 47 (2): 153–79.

Marcus, Sara. 2010. *Girls to the Front: The True Story of the Riot Revolution.* New York: HarperCollins.

Marston, Sallie A. 2002. "Making Difference: Conflict over Irish Identity in the New York City St. Patrick's Day Parade." *Political Geography* 21 (3): 373–92.

Masters, Edgar Lee. 1938. *Mark Twain: A Portrait.* New York: Biblo and Tannen.

McAleavey, Séamus. 2010. *Dialogue Paper Number One: The Role of the Third Sector in Civic Life, Democracy and Governance.* Belfast: NICVA.

McAuley, James, Jonathan Tonge, and Peter Shirlow. 2010. "Conflict, Transformation, and Former Loyalist Paramilitary Prisoners in Northern Ireland." *Terrorism and Political Violence* 22 (1): 22–40.

McBride, Ian. 1997. "'When Ulster Joined Ireland': Anti-Popery, Presbyterian Radicalism and Irish Republicanism in the 1790s." *Past & Present* 157: 63–93.

———. 1998. *Scripture Politics: Ulster Presbyterians and Irish Radicalism in the Late Eighteenth Century.* Oxford: Clarendon.

———, ed. 2001. *History and Memory in Modern Ireland.* Cambridge: Cambridge University Press.

McCann, Eamonn. 1980. *War and an Irish Town.* London: Pluto Press.

McCarthy, Mark. 2005. "Historico-Geographical Explorations of Ireland's Heritages: Towards a Critical Understanding of the Nature of Memory and Identity." In *Ireland's Heritages: Critical Perspectives on Memory and Identity*, ed. Mark McCarthy, 3–51. Aldershot: Ashgate.

McCluskey, Conn. 1989. *Up Off Their Knees: A Commentary on the Civil Rights Movement in Northern Ireland.* Galway: Conn McCluskey and Associates.

McCorquodale, Robert. 2010. "Non-State Actors and International Human Rights Law." In *Research Handbook on Human Rights Law*, ed. Sarah Joseph and Adam McBeth, 97–114. Cheltenham: Edward Elgar.

McCready Sam. 2001. *Empowering People: Community Development and Conflict, 1969–1999.* London: Stationery Office.

McDermott, Matthew. 2011. *Through Our Eyes: Experiences of Lesbian, Gay and Bisexual People in the Workplace.* Belfast: Rainbow Project.

McDonald, Henry. 2008. *Gunsmoke and Mirrors: How Sinn Féin Dressed Up Defeat as Victory.* Dublin: Gill and Macmillan.

McEvoy, Kieran. 1999. *Holding Armed Opposition Groups Accountable: A Comparative Study of Obstacles and Strategies: The Northern Ireland Experience.* Geneva: International Council on Human Rights Policy.

———. 2001. "Human Rights, Humanitarian Interventions and Paramilitary Activities in Northern Ireland." In *Human Rights, Equality and Democratic Renewal in Northern Ireland*, ed. Colin Harvey, 215–48. Oxford: Hart.

———. 2007. "Beyond Legalism: Towards a Thicker Understanding of Transitional Justice." *Journal of Law and Society* 34 (4): 411–40.

———. 2011. "What Did the Lawyers Do During the 'War'? Neutrality, Conflict and the Culture of Quietism." *Modern Law Review* 74 (3): 350–84.

McEvoy, Kieran, Peter Shirlow, and Karen McElrath. 2004. "Resistance, Transition and Exclusion: Politically Motivated Ex-Prisoners and Conflict Transformation in Northern Ireland." *Terrorism and Political Violence* 16 (3): 646–70.

McGarry, John and Brendan O'Leary. 1995. *Explaining Northern Ireland: Broken Images.* Oxford: Blackwell.

———. 2004. *The Northern Ireland Conflict: Consociational Engagements.* Oxford: Oxford University Press.

McGrattan, Cillian. 2012. "Spectres of History: Nationalist Party Politics and Truth Recovery in Northern Ireland." *Political Studies* 60 (2): 455–73.

McIntyre, Anthony. 2008. *Good Friday: The Death of Irish Republicanism.* New York: Ausubo Press.

McKeown, Michael. (2001) 2009. *Post-Mortem: An Examination of the Patterns of Politically Associated Violence in Northern Ireland During the Years 1969–2001 as Reflected in the Fatality Figures for Those Years.* www.cain.ulst.ac.uk/victims/mckeown/mckeown01.pdf.

McKittrick, David, Seamus Kelters, Brian Feeney, and Chris Thornton. 1999. *Lost Lives: The Stories of the Men, Women and Children Who Died as a Result of the Northern Ireland Troubles.* Edinburgh: Mainstream.

McLoone, Martin. 2004. "Punk Music in Northern Ireland." *Irish Studies Review* 12 (1): 29–38.

McNamee, Eoin. 1994. *Resurrection Man.* London: Picador.

McNamee, Peter and Tom Lovett. 1992. *Working-Class Community in Northern Ireland.* Belfast: Ulster People's College.

McWilliams, Monica. 1993. "The Church, the State and the Women's Movement in Northern Ireland." In *Irish Women's Studies Reader*, ed. Ailbhe Smyth, 79–99. Dublin: Attic Press.

Medeiros, Carmen. 2001. "Civilizing the Popular? The Law of Popular Participation and the Design of a New Civil Society in 1990s Bolivia." *Critique of Anthropology* 21 (4): 401–25.

Meehan, Niall and Brian P. Murphy. 2008. *Troubled History: A 10th Anniversary Critique of Peter Hart's "The I.R.A. and Its Enemies."* Cork: Aubane Historical Society.

Mellucci, Alberto. 1989. *Nomads of the Present: Social Movements and Individual Needs in Contemporary Society*. Philadelphia: Temple University Press.

Merry, Sally Engle. 2006a. "Transnational Human Rights and Local Activism: Mapping the Middle." *American Anthropologist* 108 (1): 38–51.

———. 2006b. *Human Rights and Gender Violence: Translating International Law into Local Justice*. Chicago: University of Chicago Press.

Mertus, Julie. 1999. "From Legal Transplants to Transformative Justice: Human Rights and the Promise of Transnational Civil Society." *American University International Law Review* 14 (5): 1335–90.

———. 2007. "The Rejection of Human Rights Framings: The Case of LGBT Advocacy in the U.S." *Human Rights Quarterly* 29 (4): 1036–64.

Mertz, Elizabeth. 1994. "Legal Language: Pragmatics, Poetics, and Social Power." *Annual Review of Anthropology* 23: 435–55.

Mesev, Victor, Peter Shirlow, and Joni Downs. 2009. "The Geography of Conflict and Death in Belfast, Northern Ireland." *Annals of the Association of American Geographers* 99 (5): 893–903.

Mitchell, George. 1999. *Making Peace*. Berkeley: University of California Press.

Moloney, Ed. 2007. *A Secret History of the IRA*. London: Penguin.

———. 2010. *Voices from the Grave: Two Men's War in Ireland*. London: Faber and Faber.

Montville, Joseph V. 1987. "The Arrow and the Olive Branch: A Case for Track Two Diplomacy." In *Conflict Resolution: Track Two Diplomacy*, ed. J. W. McDonald, Jr., and D. B. Bendahmane, 5–21. Washington, D.C.: Foreign Service Institute, U.S. Department of State.

Morland, Michael, Valerie Strachan, and Anthony Burden. 2011. *The Rosemary Nelson Inquiry Report*. HC 947, May 23. London: Stationery Office (TSO).

Morrissey, Mike and Marie Smyth. 2002. *Northern Ireland After the Good Friday Agreement: Victims, Grievance and Blame*. London: Pluto Press.

Morrissey, Mike, Marie Smyth, and Marie Therese Fay. 1999. *The Costs of the Troubles Study: Report on the Northern Ireland Survey: The Experience and Impact of Violence*. Derry/Londonderry: INCORE/United Nations University.

Moyn, Samuel. 2007. "On the Genealogy of Morals." *The Nation* 284 (15): 25–31.

———. 2010. *The Last Utopia: Human Rights in History*. Cambridge, Mass.: Harvard University Press.

Mueller, John. 2004. *The Remnants of War*. Ithaca, N.Y.: Cornell University Press.

Mulrine, Carmel, Jim O'Neill, and Bill Rolston. 1992. *A Report into Funding and Support for Community Development in Northern Ireland,* ed. Avila Kilmurray. Belfast: CDRG.

Munck, Ronnie.1993. *The Irish Economy: Results and Prospects.* London: Pluto Press.

Murphy, Anthony. 1996. *A Picture of the Catholic and Protestant Female Labour Force and Unemployed in Northern Ireland.* Studies in Employment Equality Research Report 5. Belfast: Central Community Relations Unit.

Murphy, Anthony and David Armstrong. 1994. *A Picture of the Catholic and Protestant Male Unemployed.* Employment Equality Review Research Report 2. Belfast: Central Community Relations Unit.

New Ulster Political Research Group. 1979. *Beyond the Religious Divide: Papers for Discussion—March 1979.* Belfast: NUPRG.

NICRA (Northern Ireland Civil Rights Association). 1978. *"We Shall Overcome"—The History of the Struggle for Civil Rights in Northern Ireland 1968–1978.* Belfast: NICRA.

NICRC (Northern Ireland Community Relations Commission). 1971. *Flight.* Belfast: NICRC.

———. 1974. *Intimidation in Housing.* Belfast: NICRC.

NICVA (Northern Ireland Council for Voluntary Action). 1992. *The Role of the N. I. Voluntary Sector: The Politicians' Views.* Belfast: NICVA Public Affairs Information Project.

———. 1993. *From Words to Action (Part I): A Response from NICVA to Government on the Draft Northern Ireland Structural Funds Plan (1994–1999).* Belfast: NICVA.

———. 1994. *Developing the Peace Process: Building the Longterm Future in Northern Ireland.* Belfast: NICVA.

———. 1995. *A Voluntary and Community Sector Proposal to Develop a Partnership and Grant Mechanism for the Proposed European Union Special Support Programme for Peace and Reconciliation in Northern Ireland and the Border Counties of Ireland. Presented to the Department of Finance and Personnel (Northern Ireland).* Belfast: NICVA.

———. 1997. *The State of the Sector: Northern Ireland Voluntary Sector Almanac 1996.* Belfast: NICVA.

———. 2004. *Designing Peace III.* Belfast: NICVA.

NIHRC (Northern Ireland Human Rights Commission). 2001. *Making a Bill of Rights for Northern Ireland: A Consultation by the Northern Ireland Human Rights Commission.* Belfast: NIHRC.

———. 2004. *Progressing a Bill of Rights for Northern Ireland: An Update.* Belfast: NIHRC.

———. 2005. *Taking Forward a Bill of Rights for Northern Ireland.* Belfast: NIHRC.

———. 2008. *A Bill of Rights for Northern Ireland Advice to the Secretary of State for Northern Ireland.* Belfast: NIHRC.

———. 2012. *Is That Right? Fact and Fiction on a Bill of Rights.* Belfast: NIHRC.

NIPSA (Northern Ireland Public Service Alliance). 2010. *NIPSA Response to the Consultation on the Draft Public Assemblies, Parades and Protest Bill*. Belfast: NIPSA.

NISRA (Northern Ireland Statistics & Research Agency). 2010. *Northern Ireland Multiple Deprivation Measure 2010*. Belfast: NISRA.

NIVT (Northern Ireland Voluntary Trust). 1995. *Peace: An Opportunity for Change: Responses to the NIVT Community Priority Survey*. Belfast: NIVT.

Noble, Michael, George Smith, Gemma Wright, Chris Dibben, and Myfanwy Lloyd, with Ian Shuttleworth. 2001. *Measures of Deprivation in Northern Ireland*. Oxford: Social Disadvantage Research Centre, University of Oxford.

———. 2006. *Labour Force Survey Religion Report*. Belfast: NISRA.

Nolan, Paul. 2012. *The Northern Ireland Peace Monitoring Report Number One*. Belfast: Community Relations Council.

———. 2013. *The Northern Ireland Peace Monitoring Report Number Two*. Belfast: Community Relations Council.

Nordstrom, Carolyn. 1997. *A Different Kind of War Story*. Philadelphia: University of Pennsylvania Press.

Northern Ireland Assembly. 2011. *Official Report (Hansard) 2010–2011 Session, Monday 06 June 2011*. Belfast: Northern Ireland Assembly.

Ó Catháin, Máirtín. 2004. *A Wee Black Booke of Belfast Anarchism (1867–1973)*. Belfast: ORGANISE!

O'Dochartaigh, Fionnbarra. 1994. *Ulster's White Negroes: From Civil Rights to Insurrection*. San Francisco: AK Press.

O'Doherty, Malachi. 1998. *The Trouble with Guns: Republican Strategy and the Provisional IRA*. Belfast: Blackstaff.

O'Donnell, Ruan. 1998. *The Rebellion in Wicklow 1798*. Dublin: Irish Academic Press.

O'Flaherty, Michael and John Fisher. 2008. "Sexual Orientation, Gender Identity and International Human Rights Law: Contextualising the Yogyakarta Principles." *Human Rights Law Review* 8 (2): 207–48.

OFMDFM (Office of First Minister and Deputy First Minister). 2010a. *Programme for Cohesion, Sharing and Integration: Consultation Document*. Belfast: Office of the First Minister and Deputy First Minister.

———. 2010b. *Public Assemblies, Parades and Protests in Northern Ireland: A Consultation Paper Published by the Office of the First Minister and Deputy First Minister*. Belfast: Office of the First Minister and Deputy First Minister.

———. 2013. *Together: Building a United Community Strategy*. Belfast: Office of the First Minister and Deputy First Minister.

O'Hearn, Denis. 1983. "Catholic Grievances, Catholic Nationalism: A Comment." *British Journal of Sociology* 34 (3): 438–45.

———. 1985. "Again on Discrimination in the North of Ireland: A Reply to the Rejoinder." *British Journal of Sociology* 36 (1): 94–101.

———. 1987. "Catholic Grievances: Comments." *British Journal of Sociology* 38 (1): 94–100.

———. 2000. "Peace Dividend, Foreign Investment, and Economic Regeneration: The Northern Irish Case." *Social Problems* 47 (2): 180–200.

O'Leary, Richard. 2009. "Christians and Gays in Northern Ireland: How the Ethno-Religious Context Has Shaped Christian Anti-Gay and Pro-Gay Activism." In *Contemporary Christianity and LGBT Sexualities*, ed. Stephen Hunt, 123–38. Farnham: Ashgate.

O'Neill, Brendan. 2002. "How the Peace Process Divided Ireland." *The Blanket: A Journal of Protest and Dissent*, July 25, http://indiamond6.ulib.iupui.edu:81.

O'Rawe, Richard. 2005. *Blanketmen: An Untold Story of the H-Block Hunger Strike*. Dublin: New Island.

Orford, Anne. 2003. *Reading Humanitarian Intervention: Human Rights and the Use of Force in International Law*. Cambridge: Cambridge University Press.

Orwell, George. (1943) 2000. "Looking Back on the Spanish Civil War." In *The Collected Essays, Journalism and Letters of George Orwell*, vol. 2, *My Country Right or Left 1940–1943*, 249–67. Boston: David R. Godine.

———. (1949) 2004. *Nineteen Eighty-Four*. Fairfield, Iowa: First World Library.

———. 2012. *Diaries*. Ed. Peter Davison New York: Liveright.

Pakenham, Thomas. 1972. *The Year of Liberty: A History of the Great Irish Rebellion of 1798*. London: Panther.

Paley, Julia. 2001. *Marketing Democracy: Power and Social Movements in Post-Dictatorship Chile*. Berkeley: University of California Press.

Pålshaugen, Lone Singstad. 2005. "The Northern Ireland Civic Forum and a Politics of Recognition." *Irish Political Studies* 20 (2): 147–69.

Palys, Ted and John Lowman. 2012. "Defending Research Confidentiality 'To the Extent the Law Allows': Lessons from the Boston College Subpoenas." *Journal of Academic Ethics* 10 (4): 271–97.

Parlevliet, Michelle. 2002. "Bridging the Divide: Exploring the Relationship Between Human Rights and Conflict Management." *Track Two* 11 (1): 6–43.

Phythian, Mark. 2011. "The Politics of Commissions of Inquiry into Security and Intelligence Controversies in Britain." In *Commissions of Inquiry and National Security: Comparative Approaches*, ed. Stuart Farson and Mark Phythian, 55–77. Santa Barbara, Calif.: ABC-CLIO.

Pinker, Stephen. 2011. *Better Angels of Our Nature: Why Violence Has Declined*. New York: Viking.

Police Ombudsman for Northern Ireland. 2006. *Report into the Complaint by James and Michael McConville Regarding the Police Investigation into the Abduction and Murder of Their Mother Mrs Jean McConville*. Belfast: Police Ombudsman.

———. 2007. *Statement by the Police Ombudsman for Northern Ireland on Her Investigation into the Circumstances Surrounding the Death of Raymond McCord Junior and Related Matters, 22 January 2007*. Belfast: Police Ombudsman.

———. 2010. *Public Statement by the Police Ombudsman Under Section 62 of the Police (Northern Ireland) Act 1998 Relating to the RUC Investigation of the Alleged*

Involvement of the Late Father James Chesney in the Bombing of Claudy on 31 July 1972. Belfast: Police Ombudsman.

————. 2011. *Public Statement by the Police Ombudsman Under Section 62 of the Police (Northern Ireland) Act 1998 Relating to the Complaint by the Relatives of the Victims of the Bombing of McGurk's Bar, Belfast on 4 December 1971*. Belfast: Police Ombudsman.

Political Vetting of Community Work Working Group. 1990. *The Political Vetting of Community Work in Northern Ireland*. Belfast: NICVA.

Pollak, Andy, ed. 1993. *A Citizens' Inquiry: The Opsahl Report on Northern Ireland*. Dublin: Lilliput Press.

Poole, Michael A. 1971. "Riot Displacement in 1969." *Fortnight* 22: 9–11.

Porter, David Frederick McKenzie. 1973. *A Study of the Urban Growth of the Shankill, Falls and Springfield Areas of Belfast from 1860 to 1900*. Belfast: Public Records Office.

Povinelli, Elizabeth A. 2002. *The Cunning of Recognition: Indigenous Alterities and the Making of Australian Multiculturalism*. Durham, N.C.: Duke University Press.

Powell, Jonathan. 2008. *Great Hatred, Little Room: Making Peace in Northern Ireland*. London: Bodley Head.

Prince, Simon. 2006. "The Global Revolt of 1968 and Northern Ireland." *Historical Journal* 49 (3): 851–75.

————. 2007. *Northern Ireland's '68: Civil Rights, Global Revolt and the Origins of the Troubles*. Dublin: Irish Academic Press.

PSNI (Police Service of Northern Ireland). 2004. *Statistics Relating to the Security Situation in Northern Ireland 2003/2004*. Belfast: Northern Ireland Statistics and Research Agency.

————. 2011. *Police Recorded Security Situation Statistics 2010/11 1st April 2010–31st March 2011*. Belfast: Northern Ireland Statistics and Research Agency.

————. 2012a. *Police Recorded Security Situation Statistics Annual Report Covering the Period 1st April 2011–31st March 2012*. Belfast: Northern Ireland Statistics and Research Agency.

————. 2012b. *User Guide to Security Situation Statistics Northern Ireland*. Belfast: Northern Ireland Statistics and Research Agency.

Purdie, Bob. 1990. *Politics in the Streets: The Origins of the Civil Rights Movement in Northern Ireland*. Belfast: Blackstaff.

Rancière, Jacques. 2004. "Who Is the Subject of the Rights of Man?" *South Atlantic Quarterly* 103 (2/3): 297–310.

Ranelagh, John. 1999. *A Short History of Ireland*. Cambridge: Cambridge University Press.

Relatives for Justice. 1995. *Collusion 1990–1994*. Belfast: Relatives for Justice.

Richland, Justin. 2013. "Jurisdiction: Grounding Law in Language." *Annual Review of Anthropology* 41: 209–26.

Risse, Thomas, Stephen C. Ropp, and Kathryn Sikkink, eds. 1999. *The Power of Human Rights: International Norms and Domestic Change*. Cambridge: Cambridge University Press.

Risse, Thomas and Kathryn Sikkink. 1999. "The Socialization of International Human Rights Norms into Domestic Practices: Introduction." In *The Power of Human Rights*, ed. Thomas Risse, Stephen Ropp, and Kathryn Sikkink,1–38. Cambridge: Cambridge University Press.

Robson, Brian, Michael Bradford, and Iain A. Deas. 1994. *Relative Deprivation in Northern Ireland*. Policy Planning and Research Unit Occasional Paper 28. Manchester: University of Manchester.

Rolston, Bill. 2000. *Unfinished Business: State Killings and the Quest for Truth*. Belfast: Beyond the Pale.

———. 2001. "'This Is Not a Rebel Song': The Irish Conflict and Popular Music." *Race & Class* 42 (3): 49–67.

Rolston, Bill and Mike Tomlinson. 1988. *Unemployment in West Belfast: The Obair Report*. Belfast: Beyond the Pale.

Rose, Richard. 1971. *Governing Without Consensus: An Irish Perspective*. Boston: Beacon Press.

Ross, Fiona. 2002. *Bearing Witness: Women and the South African Truth and Reconciliation Commission*. London: Pluto Press.

Ross, F. Stuart. 2012. *Smashing H Block: The Rise and Fall of the Popular Campaign Against Criminalization, 1976–1982*. Liverpool: Liverpool University Press.

Rowthorn, Bob and Naomi Wayne. 1988. *Northern Ireland: The Political Economy of Conflict*. Boulder, Colo.: Westview Press.

Ryan, Meda. 2005. "Tom Barry and the Kilmichael Ambush." *History Ireland* 13 (5): 15–18.

Ryan, Meda, Niall Meehan, and Manus O'Riordan. 2005. "Peter Hart and Tom Barry." *History Ireland* 13 (3): 13–15.

Said, Abdul Aziz and Charles O. Lerche. 2006. "Peace as a Human Right: Toward Integrated Understanding." In *Human Rights and Conflict: Exploring Links Between Rights, Law and Peacebuilding*, ed. Julie Mertus and Jeffrey Helsing, 129–49. Washington, D.C.: U.S. Institute of Peace.

Sampson, Steven. 1996. "The Social Life of Projects: Importing Civil Society to Albania." In *Civil Society: Challenging Western Models*, ed. Chris Hann and Elizabeth Dunn, 121–42. London: Routledge.

Sanders, Douglas. 1996. "Getting Lesbian and Gay Issues on the International Human Rights Agenda." *Human Rights Quarterly* 18 (1): 67–106.

Saville, Lord, William Hoyt, John Toohey. 2010. *Report of the Bloody Sunday Inquiry*. London: Stationery Office.

Scott, Ronnie. 1993. *A Brief Review of the Action for Community Employment Scheme*. Belfast: Northern Ireland Economic Research Centre.

Seligman, Adam B. 1992. *The Idea of Civil Society*. Princeton, N.J.: Princeton University Press.

Shankill Think Tank. 1994. *Ulster's Protestant Working Class*. Island Pamphlets 9. Comp. Michael Hall. Newtownabbey: Island Publications.

————. 1995. *A New Beginning.* Comp. Michael Hall. Island Pamphlets 13. Newtown-abbey: Island Publications.

————. 1998. *At the Crossroads?* Island Pamphlets 18. Newtownabbey: Island Publications.

Shaw, Rosalind, Lars Waldorf, and Pierre Hazan, eds. 2010. *Localizing Transitional Justice: Interventions and Priorities After Mass Violence.* Stanford, Calif.: Stanford University Press.

Sheehan, Maura. 1995. "The International Fund for Ireland: Some Preliminary Findings." *International Policy Review* 5 (1): 41–53.

Sherzer, Joel. 1987. "A Discourse-Centered Approach to Language and Culture." *American Anthropologist* 89 (2): 295–309.

Shirlow, Peter and Kieran McEvoy. 2008. *Beyond the Wire: Former Prisoners and Conflict Transformation in Northern Ireland.* London: Pluto Press.

Shirlow, Peter and Mark McGovern. 1996. "Sectarianism, Socio-Economic Competition, and the Political Economy of Ulster." *Antipode* 28 (4): 377–96.

Shirlow, Peter and Brendan Murtagh. 2006. *Belfast: Segregation, Violence and the City.* London: Pluto Press.

Shirlow, Peter and Ian Shuttleworth. 1999. "'Who Is Going to Toss the Burgers?' Social Class and the Reconstruction of the Northern Irish Economy." *Capital and Class* 22 (69): 27–46.

Shirlow, Peter, Jonathan Tonge, James McAuley, and Catherine McGlyn. 2010. *Abandoning Historical Conflict? Former Paramilitary Prisoners and Political Reconciliation in Northern Ireland.* Manchester: Manchester University Press.

Shuttleworth, Ian and Peter Shirlow. 1999. "Inward Investment and the Politics of Peace in Northern Ireland." *Regional Studies* 33 (1): 79–83.

SICDP (Springfield Inter-Community Development Project). 2000. *The Missing Peace: Development Plan.* Belfast: SICDP.

Simpson, Kirk. 2009. *Unionist Voices and the Politics of Remembering the Past in Northern Ireland.* Basingstoke: Palgrave Macmillan.

Sloan, Barry. 2010. "'Each Neighbourly Murder': Lost Lives and the Challenge of Commemorating the Victims of the Northern Ireland Troubles." *European Journal of English Studies* 14 (1): 49–62.

Smith, M. L. R. 1999. "The Intellectual Internment of a Conflict: The Forgotten War in Northern Ireland." *International Affairs (Royal Institute of International Affairs 1944–)* 75(1): 77–97.

Smith, Anne. 2006. "The Unique Position of National Human Rights Institutions: A Mixed Blessing?" *Human Rights Quarterly* 28 (4): 904–46.

Smyth, James. 1992. *The Men of No Property: Irish Radicals and Popular Politics in the late 18th century.* Houndsmills/Basingstoke: Macmillan.

Smyth, Marie Bre. 2006. "Lost Lives: Victims and the Construction of 'Victimhood' in Northern Ireland." In *A Farewell to Arms? Beyond the Good Friday Agreement,* ed.

Michael Cox, Adrian Guelke, and Fiona Stephens, 6–23. Manchester: Manchester University Press.

———. 2007. *Truth Recovery and Justice After Conflict: Managing Violent Pasts*. London: Routledge.

Special European Union Programmes Body. 2003. *EU Programme for Peace and Reconciliation in Northern Ireland and the Border Region of Ireland 2000–2005 Operational Programme*. Brussels: Special European Union Programmes Body.

Speed, Shannon. 2008. *Rights in Rebellion: Indigenous Struggle and Human Rights in Chiapas*. Stanford, Calif.: Stanford University Press.

Spulbeck, Susanne. 1996. "Anti-Semitism and Fear of the Public Sphere in a Post-Totalitarian Society: East Germany." In *Civil Society: Challenging Western Models*, ed. Chris Hann and Elizabeth Dunn, 64–78. London: Routledge.

Stammers, Neil. 2003. "Social Movements, Human Rights and the Challenge to Power." *Proceedings of the American Society of International Law* 97: 299–301.

———. 2009. *Human Rights and Social Movements*. London: Pluto Press.

Stanko, Elizabeth. 2000. "Victims R Us: The Life History of 'Fear of Crime' and the Politicization of Violence." In *Crime, Risk, and Insecurity: Law and Order in Everyday Life and Political Discourse*, ed. Tim Hope and Richard Sparks, 13–30. London: Routledge.

Stephenson, Jonathan. 1977. "Save the Shankill?" *Fortnight* 25: 7.

Stevens, Sir John. 2003. *Stevens Inquiry 3: Overview and Recommendations 17th April 2003*. Belfast: Stevens Inquiry.

Stewart, A. T. Q. 1998. "1798 in the North." *History Ireland* 6 (2): 33–38.

Sutton, Malcolm. 1994. *Bear in mind these dead . . . An Index of Deaths from the Conflict in Ireland 1969–1993*. Belfast: Beyond the Pale Publications.

Taylor, Charles. 1994. "The Politics of Recognition." In *Multiculturalism: Examining the Politics of Recognition*, ed. Amy Gutmann, 25–73. Princeton, N.J.: Princeton University Press.

Taylor, Peter. 1991. "If Cold War Is the Problem, Is Hot Peace the Solution?" In *The Political Geography of Conflict and Peace*, ed. Nurit Kliot and Stanley Waterman, 78–92. London: Belhaven.

Thatcher, Margaret and Douglas Keay. 1987. "Aids, Education and the Year 2000! Interview with Margaret Thatcher." *Woman's Own* (October 31): 8–10.

Theidon, Kimberly. 2010. *Intimate Enemies: Violence and Reconciliation in Peru*. Philadelphia: University of Pennsylvania Press.

Thiessen, Chuck, Sean Byrne, Olga Skarlato, and Paul Tennent. 2010. "Civil Society Leaders and Northern Ireland's Peace Process: Hopes and Fears for the Future." *Humanity and Society* 34 (1): 39–63.

Thompson, E. P. 1991. *The Making of the English Working Class*. London: Penguin.

Tolley, Howard B., Jr. 2009. "Seán MacBride." In *Encyclopedia of Human Rights*, ed. David P. Forsythe. 1467–71. Oxford: Oxford University Press.

Tomlinson, Michael W. 2012. "War, Peace and Suicide: The Case of Northern Ireland." *International Sociology* 27 (4): 464–82.

Tonge, Jonathan, Peter Shirlow, and James McAuley. 2011. "So Why Did the Guns Fall Silent? How Interplay, Not Stalemate, Explains the Northern Ireland Peace Process." *Irish Political Studies* 26 (1): 1–18.

Touraine, Alain. 1988. *Return of the Actor: Social Theory in Postindustrial Society.* Minneapolis: University of Minnesota Press.

Turf Lodge Development Association. 1972. *Report on Employment Survey Turf Lodge.* Belfast: Turf Lodge Development Association.

United Kingdom Parliament. 1985. *Parliamentary Debates (Hansard, House of Commons),* 6th ser., vol. 81. London: HMSO.

———. 2008. *Parliamentary Debates (Hansard, House of Commons). Northern Ireland Grand Committee Debates.* 6th ser., vol. 477. London: HMSO.

United Nations General Assembly. 1994. National Institutions for the Promotion and Protection of Human Rights, adopted March 4, 1994, G.A. Res. 48/134, UN GAOR, 48th Sess., UN Doc. A/Res/48/134 (1994).

Vance, David. 2008. *Unionism Decayed: 1997–2001.* Central Milton Keynes: AuthorHouse UK.

Verdury, Katherine. 1996. *What Was Socialism and What Comes Next?* Princeton, N.J.: Princeton University Press.

Warner, Michael. 2002. *Publics and Counterpublics.* New York: Zone Books.

Whelan, Daniel J. and Jack Donnelly. 2007. "The West, Economic and Social Rights, and the Global Human Rights Regime: Setting the Record Straight." *Human Rights Quarterly* 29 (4): 908–49.

Whelan, Kevin. 1996. *The Tree of Liberty: Radicalism, Catholicism, and the Construction of Irish Identity, 1760–1830.* Notre Dame, Ind.: University of Notre Dame Press.

Whitaker, Robin. 2010. "Debating Rights in the New Northern Ireland." *Irish Political Studies* 25 (1): 23–45.

White, Robert W. 1989. "From Peaceful Protest to Guerrilla War: Micromobilization of the Provisional Irish Republican Army." *American Journal of Sociology* 94 (6): 1277–1302.

———. 1993. *Provisional Irish Republicans: An Oral and Interpretive History.* Westport, Conn.: Greenwood.

Whyte, John. 1983. "How Much Discrimination Was There Under the Unionist Regime, 1921–1968?" In *Contemporary Irish Studies,* ed. Tom Gallagher and James O'Connell, 1–35. Manchester: Manchester University Press.

Widgery, Lord. 1972. *Bloody Sunday 1972: Lord Widgery's Report of Events in London Derry, Northern Ireland, on 30 January 1972.* London: HMSO.

Wiener, Ron. 1976. *The Rape and Plunder of the Shankill in Belfast: People and Planning.* Belfast: Nothems Press.

Williams, Patricia J. 1991. *The Alchemy of Race and Rights: Diary of a Law Professor.* Cambridge, Mass.: Harvard University Press.

Williams, Raymond. 1977. *Marxism and Literature*. Oxford: Oxford University Press.

Williamson, Arthur, Duncan Scott, and Peter Halfpenny. 2000. "Rebuilding Civil Society in Northern Ireland: The Community and Voluntary Sector's Contribution to the European Union's Peace and Reconciliation District Partnership Programme." *Policy & Politics* 28 (1): 49–66.

Wilson, Richard Ashby. 1997a. "Human Rights, Culture and Context: An Introduction." In *Human Rights, Culture and Context: Anthropological Perspectives*, ed. Richard Ashby Wilson, 1–27. London: Pluto Press.

———, ed. 1997b. *Human Rights, Culture and Context: Anthropological Perspectives*. London: Pluto Press.

———. 2001. *The Politics of Truth and Reconciliation in South Africa: Legitimizing the Post-Apartheid State*. Cambridge: Cambridge University Press.

———. 2003. "Anthropological Studies of National Reconciliation Processes." *Anthropological Theory* 3 (3): 367–88.

———. 2004. "Human Rights." In *A Companion to the Anthropology of Politics*, ed. David Nugent and Joan Vincent, 232–47. Malden, Mass.: Blackwell.

———. 2006. "Afterword to 'Anthropology and Human Rights in a New Key': The Social Life of Human Rights." *American Anthropologist* 108 (1): 77–83.

———. 2007. "Conclusion Tyrannosaurus Lex: The Anthropology of Human Rights and Transnational Law." In *The Practice of Human Rights: Tracking Law Between the Global and the Local*, ed. Mark Goodale and Sally Engle Merry, 342–69. Cambridge: Cambridge University Press.

Wilson, Richard Ashby and Jon P. Mitchell, eds. 2003. *Human Rights in Global Perspective: Anthropological Studies of Rights, Claims and Entitlements*. London: Routledge.

Wilson, Robin. 2010. *The Northern Ireland Experience of Conflict and Agreement: A Model for Export?* Manchester: Manchester University Press.

Wilson, Robert McLiam. 1996. *Eureka Street*. London: Vintage.

Wolin, Richard. 2010. *The Wind from the East: French Intellectuals, the Cultural Revolution, and the Legacy of the 1960s*. Princeton, N.J.: Princeton University Press.

INDEX

ACKNOWLEDGMENTS

I am deeply grateful to the many people who helped with the writing of this book. It was made possible by residents of Belfast who generously shared their time and knowledge. Most of these research participants must remain anonymous, but I hope this work commemorates their experiences in a meaningful way. The named research participants, Jeff Dudgeon, Michael Hall, and the Belfast Pride organization, were especially generous with their time, document collections, feedback, and ideas. I am also grateful to staff at the Linenhall Library, the Public Record Office of Northern Ireland, West Belfast Economic Forum, and the Northern Ireland Council for Voluntary Action for their patient assistance with archival research.

This research was made possible by funding from the Wenner-Gren Foundation for Anthropological Research, the U.S. Institute of Peace, and the UK Economic and Social Research Council. I am also grateful for the support and guidance of colleagues in Social Anthropology at the University of Edinburgh, particularly Jonathan Spencer, Francesca Bray, Alexander Robertson, Tobias Kelly, Magnus Course, and Katharine Dow. I am deeply indebted to Richard G. Fox, a mentor whose support has been unwavering over many years. Many other colleagues in anthropology have offered advice and suggestions as my ideas developed, especially Richard Wilson, Madelaine Adelman, and Alexander Smith. My dear friend Sarah Horowitz generously shared her artistic talent and vision for the cover. At the University of Pennsylvania Press, Rachel Taube, Alison Anderson, and Bert B. Lockwood, Jr., were indispensable guides, while the felicitously named Peter Agree patiently shepherded the book from prospectus to publication. Joanne Hindman read the entire manuscript and gave excellent editorial advice. I am also grateful to anonymous reviewers who offered generous praise and constructive critiques of the draft manuscript.

Most of all, I am grateful to my family, particularly my mother, father, and son, for their love, encouragement, and support. Thank you.